CROSS WORLDS

Cross Worlds

Transcultural Poetics

AN ANTHOLOGY

Edited by Anne Waldman
and Laura Wright

COFFEE HOUSE PRESS • MINNEAPOLIS • 2014

Coffee House Press books are available to the trade through our primary distributor, Consortium Book Sales & Distribution, cbsd.com or
(800) 283-3572. For personal orders, catalogs, or other information,
write to: info@coffeehousepress.org.
    Coffee House Press is a nonprofit literary publishing house.
Support from private foundations, corporate giving programs, government programs, and generous individuals helps make the publication
of our books possible. We gratefully acknowledge their support in
detail in the back of this book.
Visit us at coffeehousepress.org.

LIBRARY OF CONGRESS CATALOGING-IN-PUBLICATION DATA
Cross worlds : transcultural poetics: an anthology /
[edited by] Anne Waldman, Laura Wright.
pages cm
ISBN 978-1-56689-358-9 (pbk.)
1. Poetics. 2. Poetry—History and criticism. 3. Poets—Interviews.
I. Waldman, Anne, 1945– editor of compilation.
II. Wright, Laura E. editor of compilation.
PN1042.C86 2014
808.1—dc23
2013039533
PRINTED IN THE UNITED STATES
FIRST EDITION, FIRST PRINTING

ACKNOWLEDGMENTS
"Spontaneous Poetics: Australian Aboriginal Song Sticks" by Allen
Ginsberg. Copyright © 1976 by Allen Ginsberg LLC, used by permission of The Wylie Agency LLC.
    All other interviews, talks, and panel discussions reprinted by per-
mission of the respective authors or their literary estates.

For Anselm Hollo
poet, translator, teacher, friend
who crossed our worlds
in memoriam
(1934–2013)

At Evenfall

recall enormous heave of moment
la vie en rose
before some Mallarméan blows it into the *vide* or *abîme*

      (but *timing egg in storm*
      beats driving car through rock
          —Albanian proverb

sun shadow fields cast loose
drum vibes in ground moths flutter
"O Lady Time, summer was great"

but now no house of letters stands
Elizabethanly enjoying given song
paradox knots each graduate

yet she'll stay up to read & write long letters
& on still tree-lined streets attend her musings
do art   eat well   never please wicked money
        always treat language like a dangerous toy

              —*Anselm Hollo*

CONTENTS

INTRODUCTION

Anne Waldman and Laura Wright

WHILE THE UNIVERSE MAY BE EXPANDING, THE WORLD WE LIVE IN is shrinking in that we all dwell in the Anthropocene, a geological age defined by the antics and greed and curiosity and bellicose nature of *Homo sapiens sapiens.*

As we wreak havoc on our ecosystems, our land, our flora and fauna, how do we continue the conversation as poets, activists, and cultural workers? Is our talk beside the point? Isn't discourse one of our smarter human endeavors? Artists strive to do this, we believe, to keep dialogue, inquiry, and information passed on and knowledge of poetics, place, history, and consciousness moving along. To not be alone in the void. To engage in invigorated ideas and language. The poet is by nature an investigator, a thinker, a weaver, a magician: making up the world again and again. How do we come to terms with our own mind in relation to other places and cultures? How open are we? How does our creative education continue along?

We seem to be obsessively wired up, and conduct much if not most of our exchanges—verbal, literary, imaginative, business—online; we are in a new and still-evolving mode of cross-cultural, transnational, and international commerce in terms of our daily discourse. Yet we still thrive on the personal physical exchange. It buoys us up. We travel and take notes and report on where we've been, and what new contexts and persons and perspectives are circulating. We are inspired by the presence of others in the room, specifically in the zone and annals and archive of the Jack Kerouac School of Disembodied Poetics at Naropa University, from which this book derives its pulse and purpose.

This is an anthology of artist-poets, novelists, hybrid writers, playwrights, philosophers, and translators of essays "speaking" on what happens both between and across spaces, locations, languages, genres, and media. And this is an anthology that returns, again and again, to language—language as culture; language as medium; language as artifact; language as identity; language as agent of, and as changed by, globalization; language as practice; language as fact. What unites these explorations is an engagement with the other, a willingness not just to visit, but to inhabit, to occupy and explore what is between.

To translate, in its most literal sense, is *to carry across.* This collection is a chronological tour of the borderlands, the interstices, and around the complexities of translating ideas, intention, and the music of verse from one language to another. In these unmapped territories of the "between," it becomes difficult to separate the physical from the cultural and the cultural from the linguistic.

In some cases, there is less "between" than we might hope, as in Andrei Codrescu's description of Romania in 1989, in which we find much sadly still relevant to the media and public understanding (or lack thereof) of events in the twenty-first-century United States. Karen Tei Yamashita explores the effects of globalization on culture and language; Sawako Nakayasu and Michelle Naka Pierce seek to redefine their identities through peeling back their mother tongue's nuance; Cid Corman questions both the possibility and the impossibility of translation, while Myung Mi Kim interrogates one word at a time. Harryette Mullen considers the ethical obligation we have to be aware and attentive, and Hoa Nguyen illustrates the results of paying attention to personal narrative in its broader contexts. Meredith Quartermain also addresses narrative and history in terms of reinventing forms. Cecilia Vicuña, Heriberto Yépez, and Margaret Randall all present poetics as inextricable from politics; Bei Dao, Jen Hofer, and Dolores Dorantes consider how writing and translation can impact the political/social landscape. And there is hope to be found between as well, as evidenced in Judith Malina and Hanon Reznikov's resounding report on the ongoing legacy of The Living Theatre around the world.

These borders are permeable spaces unto themselves; these borders have been written and thus can be unwritten and rewritten. Bhanu Kapil speaks of an alternation between visible and invisible narratives. There are "real" borders, and physical, geographical, political borders as well. Pierre Joris talks about writing within and beyond physical and political borders in a talk on Arabic poetics presented just one week after September 11, 2001. Tom Pickard documents Basil Bunting's various connections to place. Allen Ginsberg illustrates the influence on his work of Australian aboriginal poetics, with its role in navigating both physical and spiritual landscapes. Daisy Zamora looks at poetry's role in the Nicaraguan revolution. Then there are also the borders that cultures themselves create: Alexs Pate analyzes and discourses on hip-hop lyrics; David Henderson reminds us of the roles delineated by race and class; Eileen Myles muses on what it is to be an artist in this consumer culture. Barbara Tedlock confronts the artificial borders of gender in her discussion of female shamanic traditions.

At times there is a disquietude to the between-ness. Sherwin Bitsui, C. S. Giscombe, and Ana Božičević explore being perceived as "other." Eleni Sikelianos considers "mutual infestation between the lyric and the document," the not-so-well-delineated border between art and fact. Alberto Ruy-Sánchez considers how the borders between life and death can be both strange and comforting.

Others explore borders between languages: Linh Dinh presents some contemporary Vietnamese poets, Nina Zivančević and Samuel R. Delany discourse on translating fiction, and Monica de la Torre considers, among other things, some myths about bilingualism. James Thomas Stevens discusses working with oral tradition and using old forms in new contexts. An interview with Nicole Brossard touches on space/architecture in language, and the movement between genres and between languages.

Always, we come back to language: to the practice of articulation, presented by Akilah Oliver and Joanne Kyger as antidote to the current political/cultural state of warfare; to the morality of surprise as revealed by Jack Collom; to redefinition, marking and re-marking, and the replacement of assumptions of the fiction of identity (explored and exposed by Lorenzo Thomas, Christian Ide Hintze, Wang Ping, and Victor Hernández Cruz), with questions. This is what Peter Lamborn Wilson describes as "simply another way of knowing things"; though Dennis Tedlock admits, "there are . . . moments when our own poetics displays an inadequacy of means or failure to utilize means that are already there anyway."

Finally, Anselm Hollo's life and work embodies the spirit of this anthology: Hollo was both "from" no one place and therefore "from" many places. Although native to Finland, Anselm had no one "mother tongue," and therefore had many. He truly lived and worked across worlds.

Cross Worlds is meant to be a generative compendium for practitioners of an applied poetics. The contributors to this anthology do not offer ultimate solutions on how to reside in this complex and troubling "dark age," yet at the intersection of these reflections on intertextuality, interculturality, multilinguistic, and cross-genre endeavor, we do find possible ways forward.

WOLF SONG TRANSMISSIONS

Daniel Staniforth

SPONTANEOUS POETICS: AUSTRALIAN ABORIGINAL SONG STICKS

Allen Ginsberg

WE WERE TALKING EARLIER ABOUT POETRY AS COMMUNAL SACRED dance and epic. I want to pick up on the idea of communal consciousness in poetry to expound something that I've been exploring a lot lately as a basis for prosody, a basic approach to measuring lines of poetry. My own preoccupation has been increasingly with spontaneous utterances or spontaneous forms, so I've been experimenting with that a lot. One interesting and ancient form of poetics, which is maybe the oldest, is Australian Aborigine practice. They have epic material so that it takes sometimes forty years to become a songman. To become a songman in the Pitjantjatjara tongue, which is central Australian, or in Arnhem Land among the Yirrkala tribes, involves memorizing epic material that covers a cycle of migration that the tribe takes over anywhere from twenty to forty years. That's why it might take that long to become a songman, because one main form of the epic is a long song, which is sung continuously over a cycle of twenty years, which involves travel instructions on a circular migration pattern. They eat grubs, insects, sleepy lizards. You have to have directions if you arrive at a campsite which has traditionally been used before over millennia. The last time the tribe was there, all the witchetty grubs and the sleepy lizards were eaten up, and it may take twenty or thirty years to replenish the natural foodstuffs, so that would be the length of the cycle of traveling. A wandering epic might involve the total botany of the terrain that the tribe is going to circumambulate, where you can find water holes, what kind of vegetation is around, what kind of food is around, where you can find firewood if you build any sort of fire, what are the local landmarks, how are they connected in eternal dreamtime to the origin of the earth and of the tribe, where is the best place for sports and games, what is the history of the place.

The songman uses a very simple form, a one-line verse, which is then repeated by the entire tribe, which might be anywhere from five to fifty or one hundred people. You have to have small groups if you're traveling in a continuously nomadic existence like that. The songmen use song sticks along with their verses to mark time and to lead the rest of the village in chanting. The songman is the only one that has in his head the entire stock of words and information, like what birds are around in what season, where the stars will be at a certain point, where the moon will rise and where the sun will rise, where the moon will set and where the sun will set. A lot of the older villagers can remember fragments of it, but the songman's profession is to keep track of everything. So the entire village is dependent on the poet. The poet has the equivalent of the *Encyclopaedia Britannica* in his head and is the only one who has specific instructions on how to survive in specific places.

These are Australian Aborigine song sticks [clacks sticks—they have a melodic tone, despite being a single pitch]. They are used for keeping time. Almost every elder will have song sticks, sometimes carved with maps, geographical directions, sometimes carved with messages. Those that don't have song sticks will pick up twigs; a song stick can be anything from a couple of pencils pounded together, to bottles, but generally they are little sticks, branches, or twigs. A whole village chanting together makes quite a musical din, a good racket that keeps everybody on time. Those that don't know the verse will pick up on the verse as the songman begins it. And they will chant the verse ten or twelve times. There are dances that may go along with the verses, to indicate animals such as kangaroos, for instance. Children's songs are taught to begin with—so the kids get some training. They are used for teaching a simple game as a beginning.

I met some songmen in Australia at the University of Adelaide. A group of four very old songmen who had never been out of the central Australian desert were brought down in trucks to an anthropology class and asked to perform children's songs to relate to some autistic children. The anthropologists brought in some kids that were not communicating very much and they wanted to see whether the songmen's rhythm sticks and chants would rouse any response in the kids. I sat in on the class and made friends with some of the songmen and found that they had fantastic auditory imagination. They don't have a written language so that anything that enters their ear they can remember, they can pick up anything rhythmical, anything poetical that they hear they can reproduce almost instantly. We were trading songs, so I did one verse of "Hare Krishna" and they were able to pick up on it instantly and sing it right back, after one verse. One interesting thing is that the auditory imagination is encyclopedic. Unlike our own culture, where everything is relegated to print so it doesn't have to be remembered, anything that you have to remember there, you've got to remember fast. As in the development of any kind of muscle or any kind of exercise, continuous exercise of that faculty develops it fantastically, and the capacity of people to remember is almost unlimited, from our point of view.

The song cycle will not only be the migration map, route, and all the gas stations and water holes on the way; it will also be for death ceremonies. Corpses are laid out and the songman will lead a three- to four-day or even a weeklong recitation of the path of the soul of the dead person, from the particular spot where he died, say if it's in Arnhem Land, over the geography of Arnhem Land, naming all the flowers and the birds in the air, the color of the ocean, islands in the ocean toward New Guinea, going straight north—apparently the souls went up to New Guinea for the afterlife. So there is a complete geographic and ichthyological encyclopedia of everything the soul is likely to meet on his trip to New Guinea.

There is also a conception of an eternal dreamtime; eternal dreamtime, otherwise known as the dreaming, which is where their tribe was formed and when their tribe was formed, not necessarily according to our sense of time. Large rocks or trees or natural features of the landscape are connected with the sleepy lizard or the slugs or with people north of Ayer's rock or people south of Ayer's rock. There are legends about how sleepy lizard decided to stop there and stay there, and that's why the rock looks like a lizard. But at the same time it's a continuous present. Their eternal dreamtime seems to be some sort of continuous present, which fits in with their migration cycle in the sense that some animals mentioned in the migration songs are known to have become extinct twelve or fourteen thousand years ago. This means that they have the oldest viable human culture on the planet that we know of. I don't think there is any other poetry that has survived that long. If you did, as Thomas Merton once wanted to, measure the validity or viability of a culture by its stability, the Aborigines have the most viable culture, or they had until we began destroying it.

This is a geographic migration. The tribe moving around in a several-hundred-mile journey might take a couple years, or a larger perimeter might take forty or fifty years to go around, eating up all the foodstuff on the way and then having to move on to another camp maybe twenty or thirty miles away. Then staying there several weeks or a month, as long as the foodstuff would last, and having to move on further. That's for the central Australian desert tribes, at any rate.

Their oral traditions are as old as twelve thousand years, so in that time they picked up a lot of experience. There were individuals who did make migrations outward. And there are presumably some tribes that wandered off for a long time and met other tribes. But they had their own space, their own territory, their own cycle.

I don't know what the structure of other ceremonial songs would be, I have just heard migration songs, funerary chanting, and children's chanting. The first songs I heard were children's songs. [chants, keeping time with song sticks] That translates as: *Jumping into the willy-willy one by one, jumping in the willy-willy one by one, jumping in the willy-willy one by one.* Willy-willy is a little, red sand dust storm, a child-size tornado the kids could jump in and out of. Or: *Tossing the cricket stone one to another, tossing the cricket stone one t'another, tossing the cricket stone one t'another.* That's obviously a British translation, you could also say tossing the baseball. And: *Jumping over the windbreak one by one, jumping over the windbreak one by one, jumping over the windbreak one by one.*

The migration songs involving the dead that I heard, I recorded a lot, but I didn't memorize any of them. They would be something like: *Sun rise, clouds of lyrebirds; sun rise, clouds of lyrebirds; sun rise, clouds of lyrebirds.* Or: *Sun over horizon, silver fish; sun over horizon, silver fish; sun over horizon, silver fish.* That is, simply a description of the fish and animals they would meet in the ocean, or what kind of weather it was likely to expect depending on the season. I think those soul migration songs were also involved with seasons, they would have to have specific seasonal information. I was astounded by the fact that it was a geographic structure, guiding the soul along in a William Carlos Williams–like physical world.

I tried adapting this song structure to my own use after a while. In the center of Australia is Ayers Rock, a large, red sandstone monolith. It is porous so it collects water; water is continually dripping through the center of it down to pools around the edge on the shady side and on the sunny side. It has become a sacred place for central Australian tribes to do ceremonies and stop at, because there is always water there. This is called "Uluru, or Ayers Rock," and it was written on a plane approaching Ayers Rock:

When the red pond fills, fish appear; when the red pond fills, fish appear, when the red pond fills, fish appear.

When the red pond dries, fish disappear; when the red pond dries, fish disappear; when the red pond dries, fish disappear.

Everything built on the desert crumbles to dust; everything built on the desert crumbles to dust; everything built on the desert crumbles to dust.

Electric cable transmission wires swept down; electric cable transmission wires swept down; electric cable transmission wires swept down.

The lizard people came out of the rock; the lizard people came out of the rock; the lizard people came out of the rock.

The red kangaroo people forgot their own song; the red kangaroo people forgot their own song; the red kangaroo people forgot their own song.

Only a man with four sticks can cross the Simpson Desert; only a man with four sticks can cross the Simpson Desert; only a man with four sticks can cross the Simpson Desert.

One rain turns red dust green with leaves; one rain turns red dust green with leaves; one rain turns red dust green with leaves.

One raindrop begins the universe; one raindrop begins the universe; one raindrop begins the universe.

When the raindrop dries worlds come to their end; when the raindrop dries worlds come to their end; when the raindrop dries worlds come to their end.

I tried applying that to the Vietnam War, in terms of stopping the bombing, thinking that it was such a basic form, it would be a way to get attention in large rallies and also get across a very simple message. Wandering around in peace rallies over a two-year period, I evolved a chant which I use with Australian Aborigine song sticks. It varies with the locality and it is repetitive, naturally. I'll try some of it:

Whom bomb? We bomb them. Whom bomb? We bomb them. Whom bomb? We bomb them.

What do we do? We bomb. We bomb them. What do we do? We bomb. We bomb them. What do we do? We bomb. We bomb them.

What do we do? Who do we bomb? What do we do? Who do we bomb? What do we do? Who do we bomb?

Whom bomb? We bomb them. Whom bomb? We bomb them.

Whom bomb? You bomb you. Whom bomb? You bomb you.

Stop th'electric bomb war, stop 'Nam war now. Stop th'electric bomb war, stop 'Nam war now. Stop th'electric bomb war, stop 'Nam war now.

Stop damned robot wars. Stop damned robot wars. Stop damned robot wars.

Nixon, Quaker stop your bomb. Kissinger stop your bomb. Bunker, Christian stop your bomb.

Helms Helms stop your bomb. Nixon Quaker stop your bomb. Hebrew stop your bomb.

Laird Laird stop your bomb. Nixon Nixon stop your bomb.

Stop the bombs. Stop the bombs. Stop stop stop the bombs.
Stop the bombs. Stop the bombs. Stop stop stop the bomb.
Washington Congress stop your bomb.
Columbia Capital stop your bomb.
Federal Government stop your bomb.

South Carolina stop your bomb.
Houston Houston stop your bomb.
Tallahassee stop your bomb.
Birmingham stop your bomb.
Tampa Tampa stop your bomb.
Carolina stop your bomb.
Do the Charleston, stop your bomb.
Rock Hills, stop bombs. Greenville, stop bomb.
Hot damn, stop your bombin' North Vietnam.
Florence Florence stop your bomb.
Write your senator stop your bomb.
Stop your bombs, Anderson.
Phone your congressman stop your bomb.
Spartanburg, stop your war. Stop before we murder more.
George Meany, you're a whore. Sellin' labor for the war.
Phone your senators, stop your bomb.
Federal Capital, stop your bomb.
Washington Congress, stop your bomb.
Write your congressman, stop your bomb.
Whitehouse, stop your bombs.
State Department, stop your bomb.
Pentagon, stop your bomb.
Central Intelligence stop your bomb. Central Intelligence stop your bomb.
Pentagon, stop your bomb.
State Department stop your bomb.
Whitehouse Whitehouse, stop your bomb.
Judge judge, judge the bomb.
Justice of the peace, ban the bomb.
Supreme Court war crime bomb.
Mississippi, stop your bomb.
Soldier boy put down your arms.
General Electric, stop your bomb.
Memphis, Nashville, pray for calm.
Winston Salem, stop your bomb.
IBM, stop your bomb.
Jesus, Mary, stop your bomb.
Stop Texas dropping bombs.
Western Electric, stop your bomb.
Mama, mama, stop the bomb.
Father, god, oh stop your bomb.

Sister, sister, stop your bomb.
General Motors, stop your bomb.
Army bombers, stop your bombs.
Navy bombers, stop your bombs.
Airforce bombers, stop your bombs.
Uncle Sam, you bomb the land.
Uncle Sam, don't bomb the land.
Stop, stop, stop the bombs.
Uncle Sam, don't bomb the land. Don't be damned. Stop the bomb.
Ford, lord, stop your bombs.
Kissinger, oh quit your bombs.
Rockefeller, stop your bombs.
Schlesinger, stop your bombs.
Oil industry, stop your bombs.
Auto industry, stop your bombs.
National Senate, stop your bombs.
Representatives, stop your bombs.
Illinois, stop your bomb.
Hey Chicago, stop your bomb.
Mr. Percy, stop your bomb.
Mayor Daley, stop your bomb.
Hey mafia, stop your bomb.
Righteous senator, stop your bomb.
Stop your bomb, Stevenson.
Write your congressman, stop the bombs.
Ash, Michigan, stop your war. Stop before we murder more.
Middle West, we're a whore, if we sell ourselves more war.
Middle Georgia, stop your bomb.
Birmingham, stop your bomb.
Hot damn Alabams, stop your bombing North Vietnam!

—July 23, 1976

N.B.: This transcription is of the impromptu, improvised version presented as part of this lecture. The original poem, "Hum Bom!," was published in *The Fall of America* (1971).

BASIL BUNTING: AN INTRODUCTION

Tom Pickard

'M SURE MANY OF YOU ARE AS FAMILIAR WITH BASIL BUNTING'S WORK AS I
am, and there are some amongst you who have made a more scholarly
assessment than I'm capable of, or have the inclination to do, but I want
to make you familiar with some speculations that I made about him and
that I solicited from mutual friends and admirers over the years. I
should probably preface it with a letter he wrote in response to an editor
at Faber and Faber who'd asked for an introduction to a volume of Pound's
early poetry, so you'll see just how much any attempted biography is a
transgression:

> No doubt it is fitting that maggots consume us in the end, or at least the rubbish
> we scatter as we go; but I'd rather leave the lid on my dustbin and the earth on
> my friend's graves. Piety takes curious forms: the toenail clippings of Saint What's
> His Name are revered. I don't think religion is much advanced by that. It would
> be more profitable, more to his glory, to throw away some of the poems Pound
> printed than to print those he threw away himself. I apologise for my lack of sym-
> pathy for the industrious compilers.

And there is another note worth quoting, from the manuscript note-
book of *Briggflatts* that was given to me as a boy so that I might learn the
craft from it:

> The scholar ought to be like the poet, an Ishmael, scouted and feared; a magician,
> impious, to be consulted in secrecy and shame. Only the neglected by man can
> keep either truth or beauty in view. The moment advantage has a part in his stud-
> ies or his craft, his work perishes.

The paragraph is crossed out in the manuscript and unpublished in the
final poem. He may only have been trying to get into the mind of a character, perhaps (as it is an "autobiography") that of Bunting himself. It may
also describe a deeply held belief.

I should also say that I come to this talk with as great a love for Bunting that I ever had; he was a forthright, deeply loyal, and supportive friend, but also, as Amiri Baraka has said about another much-loved friend, Edward Dorn, "he would rather make you his enemy than lie."

However, with this declaration of love for Bunting, you might ask why I'm breaking one of his cardinal rules, expressed in his lifelong insistence to friends to destroy his letters, as he did theirs, in the belief that the poetry alone should stand and speak for the man or woman who wrote it. The answer is that I have his written permission, and I'll read it to you in full so that you might take cognizance of it in relation to what I have to say tonight. When I was living in London in the 1980s, without the means to travel north and, therefore, unable to see much of my old friend and mentor, I entertained the crazy notion to know and honor a life by writing his biography. Crazy because who would enable me to embark on such a comparatively expensive exercise? I wrote to ask his permission and this was his response:

Take heed

My biography appears in Who's Who, *complete except for the date of my death which will not be delayed very long. Whatever anybody else writes must be looked on as fiction. Tom Pickard has a vigorous imagination and I hope whatever he writes will amuse you. I haven't read it; and once it's in print I shall not trouble to deny it unless it seems to libel someone else.*

So you have been warned to take it all with a pinch of salt.

What follows is a selection of material written or "gathered" over the years as fiction or documentary. I have to look at it as a way of understanding the relationship and the man. It won't be chronological either. Although some of the pieces have been published in magazines, I don't think any of the projects ever achieved completion or their aim. But it is how I've tried to deal with what I know of his life and mine as a writer. The documentary material is taken from interviews with friends and colleagues who knew him: Roy Fisher, Edward Dorn, Allen Ginsberg, and his publishers Stuart and Deidre Montgomery. The interviews were shot on film for a projected BBC documentary that fell by the Thatcherite wayside and was therefore never completed or seen by an audience. I have the footage in cans, gathering dust.

At the age of sixteen, in 1962, I somehow found a copy of the magazine *Kulchur* and saw in it an advertisement for William Burroughs's book, *Exterminator*, published by Jargon Press and I ordered a copy. Jonathan Williams responded and told me of Basil Bunting and supplied his phone number. At that time Bunting used to commute to work as subeditor of the financial pages of a newspaper in Newcastle from his home on the river Tyne at Wylam. Judging by letters to Pound and Zukofsky and others from the period, he'd given up the literary ghost and was living an English version of "internal exile" having been ditched by the Foreign Office and the *Times* in the early 1950s and at the same time rejected by T. S. Eliot at Faber's. In fact, back in the north, after being expelled from Iran, he found it very difficult to get any work at all. He says, in a letter dated 1 August, 1952, from an address in Northumberland to his line manager at the Foreign department of the *Times*,

> *Possible employers seem to believe that my expulsion from Persia must have been due to some lack of discretion on my part, otherwise the Times would not have dispensed with my services and the government would have made more fuss than it did. I don't quite see how to combat this idea effectively. Assurances are no good.*

He also sadly notes the impounding by the authorities of his largely irreplaceable library of Persian books. The sixties turned up on his doorstep bright eyed and raggy arsed in the form of myself and a young audience waiting in Newcastle's Morden Tower. The city's elegant center was blackened by industrial pollution, as were the suburbs of workers' barracks. Coal mining, shipbuilding, and armaments were the principle traditional industries and they were in decline. I left school at fourteen and joined the lengthening dole queues, and by the age of sixteen, was convinced I was a poet and had an article about teenage unemployment published in the anarchist quarterly journal, *Anarchy*, to prove it.

EXTERIOR BEACH AT BAMBROUGH SIXTIES

Long, silvery deserted beaches of Bambrough, on the north Northumbrian coastline. The dunes with sharp grass growing through them. A limited range of colors: fawn grass, thin translucent waterline, dark sea, the silvering sand. Long perspectives. Dark, low threatening sky. Solitary. A little chill. Connie and Basil are walking through the dunes. It is quite difficult going. They are a little flirtatious. Tom is following them trying to push a pram through the sand.

CONNIE: I know you like Wordsworth, Basil, but wasn't he rather solemn?

BASIL: Not at all, my dear. He is good at the ancient steady still-surviving Medieval English joke which Chaucer was fairly good at too. But Wordsworth I think was brilliant. Take his "The Idiot Boy." [*Basil pauses and looks behind him, waiting for Tom to catch them up.*] It is of course a story I have heard told in dozens of English pubs but nobody ever mentions Wordsworth. Wordsworth no doubt got it there. But he does it bloody well.

Tom is struggling to push and pull the pram through the sand while trying to stay up with them and listen to the conversation. He is failing on both counts. Basil and Connie walk on.

CONNIE: You were talking about "The Idiot Boy."

Cut back to Basil. He takes a draw on his cigarette, then continues the walk.

BASIL: Then there is "The Waggoner," which is not an ancient story picked up somewhere, but one concocted by Wordsworth himself. It is very funny. It keeps on accumulating absurdities and absurdities for pages and pages and pages, until at the very end there is such an absurd picture presented. Then you read critics and teachers who say Wordsworth had no sense of humor. It is absolute bollocks. Of the poets we've had he is the funniest of all.

He gently puts his hand on Connie's arse in an effort to help her over a sand dune (POV baby in the pushchair).

CONNIE: Do you really think so?

Tom struggling behind, trying to see what's happening. The baby (head and shoulders) being bumped along over the dunes. He sees their feet—then is bounced up at an askew angle to see the sky like a jump cut, sudden and incongruous. As though the camera (POV baby) fell from the pram.

BASIL: The thing that is most steadily overlooked is his extraordinary skill with narrative. I don't think there is any other English poet whose narrative is as complicated, as skillfully orchestrated and as good as "The Brothers." If it had been written by Henry James or by Conrad it would have a sixty-page preface to tell you why it had been done in that way. The construction is extraordinarily fine. Nobody as far as I know has told a short story like that.

Tom, hot and flustered with the effort of pushing the pram though the sand, at last catches up with them.

TOM: His mate Coleridge smoked a lot of blow, didn't he?

Cut away to POV Social Security Fraud Squad officer, hidden behind a sand dune spying on the group through binoculars. Basil and Connie walking on. Tom behind, pulling the baby in the pram. The pram has windmills blowing from each corner, and a scraggly balloon chasing the breeze. The official makes notes.

Once, pre-*Briggflatts*, when I visited him in the midsixties and was writing to London publishers to try and awaken an interest in his work, he showed me a mean-spirited letter he'd received from T. S. Eliot (it clearly hadn't lit the fire yet) in which he refused to publish BB at Faber and Faber. Bunting had attacked Eliot's *Criterion* in *Poetry–Chicago* (1932) as "*an international disaster, since he began to love his gloom, and regretfully, resignedly, to set about perpetuating the causes of it—kings, religion, and formalism. . . . I have nothing to say against his poetry, amongst the finest of the age; but against his influence on the poetry of others, the involuntary extinguisher he applies to every little light, while professing, maybe truly, to hate the dark.*"

Maybe Eliot had a long memory, but the bitterness of his letter puzzled me and in the early 1990s I asked Edward Dorn about it in an interview. He responded with his usual incisive irreverence and wit:

Well Eliot occupied the position of power and one of his strategies was to write essays and redefine what literature could be and was according to his own lights. Basil wouldn't have been a threat exactly. I mean what could threaten T. S. Eliot? But he certainly wouldn't have conformed to what Eliot wanted, as a buttressing element in his own position in the canon. We have to remember that in those days the canon hadn't even been questioned. It was assumed there was a canon and the canon was alright. Eliot was maniacal in the protection of his career. There's something very, very strange that I've never quite been able to figure out, but he had this strange prescience about his own career in the sense that somehow he managed to hit a mark down the way so far off that it's astonishing. His papers are going to be opened either the year after or the year before the Kennedy assassination papers which is going to be in 2027 or 2028. That's just amazing that he could, in a postmortem sense, opportunistically take advantage of such a mark on the board of time. This is unheard of, it's unprecedented. It's quite amazing. Maybe he killed Kennedy, I don't know. . . . T. S. Eliot was the midwife who was constantly trying to kill the baby. He was the abortionist of the postmodern movement; he controlled who was going to be born and who wasn't insofar as he could.

When I went out to meet him for the first time, he was living in a large house with Sima, his much-younger Persian wife, their two children, and his ninety-year-old mother, who played Bach on a piano and who told me she had once told Yeat's fortune with tarot cards in Rapallo. The train ride from Newcastle Central station to Wylam at that time traveled along the north side of the river Tyne to Scotswood Bridge, passing alongside and through miles of factories that manufactured tanks and other heavy armaments. Once over the bridge, the railway line followed the course of the river for another ten miles of old woodland. Wylam station consists of an open platform and I asked directions from one of the few people around. Elm Bank is a street of detached and semidetached houses set back from the road by large gardens that often concealed them. Others, like Shadingfield, the Buntings' home, had a small patch of garden in front but a long steep one at the back running down to the railway line and river. This was the first time I'd visited a house with a name instead of a number and was the kind of dwelling that my mother would work in as a charwoman. Walking up the otherwise unpopulated road thick with overhanging trees, a police sergeant stepped out of a hedgerow and asked why I was there if not for no good. As he emptied my pockets I explained that I'd come to see Mr. Bunting.

Wing Commander Bunting, you mean.

This was a challenge to my pacifist principles I'd not anticipated.

Nar, he's a poet.

He seemed disappointed that the contents of my pockets contained no more than a return rail ticket, a scrap of paper with Bunting's name and address on it, a pen, and some small change.

I've seen you before?

Don't think so.

And I don't want to see you again.

A sixty-four-year-old man with a Kipling mustache opened the door and greeted me with a handshake. Bunting invited me into his study that adjoined the lobby. It was small, but shelved all around with the books that were close to him—his Zukofsky, Yeats, Pound, Dante, as I was to discover later. There was a desk and chair and another for a visitor. After a while I was invited into the dining room to meet his wife, Sima, and her Armenian mother, recently arrived from Iran. Sima was direct, sensual, fun loving, and incredibly strong—her mother spoke no English and wore black, burka-like robes and was weather beaten. Bunting's children came through the room occasionally and I was introduced to young Tom and Maria, both going to fee-paying grammar schools in Newcastle; Tom's experience there of racism left him scarred and with a determination never to live in the northeast again. He came and borrowed some carbon paper from his father for his homework, and Basil grumbled that he only used a sheet once before discarding it. Maria was older, already conscious of her charm, and treated her father with affectionate condescension. Sima's mother had brought a large quantity of caviar for Basil, and he invited me to try some.

He won't like it. Do you, Tom? Sima said.

Before I could reply Basil said, Bring us the toast and we'll see.

Sima supplied a plate of toast and Basil began to spread the caviar thickly over the slices while she and her mother watched us.

I felt the black, shiny cluster of eggs dissolve in my mouth. Mm, it's good.

Sima translated for her mother and they both laughed. Basil took a large bite and chewed with relish. It was dusk when we finished eating and he poured another malt whiskey.

Well, would you like me to read you *The Spoils?*

I said yes, but he'd already taken the first page from an envelope. It was typed on sheet of copy paper.

Oh, we're going to go. Come on, Mammy, Sima said, and took her mother into another room.

The Spoils had been published in *Poetry–Chicago* in the midfifties, but not in the UK. Before reading the poem he poured us both a drink of malt whiskey, then quoted the line from the Koran that begins the poem, *The spoils are for God.*

All those foreign names, all that condensation, pared down images; it was complex and challenging and had it not been for his reading it aloud I probably wouldn't have made the effort to understand it—but my imagination and ear were caught and images stayed in mind long afterwards.

> They despise police work,
> are not masters of filing;
> always a task for foreigners
> to make them unhappy,
> unproductive and rich.
>
> have you seen a falcon stoop,
> accurate unforeseen and absolute
> between wind ripples over harvest? Dread
> of what's to be, is and has been—
> were we not better dead?
>
> His wing churns air
> to flight.
> Feathers alight
> with sun, he rises where
> dazzle rebuts our stare,
> wonder our fright.

I was dizzy with the drink and the caviar, the exotic sounds made by the poem, the wild and beautiful Persian wife, the big rambling house and the dusky train ride back along the river to Newcastle, and our tiny room with the baby. I don't think I ever saw the world the same way again after that. Bunting sums up the visit more succinctly in a letter to Zukofsky:

> First, about a year ago, somebody rang me up on the phone and asked if I would like to read some poetry. It turned out that the voice thought it belonged to a poet of sorts, so I said: Come out. He took the next train and turned up inside an hour, a boy of eighteen, long-haired and fairly ragged, with a fist full of manuscript.

Naturally I expected drivel, but I thought it only kind to have a look. Well there was a good deal of drivel, a good deal of useless violence, and a good deal of rather helpless filling out of lines; but very deeply buried there was poetry. I told him surgery was required, took a pen and crossed out a lot that was encumbering the stuff. He watched, then grabbed up his manuscripts and disappeared. I thought he was gone for good, offended. Not a bit of it. In two days he was back. . . . Well, I thought, if poetry really has the power to renew itself, I'd better write something for these younger chaps to read. And with the boy, Tom Pickard, and Gael Turnbull each urging me on, I planned a longish poem, about 750 lines which I finished about a month ago. I believe it is the best thing I have ever done.

NEGLECT

Roy Fisher: He didn't get through to a very wide public and that's partly chance, but I think it also expresses the way in which the modernism which he was a late figure in was gently but firmly repulsed by English literary life. It happened then, and of course it's going on now, and I put it down to a particularly English version of the old dictum that knowledge is power. The English version is more subtle; it goes: ignorance is power. It's a precious commodity; you acquire it, you nurture it, you see that it's carefully and rather obliquely taught in institutions of higher learning and an ignorance specialist will guard his own ignorance, acquire techniques for preserving it and will then pass it on and preserve a status quo in a tick-over mode. And there is power in it. It's culturally a blight and it's with us. Basil was a victim of this.

HIS LOST WEEKEND

At the age sixty-nine or sixty-eight and after the publication of *Briggflatts*, Basil Bunting's second marriage disintegrated and he fled to the depth of Northumberland to occupy a winter let that was damp and cold in the neighbourhood of King Ida's domain—low inland but close to the North Sea and the massive castles that have fortified the Northumbrian coast since the Dark Ages. It took me a couple of weeks to locate his refuge, along rain-soaked roads lined with bushes dripping sea fret. With a miserable fire burning and not much in the pantry I found him, cigarette in his mouth, reading Dante, a historical biography, and a couple of detective novels. He was wrapped in a short, woollen scarf and a woollen jacket that his wife had purchased from a church jumble sale. For the first few years that I knew him, all of his clothes were purchased from jumble sales and he walked with a stoop. When he opened the door he said,

Well, I'll be damned, what are you doing here?

Although the space was unsuitable, without much heat, he could use it to reconstruct his life with a stoicism that enabled him to meet his fate face on, whatever it threw at him. About twenty years later, a few days after his death, I dreamt of him standing on a windblown beach looking into a gray-slated North Sea at an enormous onrushing wave that was about to engulf us. This is the last verse.

> We stood by the North Sea
> a wash swirled around our feet
> furthest from the shore
> you stared towards a squall
> on the dark horizon.
> I warned against a threatening wave; swelling
> it would overwhelm us.
>
> Leaping to safety I glanced back
> and saw you,
> steady, silent, still,
> tracing the trajectory
> of the wave's engulfing curve.

"What the hell" was always his response to adversity—his or mine—but now he began to say more frequently that old people should be put out of their misery when they reached his age. He prepared a pot of tea and we sat in front of a whimpering fire burning slack coal and drinking whiskey.

When I first met him, Bunting was living in his native Northumberland and had been since 1952 when Dr. Mussadeque, who led a revolution against the British, threw him out of Iran. It was alleged that he had had a particular dislike of Bunting, who was the *Times* correspondent and a former intelligence officer in Tehran during World War II. Now, sitting at his woeful fire, he was alone, poor, and living in temporary accommodation. He would spend most of the rest his life like that.

FIRST IMPRESSIONS

Roy Fisher: When I first knew him in the sixties he hadn't turned into the very imposing old man that he became, with horned eyebrows and flashing eyes and a jutting beard. He was rather removed because he had cataracts, he had no eye contact with anybody, he hadn't got the beard, and he had that remoteness from the people around him that a person with very restricted sight had.

Edward Dorn to Charles Olson: Basil Bunting is a fine old man, very funny the way he'll stare at you with this silly grin on his face, up close, and you think he hasn't got it until suddenly he makes his answer. A real, seedy old gent, but very straight, I liked him immensely, he hasn't any of that put-off porcelainity I thought Zukofsky had . . . [1]

RF: He was, I think, resting from a trip from Newcastle to the other side of Worcester, and he was remote from a conversation that was going on. It was one of those Sunday afternoon conversations of younger people in I think the late sixties stimulated by an overindulgence in the Sunday papers, which that day were talking about the state of the novel. It was before the novelists had got uppity and really sort of taken centre stage, but there was a big discussion going on with contributions from this talking head and that about wither the novel and we were all thinking about it, and Basil exhibited a characteristic he had which was of living quite outside the time he was in. He was with you alright, but his mind was populated with people from wherever in history he chose to reside. He would plunge into Gibbon and come out again, he would talk in terms of Lucretius or Martial as if they were mates, he would suddenly in conversation savage some later Victorian critic who'd been inflicted on him at school, so you knew that his time dimension was different from yours, and this poem comes from that particular sense, and it's called "News for the Ear" because he couldn't see, but he was listening to us.

> On a kitchen chair in the grass at Stifford's Bridge
> the cataract still on his eyes,
> the poet Bunting dozed in the afternoon.
> Bored with the talk of the state of literature that year,
> sinking away under it to his preferred parish among old names,
> long reckonings, but roused at the sound of good news
> and surfacing with a rush, a grunt of delight from centuries down.
> What, has the novel blown over at last then?

Helen Egli: Bunting's life had its share of strange coincidences, and Deidre Montgomery, of Fulcrum Press, told me of this one. Shortly after they had set up as publishers in the midsixties, the Montgomerys were living in a couple of attics in Lawn Road, Hampstead, with their new baby. Despite the cramped accommodation, Basil, who had become good friends with them, used to stay there on his rare visits to London. They looked forward to his coming because he was an excellent storyteller, especially when his vocal chords were oiled with good drink, and he was happy amongst children. In other words he was an amiable, amusing, and illuminating guest. In the basement of the house in Lawn Road, a handsome but elderly woman lived. Stuart and Deidre knew her as a neighbour with a beautiful bone structure and thought it a mere coincidence that one of Basil's early poems had been dedicated to a woman of the same name, Helen Egli. One day the Montgomerys were walking around the Tate Gallery and discovered a portrait by Augustus John of a beautiful young woman whose features reminded them immediately of their elderly neighbour living in the basement. They were curious to know: was she the Helen Egli of the John portrait and the Bunting poem? They weren't on sufficiently intimate terms to ask her, but on his next visit to London they would ask Basil.

So, after the baby was put to bed, a meal and a good wine, and as the single-malt whiskey bottle was opened, they told him about the handsome old woman who lived in the basement and could she be the same Helen Egli. The cheery flush of alcohol drained from his face and the hand holding the glass discernibly trembled. Stuart said he turned white as a sheet and stood up saying I'll never come and visit you again, never come back to this house again.

According to Montgomery the affair was quite tempestuous and he couldn't get on with her at all and the child that she had by somebody else Basil's parents helped to bring up at the time. But Basil actually left England and went to France, originally, to get away from her effectively. And for years he would avoid all comment on her.

Some three or four weeks later she died, so they never met and he returned as a visitor to their house. But the coincidence didn't end there; Helen had a son who was also the local postman and he would see letters addressed to Basil Bunting care of Montgomery, his publisher. Even though he was aware of their past relationship he had never mentioned Bunting's current connection with the house on Lawn Road to his mother. After her death the son carried out the requirements of her will, to burn the letters that Basil had written to her three or four decades earlier.

POLITICS

BB's letter to Ezra: *I was on the spot when the View Pit was flooded and forty-five men drowned, I heard what the men had to say about it and the whole cursed system when there wasn't any question of politics, mining or otherwise, but just sheer human common sense. My grandfather, whom I knew pretty well when I was a kid, was a miner, son of a miner. I know the solidarity of those people, and I watched it break up in '26, when I was all the time in a mining village, took the chair at one of Cook's meetings, stuck a knife in the tires of government strike-breaking lorry, and tried unsuccessfully nearly every paper in the country to get the scandalous, faked benches of magistrates who condemned the strikers to years of hard labour shown up. Not even the Independent Labour Party's rag would publish the facts.*

Every anti-Semitism, antiniggerism, anti-Moorism, that I can recall in history was base, had its foundations in the meanest kind of envy and in greed. It makes me sick to see you covering yourself with that kind of filth. It is not an arguable question, has not been arguable for at least nineteen centuries. . . . To spew out anti-Semite bile in a letter to Louis . . . is uncommonly close to what has got to be called the behaviour of the skunk. . . . it is hard to see how you are going to stop the rot of your mind and heart without a pretty thoroughgoing repudiation of what you have spent a lot of work on. You ought to have the courage for that, but I confess I don't expect to see it.

Letter to Jonathan Williams dated 1/12/79: *I am infuriated by the unshakable naivety of people (Tom Pickard is one) who will believe any propaganda which looks as though it came from the left, and sign their own death warrants if asked in the name of Humanity of the Proletariat. The success of the Persian priests and landlords with their anti-Shah stuff is a case in point. Whatever the Shah is, he is far further to the left than the present regime or its supporters; but who is to persuade students and such?*

BRIGGFLATTS

Edward Dorn: *Briggflatts* is the great love poem of the twentieth century. This is not the most obvious thing in the world because it's the big structure, it has a musical element and a certain timing which, you know, is associated with modern poetry and, in fact, I think it's also a great modern poem in a sense that it takes geography and personal history and an incredible sense of place. But in the end it's about love and that's what makes it. Love poetry is not, hasn't been, significant in this century, which also makes this a very unique poem in that it uses the modern structure and range of effect, which, in fact actually, the academy and the academic mind feel uncomfortable with. This has been Zukofsky's problem, this has been

Olson's problem, this has been anybody's problem who wants to incorporate more and more narrative and cast the net wider and wider and Basil succeeded in doing this in *Briggflatts* in a very peculiar way.

As I'm sure you know, *Briggflatts* was inspired pretty much by the memory of his first childhood sweetheart, Peggy Greenwood. He'd not seen her for fifty years, having perhaps jilted her and feeling remorse ever since. And when he wrote the poem something remarkable happened. Gael Turnbull and Michael Shayer came to visit him and said that he had found Peggy. It was as though his creation had stepped out of the canvas. It wasn't long before he went to visit her and they had a brief relationship of sorts. Diedre Montgomery recalls an occasion when Basil was staying in London with them and on a whim Stuart took him to collect her.

Basil had talked much about the desire to see Peggy, to spend some time with her, and Stuart said—and it seemed a daft thing as this was late in the evening and it was a long way to drive—"Well, let's do it." He was not a young man, but there was a twinkle in Basil's eye at the very thought of it and that was all it needed to encourage Stuart so off they went. They came back many hours later and arrived in the kitchen in our flat and there was this small, round woman who I'd only known through Basil's poem, as a slim teenager, and there was Basil, who had the look of a boy about him. He said very little, but it was all written on his face, the delight, the pleasure, the joy and we talked for many hours that night. She really appreciated the celebration that *Briggflatts* was and the passion that's there in the poem, and it made the poem very true in the life sense of what the relationship had been. She was a very reticent woman. This was not somebody who was going to pour her heart out to anybody, but she let it be felt. They stayed with us a few days and then Peggy went back home again. She was married at the time. Her husband had been away just then. I think Basil would have liked to develop the relationship much further, but Peggy was, as she explained, a married woman, had lived a staid and steady life.

Basil was very happy and was convinced he and Peggy would be able to live together, although he was, as usual, desperately uncertain of just how he'd manage. Then things seemed to fall apart, like a dream, and he was on his own again. He couldn't seem to write himself into his own creation.

Stuart Montgomery: She took me on one side and said "I don't understand what he sees in me." She was at that time sixty-five years old, as he was, and she said, "He sees me as a small child; he looks at me and sees me as I was, he doesn't see me as I now am." He was really idealising her, and I think that's what had happened. He crystallised her with time and saw her as this young, innocent child that he remembered, and that's what made the poem. That's the driving force in that poem.

—May 1981

INFILTRATING THE MASS MEDIA: ROMANIA, 1989

Andrei Codrescu

DON'T FORGET ABOUT THE TITLE OF THE LECTURE, WHICH WAS arrived at in some moment of confusion—about infiltrating the mass media; what infiltrating? I am the mass media. But I'll talk about the media nonetheless, about a number of interesting new perversities concerning the media which occurred to me in the past year, that have to do with new levels of unreality and confusion between reality and what we hear and don't hear, that come directly from the events that I witnessed in Romania. I went there in December of 1989, I got to Romania two days after the execution of the Ceaușescus, the couple that ran the country for twenty-five years. I went there to report with an NPR (National Public Radio) crew and an ABC TV news crew that came in a few days later. What happened is, I wanted to go back very much, I wanted to go back because I left there when I was nineteen years old and I wanted to go back for a physical reason, which was to go and smell the place and hear the language spoken in its natural ways. The main thing that interested me was my hometown of Sibiu, in Transylvania, that's where I wanted to go; but I also had this job to do, which involved translating interviews for some of the NPR people—they didn't have enough translators—and also recording my own impressions. When we got there we were sure that we were going to be killed, because, according to all the news reports at the time, there was a civil war raging in Romania. We heard from all the networks that up to sixty thousand people had been killed, that so-called terrorists fighting for Ceaușescu were mounting a fierce resistance. And we saw a number of images that were very striking that nobody will ever forget who was watching television in those days: the image of the flag with a hole cut in it where the socialist anthem had been removed; the image of a young woman and her baby, killed by a single bullet, lying on the cobblestone street in Timișoara; the so-called massacre of children on the steps of the Timișoara cathedral. These are all things that were on television, sometimes by themselves and sometimes sharing the split screen with

Panama because the Panama invasion was going on at the same time. Before I left, I thought, look how slickly the u.s. army has taken over Panama City and is running the broadcasting stations, the television; the images we were getting out of Panama were very smooth and boring compared to the images of chaos and spontaneity and people on the streets, the kind of television that was coming directly from Bucharest. So there was one picture, the slick propaganda apparatus of the Pentagon, and the other, people coming in off the streets to talk on television in Romania, the new government being born on TV, the extraordinary images of the streets, the fighting—the television station was reporting itself under fire, was reporting continually on the "terrorists" (again, with quotation marks) bursting into the television station, one man came out of the wall from a tunnel and killed six people inside the TV station . . . all this stuff.

When I got to Romania we stayed at the Intercontinental Hotel and every reporter who was there was reporting the same stuff, even war-hardened veterans who had been doing all sorts of war reporting in Lebanon and elsewhere. A French reporter who had covered the civil war in Lebanon told me that for fifteen years of the civil war in Lebanon there had been fifty thousand people killed, whereas here in Romania in one week we were hearing sixty thousand dead. And everyone believed it. Our secretary of state went on *Meet the Press* and said that the United States would not have any objection if the Soviet troops went into Romania on the side of the so-called rebels. He should have known, even if he didn't know what the situation was for real, he should have known that the Romanians, for one, hated Russian troops more than they probably did the Ceauşescus, and that was just about the worst suggestion that anyone could make. So when I got there, there was the revolution, and people were on the streets, the television station was surrounded by mobs, all wanting to have their say. They were led into the station one by one, they would talk to a producer and they would be let on TV to tell their story, unrehearsed, they would just do it, a lot of them. But there were certain signs that things were not what they seemed to be. I was trying not to pay attention to them. There were a few cautionary notes sounded by people—they said, how come the fighting is all taking place at night? for instance. You'd never actually see any of the fighting. And none of the so-called terrorists who were caught were in custody, they all slipped away. The war was being conducted on television by generals, by the general in charge of the secret police and the chief general of the army, they were back-to-back with telephones telling their troops in the field what to do.

Then something happened to me. I started to have doubts about what I was seeing when in Sibiu I saw a report that the water was poisoned and a Belgian toxicologist holding a vial of water was on TV saying it was poisoned, it had a concentration of this and that; and that evening I got drunk with a correspondent from TASS, we drank a bottle of vodka together, and he told me that he'd been in Timișoara in western Transylvania where everything started on December 10 and nothing happened in Timișoara until the fifteenth, and not only him, but there were also two other Soviet TASS correspondents, three people from Hungarian radio, and two from Tanjug, the Yugoslav state TV. I asked them why they were there before anything ever happened, and he winked, you know? Now I was back in the land of signals, winks, and hand gestures, I was relearning again slowly, one of them being that everyone, when they didn't want to say something, would roll their eyes. And the other is that when someone went by or just talked to us they would go gesture to their left shoulder, meaning rank, epaulets, or both at the same time, meaning they worked for the secret police. And when I was talking with those other people who'd just gone by they would point to the people I'd just been talking to and wink and make the gesture, secret police, etc. I was not conversant in this language anymore but I was picking it up pretty fast. So, I didn't get much out of the Russian guy who'd been reporting from Timișoara before there was anything to report, except that I woke up about four in the morning horribly thirsty after all the vodka and I stuck my head under the faucet and drank about four gallons of water before I remembered that it was supposed to be poisoned. I just lay there for about three hours waiting to die . . . that didn't happen, so I thought, hmm. What about the Belgian toxicologist and all of his "concentrations"?

The people we interviewed were some of the most horrible people in the whole country. They were still in their offices. One of them was the chief architect of the regime; he was responsible personally for something called the systematization program, which was to raze all the peasant villages and move everyone into these cement blocks around factory buildings, a kind of Cambodian program in reverse, instead of driving everyone into the countryside, bring them around a Stalinist model into the city. And this guy was still in his office, but the building itself was being managed by revolutionary guards, by the National Salvation Front guards, who'd come up from the streets. Everyone had AK47s or some older kind of gun, and the young guys were in the front. Their leader, the local National Salvation Front guy said, we're going to question this great criminal architect and we're going to put him on trial. So we asked, what's he doing still in his office? They said, well, we're keeping an eye on him over there. So when we went to talk to him he said, those young guys on the first floor, they're going to get tired and they'll go home. He said, the systematization program wasn't so bad and really there are certain organic developments, the relation between country and city, it's helping something that's inevitable. Good Marxist talk, there, the inevitable and the objective. I couldn't believe I was actually hearing this stuff. I was translating for the NPR crew; so when he said, I have nothing against peasants because my father was the director of the museum of the peasant, I stopped translating; I just looked at him and I said, the people will want to have a museum of the Jew, too. And he said, that's impertinent. I said something like, fuck you, asshole—it was the only thing that occurred to me at the time. But that passed. We came back and told the National Salvation Front guy, you know that guy upstairs, he obviously thinks he's still in charge and he's going to be in charge. They said, no, he won't. Well he is, he's in charge today, he's still there. He's minister of culture or something.

Those are a few of the things that should have given me pause, but I didn't want to question it, I was handicapped by both generational optimism and idealizing the whole idea of revolution, which definitely was occurring, it was all around. Just the fact that everybody else believed it too, there was a kind of mass hypnosis going on. But when I got back . . . there were other things I saw. At that time, in December and January, I did get to see some old friends from my town, and they were all pretty well off; these were people who did very well during the regime, the ones I saw. We were happy to see each other, but at the same time they were playing a kind of interesting game where they all claimed that they had been dissidents and that they hated the Communists and now they were great National Salvation Front supporters, so they just switched the names from Ceaușescu to Iliescu, who was the new leader. And one more thing, which was at the television station: when we went there, all the foreign reporters were given revolutionary armbands and little flags; they had very quickly produced thousands and thousands of these things.

When I came back things started to unravel, and they finally found out all this amazing stuff. Fewer than one thousand people had been killed, though they *had* been killed, and possibly there were twice that many wounded. Still, that wasn't sixty thousand! Most of the images we saw on television were fakes. That famous image of the woman with the child, for instance, was a fabrication; the woman had died in a hospital from unrelated causes, the baby was from somewhere else, they were collaged together with the bullet hole put through them to make a picture for TV. The massacre of the children in Timișoara never took place. Probably the most famous of all the images was the trial of the Ceaușescus, which was also videotape riddled with contradictions (and bad translation as well on this end), and not-too-careful editing. So slowly the story began to look like the greatest media play, I thought, of the twentieth century. When the [first] Gulf War came around I thought maybe that was another one just as good or better, but much higher budget. And this is exactly the point, no one could believe, the journalists were the last ones to believe, that they had been taken in on this scale and reported a story that was in fact mainly composed of fabrications. They also didn't believe that a place so technologically unsophisticated, because Romanian television was certainly a very boring nightly event for thirty years or so, could do this sort of thing. Slowly everyone realized that actually there had been an expert team in the country whose job was to deal with tape. That was the secret police, that's all they did was tape people in their rooms, tape them talking and film them walking around in the park and in their cars, tape was their entire activity, or most of it, except for beating people up and shooting them, putting electrodes to their brain, things like that. Those were the lower echelons, mostly what they did was deal with tape. And so they produced a good one.

On my side of it . . . people who manipulate other people's realities, media people, were being manipulated; the manipulators were being manipulated, and there was no way to unravel that in any fashion. To this day nothing is clear because the people who appeared on television immediately after the Ceaușescu execution, the new leaders of the National Salvation Front, looked like they came from the streets. Their great stroke of genius was to remove their ties. They were all party apparatchiks who just took off their ties, they opened their shirts and they were wearing sweaters, Polish-solidarity style. And everybody believed it. Which is the reason the elections were set very close to December; the National Salvation Front was voted in with 80 percent of the vote in the country. So the Romanians never heard the story. We never heard the rest of the story because journalists don't go around saying, I was wrong, there were not sixty thousand people killed . . . this was done in bits and pieces but in very small type in the back of the papers, not very serious disclaimers. So for all practical purposes, delusion continues.

At the same time out there, also making tape and pictures, we were doing our share of manipulating, at the same time that we were as fanatical about details. I did get to appreciate the fanatical literalness of the media people I was with. In one instance we went to see all of these families that had been taken out of their village and put in these apartment buildings, and one man told us about his village, which had been completely razed. It was snowing at this time, I don't know how many feet of snow on the ground, and my producer from NPR, Michael Sullivan, said, let's go to Damian. And the guy said, but, there's nothing there, there's just snow. We'd gotten to this place with two insane Romanian cabdrivers drag-racing each other across the ice, so I was sure we'd end up dead. This village was fifty miles away from where we were. I said, you're crazy, what do you want to do there? And Michael said, tape the silence. It's radio, you know. It doesn't matter if it's this silence or that silence. But he said, we're going. Back in the cabs, across the ice; we got to where this village was with our guide, and Michael got out of the car and he did that [gestures/laughter]. But on the way back the man who took us there told us the whole story of how the village disappeared; it was a great story and we ended up using it. So Michael is absolved, he did the right thing. You get this—lagniappe.

The ABC news crew I worked with, I had a line in there where I walked around in the snow and elaborated on my fantasy of return to Romania. I talked about how the stepfather I hated would come and greet me because I was famous, and I would deck him. The news crew said, we have to find him, and I said, no, he's probably a very old man and I wouldn't want to do that to him; I really don't want to hit anybody, I just want to talk about it. We had a long discussion about that. And there was a line in the script— it was a half-page script that I wrote, not thinking that these people would take every word and spend ten thousand dollars trying to be faithful to every one. So one line had to do with the border and they spent a whole day at the border taking this particular shot, which was all of ten seconds in the final thing. So on the one hand there was this tremendously literal attention, on the other hand, we were missing the whole story. The entire picture was wrong. Every detail was accurate, but the picture was wrong.

What this means . . . I had several thoughts about it in the book I wrote, *The Hole in the Flag: A Romanian Exile's Story of Return and Revolution?*, but I've been thinking about other things since. In one sense it has to do with the almost total helplessness that everyone has faced with the news fact and how hard it is to get around it. But if you want to ask questions, that's a good way to do it too, because one of the things about this story is that it is still evolving all the time. There are things that are not in the book—the fact that since then, the Romanian secret police has completely consolidated its grip on the country and has become a state within a state, and the civilian front that they put in power is teetering on the verge. And another thing, which is, what we saw in Romania never happened in that form, there were no two sides in the so-called Romanian Revolution. There was nobody on the Ceaușescus' side, they had been completely and totally abandoned. There was no reason why anybody should have died. The only reason people were killed was to create corpses in order to create panic and to create the television revolution that we saw. At the same time, there was a genuine revolt, because people did come into the streets believing that they were going to effect a serious change; and they were betrayed completely, they had the rug pulled out from under them. So two revolutions occurred, one between quotation marks and one with a small r, but really not between quotation marks.

—July 22, 1991

PLOUGHING THE CLOUDS
(Annual Harry Smith Memorial Strange Anthropology Ethnopoetics Lecture Series, Part 1)

Peter Lamborn Wilson

THE TITLE OF THIS SERIES IS *PLOUGHING THE CLOUDS*, WHICH IS A phrase I got somewhere from Irish folklore, I no longer remember where. I believe it was a sort of metaphor for an impossibility or a futility, in other words it's as hopeless as ploughing the clouds. That describes my work in theory and in practice. But it also has another meaning to me, and that is, you *can* plow the clouds, you can shape the luminous and ephemeral stuff of the imagination, you can shape the air. There is such a thing as air art, like fire art and earth art and water art. This, then, is an exercise in air art, in the airiness of theory. Everything that I say is pure hypothesis and purely subjective. I'm saying this because there are real anthropologists in the audience; I don't want to be embarrassingly put into the position of defending categorical statements which I don't even believe in but I'm simply throwing around in an experimental fashion to see if any sparks shoot out of those clouds.

Another aspect of this work is that, sort of at a slant, I believe I'm doing something for Ethnopoetics Week with these lectures. By the last lecture I hope to get around to the origins of poetry, but that's going to take a long time and I may never get there. Again, everything that we are going to talk about, it seems to me, is strongly relevant to the subjects of poetics and ethnopoetics, if not in a direct sense then in the sense of what Ed Sanders calls investigative poetics. If you're just writing poetry out of your own pure subjectivity, unless you're Dylan Thomas it doesn't take you very far. To continue the Celtic comparisons, it would be better if you were sort of a Yeats, someone who actually studied something, be it, in his case, alchemy or Celtic folklore or, in this case, anthropology and archaeology and what's come to be known as ethnohistory and various other neologisms of dubious value. Poetry wants to get its hands into something, it wants to dig in the earth, and that may be more than just a metaphor. Archaeology and related studies are extremely poetically exciting. In my second lecture I'll

tell you about my own experiences last summer in Wisconsin, which I
hope to continue this summer, where I got my hands in the dirt really for
the first time. It was always book fantasies for me before, but last summer
I got into a little amateur archaeology and trespassing and being chased by
various Gothic, six-toed farmers around the cow pastures of Wisconsin, trying to see various mounds and petroglyphs. I was in a constant state of
ecstasy the whole time: the tiny little discoveries, things that we discovered
that were not in any written source, it was like pure flashes of LSD, right
straight to the cerebellum. When I try to imagine the excitement involved
in making a major discovery in archaeology, like the tomb of Alexander's
father or the gold hoard of the Achaemenian dynasty or some Mayan pyra-
mid that no one ever noticed before, of which I gather there are many, I
don't think I could stand it, I think I'd expire on the spot. I strongly rec-
ommend every poet to get a sideline in something like this. I'm just offering
this as an example of the way in which, once you get your hands in the
dirt, once you read a few books, once you've looked at a few pictures and
studied a few carbon datings, you have as much right to your crackpot theory as any archaeologist or anthropologist has to theirs. Generally speaking,
archaeology is a science which is terrified of interpretation. Anthropology
is much less guilty in this respect. But archaeology has the idea of itself as
a science, and of course it isn't, it's an art with scientific aspects, just like
any art. But there's a kind of paranoid defensiveness on the part of archaeology as an academic and professional science, in which the wild interpretations that were given in the nineteenth century, which pretty much all
proved to be wrong, about the past and especially about prehistory, have
been such a traumatic experience for archaeology that archaeologists nowadays refuse to interpret. They'll tell you, we found three arrowheads, seven
bones, and they were in such and such a relationship, and that's all. Only
the most daring or the ones with tenure are the ones who dare to interpret,
who dare to try to imagine what the life of prehistory could have been like.
Prehistory, of course, is already a loaded term; it implies that somehow
we've evolved from a prehistorical state—when everything was inchoate and
incomprehensible, and nasty, brutish, and short—to a superior state of civilized awareness in which time unfolds for us in a measured and orderly
way, and in which everything becomes known or will become known.
There's an amnesiac gulf that these kind of attitudes open up between the
present and the past, which is not so alien, which is after all just the past
of human beings, of our ancestors. There haven't been even more than a
few hundred generations since the Paleolithic age; it's really a fly speck of
time in the eyes of the gods. And it's not so hard to understand a great deal

of what was going on in prehistory. Of course, I say that as a crackpot, not as an academic.

In approaching archaeology, therefore, I believe in something which transcends what they now call interdisciplinarianism—which means that communications are cautiously open between college departments. I would like to see something that might perhaps be called "anticategoralizationism" take the place of this interdisciplinary timidity. I would like to see all the barriers between these disciplines broken down or at least breached. I'd like to see what the Russian critic Mikhail Bakhtin called permeable boundaries, divisions which are kept up for the purposes of rational discourse but which are always known to be permeable. So that not only can anthropology be allowed to seep into archaeology, and ethnography into ethnohistory, and history into ethnography, but also the findings and methodologies of all the various schools of history can be applied to archaeology and all the other so-called social sciences. This I don't think is going to happen in the academic world, or not very soon. Therefore I do truly believe, even in the moment when I try to overcome my hostility to the whole idea of academic discipline, that we amateurs, we outsiders do have some role to play, even if it's only as annoying gadflies. The English writer John Michell, who is certainly not a professional archaeologist, has made great contributions just by being open to everything: astroarchaeology, ley lines, any kind of madness. As long as you keep a kind of agnostic approach to this and don't become a true believer in any of these crackpot theories, but are able to drift creatively from theory to theory, then I think the enthusiastic or obsessive amateur has a real creative role to play in forcing various academic fortresses to open a little crack in the portcullis somewhere and let in various breaths of fresh air from other disciplines. After all, it's all just humanity; it's all just us. There's no reason for these amazingly ridiculous borders which are erected: walls, fortresses, fences. Fences might make good neighbors, but they don't make for good humanitarianism. And, in fact, Robert Frost was a well-known son of a bitch.

So I'm going to deal with subjects which are pretty much taboo since the nineteenth century, the question of origins, for example. Origins are something no one wants to talk about anymore, all the origin theories: the origin of language, the origin of art, the origin of consciousness, the origin of the Indo-European people, the origin of the megaliths. Where did these things or these peoples come from, what was their origin? In the nineteenth century, when these questions were asked, origins were seen as categorical imperatives which would exclude other origins. Once you had decided, for example, that Hebrew was the origin of all languages, because God obviously spoke Hebrew, then you could take a wild child, an enfant sauvage who had been brought up by wolves in the wild, and lock him or her into a room and record all the sounds the child made, and say that these are all Hebrew roots and therefore the origin of language is a divine origin and that's that; categorically, that's that. I would like to return to the whole question of origins, which has been dumped out of a kind of paranoia or disappointment in the failure of these theories to turn up hard, scientific data. But instead of viewing our origins as categorical imperatives, in other words, absolutes, distinct places on a line of linear thinking, I would like to construct a palimpsest of origins. *Palimpsest* is a word for an old kind of manuscript, where, when paper was expensive, people used to write one way across the paper and then turn the paper and write another way, across the writing; and then they'd turn the paper over and do that on the other side; sometimes there are even more than two scripts on the same piece of paper. I see my palimpsest written on animation cels, on transparent sheaves of paper. I would like to take all these theories that interest me, all these stories about origins, and pile them up like a stack of animation cels. Then I'd like to hold them up to the sunlight and see where the light comes through all those blobs of black. This is a kind of cabalistic approach. The old Jewish cabalists used to say that the spaces between the letters were as significant or perhaps even more significant than the letters themselves because that's where the divine illumination was coming through.

So without making any categorical statements, without giving priority to any origin theory, without making any dogmatic statements about origins or developments, I'd like to keep adding one theory to another, and hope at the end that as we drift around—the French philosopher Jean-François Lyotard has used the term "driftwork" to describe his kind of philosophy, and I also find this term very congenial—as we drift from theory to theory, maybe at least for a moment some illuminations will come through. The study of origins in this way becomes simply another epistemology, simply another way of knowing things. That knowing in itself is not an absolute; the knowing also drifts from point to point, like a wave, actually, rather than like a point. Of all the origins that we are interested in, it's the origin of consciousness which is the most fascinating. When does the animal become the human? When is it no longer instinct—if that's what animal thought is, and of course that's a deep question in itself—and become self-consciousness? Not even reason, but simply awareness of self as self, as separate from all that other. What is the origin of this consciousness? What is the origin of this self-consciousness? Some people would say, for example, it's fear of death, that once the human brain gets big enough it begins to project thought into the future, it no longer lives for the moment. As soon as that thought, or even perception, is projected a moment into the future, then it is possible to become aware of one's own death. And having become aware of one's own death and the obvious inevitability of it and the obvious meaninglessness of it—or let's say the impossibility of its meaning—then thinkers of this school would say that from that moment on self-consciousness exists and, therefore, culture exists and, therefore, civilization exists and, therefore, the whole ball of wax. Instead of taking this death view, which, by the way, is somewhat, although not precisely, related to Freudian thinking, you could also take another leaf from the Freudians and talk about sexuality as the origin of consciousness. Once sexuality is separated from instinctual behavior, whatever the hell that might be—there was a PBS special on the love life of the animals, sort of PBS animal porn, and the stunning variety of ways of making love that exist in the animal world certainly puts a very big question mark next to the whole idea of "instinct"— but let's assume that the beasts have instinct and humans have something more, and that something more is desire, which, again, is a projection into the future. Even when the beloved object or the desired object is absent, one desires the object, the person, the thing. So that passion or sexuality or desire then becomes the spark that brings consciousness into being. Another theory, which I like a lot, the chief proponent of which at the moment is Terence McKenna, another Irish American bullshit artist, is that consciousness arose because of the ingestion of psychedelic plants. This sounds funny but the more I think about it the more I realize it's certainly a theory that deserves to be layered into that palimpsest along with the other theories. To look on it as exclusively true, the way Terence does, gets you into various kinds of conceptual difficulties. But to look on it as *also* true, along with other theories, that makes it very interesting, that suddenly restores its interest as a theory. So you can imagine that an early hominid, some australopithecine or Peking man or woman or Java man or woman or *Homo habilis,* or one of these very prehuman humans, if you can think of them that way, in browsing over various plants, not knowing whether it's good or bad, accidentally ingests some *Amanita muscaria* fly agaric, or ergot, or some other naturally occurring psychotropic. In the "new world" there are hundreds of such plants; the "old world" in some ways seems strangely poor in psychotropic plants, but it is certainly not lacking in them. Another point about psychotropic plants is that some of them are only activated by a process, they have to be processed in some way; ayahuasca, for example, has to have other plants added to it before it becomes a viable psychotropic. In any case, Terence's image is that a kick start was needed for the human condition, that these hominids needed a boot in the ass to set them on the way of being human, whatever that was going to be, and that some mushroom supplied this kick.

Then there's a theory I'd like to bring in tangentially, which is the theory of Georges Bataille, who, in his book *Theory of Religion* and also to a certain extent in *The Accursed Share*, discusses the question of the origins of consciousness and of sexuality. He speaks of a hypothetical original "order of intimacy," in other words, hypothetically for him at the beginning of human consciousness there is no separation, there is somehow consciousness without separation; the human condition has already been reached but there is no self-awareness in the sense of self-alienation, there is no potential psychotic split or abyss that has yet opened up within human consciousness. This is the stage that's referred to in every body of myth or folklore as the time when the gods walked the earth, when the animals spoke like humans, when all the orders of existence were on a single, horizontal plane and in direct communication and, as you might say, ecological relation with each other. Bataille's weak point is that he is unable to describe or explain why this order of intimacy should be broken. What would induce the doubling of consciousness in a situation like this? This surely would be perfection. This would be like a permanent psychedelic stage in which one was always acting on the basis of what we might call a transcendent consciousness, which is also imminent at the same time and involved in things, involved in the world, in nature. So what is it that causes what Bataille calls the "violence of the sacred"? Presumably under the order of intimacy there is, in fact, no consciousness of the sacred, just as in Bali there's no word for "art." The artist is not a special kind of person but every person is a special kind of artist. So, projecting backwards into the Paleolithic, or into the origins of humanity, wherever or whenever they may be, this also pertains. What possible shock or catastrophe could have occurred to break that original order of intimacy, and make future generations view it as a hideous chaos instead of as the golden age? That is the question—and there are many other questions about breaks and abysses and separations—that is the question I'm proposing; and I'm not proposing to answer it with any one, single, simpleminded answer. I want to create a complex web of references to various theories about this moment, this tragic, catastrophic moment, which may of course have been extended over centuries or even millennia of time, but which appears to us in retrospect obviously as a moment, a crack, out of which time and space, as two different things, emerge.

This also leads directly to the whole question of art and writing. In the hypothetical original order of intimacy, when the animals spoke to man and the gods walked on the earth, what would have been the point of art or writing? Obviously there would be no point. Just as all consciousness would be a kind of perpetual psychedelic trip or high, so also all art would be life itself. It would be totally indistinguishable. Not only would there be no word for it, there would presumably even be no words as yet, at all. But at some point in the development of the human, *techne*—the Greek word for technology—*techne* comes into being. And *techne* obviously represents the interface between my consciousness and that world out there. Now my consciousness is going to manipulate that world, it has taken that world for the object, no longer the subject of its thought. Formally, as Claude Lévi-Strauss says, animals and plants are good things to think with, they are actually part of a process of thinking. So if you look at ancient myth or if you look at the paintings on walls of the Paleolithic caves, you see a process of thinking *with* the things of nature, in other words, nature is still the subject of the thought to a large extent. Afterwards, as art and language come into being, the split, the medium, the in-between stage of *techne,* comes into being; now there's something that's in between me when I grasp reality, something interposes between me and that reality. It is no longer part of me, it is a part of some other. So out of this is the origin of art; at this point one wishes not only to manipulate the world but to create beauty in the world. Before, everything was beauty so there was no concept of beauty. Now there is something which is unbeautiful, it is inside, it is the psychoid split which has occurred, this alienation of self from self. And therefore something needs to be rectified, a balance needs to be restored. So art comes into being, ritual comes into being, the whole order of the sacred, which includes art, now comes into being. This is the point at which we get, let's say, to Neanderthal man: 60,000–40,000 BCE, flourished before the last ice age, they are still arguing as to whether Neanderthal was *Homo sapiens* (or wise, wise man as we like to call ourselves), or whether Neanderthal was some lost branch of evolution that didn't make it, or whether in fact it was an evolutionary precursor to *Homo sapiens sapiens,* or what. It's still a mystery. Neanderthals had bigger brains than we do. If we are going to talk about evolution then we are going to have to ask why these primitive creatures had bigger brains; what did they need those extra brains for? Very curious. My own poetic fancy is that they needed bigger brains because their perceptual world was so much bigger than ours, that they were still closer to this order of intimacy and therefore the myriad things, the ten thousand things, as the Chinese say, were much more perceivable, much more perceived by them. For example, if you visit a South American tribe now you'll find that you walk through a jungle with them and they see everything, the forest is a book for them, it is a text; they know what everything is, they call forth everything, they evoke everything, they live with everything. And you're seeing what? A hellish, green chaos of perception, out of which nothing appears to you as meaningful. So assuming that old Neanderthal was closer to that world in a way which even our modern tribal people can no longer be, there were many more things that Neanderthal had to think *with*. This is a strange way of looking at things because we feel that civilization of course has created the many things and before that there was only a kind of brutal simplicity, what John Michell calls the Urdummheit theory of humanity, that human beings were originally stupid and only recently became clever. It's a very unsatisfactory theory—this has to be said, as stupid as it may sound—because this is still to a large extent orthodoxy within the archaeological world. When I see the burial sites, for example, of the Neanderthal, which is just about all we can recover of their culture, I don't feel this brutal stupidity; I feel something very profound. There's a wonderful dig in Iraq that I've read about, called the Cave of the Flowers [Shanidar], which is a Neanderthal burial site, where a pollen analysis was made of the dust in the graves, and it was discovered that the burials had been made with heaps and heaps of flowers and herbs, they had been piled into the grave, on top of or underneath the bodies; they were able to identify them all, and many of them turned out to be plants which are still used in Iraq, in that region, today as medicinal or magical plants. So here's a cultural continuity going back to 40,000 BCE, which speaks directly to us. I've lived in that part of the world and used those herbal remedies; that was a direct contact between me and the brilliance of Neanderthals. The use of red ocher in graves already begins with Neanderthal and continues right up to the present. Ocher is perhaps the original religious symbol, red earth; it was put into the graves, perhaps to symbolize blood, the blood is the life, perhaps to symbolize light, red sunlight, but obviously having a whole complex of lifelike symbolism connected with it and indicating, some people would say, already a belief in immortality or a continuance of some kind of life beyond the grave. So: religion, in toto, the whole ball game, already there long before Cro-Magnon, long before "modern man."

As a matter of fact, just as a footnote, somebody, I think it was Andrew Schelling, was talking at the panel yesterday about writing, and he dated it as beginning, as we've all been taught to see writing as having begun, in the late Neolithic, in Mesopotamia, which is already very late in the story of prehistory. In fact, it's the end of the story because once writing comes along and succeeds then history begins. But first of all the scholar Marija Gimbutas, who was a wonderful archaeologist and I'll be referring to her work a lot, has already discovered that the early Neolithic, seventh millennium, in the northern Greek and Balkan and western Anatolian regions, societies which she describes as very early Neolithic, far earlier than Mesopotamia or Egypt, already had developed some kind of a symbological system. We can't decipher it at all, although she made some interesting stabs at doing so; but her arguments basically lead to the conclusion that writing itself is far older than we believe and, in fact, is prehistoric. Alexander Marshack, another great archaeologist with a vivid imagination, traces notation at least, if not writing, way back into the Stone Age, even into the Paleolithic, on a number of objects which he has studied which had never been studied before because they were so embarrassing and impossible to understand. They are objects which have scratches on them and they're obviously not decorative. They're not at all interesting to look at, some of them are very worn, as if they'd been carried around in somebody's pocket or used over a long period of time, and they have little nicks and scratches or marks in them. No one had ever asked what these things meant until Marshack came along and suddenly saw them as a form of notation. Because, of course, according to the *Urdummheit* theory, these people were too stupid to do something like that; ergo, these things were meaningless or perhaps decorative, but basically meaningless. Marshack asked if they might not be notative and he started counting the scratch marks, adding them up, seeing where they were divided, and over and over again he began finding numbers which related to the lunar cycle: thirties, twenty-eights, sevens, numbers like that. So he hypothesized and wrote a great deal, he did painstakingly careful work to propose his theory that these were in fact the origins of calendrical mathematics; and that for reasons unknown but perhaps understandable or recoverable through ethnography, these Paleolithic hunters and gatherers were already interested in the calendar, which was previously thought to be a Neolithic invention, dependent upon agriculture or perhaps giving rise to agriculture, but having nothing to do with the hunting societies.

So every origin can be pushed back, that's the point I'm trying to make here. All the origins can be pushed back. You begin, as I did, with a fascination with early classical societies like Greece and Mesopotamia and then you start going back. Under every fact a trapdoor opens and drops you down, down into an archaeology of time. You discover that all those layers are still present, none of this has vanished. I'm not talking just about archaeological stratigraphy, although that's part of it. Within every consciousness there is and remains the hunter-gatherer consciousness, a Neolithic peasant consciousness. We are all still those people. It's only been the merest, briefest time since we were not those people. Secretly we are still those people. We have strong links of consciousness which connect us to those people, which have been denied, vigorously, hysterically, rigidly denied ever since the rise of civilization in the Fertile Crescent, whatever you want to call it—actually it was northern Anatolia, I'll get to that later. As soon as we have a mythology to look at, it's a mythology of denial: denial of this connection. It's a mythology which tells us that those ancient people were chaotic, evil, and bad, and that we, the agriculturalists with the priests, the kings, the storehouses full of grain, we're the good guys; those primitive tribespeople, those are the bad guys. Those are the avatars of chaos and we are the avatars of order. So history itself is founded on a total dualism, on this dichotomy, on this split which was perceived to have taken place in time, between a primitive chaos—this theory has been identified with the line that the life of primitive man is nasty, brutish, and short, as Hobbes said. This has been the point of view ever since Mesopotamia rose itself from the slime of prehistory, and it remains the ideology of today, obviously. Otherwise we, as a culture, would not still be engaged in desperately trying to wipe out every last vestige of the Paleolithic, on one level. We heard all the "eek, eek" stories from the panel the other day about how this language is disappearing and that tribe is disappearing; this is not a joke, this is happening. On the other hand, we, right now, are living through what I would call a return of the Paleolithic. By that I mean that nothing disappears. Finally now, after all these centuries, certain weights have been lifted from our consciousness. Civilization itself has failed so miserably, in certain respects anyway, that we have regained our vision of this prehistoric past and we've reinterpreted it. Now we have a new interpretation of it. That's why we have neoshamanism, neopaganism, green philosophies, Gaian philosophies, ecological activism; all those kinds of forces in modern society are coming out of what I call not a return to the Paleolithic, no one wants to bomb themselves back to the Stone Age, but a return of the Paleolithic.

So these dichotomies are set up: order and chaos, cultivated and wild; St. George and the dragon is a good example which can be traced back to one of the earliest Babylonian myths of Tiamat and Marduk. Tiamat was the dragon, or rather the dragoness. She was the earth mother, her progeny were monsters, and she had to be removed from heaven by Marduk, who was the male, phallic, patriarchal god: the warrior-priest-king god, who slaughters the female Tiamat, who is symbolic of water, chaos, and shapelessness, and cuts her, and her consort Kingu, a kind of Adonis figure, up into little pieces; out of those pieces human beings are created. So human beings are gobbets of carrion from the dead body of the matriarchal dragon; and human beings are created for one purpose, and one purpose only, by this act of Marduk: that is, to work for the priests and kings, to fill up the temples with grain so that there will be wealth for the priests and kings. It says so; go read it in the book. I'm not making this up. That's what the myth says, and I take it quite literally. St. George has pinned down dragons all over Europe; if you go travel around Europe from church to church, wherever there's a church dedicated to St. George, there's a dragon underneath with a lance through it, sticking it into the earth where St. George pinned it down. In this way the Marduk consciousness—St. George is definitely Marduk—the Marduk consciousness, by pinning down these dragons, actually creates the landscape of culture. Before there was only chaos, only wilderness, only forest, only what the Cuban magicians call *el monte*, the forest and mountain combined into one concept, the wildness, the *out there* which is not us. By slaying the representative of that otherness, which is a dragon or a snake, and pinning it down, St. George actually creates the landscape of Europe. This is called *landnama* in Icelandic: the emergence of cultured landscape out of nothingness, out of supposed chaos. Of course as I said before, it's not chaos for the tribal hunter who lives inside it. The rainforest is not chaos to the Mbuti Pygmies, it's their home, their text, their everything; they have no concept of a cultivated space separated from this forest, no concept of an *other* place or an *other* time. They are still, as it were, not only living in dreamtime but in dreamspace. But for the modern consciousness, which begins already with Babylon, just like the Bible implies, for modern consciousness, which begins with these great Mesopotamian civilizations, they look on it as a process of actually creating the earth. If you read the mythologies of these people, this is a process of creation; Marduk creates human beings. Before that there were no human beings, there were only wild monsters who inhabited the forests. In Gilgamesh, the first epic of the human race, we have the character of Enkidu, who comes down from the mountains—Gilgamesh, who is the great king, the Marduk figure in the tale, his best friend is Enkidu, who comes from the mountains, from *el monte,* from the forest, from the wild place, and he is "an hairy man" as the Bible says of some character, he is a hairy fellow, a sort of a Sasquatch character. He comes down out of the mountains because Gilgamesh tempts him with a woman; desire tempts him to become civilized. Then he and Gilgamesh fight a terrible battle and afterwards they become the best of friends. No culture could survive forever with this schizophrenic split going on all the time, this intense, rigid consciousness of fences and fencing off of space, it would be too psychotic. So there's always a reconciliation that occurs, first a split into two, first a separation, a thesis and antithesis, and then, using Hegelian terminology, a synthesis or, as I would prefer to say it, a dialectical reconciliation between these terms. The wild is absorbed into the civilized and the power of the wild is used and understood. Sometimes it involves a contract or a contact with the rem-nants of the wild people who live out in the woods; sometimes their magic is more powerful than our magic. And if we civilized ones want to, for instance, be cured of some dread disease or put a spell on our wife, then we go to the old sorceress of the forest, the witch who lives on the other side of the clearing. If you read fairy tales about witches, they are always on the other side of the clearing. So the remnants of the wild people remain necessary. Once the last indigenous tribe is erased from this earth, if that's going to happen, that will be the millennium, that will be the end. Because without that existent consciousness of the wild, the existent consciousness of cultivation and of culture will die, it will lose its root. Even if this root is surrounded by images of violence, it is still legitimately there.

So, we are looking at a gradual process of separation. I don't believe that we can take one moment in time and say, "that was it, if we could only go back before *that moment* . . ." Be it the 1960s or the Paleolithic, there's a spec-trum of moments, a continuity of moments, a chaos of moments; there's a moment that occurs over and over again. It's always a moment of separation. The separation is always new in its terminology, new in its terms, but never new in its structure. That's why the same old myth of the dragon slayer gets trotted out again, and it's still going on. If you pick up a newspaper and see the way, let's say, the Arabs or the Muslims in general are depicted in our society, I wouldn't be surprised if you found the term "snake worshippers" used at some point. They, at present, are the wild other we're dealing with. In their own minds, of course, they are highly civilized people; in fact, they are more civilized that we are, but that's another matter.

Let's say we want to identify some of these key points or ambiguous moments of separation, when some order of intimacy is broken and replaced by an order of separation. We might, for example, go back to the [last] ice age. There's an interesting fact, that amongst hunter-gatherer soci-eties—and I should point out that for about ninety-five percent of its exis-tence as an entity, humanity has been involved in hunting and gathering as an economy, it's only the last five percent which involved pastoralism, agri-culture, and industry—so amongst all the hunter-gatherer societies we can look at now, gathering is much more important than hunting. And gathering is the province of the women; hunting is the province of the men. This is almost universal. But the hunting, as it turns out—this is from a collection of essays called *Man the Hunter* that came out from the University of Chicago Press in 1968, it was interesting that it came out in 1968 because I think this idea of the hunter plays into the psychedelic movement and the rebellion of the 1960s—but the finding was that gathering is much more important economically; the hunting is prestigious, it's exciting, adventurous, secret societies are formed around it, rituals are formed around it, religions are formed around it, as you can see if you look at the cave paintings in Europe which are ninety-nine percent depictions of animals. The figures range, among modern tribes, from ten percent hunting and ninety percent gathering, among some African tribes, to a more even balance among the Eskimos. Of course the Eskimos are in a part of the world where hunting would obviously be more important than gathering, and a large part of the Eskimo diet is meat, because that's what there is to eat; only about thirty percent of the Eskimo diet comes from gathering. So we could project backwards. Here's a place where ethnology could throw light on archaeology. We could project backwards to those Neanderthals as the ice age, the *Würm* glaciation, the last big ice age, begins to creep up on them. Presumably they had some sort of gender egalitarian thing going, I like to believe this anyway. Gimbutas and a lot of other people believe it now, that original human society—*original*, there's that word again—original human society was a gender-egalitarian society. It may have been matriarchal in the strict sense of the word, that is, descent was marked through the female line, because before marriage is invented you don't know who the father is. So clearly, if you're going to have any idea of kinship at all it has to be based on the female. But this doesn't necessarily mean that there was some kind of society of huge, strong women lording it over supernumerary men. It's much easier to see, for example, that hunting arose in prestige precisely to balance, to rectify an imbalance that would have occurred because gathering was economically so much more important, and because kinship was traced through the women. The prestige of hunting, the cult of hunting, may have been a response to that imbalance. But then along comes the ice age and the whole thing is thrown into a new imbalance. Now hunting, which gave itself prestige, has become more economically important than gathering; and so a terrible imbalance may have occurred in Neanderthal society, in fact that may be why they disappeared. The same imbalance would hold true for us too, because we, modern *Homo sapiens sapiens* Cro-Magnon types, emerge out of the ice age. That's where we first see ourselves, emerging out of the ice. I think that's why that frozen fellow in the Swiss Alps* has been so fascinating to everybody; everyone sees their origin in this frozen corpse.

This theory would go on to explain that men in the ice age achieved an unfair balance of power in society. And therefore, once the ice went away, women, who still remembered how to gather, began to really push it as a new economy. And gradually this pushing of gathering and returning every year to the site where, say, certain grasses or fruits were found, and the discovery that you could reseed those areas on purpose, this intense new activity of the women created the beginnings of agriculture. Therefore, another flip-flop now takes place in human society, and once again women are on top. The famous Neolithic matriarchy, the age of the goddess, which we now think we know so much about, although we may not have very much *accurate* data about, comes into being. Maria Gimbutas, in her book *The Civilization of the Goddess*—which has the most beautiful photographs of any book on the Neolithic, she photographed stuff nobody else apparently dared to photograph because it would have screwed up their theories, endless Neolithic goddesses of all kinds, overwhelming evidence—something like ninety-five percent of all the mobile art found in the Neolithic is statues of goddesses and only less than five percent is the little phallic consort-deity of the goddess, the male as consort of the goddess goes along with it. So to continue with this gender-war theory of human development, at the end of the Neolithic, with the introduction of a new *techne*, metals, which are apparently brought in from the east, according to Gimbutas, by the proto-Indo-Europeans. Kurgan people, that is to say, most of us, the Indo-Aryans, whatever you want to call them, brought in bronze and this created yet another rebalancing effect on human society. Since metallurgy was magical—it involved digging into the body of mother earth in a much more intrusive way even than agriculture—it therefore has always been and is still surrounded with intense taboo, and has been largely a province of men. Metallurgy, then, changes the balance once again. Now we have the image of the great patriarchalist societies of the early classical period, the Greeks, the Mesopotamians, the Marduk and Zeus worshippers, the sky-god people, that big Nobodaddy phallus lightning bolt in the sky. And men take over; the king replaces the queen; now the goddess is the consort of the god, not the other way around. The Neolithic goddess survives, but gets smaller and smaller, and more and more creepy, until finally she becomes Hecate, the witch goddess and a principle of evil. Which goes right back again to the idea of Tiamat, this feminine principle, the principle of water, being the evil, chaotic principle, while the male principle, of day as opposed to night, light as opposed to darkness, strength as opposed to weakness—all these mythic dichotomies come into play, and we have a new propaganda in the world, the propaganda of the fathers as opposed to the propaganda of the mothers.

It's a very clever, neat theory, but I don't think it's a categorical imperative, I'm not adopting it as dogma. For one thing, it's oversimplified, it's like a Punch and Judy show. For another thing, there's too much actual, hard data in the way of it. And for another thing, I just don't like it; even if it was true, I would reject it. However, I don't think it's a useless theory by any means. If I were to take Gimbutas as the major representative of this theory I would bow down to this woman—why? Because even though she is a professional archaeologist she dared to have an interpretation, she dared to have an opinion about what things were like in prehistory, instead of just saying, well, we found eighteen figurines of plump female figures, not goddesses, or we don't know for sure, maybe it was primitive pornography—that's what I call the R. Crumb theory of the Neolithic goddess. At least she dared to construct a theory and we can bounce off it, we can have a conversation now. What a relief. We're no longer being stiff-armed by these academics who say, sorry, you don't have any right to interpret that because we're experts and even we don't know what it means. I know somebody who used to work with Gimbutas, and he said that in the daytime she would be on the dig, behaving just like a good, scientific archaeologist, but at night she would take one of the plump female figures and go back and sit in the moonlight and listen to it. So she gives us this lovely attack from both sides, not only the scientific, but the intuitive, not only the dry, academic work in the dust, which she makes very exciting by the way, but also that nighttime intuition, the realm, as Hesiod said, of Chaos, Eros, Gaia, and Old Night.

So that's her theory. I don't want to oversimplify, you should go read her work, I'm not trying to make her into some kind of avatar of vulgar feminism—far from it. There are people who have used her work in that way, but that's not her fault. So that's one theory. Now we could talk about other theories—and I'm just going to come across them as I go along. What we're looking for always, again, is the break, the split, the abyss that opens up in consciousness between the old gender-egalitarian tribal setup, which we could call a society, and the new hierarchical, class-divided society in which for the first time there is surplus and scarcity. The hunters may know hunger, but hunters do not know scarcity. A hunter can die of hunger, but a hunter does not die of scarcity. Scarcity and surplus: that dichotomy comes into being with agriculture. Here we come to one of my favorite books, *Stone Age Economics*, by Marshall Sahlins. Sahlins was particularly offended, as an anthropologist, by the "nasty, brutish, and short" theory of "primitive" "man"—all those words in quotes, please. And he set out to do a statistical analysis of all the fieldwork he could gather concerning work and food gathering among existent hunting and gathering societies. I think he found fourteen or fifteen of them. He pointed out that these are people like the Bushmen, the Pygmies, the Eskimos, who have been pushed out to the bare margins of viability in this world. We powerful, agricultural-industrial types took all the good land; all that's left for these folks is the tundra or the steppe or the desert. Right away you would think, if anyone's leading a nasty, brutish, short life, it must be these folks. So Sahlins went and collected all the data that he could about the amount of time spent in food gathering by these people; and then he compared it to another statistical analysis he made of primitive agriculturalist societies, slash-and-burn types, and found out how many hours a day they had to work. I may be getting the figures wrong, but it was something like this: the hunter-gatherers average 4.2 hours a day of work, and that means a lot of them work even less than that. The primitive agriculturalists average fourteen hours a day of work. The larder, that is the number of foodstuffs known to primitive hunters, he found, averaged out to about two hundred different things to eat. The larder of the agricultural societies averaged out to twenty things, one tenth of the menu. So the idea that agriculture came into being because human beings were tired of eating bugs, a kind of culinary explanation of the rise of agriculture, doesn't hold true. The diet of the hunter-gatherers was far more complex, it was much more of a cuisine than a mere cookery. In fact there's a wonderful story about anthropology that I believe I got from Sahlins: he says that there was a tribe of Australian Aborigines who appear in the original literature as very nasty, brutish, and short; and the clue to this is that every year they walk over a hundred miles through the desert to get to a place where there are some fallen trees and pry off the bark and eat these grubs. Any people that does that must really be desperate, right? Later on, another anthropologist went and actually deigned to ask the people themselves what they were doing. And they said something like this: well, we have nothing better to do at this time of year, and we love to go walkabout, we love to wander through the desert, and we get to this place, and wait till you taste those witchetty grubs—mmmmm. It's as if we would say, and then I went to the Riviera and lived on caviar for a week. Sahlins developed this kind of anecdotal and statistical material into a picture of Stone Age economy, and he coined the term "the original leisure society" to describe this. I don't actually like the word *leisure* anymore, it has too many negative connotations from TV land, but let's think of it as the original society of excess, of having far more than anybody could want or need. If you study, let's say, the Northwest Indians, the people up around

Washington and Oregon, or what you can recover of knowledge about the Indians who lived around the Chesapeake Bay, they probably worked, on the average, about half an hour a day on food; work took up about half an hour of the day in the life of a people like that. Where do you think all that fantastic art came from among the Northwest coast Indians? They had time, they had leisure, they had time to devote themselves to an amazing explosion or excess of creativity. Georges Bataille talks about this too, by the way, in *The Accursed Share*; he talks about how a society which experiences excess will have to blow it off in some dramatic way. For example, the potlatch would be the way in which the Northwest Indians blew it off. Every once in a while some rich person would say, I'm going to prove myself the most generous dude within fifty miles, I'm going to give away *everything*, and hold a big party. I just saw a wonderful show on this at the museum in Seattle, soup bowls twice the size of this table and spoons, they weren't ladles, they were spoons, each person got one of these spoons to dish up candlefish oil, which was a great delicacy for them. (When you live in a cold climate you get into that greasy food.) They just spent all their time doing this until "we" arrived and blew the whole scene, and finally actually made the potlatch illegal. Up until a few years ago [from 1885–1951], the potlatch was a crime and had to be practiced underground. So the whole practice of potlatch got distorted by contact with Europeans; but originally it was an expression of social excess, a sort of bounteous exuberance of overdoing it. This is why so-called primitive peoples have these blowouts: when something is in season, they go where that thing is in season and they eat themselves sick, dance themselves ragged, make love, and have fun—and it happens a lot, it happens quite frequently. Even in the Middle Ages there were still 111 official holidays in Europe, a third of the year off. What is that now, twelve official holidays a year in this country?

I'd like to leave that as a point that you should keep in mind as I continue to talk about the Stone Age: we are *not* talking about the nasty, brutish, and short, we are talking about a great culture which is not yet a civilization and therefore is hard for us to recognize as a culture. But it is a *great* culture, and it is a culture of permanent excess. This is my interpretation. The reason why the folks in France spent all that time decorating caves was because they were so well fed and happy that they wanted to do art. It's an impulse we can all recognize, or at least dream about. In about 1876 a French writer, I think he was an archaeologist, stumbled by mistake into one of the painted caves in France. This anecdote is recounted by Marshack, but I've forgotten the details. He wrote later on in his diary [that] there seemed to be some daubs of colored something smeared on the wall. He couldn't see it, he could not understand that it was art. What it appeared to him as was just rubbish on the wall. This is exactly like those famous so-called primitive tribes who can't recognize a photograph when they see it. I remember these stories from my childhood, pictures of guys with bones in their noses holding a photograph upside down and we would laugh, "they don't understand photographs, how primitive." Well, this French savant in the late nineteenth century could not understand that Lascaux is the greatest work of art in Europe, or at least one of them. He couldn't see it. We couldn't see it until very recently. The entirety of prehistory, as we now understand it, is a very recent discovery. It began with a few sort of disgusted English, German, and French gentlemen who really thought that primitive things were kind of disgusting but they didn't have anything better to do so they would mess around and look at these things; people like James Frazer, author of *The Golden Bough*, who actually hated all the stuff he wrote about, or at least so he said, thought it was evidence of *Urdummheit*, of how stupid people were before the British came along to correct them. Nevertheless he dabbled in it for twelve huge volumes. So beginning with those kind of people, who could sort of half see, by focusing through binoculars made out of classical literature—the Greek classics contain innumerable clues about the so-called prehistoric period—they could begin to reach back. Or Johann Bachofen, a contemporary and friend of Nietzsche, who wrote the book on "Mother Right," invented, or rather reinvented, the whole concept of matriarchy, and as far as I can make out thought the matriarchal period was a scandal that involved a lot of men who were being dominated by women spending all their time screwing around, literally, fucking, orgies, culture of orgiasticism. That's the way he saw it. And he thought that the real Hellenes, the real Greeks, the real patriarchal people represented this great step forward in social evolution, to get rid of the female, to get rid of the chthonic, to get rid of the Paleolithic, the dragon, the mothers, the water, and replace it with this wonderful image of Greece as the epitome of reason, bare, white stones—we forget that those temples were painted like Hindu temples and that the statues were painted like the statues in Hindu temples, and that even these great Hellenes, who were so patriarchal and masculine and platonic, themselves were far closer to what we would consider wild-ass paganism than we can ever imagine. So Bachofen, burrowing back through that wild-ass paganism, recovered the matriarchy, and he thought it was awful. He was shocked. Actually, I think he had mixed feelings—sometimes he kind of liked it. How can you dislike the orgy, after all? But he couldn't admit it, it would have been *pas comme il faut* in the Victorian era to actually admit to nostalgia for this matriarchal orgiasticism. And his work has been taken up and reinterpreted by some smart feminist students of prehistory, including Gimbutas.

I would like to shift the focus of the question now and question the origin of the state. We've talked about how for millions of years human beings live in a state of egalitarian, surplus economy. Hunting and gathering goes on for millions of years and no one ever thinks to change it. This, of course, from the point of view of progress and evolution, looks like degeneracy. However, from the post-postmodern point of view, which views civilization as a mixed blessing at best, this Paleolithic past begins to look more and more like the golden age. Politically, the kind of tribal structure that we're talking about is not and cannot be considered as "the state." In fact, anthropologists and archaeologists no longer consider that there was in those days such a thing as "the state." Society, yes; of course there was society. Human society itself begins with that original moment of splitting apart, which immediately then demands its antithesis in coming together. If you want to ask about the origins of human society, it is also in that mythical moment of falling apart, of the primordial split of consciousness. But the state is something that comes much, much later—only a few minutes ago, really. It arose in the form that we know it now pretty much in the Neolithic, I think in the late Neolithic. If you look at a place like Çatalhöyük, which is the first city in the world as far as we know—it's in Anatolia, Turkey, and was dug up in the late 1950s or early 1960s by James Mellaart, and has still not been paid very close attention to. It turned out to be a town with streets laid out in a grid pattern, like New York. So now we're faced with another mystery. First we had the mystery of gender, then we had the mystery of agriculture—why would anyone want to give up hunting and gathering for such a shitty deal as agriculture?—and now we have to ask ourselves about the state. Why would anybody give up egalitarian society, which persisted well into the Neolithic according to Gimbutas, a society which moreover has revealed almost no signs of warfare or violence as we understand it. There's no human sacrifice to be found in the Paleolithic and early Neolithic, no evidence of cannibalism—or some people think there is but I disagree, I have a different interpretation of all of that material. Warfare begins with the Bronze Age and seems to coincide with the invention of "the state" as a means of organizing society. What earthly reason could there have been to give up what I call a million years of anarchy in favor of this tight-assed form of order, in which a few people are in a much better position than ever—the kings and priests—but most of us are beginning that long history of work, consume, die. Why? What was in it for us? Why should we ever have adopted agriculture, why should we have adopted the state? All the old evolutionist views that these were "steps forward," that agriculture would provide more and better food, and that the state would protect people against violence—what violence? But don't ask, there's violence out there in the forest, I can feel it! But why? Was this a scam? How about the conspiratorial theory of history? An elite which bands together to enslave the rest of humanity and constructs out of nothingness a new religion based on the idea that you are nothing but a piece of dead flesh cut off from the primordial dragon, and it is your duty to do nothing but slave for the priest and the king and to fill up that storehouse with grain, to make that surplus on the one hand and that scarcity on the other. You are in the scarcity, the king is in the surplus. What caused this? What on earth could have caused this? The French anthropologist Pierre Clastres has two books which are very germane to this question. One is called *Society Against the State*, and the other one is the book Clastres was working on when he died, and Autonomedia published the English version, called *Archaeology of Violence*. In these two books Clastres puts forward a theory that society itself is a structure which is meant to resist the emergence of the state. It's not just that people were happily bumbling along through the whole Paleolithic and they never thought of it—they never thought, oh, we could enslave all these people and make them work for us; the thought occurred countless times, to countless sons of bitches—it probably occurred to the second Australopithecine that he could enslave the first. It's a very old idea. But it never worked. Clastres, by the way, doesn't give this fantasy about the past, he sticks strictly to his fieldwork amongst the Guayaki Indians of South America. But I'm extrapolating. Later on in his book on primitive war he did begin to extrapolate back into the past. So Clastres sees society itself as a defense against these sons of bitches who come along from time to time and try to invent the state. Everybody knows this happens, you can find stories about it in the mythology; you can work in comparative mythology and separate this out as a motif in folklore. We've always known that these potential kings and priests were around, but we've resisted them, apparently. Clastres looks at the tribal societies he studies and he sees many of the social institutions in a new light because of this theory. So he rejects Levi-Strauss and all the earlier work, which his is in part based on, and comes to a new theory about primitive society, that it is in fact a kind of freedom machine—that's my phrase, not his—it's a mechanism for the preservation of social freedoms. And these things are very well understood, at least on the level of folklore or mythology, by the societies in common. In his second book, *Archaeology of Violence*, which he unfortunately never finished, he began to focus in on the question of warfare. Gimbutas points out that there's very little evidence of warfare all the way up through the Neolithic. There are no fortified settlements, no huge caches of weapons, very few examples of skeletons that seem to have been victims of violence or murder; and if you look at so-called primitive tribes you find the same thing. There's very little evidence for organized, continual violence, what we call warfare, amongst so-called primitive people. In fact the last surviving example of this might be the Yanomamo, the wildest-ass tribe in the world, I think. They have continually resisted the onslaught of civilization, and they do it because they're somewhat like, if you took the Hell's Angels and dropped them in the middle of the jungle and came back five thousand years later, that would be these people. They are wonderful, I really admire them; they are completely given over to violence, their entire way of life revolves around violence. On the slightest excuse they take clubs out and start bashing each other over the head. There's a wonderful ethnographic film, apparently, of some anthropologists who were fortunate enough to be in the village one day when these fights broke out and, with their jaws hanging to their knees, filmed this going on: incredible violence. The first anthropologist who really studied them, Napoleon Chagnon, had one of the classic anecdotes of modern anthropology. As a young anthropologist he went to study these people and they gave him shit continually—they laughed at him, they wouldn't anwer his questions, they stole his food right in front of his face, they pushed him around, they made fun of him constantly, and he was the saddest little anthropologist in the world. He saw his whole career going up in smoke from these sons of bitches who wouldn't pay attention. One day at the lowest point of his depression he was sitting in his hut with one can of sardines left and the lowest guy in the pecking order in the tribe, some cripple everybody laughed at, came into his tent, kicked him out of the way, and stole his last can of sardines. It was the last straw and he lost it. He rushed out to the guy and in front of the whole tribe started pounding on him. "Give me back my fucking sardines, you son of a bitch!" And after that the elders of the tribe came up to him and said, sorry, man, we didn't know you were human. Now warfare among these people is clearly not a force for centripetality, for moving in toward the center and toward ever more severe forms of social order. Warfare among folks like this is centrifugal, it scatters every social force to the winds, it dissipates. Again, it's a form of excess, it's a form of working off that excess of Stone Age economy, this time in the form of violence. And of course it involves the expenditure of great amounts of wealth to do this. You have to raise up a troop of your friends and you go have this adventure, you have to leave your fields behind, you can't do any hunting; by their standards it's very expensive. So it's a form of waste, they waste the excess in this means, through primitive warfare. Right up until very recently, the pictures of war that we get from, for example, the Plains Indians of the nineteenth century, it was still very much this way. It's not a warfare aimed toward the creation of a state, in other words toward the conquering and enslaving of an entire people; it's a dissipative warfare, it spreads itself out in every direction and it's actually not that violent. One of the big problems that the Plains Indians tribes faced when they first came in contact with the Europeans was that counting coup was considered to be a far groovier thing to do than killing somebody. If you could take your coup stick, which was a symbolic weapon, it couldn't be used to hurt a fly, and get close to one of the enemy on your pony, and touch him in sight of everybody, and get away—you leave the guy alive, but his face is completely gone, he's been touched. Counting coup was far more sophisticated in a really cool way for the warrior to act than to actually kill somebody, which is messy and kind of crude. But the Europeans didn't understand this. Even after they were touched with the coup stick they would go right on firing with that damn firestick, wiping out the warriors who had done the really brave thing, who had counted coup.

This is primitive warfare. It is not, repeat, *not* war as civilization knows war. According to Clastres, if I read him correctly—the essay breaks off at the point that he died, and he promised he was going to go on and analyze what could cause these social structures to break down and give way to the state—he was going to try to answer the question of the origin of the state, and I think he was going to find that origin in a breakdown of the primitive warfare structure, in that there would come a point at which, inadvertently almost, primitive warfare would result in the conquest and enslavement of another tribe and therefore the creation of a class structure. In order to manage that class structure, the state would have to arise. Again, it's really not explanatory, because why did that accident occur? Nevertheless, it's very close to being an explanation and it's an interesting concept.

So now we have the state. We have social hierarchy, we have property. And let's leave it at that, the mystery of the rising of the state. I will arbitrarily break off here because I want to leave some time for questions. Next time I hope to focus in on a fascinating example, which has to do with my studies in Wisconsin last summer, of a society which apparently moves backwards through this supposed developmental system, who were at one time agriculturalists but gave it up to go back into the woods and become hunters and gatherers again, and what role psychedelics played in that story, and what role economics played, what role art played . . . in a society that created some of the most beautiful art in America, the effigy mounds of Wisconsin.

—July 12, 1994

NOTE (2009): See now in Peter Lamborn Wilson's *Escape from the 19th Century* (Autonomedia) "The Shamanic Trace," which contains his conclusions on the Effigy Mounds; and *Ploughing the Clouds: The Search for Irish Soma* (City Lights), with his "megalithic" meditations.

*Otzi the Iceman, also called Similaun Man, Hauslabjoch Man, or even Frozen Fritz, was discovered in 1991, eroding out of a glacier in the Italian Alps near the border between Italy and Austria. The human remains are of a late Neolithic or Chalcolithic man who died between about 3350–3300 BCE.

BORDER ZONES:
OTHER PARADIGMS OF LANGUAGE

Wang Ping; Christian Ide Hintze, director of the Schule für Dichtung in Vienna; Elsa Cross; Ilya Kutik; Lyn Hejinian

WANG PING: Probably I should talk about why I write in English. Chinese is my native language. But except for a few Chinese poems I always write in English. Technically, I grew up in China, until I was twenty-eight, when I came here. The Cultural Revolution began when I was in the third grade, which means that my school education was stopped at that time. So I was a self-taught student until I went to Beijing University in 1980. Just by pure accident I got into the English Department. The reason I got into the English Department was because after I graduated from high school I really had nothing to do, there was no work, there was nothing except going to the countryside, and I was only fourteen, my mother wouldn't let me go. So I stayed home cooking meals, shopping, and I was very bored. My father had a friend whose major was English, and, I don't know why, but one day he said, "Do you want to learn English?" And I said, "Sure." So we went to a schoolyard every morning—it was like a date [laughs]. And we started learning English. It didn't last too long, but I continued after he stopped—maybe his wife protested, I don't know—he suddenly stopped as abruptly as he started teaching me English. But I continued, though that was not much.

Also, I went to the countryside as a farmer and three years later I had a chance to leave. That was the goal—we went to the countryside in order to get out, because there was no work at all at that time, the only way to do anything was to go to the countryside. So I went to the countryside and three years later I had a chance to go to a foreign-language school in the city, so I went there. And then I continued.

So my past to what I'm doing now was pure accident. But I ended up at Beijing University, studying English literature. My school training for writing started then. It was very strict training; it was the best university in China, so there were all the great scholars from all over the world: Oxford,

Columbia, Harvard. I was lucky in that sense; I was trained strictly from the very beginning. I always wanted to write but I never had the courage. Maybe I had to leave that culture, that language, in order to write. I am Chinese, I am very Chinese in a way, and very proud of being Chinese, but I couldn't really write in Chinese. My way of thinking in Chinese is very different from how I think in English. Images, emotions, everything is very different. If you look at my Chinese poetry, it is very different from my English poetry. I can say anything in English, I can curse, I can say whatever; but in Chinese I would never even think about cursing. I tried to translate some, and when I gave it to my Chinese editors, it's not even a cursing word in Chinese, it's just very inelegant. It was something about female sexual organs and they didn't like it, they wanted me to change it. I asked, what's wrong with that? And they said, it doesn't look good. They changed it, finally, without my permission, in order to publish it. Our Chinese traditional poetics is very different. I remember at that time Chairman Mao was also a poet, he is a great Chinese traditional poet, he is very good—he was not a chairman for nothing. Anyway, one day I remember, I got up, and at that time in China every word Mao said, even if he farted, it was a big deal. People would have a parade at midnight to celebrate Mao saying a word, or yawning. In the 1970s, he was already old and deranged, he wrote a poem, and it said "no need to fart." We were all shocked, how could he say this kind of word in a poem? But since he was Chairman Mao, every word was sacred, so we all accepted it. And I think in translation they changed it. That's just an example of how differently we think, especially in terms of poetry.

When I came to America, life was very different. By accident I got into Lewis Warsh's writing workshop, and I started writing. Also by accident I got to translate for Allen Ginsberg at the International Poetry Festival that was for Chinese and American poetry. I also translated for Bei Dao, Gu Cheng, and they went to Santa Fe and worked with Arthur Sze. At the same time, maybe it's karma, I got a job teaching gifted children in elementary school, and I happened to come across Kenneth Koch's book, *Wishes, Lies, and Dreams.* So I started teaching poetry to kids. These three things combined together and I suddenly started writing. And now I cannot stop, I am still writing, in English. I feel great freedom to express, I have so much to tell, all the things I have seen, I have lived through in China, and also things I have seen here, feelings I have had in America. English right now is the only language in which I can express how I feel. But someday my wish is to go back to China and pick up that language again, to write in Chinese. I'm not a nationalist—China has done terrible things, especially to Tibet—but the Chinese language is very special because it is one of the few ideogrammatic languages in the world. I think people who grow up learning these strokes and a language based on pictures and images think or look at things differently from people who grow up in a language with an abstract alphabet. I don't know if you have read Ernest Fenellosa's little book, *The Chinese Written Character as a Medium for Poetry*, edited by Ezra Pound. There are a lot of mistakes, but it is very imaginative and inspiring, even for the Chinese. Sometimes probably it takes an outsider to see the great truth; I think Fenellosa somehow saw and grasped the great truth about the Chinese language and poetics.

CHRISTIAN IDE HINTZE: It was great to hear from Wang Ping that she is proud to be Chinese. I am not at all proud to be Austrian. All my life I have been trying to find another identity. Vienna is the city of two names: Sigmund Freud and Adolf Hitler; Hitler took his ideas from Vienna. You will find these two energies in Vienna. I don't want to talk too much about my personal history, but my ancestors—all my life I've tried to recreate myself and my name is not the name I was given by my parents. I never had the ambition to become a poet or to live like a poet. When I was nineteen years old I quit everything, I left home and lived in the streets for five years, producing little pieces of paper, leaflets which I was handing out to people in front of football stadiums or concert halls or at demonstrations. The main thing was I wanted to know something more about communication structures, the most important thing was my name on the piece of paper and my telephone number and address. I produced one million five hundred thousand of these pieces of paper. I was traveling around with these papers all through German-speaking countries, also to the then-existing East Germany where the police were like my best friend. Step by step I developed a way of filling the paper with words, I got a certain routine by filling paper with words. After five years I was completely exhausted by that way of living and I tried to do something else. What could I do? I was just continually filling papers with words. Whenever there was a poem there, writing was always very difficult for me, in fact it was the most painful thing to me. There were so many other things occurring in my body, in my voice, and poetry as I experienced it had much to do with melodies, rhythms, visual experiences. I developed a four-dimensional concept of poetry: first is written poetry, published in books; second is acoustic poetry, composed with the voice, published on CD; third is visual poetry and performance poetry, body poetry, published on video; and the fourth dimension is what I call the infrastructural poetry, the poet himself or herself dealing with the infrastructure of poets, organizing festivals, organizing demonstrations, organizing poetry schools. This is where I am working.

The workshop I am giving here is sound poetry and performance poetry. *Lautdichtung,* in German, is the kind of poetry that is only spoken sound. *Lautdichtung* is nonverbal. The other part of the poetry I am teaching here is performance poetry. Once I was invited to give a reading and I forgot all my materials and had to improvise. I think something new came out. I'll give an example of that too; it's complete improvisation: [performs improvisational poem, something like this]:

Sa!
Ts'owww. Oms nyieh mogh.
Si-be. Si-be. Ma. (M)maa.

In 1980 I met Allen Ginsberg in Vienna and he invited me to come to a poetry school in Boulder, Colorado, which sounded very strange to me. In fact, it was like he was insulting me, because he told me I should go there and for European ears that sounds like, you're not a genius, you need to go to school. It took me ten years to follow that invitation. Together with Chris Loidl and Christine Huber, two other Viennese poets, we founded the Schule für Dichtung in Vienna in 1991. It is some kind of sister institute to the Kerouac School. We learned a lot; mostly the principle that the school should be organized and directed by poets, not by politicians, not by scientists, not by journalists . . . I have some principles written down, but maybe that's a little boring? Allen Ginsberg was there, Anne Waldman was there, in Vienna, Anselm Hollo was there already, Jack Collom was there, Jackson Mac Low was there, Anne Tardos was there; we built up tight relationships. I think the idea is that there is a global poetry, a poets' network, growing, and it needs to be organized. I think there is a new type of poet emerging that I call the infrastructuralist, a gifted poet and a gifted organizer. For me, Anne Waldman is the paradigm of that poet.

I have discovered some more poets who are very gifted in that respect. Two weeks ago I was in Colombia at, I think it's the biggest poetry festival in the world, in Medellín, which is well known for the Cali Cartel and the Medellín Cartel, the cocaine cartel. The first thing that struck me there was the audience, the opening reading was attended by five thousand people and each reading was attended by one thousand people. I am not a known poet in Colombia and one thousand people attended my readings there. The people directing it, Ángela García and Fernando Rendón, are true visionaries; they follow the same ideas. They want to build up a house of poetry in Medellín, they want to build up a temple; they are supported by many people. Poetry in Colombia has achieved a status which is very unusual, it is the only [*instancia*] which they believe in. By the time the festival took place there was a massacre going on, the bomb attack in which thirty people died and two hundred were injured. It was an act of revenge by the cocaine cartel. So the cocaine cartel is one violence and the other violent power is the guerilla; the poets there manage to find a third way and say, political manifests are decadent, no political manifests, only poetry—and that works really well.

ELSA CROSS: Ide was just telling me a while ago about his trip to Colombia. He also came to Cuba and Mexico. It struck me, the impact this trip had on him. I was thinking about, and telling him, the impact my trip to Paris had on me last year. He was wanting to go to Latin America; I just want to go back to Paris. So I was wondering about this transculturation, I'll call it, that is something so easy for poets nowadays but could be so much more difficult in the last century. Now one can travel easily and be in contact with many cultures. There are so many different accents and voices at this table. That is one aspect of this changing view of one poet who is directly influenced by different places and traditions, and voices.

I was thinking also about my own trajectory as a poet and how the first book I wrote, *El diván de Antar,* was made up of many images and symbols from the Middle Ages. I wonder why, being born in Mexico, all this stuff came to me? It started flowing out in a very spontaneous way and it came out as a book that was published and even won an award, which was still more surprising. Then I traveled to India some years ago, and I felt somehow I had always lived there, it was so familiar to me, so close. I cannot find an answer to that ease with which I can grab things and make use of them in my poetry.

ILYA KUTIK: I have discovered that I have lots of things in common with my colleagues here. I was born in Austria, which was not Austria at that time, but the Ukraine; I was born in Lviv, the second-biggest city after Vienna, during the Austro-Hungarian Empire. Then, also, Stalin was a poet, he composed poetry; he wasn't as good as Mao was, but still . . . Also, Lyn Hejinian was the second American poet I ever met; the first was Ginsberg. He came to Moscow and had no opportunity to perform his poetry. They sent him to exile, to Tblisi in Georgia, and we hitchhiked around a bit, that's how I met him. I met Lyn about ten years ago.

What else? I started to translate poetry because I was not allowed to publish my own poetry before the so-called *perestroika*, and translation was the only way to survive somehow. So I translated miles and miles of English and American poetry, and French poetry. My first book came out in Denmark, in Danish; it was only after that my first Russian book came out. This group was very underground and it was called the Metarealist Poets.

We also have a unique school in Russia for writing, called the Gorky Institute. I graduated from this institute and it was strange; the director of this institute was a famous Stalinist and that's why the institute was very progressive, because he didn't allow anybody to approach the program, so ninety percent of the teachers were dissidents somehow, hired by this Stalinist. It is a paradox, but it was like that. It is a great school, it was better than Moscow University at that time. So the education for writers was very good.

What we call translation in Russia is not translation at all because we usually ruin the poem we are translating. First of all, Russian poets, most of them, write only rhymed poetry. Free verse does exist, but only occasionally. That is why when I translate poetry which is unrhymed into Russian, I usually rhyme it. The logic behind this is very simple. If they translate me into different languages and they do not rhyme my poetry, why should I keep their poetry free? [laughter and applause] So call it translation—I call it versions. This tradition comes from the beginning of the twentieth century; the first who did it was Boris Pasternak, a Nobel prize winner for his awful, lousy prose, *Doctor Zhivago*, but he was probably the greatest poet who ever lived on Russian soil, which you can't tell because you read awful, unrhymed, American translations of Pasternak. So I can't help you.

So we translated just to survive. After our books started to come out, I tried not to translate. But I lived in Sweden for four years, it is a very boring country and there is nothing to do. You can't always write. I still believe one can write only if it is some kind of dictation from above somewhere. That's why I translated a lot of Swedish poetry into Russian. And again, I was rhyming, it was like being very wild. It is very good rhymed Russian poetry now, this Swedish free poetry.

Anselm Hollo asked me to tell you what metarealism is. There are two groups in contemporary Russian poetry, which appeared in the early 1980s. One of them is called conceptualism, which is mostly poetry for entertainment. It tried to make a parody from all the Soviet mythology. I still believe, and everybody does, I think, that Soviet mythology, the same huge mythological body, is no less than the Greek one. You can use it two ways: first, to make it ridiculous, and then to fix it as some kind of mythology. Conceptualism did that. The other group, called metarealism, is difficult because the term is not mine; however, I like it. You can decode it as metaphysical realism. What does that mean? It means that to express, to write this confessional poetry which, in the 1960s in the Soviet Union became boring; you usually express yourself from inside, telling how you are nervous, etc.—I got the idea that it is better to write, not that *I am nervous* but . . . "grab the life of my nerves." So if I say "my nerves" rather than "I am nervous," it means almost the same thing, but from different points of view. I try to be, if I can say this here, epic about myself; I try to describe myself from the outside, not from the inside. This metarealism also means that there are lots of realities, that they exist but we don't know anything about them. For instance we have some kind of world inside of a tree but you cannot see it, you can only imagine it. So it includes the description of some realities which are hidden. It is a different point of view. Actually this poetry is a kind of reflection of hatred toward lyricism; it is more epical somehow.

LYN HEJINIAN: Ilya's discussion of translating into rhyme brings up a larger question. It has been my long-standing interest to imagine expanding the paradigm of what poetry is and what kinds of projects poetry can undertake appropriately. Ilya and I have a mutual friend, Arkadii Dragomoshchenko, a poet who does not rhyme, at least not often. He was giving a reading in St. Petersburg, or Leningrad, as it was called then, with Ilya, and at the end of his readings somebody from the back of the audience yelled, "That's not poetry!" Arkadii said, "You are right, but excuse me, please, you are also wrong." That is, it didn't sound like a Russian poem, and for someone who had an expectation of what a poem would sound like, it didn't fit; but it also *was* a poem if you could expand the definition of what a poem would be. Then it would be a poem because there had been a big paradigm shift.

I say this by way of a preamble to something that I've been thinking about in the last few years, teaching a lot of theory and philosophy in the context of the poetics program at New College [of California]. A great deal of French contemporary philosophy, that is, Derrida, etcetera, is somehow anchored in a famous dictum of Theodor Adorno's, that "to write poetry after Auschwitz is an act of barbarism." That is a line also that the famous Jewish/Egyptian/French poet Edmond Jabès quoted at the beginning of his enormous, multivolume project. And it is a line that I have thought about a lot, because my own coming into adult consciousness as a poet but as, I hope, a socially responsible one, was in the context of several atrocities. The Holocaust must be regarded as a singular event, but it can be taken also as a kind of metonym for other atrocities, and my own coming into consciousness occurred in the light of—I was shocked into awareness by—two ongoing atrocities occurring under the aegis of the u.s., namely antiblack racism and the Vietnam War. Those two things interlocked in my mind.

And, in more recent times, in the lingering context of historical atrocities but also in light of contemporary philosophical trends, I began to think about a double interpretation of this dictum of Adorno's. One would be precisely in the negative sense, that after atrocity, meaning is forever altered, altered into a condition of impossibility. That is, we cannot make meaning of an atrocity, to do so is in some way to allow it to exist, to accept its terms. The second way that I have thought about the dictum, however, was to think about what barbarism means. It comes from the Greek word *barbaros*, which is an onomatopoeic imitation of babbling; it was the Greek word for people who don't speak Greek, they babble. I have come to think of a possible position for the poet, which is precisely to be a barbarian, precisely to refuse to speak the language of atrocity and to endlessly be searching out other paradigms of language, other ways of speaking that will defy the language of atrocity. Since atrocities replicate themselves constantly; that means that poets are always having to rethink the question of language and position themselves constantly in a kind of barbarian territory, which, in this big metaphor, is a kind of border zone. There is always a barbarian at a border, where different languages are encountering each other, mores are confusing, etcetera. I think that is an important territory for poetry not only to occupy but to constantly re-create.

—June 26, 1995

PARALLEL VERSE, TRANSLATION, *THE POPOL VUH*

Dennis Tedlock

IRST, A POLITICAL STATEMENT: ANY EFFORT TO TRANSLATE AND INTER-
pret a distant poetry necessarily raises questions about the current
state of poetics in the language and culture of the translator/inter-
preter. There may be unexpected moments of familiarity across
great distances, as Jerome Rothenberg was so good at pointing out
in *Technicians of the Sacred*. But there are other moments when our own poetics displays an inadequacy of means, or failure to utilize means that are
already there anyway. Recent North American poetics, the more formal side
of it, is really in kind of a chaos right now. Going back, then, to the most
recent time when it made some kind of sense, North American poetics
seems to have been spiralling recently inward upon its own innermost
recesses. In Michael Palmer's anthology *Code of Signals*, out of twenty-eight
contributors, only three make passing mentions of poetry and languages
other than European ones. And not one single line from such poetry is
quoted or translated. The only languages mentioned, by the way, are Latin,
Greek, and French.

We don't have to go all that far back or all that far afield to find examples of a poetics that does its main formal work at the level of grammar or
syntax rather than the more familiar lexical and phonological levels.
Western poetry of the last I don't know how many years—decades, generation—does its main formal work at those very small-scale levels. But among
the twenty language poets anthologized by Douglas Messerli in the book
"Language" Poetries, the New Directions book, fewer than half make use of
syntactical parallelism, that is, overlapping repeats of the same grammatical
structures but with different words stuffed into them; and only two of those
poets carry that parallelism beyond the making of lists of adjectives or
nouns. Those poets happen to be Jackson Mac Low and Lyn Hejinian. One
might say that language poets underplayed and even short-stopped syntax
rather than making its structures directly visible or audible, almost as if mainstream English language poetics, which is to say the poetics of phonology,

were holding them back from a full rediscovery of the rest of what's in language, including grammar and syntax. Clark Coolidge (as well as a few other people) occupies a kind of strange position here, where he is sort of doing battle with syntax; he knows it's there but he sort of tries to destroy it. If you hear him from a distance he almost sounds like he's speaking normal sentences, but when you listen close up you discover that the intonations of normal sentences are disguising all kinds of wonderful hatchet jobs on syntax or grammar, juxtaposing things that don't belong together in the same sentence, and so forth.

Mikhail Bakhtin characterized poetry as monological, and prose, prose fiction in particular, especially Dostoyevsky and after, as dialogical or polyphonic, having many voices. But he didn't think about the poetics of parallelism, which James Hightower, a Hebrew and biblical scholar, was calling polyphonic long before Bakhtin's work came to general attention. He used that word, *polyphonic,* which Bakhtin's translators are also fond of. Bakhtin writes of a force he call dialogism, or his translators call dialogism, which operates even at the level of individual words, since a given word exists in an environment of other words that could have been used with reference to the same object, words that may come to the mind of the hearer or the reader even if they are not there on the page. What happens in parallel verse is that one or more of these other words—or phrases or sometimes whole sentences—is actually given voice. Here's an example from the K'iche' Maya book known as the *Popol Vuh:* [reads from the original text] "By sheer genius, by sheer acuity, they got it done." In a converse process a single word may conjure up differing objects. In that case parallel verse may introduce a further word that works with the first word or phrase to refer to a single object. The sinologist Peter Boodberg once compared this effect to stereoscopic vision, a notion James Fox explores in the book *To Speak in Pairs.* I think Jean-Jacques Rousseau came closer to the mark when he said, "The successive impressions of discourse which strike a redoubled blow produce a different feeling, a different effect from that of the continuous presence of the same object." Here is an example from contemporary K'iche': [reads original text] "The dream came out bright, clear; it was gleaming, glittering." The effect of this passage is one of scintillation rather than of an object with a focused and static solidity. Alternatively a second word may move some distance from the first, opening up a whole range of possible objects. The two words together become complementary metonyms, not just any old metonym sort of referring sideways to something, but complementary metonyms for a large range of objects that's neither named by a single, abstract term nor listed in detail. In Mayan languages, as in Chinese, the paired terms may be pronounced in a single word, as in these K'iche' examples. In Mayan languages and in Chinese, you can produce large, abstract concepts by making one word out of two words. Some of the commoner K'iche' examples are: *kajulew*, which is composed of *kaj*, "sky," and *ulew*, "earth," as if to say "skyearth" as a single word in English. That's the way they say "world," without reducing it to some imaginary singularity. Another one is *q'ij-ik'* which means "sunmoon," and that's a way, a pair of metonyms for referring to all of the movable heavenly bodies, sun, moon, and planets; *kej- tz'ikin*, "deerbird," all the animals of the land and the earth, the four-footed animals and the winged animals; *kar-tap*, "fishcrab," that's all the aquatic animals, not just what we would call fish, properly speaking, and crabs, properly speaking, but everything else that's in the same category with those two things. But whether a parallel verse evokes a single object with near synonyms or opens up a range of objects with something more like antonyms, any notions of an isomorphism between language and the world is constantly undermined. Mayans and their cousins all up and down North America would never have concerned themselves with the notion that there was once a perfect language which had the right name for everything and then along came the Tower of Babel, which spoiled it all. That's a very distinctly old-world, Western notion and involves incredible essentialism about language, which is completely foreign to most Native Americans and especially to Mayans and other Mesoamericans.

So in the one case here two different words or phrases, or there could be three or four of them, refer to the same object, while in the other case two words may point to many objects other than the particular ones they happen to name. To paraphrase and contradict the famous dictum of Robert Creeley as voiced in Charles Olson's essay on projective verse, form is always other than an extension of content.

A syntactical poetics, a poetics of parallelism, a poetics of grammar, stands directly opposed to the philosophical or scientific project of developing and object language with no polysemy and no synonymy. Periodically scientists yearn for such a language, where each word in it refers only to one object in the external world. Even a particular person or place, in these Mayan languages and other Mesoamerican languages too, will tend to have more than one proper name or at least a name and one or several epithets. Here is a Mayan hieroglyphic passage, now decipherable, from the seventh-century temple of the cross at Palenque, in which the same god is referred to in four successive phrases: [reads in Mayan] "Dwarf of the red corner," "sustenance personified," "third-created god," and "sprout of sustenance." But it's all referring to the same guy. One of the interesting things that happened when the first missionaries, beginning in the sixteenth century, tried to adopt Mayan and Aztec poetics to European theology was they saw the need to have pairs and even threes of names for god. And they got in trouble because no sooner did these names they invented, such as "Maker" and "Modeler" for the god as creator, escape among their parishioners, than the parishioners started using plural verbs with them, or sometimes singular, sometimes plural, as they pleased. Now you see one, now you see two. So in the long run the efforts were completely defeated by the poetics. I like that picture of poetics as able to defeat a monist ideology. The same thing is [true] with proper names of places. If you ask a Mayan, what is this place called, they feel at a loss if they can't give you at least two names and better three or four for it. Here's one, going back to the seventh century inscriptions again: [reads in Mayan] "Lifted-the-sky place," "eighth corner house is its holy name," "house of the north." All referring to the same place. We don't know where that place is, it is probably up there somewhere.

In a poetics that always stands ready, once something has been said, to find a second and even a third way to say it, there can be no fetishization of verbatim quotation, which is at the very heart of the commodification of words—witness the copyright laws. Saying the same thing that was said previously doesn't necessitate using the very same words. In the case of the Mayan poetics of the last eighteen hundred years—that's about the length of the history of Mayan literature, which is a longer history than quite a few European literatures, especially including English—in the case of Mayan poetics not even writing, whether hieroglyphic or since the sixteenth century Mayans have been using alphabetic writing, neither kind of writing requires verbatim quotation. When Mayan writers cite previous texts, and even when they cite earlier passages in the same text, they unfailingly construct paraphrases and unflinchingly treat them as if they were direct quotations. If you confront modern speakers on this, having transcribed, let's say, a rural folktale and you say, when you had the character quoting what somebody else said actually it turned out different, they'll say it's not different, it's the same. Then if you show them on a piece of paper they say, yes, yes, I know the words are slightly different, but it's the same. The authors of the *Popol Vuh* tell us that messengers sent by the lords of death "delivered their words in just the same order" as they were given. But the comparison between the message that was sent and the one that was delivered reveals what looks to literalist eyes, at least, like a discrepancy. This Mayan is already using the Latin alphabet, in this case, but writing in their own languages. I'll read the two messages, the original message and the way it was, first in K'iche' and then in English. Here is the original message as sent: *Chikik'am k'u uloq ri kichoqonisan,* and delivered: *Chik'am uloq ri ronojel ket-z'ab'al.* In English it comes out something like this: message as sent is "so they must bring along their sports gear," and message as delivered is "he must bring along their gaming equipment." So whatever their differences, the two sentences are at least parallel in their construction and they have the same object in view, which is that the people who are being summoned are supposed to bring their equipment with them. Our own notions of accurate quotation of course have been profoundly influenced by print technology, which makes exact reproductions of texts. I've always marveled how a lot of poets seem so tied to this notion of exact reproduction that when they are at a poetry reading, poets will stop when they say something wrong, they'll stop and go back and correct it even though their audience would never know the difference. They always stop and say, "whoops," and then they back up and say it the way it was on the page instead of the slightly different way they said it spontaneously. When you find yourself doing that, by the way, that's a very good indication that perhaps you should rework that passage, that it was easier to say the way you said it wrong rather than the way you had it on your page. Anyway, the movement between or among alternative means of referring to the same object, in this parallelistic kind of poetry, entails a kind of translation, what Roman Jakobson called intralingual as opposed to interlingual translation. In parallel verse, not only in theory but in practice, the further step to interlingual translation may take place, with words from two different languages converging on the same object. That zydeco song I quoted, which had Cajun French and sort of Tex-Mex Spanish and sort of standard English all in the same song, is an example, and that Belizian poem, which had four languages in it, is another example. In sixteenth-century K'iche' poetry similar moves were made between K'iche' and Nahuatl, and today they are made between K'iche' and Spanish. When somebody is talking to you, even conversationally, and being highly poetic in K'iche', and if they can't think of a way to rephrase something in different words in K'iche', sometimes they'll throw Spanish in instead of alternate K'iche' words. This is not totally strange to Western tradition in the so-called macaronic—as in macaroni—verse of medieval Europe; the moves were between Latin and the vernacular, whatever their local vernacular was, in the same poem.

So we can now see that the popular notion that poetry is untranslatable, or, as Robert Frost put it—we can always trust him to give the purest statements of some of these Western notions of ours—poetry is what is lost in the translation, we can see that that notion is an ethnocentric one, we might say a linguocentric one as well. It is rooted in a poetic tradition that is given to manipulating language sounds at a level below that of words and phrases, which is to say below the level of segments that would have any meaning out of context and below the level of translatability. To put that yet another way, at the level where languages are most different. In parallel verse, translation takes place within the poem itself, and each time it takes place it implies, or even invites, the possibility of further translations, whether the present poem realizes them or not. There are rhymes in the broad sense of recurrent figures of phonemes in parallel verse, and in fact the sounds of a couplet or triplet may rhyme in as many or more of their syllables as they don't rhyme—I'm using rhyme in a very broad sense. Here's a passage from a K'iche' prayer: [reads in K'iche']. But these rhymes are gen-erated at the syntactical level by rephrasings, substituting different words, which is to say that recurrent figures of phonemes, which are heard in this kind of poetry, also produce recurrent figures of meanings. You can hear this play of sound in this kind of poetry in languages you've never heard before; you don't even have to know what language it is in to hear what's going on with these substitutions, the constant play of sameness against difference. You can spot it right away, the first time you ever hear a record-ing of somebody reciting in a language from any part of the world. What's foregrounded in this process is the parts of successive sticks of parts—parts of verses, parts of couplets, parts of triplets—that do *not* rhyme, the mor-phemes or words that change from one stick to the next without changing their positions within it. What connects them is their meanings, not their sounds. This can be heard in the English translation of what I just quoted in K'iche': "world of the sunrise, world of the sunset, all worlds whence come these yellow seeds white seeds, yellow beans white beans, yellow bundles, white bundles." That yellow/white, yellow/white, yellow/white throws forward seeds, beans, bundles, the part that doesn't rhyme.

Syntactical sound patterns can be iconic in their relationship to their objects, but this is not because they produce images or echoes of their objects, but because they produce diagrams of the relationships among them. As when the direction of sunrise is mentioned before the direction of sun-set, or lists are constructed according to scales of differentiation, or actions are laid out in chronological order. Those all happen to be examples of the alleged arbitrariness of language. In fact there are all kinds of things about language, right from the ground up, that are not arbitrary at all. One of those is that in every language it is easier to describe two sequential actions in the same sentence by naming them in the order in which they occur; that is, language is imitating the world, syntax is imitating the world. In every lan-guage you can also construct a sentence in which you say something like "I drank a glass of water, but before that I spoke into the microphone," but in every language it is more complicated to say it that way; the simplest way is to put the actions in the order in which they occurred. There are many other things about grammar, about syntax, that are the same way; they are actually mirroring experience, or *diagramming* experience would be a better way of putting it. Directionality, the way time elapses, you can always reverse the stream, but that's when your grammar gets complicated.

In a phonological poetics, alliteration, assonance, and positional rhymes create sound patterns that are independent of syntax. In English we are told we are cheating if we just use two verbs with the same ending to make our rhyme, that's too close together, that's not really a rhyme. We are always trying to liberate the sound pattern from the patterns of the meaning at that level. Such a poetics strives to increase the iconicity or echoicity of language at the level of the image or the echo rather than that of the diagram, producing new relationships among words by means of what Jakobson calls poetic etymology, as if you had discovered another meaning for a set of sounds. Objects are drawn closer together by making them sound alike, whereas a syntactical poetics draws objects together by positioning them within a structure. Rhyming, sound patterns of the kind that are independent of syntax, do occur in K'iche', but they take the form of deliberate puns rather than subtle resonances. Instead of thickening the atmosphere around the set of meanings already in place, puns suddenly add new meanings, and these new meanings may in fact be appropriate to the matter at hand, but they are unfolded independently of verse structure. The auguries for the days of the K'iche' calendar are often produced in this way. For example this past Saturday's date would be pronounced together with its divinatory meaning so that to translate it into English in a way that respects the sound patterning, it is as if to say "ten dog a jealous god." One of the ways they play on sounds is metathesis. I just did a metathesis when I took "dog" and turned it into "god." You could also say something that translates into: "ten dog it's all in a fog." This past Sunday goes like this: "eleven monkey right on the money." Or, "eleven monkey, matrimony." Yesterday went like, "twelve tooth on the tried and true root." Or, "twelve tooth, the wayward youth." And today with its augury sounds like this: "thirteen cane plant, domestic slant." If you are interested about that, watch for things going wildly out of control in your household, your institution, your tent, anything analogous to a house or household. This is a day where things are almost too much related to that.

Now there are rhythms in parallel verse but they operate at a larger scale than those of metrical verse. Each of the two or three sticks that makes up a parallel couplet or triplet may repeat the same rhythmic sequence; but each of the feet in this rhythm, if that is the proper name for them, is likely to be as long as an entire hemistick, that is, half of a couplet. Further, the passage from one couplet or triplet to the next is likely to carry with it a change in rhythm. This is a poetry of changing rhythms, not of picking your rhythm and doing your whole poem in it. In the following pair of couplets from the K'iche' drama known as the *Rabinal Achi*, the first has stressed/nonstressed syallables in the sequence dada dedada dada dedadada and then it shifts in the second to deda deda deda, deda deda dedada. Notice there is variation even within those feet. [reads in K'iche'] "Dance on and on, sir. Dance around and round, sir; inside the great fortress, inside the great walls." North American song lyrics operate in the same way, where, after two or three lines the rhythms all shift. As a result people scanning K'iche' poems, or ethnomusicologists trying to transcribe North American Indian songs, have to keep changing the time signature every so often; the songs are never composed all in the same time signature, the same meter, from beginning to end. In musical terms these are called isorhythms, and they produce the poetical equivalent of a musical composition that can't be written out with one time signature. And we have those in the West too, medieval motets operate in the same way. This is music and in the case of poetry without music, rhythms, operating with a little more respect for what's already there in language than they normally do. Language is not being hammered out and forced to follow one pattern of rhythms, but it's a compromise between the desire for repeating rhythms and what you want to say. There's a dialectic going on there.

To end on one further point that picks up on something that came up recently concerning nonsense syllables or sound poetry that doesn't use words as we normally understand those—there was one mention of Comanche music and that's what I am picking up on—but all over North America there are many songs in which the lines with words and lines with vocables (that's what musicologists call them), the so-called nonsense sylla-bles, something like scat singing in jazz, you always find these things closer to the familiar than you expected to when you think about it. In all of those North American examples you have very commonly, let's call them verses for the sake of making a parallel, the verses of the song may be in words and the refrain may be in vocables, so the tension between these two things is brought together in the performance. Very different from a language poet, say, deciding, I want to escape from language as given and do something that's completely outside of translatable, it may sound German to you, or French or Spanish or English, but it "has no meaning." In these traditions, this so-called nonsense, this thing that's partly other than language, is always there, juxtaposed to the other thing. In the most wonderful songs of all there are things in the refrain of vocables that sound almost like words, and on the other hand the words may be encased in vocables, so that around the edges of the verse part that has words, lyrics to it, the vocables have invaded that space, so you have this dialectical relationship between the two things.

JACK COLLOM: I heard this with delight, but a couple of questions were raised in some of your emphases. For example, I realize that a slip of the tongue might be an indication that a poet think about altering the original run of words, but it seems to me that you were saying he is *necessarily* foolish in going back and trying to correct himself, as if Rembrandt were painting and he stumbled and jabbed his brush into the canvas, this new stroke would necessarily be the best thing for the painting.

DENNIS TEDLOCK: That's a nice analogy. The difference is, though, that I can still remember how it was said wrong, whereas I need an x-ray to find out whether Rembrandt corrected a mistake. And my other analogy, when you get into arts that are more deeply into performance, like drama, good actors don't correct their mistakes, they go right on.

JC: That's certainly true. A poetry reading might be different than the creation of an image or an illusion, it might be different in an actor's aim than in a poet's. I'd like to ask too, briefly: Frost, whom I don't usually like, made this nice remark about poetry is what's lost in translation. Now he may not have meant that so absolutely as he stated it, but were you saying, did I catch you right, this is necessarily ethnocentric of him to remark even that poetry is difficult to translate?

DT: He's saying it within a tradition that retreats into the aspects of language that are most peculiar to particular languages. Whereas this kind of poetry is imminently translatable and is focused more on the way meanings are put together at the level of whole words and whole phrases. That makes it very translatable compared to a poetry that is very wrapped up in the sound patterns it creates below the level of meaning.

JC: Isn't every poetry, whether consciously or not, wrapped up in the exactitudes of sound to the nth degree?

DT: I'm trying to make a difference, saying there are poetries that are less wrapped up in the sound. There is sound here too, but as I was saying in the parallelistic poetry—Jakobson said that in unwritten poetry, the poetry is the grammar of the language. Poetry is always putting on display these large structures of the language. Again, this is the level where meanings are juxtaposed and manipulated quite directly. So if you begin to hear sound patterns in parallelistic poetry it will be a good reflection of the way the meanings are arranged. Whereas in a poetry that's focused on alliteration, assonance, maintaining a certain meter, that's all running along below the level of meaning. You can choose a certain meter because it is more appropriate to evoke a certain range of meanings than some other meter, that is true, but it is still operating at this subconscious—in the hearer at least, not in the poet if you are desperately trying to correct a gap in the scansion in a line.

—June 27, 1995

HIDDEN FEMALE SHAMANIC TRADITIONS

Barbara Tedlock

'LL BE TALKING TODAY ABOUT HIDDEN FEMALE SHAMANIC TRADITIONS. THIS is something that was beginning to happen in my head last summer when I was here. For a long time I've wondered why it is that the tradition and the writing about shamanism is primarily about males, in this tradition, and why it gets talked about in terms of hunters and warfare; we have a lot of rich imagery. Is there another voice of shamanism? Although growing up I heard many stories about my mother's mother, a Cree Ojibwa person who was trained as a shaman, I had no idea and I was not prepared for the possibility of ever training as a shaman as my husband and I did in Guatemala. That shows how you can be so divorced from a possibility of participating in a religious worldview because of gender and because of general ideas of it, that you are completely shocked out of your mind when you are included. The historical neglect and the misconceptions about women in shamanic practice result from a convergence of factors, I think—I'm just trying these out on you—including cultural assumptions regarding women's proper place in society, theoretical orientations within academia, and observer bias. Those are the three I've figured out. There are probably some other reasons too. Evaluations of female religious practices have too often been based on opinions refracted through the eyes of male observers and explained by means of concepts taken from the strongly male-oriented intellectual traditions of the West. If you don't believe me, just look at all universities. From the earliest missionary observers to current analyses of cultural symbolists, women have been peripheral to the mainstream of interest in the whole field of religious studies; I'm not just talking about shamanism. In discussions of ritual activity women are typically portrayed as objects of male power elites in androcentric religious symbol systems. Rarely are they described as subjects and creators of their own religious realities.

So in order to begin to hear women's voices, let's listen to a direct testimony of a powerful Yurok woman talking about her selection as a shaman, her strenuous training ordeal, and her successful shamanic practice.

I began with a dream. In the dream I was on Bald Hills. There was a Cahuilla man, who fed me deer meat, black with blood. I did not know this man. He was a short-nosed person. In the morning I was ill. A doctor was called in to treat me and diagnose my case. Then I went to the sweathouse to dance for ten nights. This whole time I did not eat. I danced until I became unconscious and they carried me into the living house. When I revived I climbed up the frame-work of poles, those poles for drying fish. I escaped through the smoke hole. I ran to another sweathouse; I began dancing there. I ran to another; I danced; I ran. On the tenth day while I was danc-ing I obtained control of my first pain, my shamanic power. It came out of my mouth. It looked like salmon liver. And as I held it in my hands blood dripped from it to the ground. This is what I saw in my dream, on Bald Hills. I thought that it was merely venison, but when I ate the venison the pain entered my body. All that winter I went daily high up on the ridges to gather wood and each night I slept in a sweathouse. At this time I drank no water. Sometimes I walked along the river, put pebbles in my mouth, spat them out. Then I said to myself, when I am a doctor I shall suck and the pains will come into my mouth as cool as these stones. I shall be paid for that. When day broke I faced the door of the sweathouse and I saw a long dentillium. [A dentillium is a type of shell bead that was used as money in this part of California.] And this shell was looking in at me. When I went out to gather wood I kept saying, that shell has gone before me, I see it, I see its tracks. When I filled my basket with wood I said, that large shell, it's very heavy. When I swept the platform before the sweathouse I said, I see shells, I see shells, I see shells; I am sweeping them to both sides of me. So whatever I did I spoke of money constantly. I was not alone in the sweathouse. Others were present to watch for fear I might lose my mind and do myself some form of harm. Once I dreamed I saw an uma'a, a spirit, coming. One of his legs was straight, the other was bent at the knee; and he walked on this knee as if it were his foot; and he had only one eye. Then I shouted and I dashed out, I ran down along the river; my relatives pursued me, running, running, brought me back unconscious. Then I danced for three nights. At this time I received my four largest pains. One of them is blue, one is yellowish, another red, the fourth one is white. Because I received these in dreaming about the spirits, they are the ones with which I cure sickness caused by spirits. My smaller pains are whitish. They are less powerful. It is they that came to me in my first period of training. The pains come and go from my body, they come and go. I do not always carry them with me. Today, though, they are inside me. In my dancing I could see various pains flying above the heads of the people. Then I became beyond control, trying to catch them, catch them, each one. Some of the pains were very hard to drive away, they kept coming back. I tried to catch; they hovered over certain people. Such people are likely to become sick. Gradually I obtained more control of my pains, until finally I could take them out of myself, lay them in a basket, set this at the opposite end of the sweathouse, and then swallow them from where I stood. All this time I drank no water. I gathered firewood for the sweathouse, slept in it, and I constantly spoke to myself about this shell money. This I did for two years. Then I began to be ready to cure. I worked hard and long at my training because I wished to be the very best doctor of all. During all this time, if I slept in the house at all I put angelica root at the four corners of the fireplace, and I threw some of it into the blaze, saying, this angelica comes from the middle of the sky, there the shells and the woodpecker scalps eat its leaves, that is why this root, this angelica, is weathered; then I inhaled the smoke of the burning root. Thus the shells would come to the house in which I was. My sweating and refraining from water was not for the entire two years but just ten days at a time, then a rest, then ten days at a time. At some periods I would gash myself on my arms and I would run young fern fronds into my gashes. In the seventh moon, after nearly two years, I stopped my training. Then I danced about the fire. This cooked me, cooked my pains inside me. After this was done I did not need to train anymore.

While this Yurok woman's story follows a classic shamanic pattern, what's unusual is her candid admission that during her ordeal she thought constantly about her future financial rewards. Since Northern California shamans were only paid if they were successful, this is a measure of her confidence in her control of her shamanic powers. And, indeed, she was the most powerful woman or man shaman in that whole area of California.

The disappearance of women shamans from the historical record is subtly coded within the word *shaman* itself. This word comes to us from the Tungus language of Siberia. When it was borrowed into English, the last syllable, m-a-n, man, which originally meant, in Tungus, "one who," took on the English connotation of male gender. Thus the borrowed word played a role in the privileging of males over females as the shamanic norm by English speakers, who have unconsciously linked male gender with the institution of shamanism.

At this point I'm going to skip a detailed discussion I've written about the evidence of women in Paleolithic shamanism, but I'll give you one delicious fact which you will never find in Eliade or any of the other male scholars, which is that the earliest-known burial of a shaman, complete with rattles, red ocher, and amulets, when the bones were studied by physical anthropologists, they turned out to be those of a woman. This is the oldest skeleton of a shaman in the world by more than ten thousand years. It's in what is now the Czech Republic. I'm also skipping over here some very important new findings that in classic Mayan society, in a city called Yaxchilan, noble females are portrayed letting blood, which resulted in visions which enabled them to practice as diviners, as priests, and as midwives. One wonderful example is Lady Xook, who sees an enormous serpent—and on my arm I have a tattoo of her vision. This is new information. It seems like whenever studies go on for a long time we talk about the kings but we never find out about the queens, we never find out about the women healers. Now Lady Xook is coming to the fore.

Due to the prejudices of Roman Catholic priests, the unique role in shamanic practices of midwives remains poorly known today. The famous Franciscan priest Bernardino de Sahagún ambiguously described Aztec midwives as "knowledgeable herbalists, bonesetters, physicians, and seers," but then he denounced their practices as a combination of black magic and cynical fraud. This is a quote in English from Sahagún: "she deceives people, ridicules them, reduces them, perverts them, bewitches them, blows evil upon them, removes an object from them, sees their fate in water, reads their fate with cords, casts lots with grains of maize, draws worms from their teeth." That this view is more Spanish than Aztec is revealed by the fact that during the festival of Toci, which means "our grandmother" (and our grandmother of course is an aspect of the earth mother), all female curers and midwives wore the tobacco pouches of priestly status. Even though the Mesoamerican two-hundred-and-sixty-day calendar had its origins in divinatory rites pertaining to human pregnancy, the Spanish chroniclers saw nothing special at all about midwives. Although they reported that they had heard from the women that they were divinely elected to practice as midwives, the priests missed this information and lumped them together with all the other nonshamanic healers. Father Cobo for instance, who resided in Peru during the early seventeenth century, reported that among the Quechua, "there were also women midwives, some of whom said that in their dreams they had been given this office, and they had to perform many ceremonies, many fasts and sacrifices."

In the Andes, dreams and visions also revealed religious vocations, and midwives, as earthly representatives of the earth mama—there, it's Pachamama—attended specific rituals that prepared them to directly communicate with the sacred. So these colonial priests attempted to undermine women's ritual organizations also, and in some indigenous communities women found ways to circumvent them and continue to practice in Andean structures of community religion and government. The Jesuit priest Bocanegra inadvertently discovered that individual women would confess to native women before they went to the local Roman Catholic parish priest. He said, "The Indian women teach other women to confess to them by means of these knots and these signs on quipus (quipus are knotted strings), which were multicolored in order to classify sins and the number that were committed." Under the guise of Catholic confession of sins, these Andean women priests were continuing the pre-Columbian religious practice of annual ritual confessions. This of course outraged the priests, since by concealing their heretical activities, native priests were able to preserve both the practice of indigenous rites and also very different concepts of sin, guilt, and responsibility than those that the priests were trying to teach them.

Seventeenth-century Europe was convulsed by witch hunts and women held central place as the victims, making up fully eighty-five percent of all of those humans who were executed for sorcery. And in accord with the European social stereotype of the witch, the persons most likely to be responsible for performing black magic were, you guessed it, *old* women. Midwives, who were generally older women, were considered especially harmful because they eased women's pain during birthing. This was said to be against the will of God, who had imposed this pain as divine punishment for Eve's original sin. Not only midwives, but also women who appealed to them for help during difficult labor, were condemned to death.

In our own time, women's shamanic practices are not so much suppressed, as they were in the Colonial period, as now they are downplayed or erased from the record. Thus the great Swedish ethnographer, Åke Hultkranz, in his famous book *Shamanic Healing and Ritual Drama*, asserts that although there are medicine women among the Shoshone they are few in number and their powers are not as great as the powers of their male colleagues. That he did not encounter powerful female shamans during his more than ten years of research in the Great Basin is stupendously strange to me, given that other observers, in fact all of them, have noted that

Shoshone, Ute, Paiute, and Washute peoples have about an equal proportion of very powerful male and female shamans. He's just sort of outside of
it there. Hultkranz also stated that among the Inuit, some women occasionally perform as shamans but it is only "with difficulty" that they achieve
the same magical effects as their male colleagues. However the written
sources I've found reveal that Inuit women and men perform equally but
differently as shamans. While male shamans are known to engage in competitive and very flashy conjuring contests, I find no evidence of female
shamanic rivalry. So I'm trying to figure out, are we dealing with different
traditions of shamanism? How many of them are there?

That women's and men's shamanic roles are different but complementary, I believe, is nicely illustrated in South American traditions. In the practice of shamanizing, the Canelos Quichua, these are people living in
Ecuador, female and male shamans work together in healing teams, men
and women together. Whenever a male takes one of the hallucinogens, like
ayahuasca, soul vine, and/or datura in order to diagnose an illness, one or
more of his female relatives snuff a psychoactive tobacco water in order to
clarify his vision by naming it. They speak as poets with the voice of the
vision, with the images. And this is what the women sing: "I am black
jaguar, I am black anaconda, I am red jaguar, I am red anaconda." As they
see and share in the male's imagery they sing it for the audience. Quichua
women also tend their own datura trees and they brew the leaves, flowers,
and roots as a tea for use during all female ritual occasions. Under the
influence of the drug they experience the unity of time and space, seeing
back into the ancient past, forward into the distant future. In dialogues with
the earth mother they actively seek knowledge of their body-souls, intellectual and artistic integration with mythic structures and pottery designs.
In other words, they are involved in using the drugs to bring forward certain beautiful artistic traditions. They carefully study local petroglyphs,
which they describe as ancient soul carvings, in order to intensify the symbolism of their own dreams.

The woman's shamanic path among the Huichol of Mexico also focuses
on the acquisition of a specifically female craft. The process of learning to
weave parallels and merge with the shamanic path in such a way that
women master weavers are all also trained as shamans. Huichol shamanism
runs in families, as in the case of the well-known shaman Ramon Medina
Silva, whose mother, sister, and wife were all well-known shamans or
mara'akame. Throughout his life Ramon's shamanic teacher was his mother,
who instructed him in the practical and esoteric lore of the animals, birds,
and weather. She taught him history and myth, sang long song cycles, and

described details of the supernatural environment. She was called to the profession during a dream in which the ancestors told her that she was to become a shaman. Ramon's wife, Guadalupe Rios, helped him in his shamanic practice throughout his life and after his death became a curer, singer, and family matriarch. On a recent trip to Sante Fe, New Mexico, she explained that her husband had been killed by sorcery and that she and others of her family had been victims of black magic sent by envious neighbors. Despite these setbacks she had established a ranch near Santa Maria del Oro, which is in Nayarit, Mexico, where she holds ceremonies and teaches traditional knowledge and skills to a number of young Native Americans. She has also become a cultural ambassador to quite a number of Amerindian nations, including the Cree of Canada and several New Mexico pueblos. Yet the story of Ramon Medina and Guadalupe Rios is not unique, as indicated by the careers of another well-known shamanic family, that of Don José Matsuwa. He is a healer and ceremonial leader revered throughout the Sierra, who was succeeded on his death by his wife. Both he and his wife had trained their daughter. These are two very famous women healers. The daughter has taken many people, both Huichol and gringo, on pilgrimages. But what is odd here is that although we have the written words of the men in these cases, we know about Ramon and Matsuwa, no one has collected the words and the healing powers of the women. The Huichol case fits an established pattern, where it is mentioned in passing that there exist both male and female spiritual healers within a particular culture, tribe, or nation, but then none of the women shamans are interviewed or allowed to speak for themselves.

This may partly have to do with a problem that we have relating to how women who help their husbands shamanize or who work within families are denigrated. They are considered to be incorporated into their husbands' careers in the same way that in European and American society politicians, policemen, diplomats, corporate executives, and, I'm sorry to say, even scholars are informally and often invisibly incorporated into their husbands' careers. In academia this insidious practice of female erasure has been called the "two person, one career" pattern. And the career of course is his; it goes under his name, and it is particularly common at all the Ivy League institutions; the Department of Anthropology at Yale is almost all two people, one career. There is some very good evidence that the wives of shamans, however, are trained as shamans and they are formally united with their husbands into a dual or coshamanic practice. So for instance in the Orinoco Delta of Venezuela, all the wives of high-ranking Warao shamans undergo shamanic training; in fact the men cannot be shamans unless their wives undergo this training. These women specialize in healing sudden illnesses, especially nicotine seizures, which males experience during their shamanic séances. A woman shaman cures them by asking the tobacco spirits, who typically reside inside these male shamans' chests, to release the men. The women, who are referred to as "mothers of seizure," are crucially important shamanic healers for the male tobacco shamans; they would die without the women shamans. Their role is directly modeled after that of a mythic wife of the first shaman, who upon entering the celestial house of the tobacco smoke saw a swallow-tailed kite suffer a nicotine seizure. If you've never seen someone suffer a nicotine seizure, it's frightening. Immediately she changed herself into a frigatebird; she covered the tobacco spirit with her body and her wings, healing him. In return the spirit ordained her as the healer of seizures. Among the Waorani of the Ecuadorian Andes, shamans consist exclusively of married couples; they are called jaguar father, jaguar mother. Together they take ayahuasca and they send out their spirit familiars, which are known as jaguar children, to discover the location of herds of peccaries, report on the welfare of relatives who live far away, and identify culprits responsible for illness or death.

On the North American plains in the Crow Indian nation, couples were regularly adopted together into the tobacco society and birth attendants were usually couples. Gray Bull, for instance, and his wife, Muskrat, practiced together as midwives. Muskrat had been a visionary long before she married Gray Bull; she had been initiated into the weasel chapter of the tobacco order. She had been given a fabulous emblem by an old couple. Later, for some reason that nobody really understands, they took it away from her. She was so unhappy about this she went out and grieved over this loss of power and went into the mountains to fast. A storm came up; she went into a rock shelter, there she lay down to sleep. As she slept a weasel came into her dreams. He stepped on her neck; he entered her stomach. She heard him whistling inside her, and he said, "That is what we want to give you, we want to give you that." He gave her a whistle and a song: "The weasels are coming out, I'll make tobacco come out. The weasels, they are coming out, the tobacco is coming out." Her dream weasel then warned her never to allow anyone to strike her in her kidneys. Later when Muskrat was again fasting, a gray horse went into her stomach. As a result she was able to cure horses that had difficulty in urinating by chewing tobacco and placing it in the horse's mouth. After marrying Gray Bull she obtained knowledge of midwifery from a visionary to whom she paid a gray horse. She and her husband practiced together as a team, easing the pain of delivery.

Among the Cheyenne, no man could ever become a healer by himself. Even if he personally received a curing or visionary power during dreaming, his wife had to be taught or he was not considered a shaman. Gros Ventre pipe keepers were always husband-and-wife teams, who shared the care of the sacred pipe. The current keepers of the sacred pipe of the Lakota nation, Arvol Looking Horse and Carol Anne Heart, together are charged with promoting their culture. As Carol Anne said, "If I were to summarize what Arvol's and my responsibilities are, it would include the preservation and reinforcement of our nature, our spirituality, and the language and the ways of the Lakota and the Dakota people." She talks about how difficult it is for them to practice, because they have to be so pure and better than other people.

So there is a role of a cokeeper or a coshaman in many Native American traditions. It may seem strange, in fact I know it does, to Euro-American feminists. Feminists get very unhappy hearing about this. But as the Cherokee scholar Rayna Green explained, "Native American feminism is different. It is neither revolutionary nor oppositional toward society or men. Native feminists insist on retraditionalization or return to forms which they insist involve women and men in complementary and mutual roles." This is hard stuff for pure feminists to take, but this is the way Native American feminism is. That shamanic husband-and-wife teams are not the result of unique historical accidents or some kind of special ecological circumstance is suggested by my own shamanic training in Central America in Momostenango, where husbands and wives are ideally trained together, as were my husband [Dennis Tedlock] and I.

There are many other traditions, such as among the Inuit, where women healers practice alone or with other women. So there are women who practice with men, women who practice alone, and women who practice with other women. With the Inuit we have a situation where usually they come upon their shamanic power in a spontaneous dream or visionary experience. Uvanak went outside one winter evening when the moon wasn't visible and all of a sudden a glowing ball of fire rushed from the sky to the earth. It struck her. A split second before it entered her body she perceived that one side of this fireball, this meteor, was a bear; the other side was a human with bear fangs. When it struck her she felt herself filled with flaming light. Then she recovered and she ran home singing: "The great sea moves me, the great sea sets me adrift. It moves me like algae on stones in running brook water, the mighty sea. The mighty weather storms through my soul, it tears within me, I tremble with joy." Whenever she sang this song everybody who heard her felt their minds cleansed of any kind of evil thoughts and released into joy. So instead of being a man on an ecstatic flight, like the ideal protoshaman that Mircea Eliade thought of, Uvanak was the woman who incorporated into her own body another persona, that of a half-bear/half-person fireball. In the process she became a medium or a channel to the elemental world. All good shamans are channels to the elemental world.

Eliade rejected possession or transmediumship as shamanic because he felt that it involved a lack of control over the spirits, while ecstatic soul journeys required shamanic control. So there's a notion of a lack of control and a notion of control. Eliade's passive/active, controlled/uncontrolled dichotomy has been elaborated by a lot of other scholars. There is a tendency to associate women with spirit possession or mediumship, which is considered uncontrolled, and men with this ecstatic soul flight, which is considered controlled and shamanic. It has been argued by feminists, and this is an interesting argument, that leaving one's body and sharing one's body are completely different phenomena, and that these activities directly relate to the differences between men's and women's socialization. Thus, a classic shaman, by which I mean a male shaman, transcends his human body—which makes sense, they argue, in that males are raised to develop their gender identity and sense of self in negation and separation from their mothers, rather than in agreement and connection with their mothers. While this is a very beguiling hypothesis, I know of no examples of true possession, by which I mean a splitting of the ego, among Amerindian shamans. Instead shamans identify with, combine with, or assimilate their helping spirits. Among the Inupiat of Alaska, both men and women carve masks depicting shamanic journeys, and they represent the fusion of two spirits, the shaman's own spirit and one or more of their tutelary spirits they use in healing.

I'll talk a little about a Wintu shaman some of you may have met. Her name is Flora Jones. At the age of seventeen she was playing cards, she was actually playing Hearts, with some of her friends in Northern California. Suddenly she felt a burning sensation, a ringing in her ears. "It was like a hot bullet shot through my ears," she said, "the pain flashed through my body and I was unconscious for four days." Can you imagine: you're playing Hearts in your kitchen and then you're unconscious for four days? Her threshold experience of heightened sensory awareness preceded her visionary trance. When she finally awoke she was surrounded by four shamans singing and healing her. They told her that this was an encounter with the star spirit—in this part of California the star spirit is the main, most powerful shamanic spirit. In the following days her helping spirit taught her doctoring songs and the healing arts of the shaman, and over the years she gained more and more tutelary spirits. You are never just made a shaman in one day and then you are a shaman forever; you are always being trained and gaining more powers as you go along. When she shamanizes she forgets what she says, she can't retain it. This is true for a lot of shamans. So she used to have an interpreter, somebody who would come and listen to her and tell her what she had said in her séance. Now she uses a tape recorder and plays it back to hear what she said. She uses wild tobacco in order to help her get into a trance state, and then, as she says, "I feel for sores, I feel for aches, for pains. When I put my hand over the body I can feel every little muscle, every little vein. I can feel the soreness, it hurts me. If my client hurts, it hurts me. If they have heart trouble my heart, my heart just beats. Any place they are hurting, I hurt, I become a part of their body." This kind of identification with the person you are healing is very common.

Pomo shaman Essie Parrish also obtained her shamanic power involuntarily, through the auditory channel. At the age of eleven, she was sleeping and a dream came to her.

> I heard singing in the sky. Because I was little I didn't know what it was, I didn't pay attention to it, I just listened. There was a man singing up there. Then he made it known to me, it was as if it entered deep into my chest, as if it was a song; the song was singing my voice box. Then it seemed as if I could see it, as if I could just make it out. After I woke from sleep the song was singing here, inside of me. Even though I didn't want to sing, I wasn't singing, still the song was singing, singing in my voice box.

The trances and dreams of several of these women call into question the separation of mediumship from shamanism. Spirit possession and ecstatic soul flight might better be described as components within the same shamanic complex, would be my argument. In other words the descent of spirits and gods and the ascent of your soul or spirit are similar. And that is experienced by both men and women. You cannot separate male from female. Some women fly out of their bodies, some women incorporate into their bodies, and the same with men. It seems to be very difficult for people to understand that in shamanism women are not submerged or dominated and thus they do not struggle with men for spiritual equality. Within these shamanic systems the maintenance of female-male relations involves a dialogue based on transactions between the sexes. I have never seen a dominant-submissive situation between male and female shamans. At Zuni Pueblo, it is very interesting; there are equal numbers of men and women shamans in the medicine societies, and both the men and the women have admiration for women. They always talk about how lucky they are they were born *teha*— precious, powerful—just by being women, whereas men, they have to work a lifetime in order to become *teha* or valuable, powerful. So shamanism for them comes more easily for women than for men, and they describe it in that way. This is not unique. Cree healer Vernon Harper says this: "We are taught in our Cree tradition that a woman is a complete being. A man is not. The woman is what we call the caller, the fire, the life. This is what I tell the young women who are scared to come in to the sweat lodge. I say, don't be scared, because it is going to be easier for you in here than it is for the men. I have been running lodges for close to eighteen years now." He does these in prisons by the way, all over Canada. "And in all those years there have only been two times that men were more together psychologically than women. Basically, women don't need men; men need women. We are not complete; that's the reason we men find partners." Although the majority of shamanic accounts recorded from Plains societies concern men's experiences, you can just think of Black Elk, there are all kinds of wonderful male experiences recorded, in a number of groups the gender of the shamanic candidate was (and is still today) never a major consideration. Among the Plains Cree the sun—which by the way is not a male power, it is a female power—gives visions equally to women and to men. Bear shamanism, which is probably one of the most powerful forms of the healing tradition, has long had a mix of female and male practitioners.

When Amerindian women shamans are mentioned as important spiritual leaders or healers in their own right, many authors set them aside in this very strange, linguistically marked, awkward category of "shamaness." Or else they construct them as powerful but nevertheless evil sorcerers. I'll give you an example from our popular culture. Taisha Abelar, who is a member of the informal society of sorcerers that includes Carlos Castaneda, illustrates the pattern beautifully. She has a book called *The Sorcerer's Crossing*. Here we are treated to the story of her apprenticeship in Sonora, Mexico, under Clara Grau and other sorcerers who instruct her in kung fu and karate-like martial arts, together with the use of what she calls crystal weapons, to expand her perception and prepare her to separate her body from her double in ecstatic flight. She dressed in jungle fatigues, lived in a treehouse, and underwent months of grueling training in the hands of what she describes as ruthless female and male sorcerers, who order her about, abandon her, and otherwise mentally and physically abuse her. When women write works of nonfiction centering on firsthand accounts of shamanism which include actual apprenticeships with identifiable, real people living in places, known communities—we can go and meet their teachers—they reveal quite a different narrative of female shamanic initiation. There have been some recent doctoral dissertations that indicate that in Peruvian society there is a dramatic oppositional curing ideology; Eduardo is one of the great practictioners, and there are several books about him in which they fight with spirits; it is all really quite remarkable and showy. The women who have gone there and have worked with the women shamans have found that there is a different model of healing and curing there. What these women shamans do is emphasize the need for the patient, whether male or female, to actively participate in and take responsibility for their own healing. In the male practice the patient is passive and the male shaman does all the battle with the spirits to help the person. In the female tradition you encourage your patient to take part of the workload. Instead of transcending illness by fighting with it and ordering around these things, they practice what I like to call a more immanent or a more experiential model of healing that insists on a patient's self-awareness, a patient's self-purification, an acceptance, a surrender. They work on healing imbalances within. One of the things they talk about is straightening the umbilical cord in order to allow blocked spiritual energy to flow between power sources and the patients. So they work on the umbilicus, and I'm finding this in a lot of the women's traditions, there is a lot of discussion on the umbilicus, and for good reason. Women are trained as midwives in that kind of tradition, and also this is the way to connect the inside and the out, the self and society.

Among the Mazatec there are some wonderful recordings of male and female shamans that you can listen to. What's incredible is the women's language and the men's language, the way they describe what they are doing with powers is so completely different within the same tradition. It's fascinating. There's a woman by the name of Eileen Penera; in her chants she talks about giving birth, she talks about agricultural growth, and the words she uses frequently are words like *freshness, tenderness, happiness.* She describes herself in the third person, this is what she chants: "Woman of medicines and curer who walks her appearance and her soul, she is the woman of the remedy and the medicine, she is the woman who speaks, the woman who puts everything together, doctor woman, woman of words, wisewoman of problems." Now Ramon, who is in her same family, on the other hand chants quite differently; he talks about himself as a mediator between the elemental powers that determine your ultimate fate. He talks with father in the sky and father as the source of fright, and identifies himself specifically with the crackle of bolt lightning. "I am he who speaks with father mountain, I am he who speaks with danger, I am going to sweep the mountains of fear, in the mountains of nerves, I am he who speaks with the dangerous mountains says, I am he who speaks with mountain of ridges says, I am he who speaks with father says." Then he shifts between first and third person, makes himself subject and object, revealing a two-ness of language, his own and that of the natural world speaking through him. "I am dry lightning says, I am the lightning of comet says, I am the dangerous lightning says, I am big lightning says, I am the lightning of rocky places says, I am the lightning of the dawn, the light of day says." Whereas the female healer's language centers on searching, questing, releasing, disentangling. She directs the psychedelic mushrooms that they both have taken, directly, saying, "We are going to search and question, we are going to untie and disentangle, let us go searching for the path, the tracks of her feet, the tracks of her nails, from the right side to the left side, let us go, let us look. So while Ramon chants of fear, terror, and the father in the sky, she is chanting of sweetness and goodwill. These key gender differences have been merged in the practice of family shamanism. This is where mothers, fathers, aunts, uncles, children all get together and eat the hallucinogenic mushrooms in a single ritual setting. This is another whole dimension of shamanism that's rarely discussed, the practice of family shamanism. You might wonder, how do shamans learn about this? They learn about it in the family, usually. In this culture women and men learn how to experience or talk about, one or the other or both, the shamanic ecstatic journey differently by picking up same-sex unconscious images and kinesthetic responses. The same is true, I believe, in other cultures when men and women are encouraged to enter the shamanic path.

Within the long Christian tradition of branding shamanic practitioners as witches and sorcerers, midwives have been singled out over and over again as particularly evil. These women were perceived by many men as not only interfering with God's realm but as a direct threat to the male monopoly on medical knowledge and practice. In this way women's shamanic knowledge, including healing, birthing, trancing, dreaming, and prophecy, became hidden.

—June 27, 1995

NOTHING I WITHHOLD: A SOCRATIC RAP

Cid Corman

WILL TELL YOU THE SECRET. WHAT IS IT? YOU ASK. I KEEP TELLING YOU. LIS-
TEN. I don't really know what I should say to you that my poetry does-
n't say better. That's what it's about, you say it better. And in a way that
can be transmitted through you.

In 1960, after being away from America for six years, in Europe and
Japan, I was so anti-American that I thought I'd better come back and see
what it was all about. I had just published, in Kyoto, "A" 1–12 of Louis
Zukofsky, the first printing of it. And what I did when I came back, after
staying awhile in San Francisco, which was my base the two years I stayed
back in America, I had to go back to Boston to see my parents and family,
and I read, crossing the United States; I traveled by bus across America and
stopped every eight hours and gave a reading at every stop. I had arranged
this all. I arrived back in Boston with all my travel expenses paid; although
I didn't have much in my pocket I still had more than what I started out
with. I read from "A" 1–12, I didn't read any of my own work, I just read
Zukofsky's work. And he said, when I met him in New York at the end of
the trip, he said I was wasting my time. I said, Louis, for me, if there were
one person, say, one woman in the audience who got something out of it,
something of it stuck in her head, and she transmitted that to a child of
hers, it would have been worth it, all the readings. That's my feeling. It may
be that the work I read may not do much for you beyond leave a trace in
your memory, but you too will transmit it, perhaps, a few of you, to someone else again. For me, that transmission is what it's all about, to bring it
through from one generation to the next, what I believe is the lifeline of
human beings, poetry.

Maybe I can give you an idea of what I mean by reading other people's
work, people whose work you would not likely know. This is a young
poet, a dear friend of mine, who lives in San Francisco. I had hoped he
would be here, but because of economics it's impossible for him to be here.
He is an extraordinary poet and human being. George Evans is his name.
Let me tell you how we met. When I started my cake and coffee shop with

my wife in Kyoto over twenty years ago, we had poetry readings; it was a shop unlike any you have ever known or anyone else probably ever will know. It was designed not to make money—that's my style; I have written a book called *How Not to Become a Millionaire*. I had never done a business thing before in my life; at age fifty I went into business and became a baker and an ice cream maker and ran the shop with my wife, who also had no such experience. She had only worked in filmmaking before that; she was a news editor on a television station and had worked as a script girl. She had met most of the famous Hollywood names when she was a youngster; she had met Marlon Brando, John Wayne, everybody in the film industry when she was practically a child. But she had had no business training whatsoever. So we did this thing because she wanted to do something outside of the house and I wanted to do whatever she wanted to try. I, of course, was not going to stop writing poetry, but I could do my work in the morning and the shop opened around noon. She would go in a little earlier and get things ready and then we would work together. But of course business was very slack, always. If we had five customers in a day we had done pretty well. We only later found out we were undercharging. I had a friend who was an accountant come in and check what we were doing and he said we had to double our prices if we intended to make any money. We had to learn the hard way. The shop is still going and it's doing much better under my brother-in-law's handling than it ever did under mine. But I also had many poetry readings there, three times a week we had poetry readings and discussions, a lot of good things happened, many good people stopped by to give readings, the best known of whom was Kenneth Rexroth, who gave a terrible reading. He thought he would try to read his poems in the old Yeatsian way, so he half chanted and sang them. It was not successful, which was unfortunate because some of his work is very fine—but that's the way it goes. His wife read the following week.

The shop is named after me, it's called C.C.'s—in fact, I'm best known for cake and ice cream in Japan—and one day this young fellow came in, about twenty-five or twenty-six years old. I'd never seen him before. He knew my name apparently and he asked to speak with me. Nobody was in the shop, so it was very simple. We sat down together and he gave me this large manila envelope full of poems; he asked me if I would look them over and give him my honest opinion of them. I said of course, I will. In my usual fashion, when he went off, I read them at once. And I was flabbergasted. They were unbelievably good for a youngster, I could hardly believe what I was reading. Only once before in my life had anyone come to me, unsolicited, and delivered such poems to me, that was Ted Enslin way back around 1951. The rest of the work that I published, I always solicited, I went out and got it. So this was remarkable. But, what happened? Where was George? A year later he came back to find out what I felt about the poems! He was doing Zen by himself in Kyoto, he had come to meditate for a year in Japan. So I told him my opinion and we have been friends ever since. I featured him in *Origin* twice. And if the last series had been allowed to continue he would have been seen in considerable quantity, because I do very much admire his work.

Some of his work is really prose, written out of his Vietnam experience. He was in Vietnam as a teenager and he worked in the medical corps. George never went to university, he went into the military right out of high school and he had had a strange life even before that. He had wandered all over America. His parents had sort of told him to get out of the house when he was about fifteen and he wandered all over America and lived a good deal of his early life in Pittsburgh. In more recent years he's been mostly on the West Coast. He speaks, reads, and writes Japanese, he is very adept with Japanese.

Next I want to talk about something quite different, from another poet whose name will be unfamiliar to you, an old-timer, he's in his mideighties now. I've known him most of his life. When he started out teaching he was on the campus where I was studying as an undergraduate and I met him at that time, during the war. His name is Lyle Glazier. He lives in Bennington, Vermont, on property that his wife's family owned, that Robert Frost once tried to buy; it's on a hill overlooking Bennington. He is Bennington's most conspicuous citizen, and I mean *citizen*. He has made more hell for the city than any single person they've ever had. Many of them wish he were dead, especially the rich. He put the richest man in town in jail, catching him for stealing the city funds. He was laughed at for two years for accusing the man and then he produced all the documentation and the man was put away. He keeps his eye on things. He is very concerned that the working-class people are treated like human beings.

This book is features of a long poem called *Azubah Nye*. Lyle Glazier comes from a family that came to America on the Mayflower, literally. Unfortunately or fortunately—it depends on how you look at things—his mother and father were dirt poor, very poor as the poem makes clear. But he likes to believe that among his ancestors was an Indian woman, and this is the name of the woman, Azubah Nye. He's not got absolute proof, but he likes to believe that. This is the same man that introduced Black Studies into the American curriculum; I don't know that there are many black people that realize it. He has helped more people, black students of his, to find jobs than anyone I know of, and he does it quietly, so that he isn't known. He is retired from teaching; he was a teacher most of his life at SUNY Buffalo.

This poem, then, is a longish poem telling about his family, the lineage and the type of life they were living. In the last part, the last pages of this which I want to read to you, he tells of the desperation of his family. His mother's name is Myrtie and his brother's name is Mel. He also speaks of his grandpa and Perry, who is an uncle of his. He opens telling of how his father was fired from his job.

That was after
Pop has his job
in the stockroom
of Millers Falls Tool Company.
A calculus whiz
he kept books for the foreman.
When he was dead Gramp realized
"I should've mortgaged
the place to get him
an education, I
never did know nawthin."
Anti-union
Pop thought himself
potential management
not a laborer.
Promoted when his boss retired
he was so grateful
he never got the raise
that should have come with the job,
went on working
at $30 a week
nine hours a day
& Saturday mornings
he working along with his men,
never dressed to be foreman.
He must have gone stark crazy
the morning he was called in
(October '33)
"We have to let you go."

His mother and father both committed suicide and the two boys were left in the care of their grandparents. With great difficulty Lyle worked his way to university, graduated Harvard with a doctorate, and wrote poetry all his life. But it was only in later years he began to publish some of it, he never had time to push it. He has taught in many parts of the world; he's taught in Turkey, Yemen, India. He is also bisexual, and this has led to a curious life. He is writing his autobiography now and it's a story, and he tells it beautifully too, honestly, and in remarkable detail. He was married to a woman and had three daughters who are all grown up now, and he has grandchildren; he lives alone; his wife died five or six years ago. She was a nice woman, I met her once or twice. She was most of her adult life in a wheelchair, her health was very poor. The curious thing is that when he writes about the last year or two, when she was dying and he was aware of it and she was too, it was like a romantic fairy tale, their relationship was so beautiful it is unbelievable. And yet he is a man who continues to have relations with other men and is open to affairs of any kind, he remains very sexually active. He really amazes me. When his wife died, a woman in the neighborhood, ninety years old, came to him and said, would you please have sex with me? I've never made love to a man, I'd like the experience, to know what it's like before I die. [laughter] He refused. He likes to enjoy himself. [more laughter] But only Lyle would be approached in such a situation.

ANNE WALDMAN: It's interesting to me—the stories of so many of the writers you present and your interest in the narrative poem; could you talk about biography and how the work is refined into poetry?

CC: In my own case, my life is worked directly into my poetry. There is nothing I withhold, of my life, in my poetry. Although many years ago Kenneth Rexroth wrote of Allen Ginsberg and myself as two saints, I don't think that's true of either of us. It is part of my life to say it the way it really is, not to distort, just to lay it out the way it is. So unlike many writers, like T. S. Eliot and my friend Louis Zukofsky, whatever letters of mine remain, let them be the way they are. If they are misunderstood, as they are likely to be, it's all right too. That's part of living, and I don't feel it's right to distort the actualities. Let people know what it was all about as much as you can. It's hard enough without all the added ornamentation, the cutting away and the deceptions that go on in life. We do love to deceive ourselves, that's part of human nature. But even so, it is part of my sense of it to make it as open as possible. So you'll find all my flaws of nature in my poetry, I make no bones about it. I'll give you an example. This is a piece that is in answer to a poem by George Evans, it's called "Enuresis." Some of you may not know this term. It's the medical term for bedwetting. He wrote a poem about terror and this is my answer:

Terror is not—Ed—
sitting in one's piss.
I know—I've sat there—

I've slept there and did
most of my childhood.
That was warmth—in fact—

and comfort—in spite
of the unconcealed
unconcealable

smell. Terror? That was
and always will be
Mother cursing Dad

and there there I am
alone in that night
hearing that door slam.

AUDIENCE MEMBER: Can I ask you about your friendship with Stephen Jonas? What were the circumstances of your meeting? How did you see his development as a poet and could you relate that, possibly, to his flamboyant, biographical, tragical maudit?

CC: Well, I'll tell you what I know because I was away from Boston during much of his last years. I did see him once within a few years of his death. Steve and I met through a poetry group of mine. I started many poetry groups in Boston. These were public, free affairs held in the public library system. I had worked in the public library system and I asked if I might use a room in the evening before they closed, the last hour in their service, to discuss poetry with whoever wanted to come—dealing with modern poetry only. Steve was a member of the group I had in the poorest part of town, the West End Library it was then—today that is part of what is called Government Center in Boston; it's a completely changed area.

It was the immigrant area of Boston, mostly European immigrants then, and a very shabby area. It was a mixed group we had: very old people and very young; some were just curious and some were probably writing, Steve was one of them. We became quite friendly at that point. I saw him a good deal beyond the group. He had a flat in the downtown area, a shabby place in the red-light district of Boston. This was the combat zone, where the sailors hung out during the war period, all the burlesque theaters, he lived on the fringe of that. And I used to go over to his place. There were usually a couple of young men staying with him. I wasn't concerned about his private life, I was concerned of course with poetry, and that's what we were focused on. He was writing then and showing me work. This was before I started my magazine, so it was the late 1940s, 1949 perhaps. He was in his early twenties; I was still in my twenties also, a little older than him. He showed me his work as he was writing, most of it was very influenced by Pound. He was enamored of Pound's work, and he used a kind of musical line, he was very caught up in logopoeia, phanopoeia, melopoeia. The work—there was something there, but it wasn't satisfying to me. Later, when I came back in 1961, when I was in Boston I visited with him and he was quite a different person. He looked quite different, he had put on a lot of weight and he looked very shabby; he had just come out of hospital, he was on chemicals that the hospital had prescribed and he was very excited that these people, he thought, were helping him with these chemicals. I wasn't at all sure. He was living in an awful flat, it was dirty and everything looked very bad. It was a dark place, and I had the feeling he might be very lonely there too. It was not very far from the Massachusetts General Hospital, near the Charles River, still in the downtown area but in a different part of it. Then he showed me work, some of which I took and published. That work seemed to me considerably better than what he had been doing. It was more terse and it was more solid in its feeling. He was coming from a different place. That impressed me, and I tried to encourage that. But I had no more contact, apart from that, with him then. It's only been recently that I have heard all these other things about him, as the people who have been interested in Steve have brought forth a lot of information, which I was oblivious of at the time, and he said nothing about. I normally don't probe into people's private affairs unless they really want to talk about such things. But he was a person I liked. Oh—and of course the most famous thing, with John Wieners, that famous scene when Charles Olson came to town and Steve came and brought John Wieners and Ed Marshall with him. I didn't know them and he introduced me to them; they stayed for the four-hour reading along with many others. I didn't know them until some years later when Ed Marshall met me again by accident in San Francisco and told me what happened, that they followed Olson back to Black Mountain. One of the beautiful things, how people coincide.

AW: I am curious about your advice and suggestions toward young writers. There's the attraction of the internet, that kind of publishing; there are many more readings than there used to be, and probably more bad poetry out there . . . Here at Naropa we try to encourage the sense of the poet in the world, active and engaged, a kind of cultural worker. What could be transmitted, from your experiences, to the young people present.

AUDIENCE MEMBER: In light of that comment, I wanted to ask you also to comment on the next century that we're moving into. What kind of responsibilities do we have as artists, as writers and poets? What kind of questions should we be asking ourselves and what kind of demands should we be making on ourselves, from a broad perspective?

CC: I'm not the kind of person who likes to tell somebody else what to do or how to do it. But the main thing is to stay open to others, to listen, that's the secret, and to look around you. If you are planning or intend to start a magazine, it's up to you to go out and find the poets, not to wait for them to find you. You read. And if you see somebody's writing that interests you, write to that person. You can always make contact and they are always delighted to hear, because there isn't so much feedback—I'm talking about little magazines in particular. Whatever format you choose to use it will still be pretty much the same issue. To start a little magazine it's a good idea to have already, in your hand as it were, a few people whose work already interests you and with whom you've had a little contact, so that you have the nucleus of something. And I very much believe that a little magazine should be prejudiced, that it should reflect one person's mind. Once you have a staff of editors you're going to compromise, you have to, there's no way two people are going to see exactly alike—nor should they. This makes for a very mixed bag and no coherent policy. You don't maybe start out with a coherent policy, you may not know exactly what you're doing. But you will find gradually through the work that you publish, the people that you find yourself related to, you will find there is a kind of unspoken policy. I never wrote any editorials in my magazine. I left it open to what was going to happen, which I couldn't possibly predict. I wouldn't have known. The people that came into the second year of my issues were people I hadn't known when I started the magazine. But I did read all other little magazines religiously, from many places. As soon as I started, and even before, I was already doing this even before I thought of starting a magazine. In fact it wasn't my idea; it was the rich lady's idea. It hadn't crossed my mind, even. Mostly because I didn't have any money and I knew there was no point, and I didn't ask her for money, she volunteered it, it didn't even occur to me to ask. Later of course when I asked her, I got nothing, ironically. If you can get it, it's nice. I never had much patronage and I still don't.

AUDIENCE MEMBER: A visiting writer last week juxtaposed two words: *translator* and *traitor.* I am curious how you respond to that.

CC: That's famous: *traduttore, traditore.* Translation of course is a thing in itself; it's almost a world in itself. I will only talk in terms of poetry translation; prose translation has its own particularities. I have translated from the most ancient writings of antiquity up to yesterday's poetry. Actually, a translation I made six weeks ago is already published. The author was flabbergasted because he was visiting me, and when he got home he already had the translation printed. He had written it just weeks before. He sent the poems to me, I translated them the moment I received them and sent them off to my friend Bob Arnold, who printed them the day he received them and sent copies off immediately to the author in France.

There are certain obvious features in translation. One, there is no such thing as a perfect translation. That means anybody can be put to fault with a translation. You open yourself immediately to criticism when you translate something because somebody is going to find fault, necessarily, with what you do because there is no final translation of anything. There are translations of course that are taken as gospel, like the Gospel. You'll find that translations of the Bible in many languages are taken as the final word, it's that kind of thing. I have written into my books, when I have made a translation, I have said, if you can translate it better than I can, please do. If you can change even my own poetry, if you can add a comma or take away a comma or change a word of my poetry, and make it better, it's yours. I'm delighted. You don't need to mention my name. That's what, for me, poetry is all about. I'm concerned that when you translate poetry, that it become poetry, that it *be* poetry. That first of all. Then you try, as far as you can, to bring through what you felt, what you found in the work yourself; and some sense, as Walter Benjamin understood, to bring across something of the genius of another language into your own. The way Hölderlin brought over some of his Greek translations into German, which Goethe despised when he saw them, but which gradually have taken effect and which Benjamin uses as his models of translation. The thing is, unlike Goethe, who did translations too, Hölderlin lived his translations; he translated into his life as well as just translating words. That's another thing. It's very hard to translate Tu Fu, for example, in Chinese, without entering into his work, his very engaging work; it's hard not to feel, or try to transpose yourself, into that world that he lived. It is such an exacting world, such a difficult world. Men who have to pass exams, get into a court service, and then are translated into all sorts of activities which are not true to their lives, but they have to go through it and in an environment full of wars and separation, isolation from family. A very tough world to live in. And we feel it, we share that feeling, and he communicates it incredibly well, so that we still feel it.

AUDIENCE MEMBER: I've been thinking about what you said about how much poetry you write. How much of the poetry you write do you edit? And what is your editing process?

CC: What I do, I write a poem and I put it away for a year, at least. Because there is what I call a "halo effect." When you write something it always seems a little better than it really is. You think you've done something that you haven't done because your feeling is still overlaid with the words that you've set down, especially in poetry where you are writing often out of a great intensity of feeling. So I put it away until I don't recognize the poem when I come back to it. I have to find out if it moves me, if it does anything for me, if it works, simply. If it doesn't, and I find nothing there, I throw it away. Otherwise I may find something there that I may be able to work with, that stimulates me either to improve it, or to take off and do a different poem altogether, or that rare, lucky thing when it turns out I did o.k. and I'm satisfied with what I find. Sometimes I am really shocked at how well some of the poems came off, but that's only after many years of writing; this was never true in my earlier years. I always found I had more work to do, even though it may only have been one or two words changed. I have probably worked longer years on a single short poem than anyone in history, twenty or thirty years on a single poem that ends up with maybe five words in it. And it was short to begin with.

—July 6, 1995

TALKING BACK TO WHITMAN

Lorenzo Thomas

'LL BEGIN BY CITING A COUPLE OF POEMS, BECAUSE WHAT I WANT TO TALK about is the relationship between literature and identity and American society as we understand it today. There's a marvelous poem by Amiri Baraka that he wrote during the height of the Black Arts movement period, throughout the 1960s. Scholars say the Black Arts period ended in 1975—at least that's what it says in the Norton anthology of African American literature. At that time African American poets were writing specifically to African American audiences, and one of the concepts of the period was a concept called "nation time": the idea was that African Americans constituted a nation. In that period Amiri Baraka wrote a poem; there are some beautiful lines in that poem. He says, "The nation is like ourselves. Whatever we are doing or not doing is what the nation is doing or not doing." Whoever he intended that poem for, and I guess he read it at demonstrations and in basements of community centers, the words are still absolutely true. The nation *is* like ourselves; whatever we are doing or not doing is what the nation is doing or not doing. In other words, there is no "they"; it is us.

What does poetry have to do with that? There is another poem I want to quote a bit of, because I think it is relevant, a poem of Allen Ginsberg's from *Cosmopolitan Greetings* called "Improvisation in Beijing." It has the premise that here he is in Beijing and [he] wonders what to tell these people that don't know who he is, so he makes up this poem.

> I write poetry because I want to be alone and want to talk to people.
> I write poetry to talk back to Whitman, young people in ten years, talk
>   to old aunts and uncles still living near Newark, New Jersey.
> I write poetry because I listened to black Blues on 1939 radio, Leadbelly
>   and Ma Rainey.
> I write poetry inspired by youthful cheerful Beatles' songs grown old.
> I write poetry because Chuang-tzu couldn't tell whether he was but-
>   terfly or man, Lao-tzu said water flows downhill, Counfucius said

honor elders, I wanted to honor Whitman.

I write poetry because overgrazing sheep and cattle Mongolia to U.S. Wild West destroys new grass & erosion creates deserts.

I write poetry wearing animal shoes.

I write poetry "First thought, best thought" always.

I write poetry because no ideas are comprehensible except as manifested in minute particulars: "No ideas but in things."

And then Allen Ginsberg goes on to say some more reasons why he writes poetry. What I find fascinating about that poem is that it reveals the poet as a wise and kind man, which Allen Ginsberg was, and also in a short compass, whether for an audience in Beijing or one here at Naropa, it explains precisely the culture that this wise and kind man had been shaped by. It expresses his immediate concerns at that moment, in 1984, when he wrote the poem. He has religious concerns, political concerns, personal concerns, familial concerns; all of that is beautifully expressed in the poem.

We are in the midst right now of trying to figure out what the question of American culture is. Not everybody is as self-aware as Allen Ginsberg was. Not everybody is able to see through the immediate political or personal need of the moment and write words that express that reality in a dimension that lasts and is applicable to all situations, such as Amiri Baraka did in his nation time. So the rest of us are left squabbling, questioning, posturing, and trying to figure out what is American culture. "What is *my* culture?" is the way it is usually put, because this is America.

I will start with the premise that ethnicity—which is what this usually boils down to eventually, race or ethnicity—ethnicity in the United States is a fiction. I'm not talking about what used to be Yugoslavia; I'm not talking about South or Central Africa; I am talking about this place that is now the United States of America. And in this place ethnicity is a fiction; all ethnic groups are fictitious constructions, they are political fictions. They are designed to allow group identity, and once they do that they are a means of political leverage. So these fictions, the book-type fictions, written by so-called ethnic writers in America, are double fictions. They are written to define or reinforce group identity, and to assess the chances at that moment, or in the future, of the group being accepted in the American mainstream. I'll go further then to just say ethnic or racial groups and use the word *subculture* and it's the same thing. Literary avant-garde's purpose is to define itself and its members and to assess its chances of succeeding. And for an avant-garde to succeed, it means it is going to become the academy. If you don't think that's true then you don't understand English or French or Italian. The avant-garde comes before taking over the castle, that's what that's about.

I say that American ethnic groups are fictitious. If you take for example the category Asian American, this is supposed to include people from India, Pakistan, Korea, Laos, China, Japan, the Philippines, and a few other places. In a book edited by Ishmael Reed called *Multi-America*, Amrijit Singh, a wonderful literary critic whose speciality is the Harlem Renaissance, points out that the categories South Asian or Asian American are very conscious political decisions made by people in the United States of America and the United States Census Department to create a political entity. Looking at the concept of Hispanic or *Latino*, which, by the way, I think is a terrible word for etymological reasons, that too is supposed to embrace people of Mexican descent living in what is now the United States that used to be Mexico, people from Puerto Rico who are American citizens since the beginning of the twentieth century, people from Central and South America, and perhaps even people from Spain or the Canary Islands. Again, if you think about it, people from these different areas don't speak the same Spanish; there is a difference between the Spanish of Nicaragua and that of Mexico, that of Puerto Rico, etcetera. African American is a fictional quantity in another sense, less so perhaps than Asian American or Hispanic American because African American simply means people of African descent—that is, people of *noticeable* African descent. But when we use that phrase it includes people who are five-star generals, chief executive officer of the largest food corporation on Earth (Reginald Lewis at Beatrice, Incorporated), and people who live in communities where forty percent of the black men are unemployed, and everybody in between. Somehow all of this is the "African American" group. The other group, White, is even more of a fictitious construction than the others. Not as recent vintage as Asian American or Hispanic American, but of more recent vintage than African American, the category White doesn't appear until really about the time of the Civil War, after the middle of the nineteenth century. Today, it embraces anybody who is not Asian American, Hispanic, or African American—then, you're white. Again, this is meaninglessness. Why these groups? The reason for this fiction is for political power, to define a group, identify its members, and then pursue the group's perceived interests. The "founding fathers," by the way, I think, understood this; they didn't have these categories but they understood what has created them. I was at a lecture in Atlanta that Adrian Piper was giving—a wonderful artist. She had done a performance, a piece where it appeared to us in the audience [that]

Adrian Piper was arguing with another speaker that we assumed was a white man; later on she announced to us that Adrian Piper did both voices and one half of the script was electronically manipulated at the mixing board to change her voice into that of what we assumed was a white man. That's what she does; she masquerades as all kinds of different people besides herself; it's conceptual art. During this lecture a young woman in the audience asked a question, after Adrian Piper had talked about all these confrontational art things she had done in the sixties, whether on race or gender issues or inclusion in the Museum of Modern Art, how she had marched and demonstrated, etcetera. This young woman was almost in tears, saying, but Dr. Piper you did all this twenty years ago, but we're still having to confront that here. This was a top student at an elite university who had somehow come to believe that "been there, done that" means something real. So Adrian Piper had to explain that yes, we did march twenty years ago, and thirty years ago, and they marched forty years ago, and fifty years ago; and the voting rights act of 1964–1965 did nothing except reinforce what African American people already had by constitutional right in 1865—the point being that the founding fathers thought of this democratic republic as not something that had anything to do with majority rule. A democratic republic was a means, a system of negotiating interests. In Philadelphia, at the constitutional convention, they all realized that they were there in their own personal, private interest. The purpose of the Constitution and the other documents was a way of negotiating those interests so that everyone got a share of their interests. Which means that it is a constant negotiation; there is no "been there, done that." If you want your interests reflected in the mainstream you must constantly negotiate that position, because there are some other people with conflicting interests. Like the speaker of the House of Representatives at the moment, Newt Gingrich. And to turn this back to literature, the "Contract with America" that Representative Gingrich and others wrote says nothing that is not in James Fenimore Cooper's *The American Democrat*—except *The American Democrat* is much more eloquent and annoying and insulting than the "Contract with America." James Fenimore Cooper did not predict Newt Gingrich. But if you read *The American Democrat,* he explains Newt Gingrich, because he eloquently points out the interests that Mr. Gingrich and others are out to negotiate for themselves, the interests that they serve.

In addition to this idea that this country, as a democracy, is a negotiation of these many interests—and the reason I want to be African American is so I can have a whole bunch of people with me, supporting my interests, the reason that I want to be Asian American is because a Filipino American will never get to be the mayor of Houston, but there might be enough Asian Americans that a Filipino man or woman who is identified as Asian American can become mayor—in addition to this idea, the other side of this was the idea of the American people or the American polity as a new nationality. Not these fictions of ethnic origin, but a new nationality. That idea goes back to the 1780s. J. Hector St. John de Crèvecoeur, in a book called *Letters from an American Farmer,* written as propaganda to support the American Revolution in France by saying how great it was to be in these colonies now becoming free, points out that the American is not French, is not English, is not Dutch, is not German; the American is a new man. Because all these people coming here now become not Dutch Americans, French Americans, etcetera, they become Americans. This concept is later called the melting pot. And he has a point, because anybody that came here in the 1780s was not doing so damn well in Europe, otherwise they wouldn't be coming here. So you don't owe them anything; you get here, you're an American. I guess the same might be true for Africa. If you were a prince and you wound up in Georgia, there was something wrong with your princedom, if you were the one that ended up on that boat. I digress. People ask me, though, they say, the melting pot, that's a ludicrous idea, how could that be. De Crèvecoeur said all these people—French, Irish, Dutch, etcetera—all these people become a new person, a new American, but that's impossible, that's ridiculous. And then I look at the African American. They are all these kidnapped people from all over the continent of Africa, kidnapped and wound up in Senegal and Gambia and Ghana, where the slave depots were, speaking different languages, having different religions. They all wound up here. And all of these people became *a people.* So tell me that the melting pot is impossible; African American proves that it is not. And that's not what de Crèvecoeur was talking about; but the concept, as Allen Ginsberg says—ideas are demonstrated in minutiae, in the things. So if the idea of the melting pot existed in de Crèvecoeur's head, the reality of it existed in Charleston, South Carolina, and elsewhere. In Vermont, too, where de Crèvecoeur bases his idea on the fact that one farmer was Dutch, but his daughter married the daughter of a farmer who was English, and their kids married the folks down the hill who were Swedish, and therefore became American. He didn't use the word *white.*

Also in the *Multi-America* book that Ishmael Reed edited is a wonderful essay by David Lloyd, where he points out that all of the nationalities, everyone who came to this continent, were mistreated by whoever else was already here in the mainstream and had to fight for their interests. He points out that something peculiar happened after the Civil War, when the Germans, who lost the revolution in Germany in 1848 and had to flee to places like St. Louis, and were not wanted, or the Irish, who had to flee significant problems in Ireland, came here. They used to have signs at jobsites, "No Irish Need Apply," and they'd have signs at eating establishments that said "No Irish or Dogs." Somehow, David Lloyd says, after they fought their way through they forgot about how they had had to struggle for their interests and were happy to join this new category called "white," thinking that their interests were against the interests of all those other so-called ethnic groups.

The word *ethnic* itself is an interesting word. At its most polite it means "other." The word is Greek, *ethnikos,* meaning tribe or nation. But the Athenians didn't apply the word to themselves; it applied to the Spartans or the Turks, so it means "other" in that sense, another tribe. By the time it comes into English, in the fifteenth century, it not only means other, it means heathen, people whose religion is not in a book. We didn't really like Jews, but they had a book, in fact, it was our book too, half of our book, so that's cool. But all those people weren't in the book, they were ethnic and they were heathens. So today when we use the word flippantly in American discourse, I wonder if people know what they're talking about, what they mean when they use the word *ethnic.*

The concept of whiteness is interesting. If you're interested in it I'll ask you to read a book by George Schuyler called *Black No More,* a very funny novel from 1932. In this book a scientist discovers a way to make black people white; they step into a chamber and get radiowaves or something, it's very painful, but they emerge white. Then of course strange things happen, like one of these former patients becomes head of the Ku Klux Klan. It's a fascinating book if you want to understand this business of whiteness. The people that Schuyler was satirizing were people like Lothrop Stoddard, who wrote a book called *The Rising Tide of Color against White World Supremacy,* a best seller in 1925; it was endorsed by the president of the United States, Calvin Coolidge, who told people that they ought to read this book. Stoddard's idea was that white people were being overwhelmed by the "colored races," and he was basing this on the Russo-Japanese War, which the Japanese won. Then suddenly, because the Japanese won, the Russians became white people. The English and others had never quite thought of them that way before. Another book is by Madison Grant, who was supposedly a scientist; he was a big donor and the president of the New York Zoological Society, that is, the Bronx Zoo. I checked it out. It sounded so impressive and then it was just the Bronx Zoo. Madison Grant was a big-game hunter; he was also a Harvard graduate. And that qualified him to write books on race and ethnicity. That's what Schuyler's *Black No More* satirizes.

I'm saying all this to suggest that in our own moment, when we look at our literature, if we continue to think that there is a separate Asian American culture or a separate Latino culture or a separate African American culture, we will have a strange way of understanding the literature written in English that comes out of what is now the United States of America, or that has come out of the United States of America for the last two hundred and twenty years. When we talk about inclusion we have to be very careful about exactly what we mean by that. Is this another way of reaching toward homogenization, or is this another way of disguising the conflicts of interest groups—which eventually doesn't serve anybody because the framing notion is that interest groups meet in Congress and negotiate the best interests of all. Nobody gets everything they want if you are negotiating; you end in some cooperative situation.

The poetry written by African American writers, just like all these other ethnic fictions, reflects historical definitions of the group. What is the self-definition the African American people share at a particular time, or that their writers are empowered to try to get them to subscribe to, embrace, and share? Besides those definitions of what the group means, it also assesses the relationship of the group to the mainstream. That is not of course everything that African American writers write; writers write all sorts of stuff. But that is one way we can understand the literature marked "African American." Its first work is to speak to African American people and define what African American is and to assess the relationship of this group to the mainstream. It is a conversation intended to be overheard by everybody else. Like any text, a poem reflects and records the period that created it.

So I thought that I might spend a few minutes offering a brief anthology of poems by African American writers that provide a sort of timeline of that definition within this polity, this society, this culture. I'll start with Phillis Wheatley. The most famous poem of Phillis Wheatley's is "On Being Brought from Africa to America," published in 1773, written earlier. Wheatley started writing when she was about fourteen years old; her book appeared when she was twenty. When she came back from England, for her twenty-first birthday, the Wheatley family emancipated her.

'Twas mercy brought me from my *Pagan* land,
Taught my benighted soul to understand
That there's a God, that there's a *Saviour* too:
Once I redemption neither sought nor knew.
Some view our sable race with scornful eye,

"Their colour is a diabolic die."
Remember, *Christians, Negros,* black as *Cain,*
May be refin'd and join th'angelic train.

Now that's a spooky poem. If you read that poem carefully—and James A. Levernier, a critic who has written a lot of studies on Phillis Wheatley, in a number of *Legacy* [issues] (a journal on women's literature in English), wrote a piece on Wheatley where he points out what shouldn't have to be pointed out. First of all, Phillis Wheatley is a neoclassical poet in the mode of Alexander Pope. Anyone who could possibly pick up a neoclassical poet and not understand that their primary mode of discourse was irony should not have gotten out of sophomore class. Except that everything you learned about neoclassical poetry, when you confront the slave poet Phillis Wheatley, goes out the window because she's black. How could she possibly be ironic? She was ironic because she was studying Pope. This poem presents her as a neoclassical ironist in the grand tradition; it also presents her as a partisan for the abolition of slavery; and this and other poems present her as a member of the group of her day that was promoting the rights and the equality of women. There are some interesting tricks in this poem. When she says "their colour," speaking in the voice of the slave masters and the hypocrite Christians who support slavery, they say "their colour is a diabolic die"— Levernier points out the dye she is referring to is indigo, which is why slaves were brought here, to work on the indigo plantations. Which is why the Quakers refuse to dye their clothes, because dying their clothes would support the indigo plantations. And sugar. She says, "Remember, Christians, Negros, black as Cain [i.e. cane],/May be refined." Quakers don't put sugar in their tea either, because that would support the slave system. So anyone who reads that poem and says Phillis Wheatley just thanked Jesus for being a slave didn't read the poem in the way neoclassical poetry is intended to be read. Poets play with words and present them in an ironic fashion. In that line, by the way, there is a comma after "remember," a comma after "Christians," a comma after "Negroes"; and if you want to do a Chomsky tree on that it's very interesting—are the Negroes black as Cain or the Christians black as Cain? Or both? It doesn't matter because according to Phillis Wheatley's Jesus, they both can be saved.

Here's another poem. This one is by Sherman Alexie, a Spokane Coeur d'Alene from Washington, from a book called *Reservation Blues.* These guys sitting around on a reservation eating government cheese meet up with Robert Johnson, who is trying to escape his past and wanders in with his guitar; he is there to see Big Mom, who spookily enough turns out to be like a caricature of Willie Mae "Big Mama" Thornton, but if you don't know that, you think it's some kind of Indian tribal thing that Sherman Alexie is talking about. Robert Johnson didn't die, by the way, in 1938; he faked his death and has been wandering around the country ever since . . . and then shows up on this Indian reservation to see Big Mom, because he's heard about her from Elvis and Janis Joplin and so on. There's a great line that says, yeah, Big Mom was a musical genius, she was a teacher of all these great musicians who shaped the twentieth century—he mentions Les Paul, Paul McCartney, Jim Morrison—still Big Mom had her heart broken by many of her students, who couldn't cope with the incredible gifts she had given them: Jimi Hendrix, Janis Joplin, Elvis; they all drank so much and self-destructed so successfully that Big Mom made them honorary members of the Spokane tribe. This is a poem that Sherman Alexie sort of sticks in this novel:

My braids were cut off in the name of Jesus
To make me look so white
My tongue was cut out in the name of Jesus
So I would not speak what's right
My heart was cut out in the name of Jesus
So I would not try to feel
My eyes were cut out in the name of Jesus
So I could not see what's real

And I've got news for you
But I'm not sure where to begin
Yeah, I've got news for you
My God has dark skin
My God has dark skin

I had my braids cut off by black robes
But I know they'll grow again
I had my tongue cut out by these black robes
But I know I'll speak 'til the end
I had my heart cut out by the black robes
But I know what I still feel
I had my eyes cut out by the black robes
But I know I see what's real

And I've got news for you
But I'm not sure where to begin
Yeah, I've got news for you
My God has dark skin
My God has dark skin

Lovely poem. Somehow when we start talking about inclusion and diversity, we're going to have to figure out a way for Sherman Alexie's "My God Has Dark Skin" to sit side by side with Phillis Wheatley's "Being Brought from Africa to America." These two poems are saying two different things about Jesus. You might say no, because Phillis Wheatley was attacking those hypocrites who go around using the name of Jesus while they do things like slavery and oppression. But you'd better think about it before you simply say everybody's included and on the same level and for the same reason and so on. Wheatley is not an anomaly, so to speak. We have been taught she is, but in a certain way she is not. There is an interesting collection by Vincent Carretta called *Unchained Voices*, which is an anthology of other African writers in English in the eighteenth century, from North America, England, and the Caribbean, some of whom were slaves and some of whom were free men, and some who were slaves and then free. It will give you a place to put Phillis Wheatley. There are lots of arguments too; Amiri Baraka has a different view of Phillis Wheatley than I do, as do other people. This is something that needs to be read and thought about, not simply dismissed on a political sloganeering basis.

About the beginning of the twentieth century—slavery of course ends at the end of the Civil War, and at the end of the Civil War African American people are considered to be bonafide American citizens with the right to vote, which, for the next thirty years, interests in conflict with that do their best to undo. So that by the beginning of the twentieth century, you have a poet like Joseph Seamon Cotter, Jr., a very talented young man. He wrote sonnet sequences and died very young, I believe of tuberculosis. He lived from 1895 to 1919 and wrote some beautiful poems. This one is called "Is It Because I Am Black?"

WHY do men smile when I speak,
And call my speech
The whimperings of a babe
That cries but knows not what it wants?
Is it because I am black?

Why do men sneer when I arise
And stand in their councils,
And look them eye to eye,
And speak their tongue?
Is it because I am black?

Now think about that poem for a minute. Here is a man whose father was a poet and a minister of the gospel, a man whose legacy, if you want to call it that, extends to the woman who wrote excellent neoclassical poetry a few years before the American Revolution. On what possible basis could anyone in 1917 say of this young man, as he stands up to read a sonnet, how did this happen? That is the question. It doesn't make sense, does it? He read Shakespeare, he read Spenser, he read Wheatley, he read Milton; why in 1917 should someone ask him, "how is it that you write sonnets?" He is a fascinating poet and the sonnets are beautiful.

Another poet of the same era, Angelina Weld Grimké, is a fascinating poet who published much too little. She was born in 1880 and died in 1958. She was a schoolteacher in New York City. Just around World War I and into the Harlem Renaissance, she was active in publishing her poems and stories and plays. She wrote a play called *Rachel* and many other plays that were performed by the beginnings of the Little Theater movement in that era; and there was a black Little Theater movement at the same time, by the way, not just the one in Provincetown or Chicago. This is part of modernism, this is part of that movement. Angelina Weld Grimké is a descendant of the black Grimké family. If you've studied slavery you know about the Grimkés, who were staunch abolitionists. There was a Grimké family that was supposed to be white, and there was a Grimké family that was supposed to be black. Of course it was all the same family. Charlotte Grimké is the one that is most remembered as an abolitionist and feminist from the antebellum period.

Angelina Weld Grimké was very much involved with Margaret Sanger and the women's rights and birth control movements. You can read about her in a book by Claudia Tate called *Domestic Allegories of Desire*. Claudia Tate studies the novels of Frances Harper, *Iola Leroy,* and a whole slew of others, novels primarily written by black women and that essentially spoke to the middle-class yearnings of black people—like the novels that are popular today, except these had a positive message. Tate points out that the Black Arts Movement and some of its concerns have somewhat eclipsed scholarship into this popular African American literature of the late nineteenth and early twentieth centuries, because the messages being sent, on a middle-class level, were not the messages that the revolutionary poetry of the 1960s was willing to deal with, just like it wasn't willing to deal with the subtleties of Phillis Wheatley.

This is Angelina Weld Grimké, "A Mona Lisa."

1.
I should like to creep
Through the long brown grasses
    That are your lashes;
I should like to poise
    On the very brink
Of the leaf-brown pools
    That are your shadowed eyes;
I should like to cleave
    Without sound,
Their glimmering waters,
    Their unrippled waters,
I should like to sink down
    And down
        And down . . .
            And deeply drown.

2.
Would I be more than a bubble breaking?
    Or an ever-widening circle
    Ceasing at the marge?
Would my white bones
    Be the only white bones
Wavering back and forth, back and forth
    In their depths?

Sometimes it's hard to tell, in reading people like Grimké, what race has to do with what they are writing, until you remember that they are writing in a period when somebody will come along and ask the questions that they asked Joseph Seamon Cotter, Jr. People like Cotter and Grimké set the stage for the Harlem Renaissance, for writers like Langston Hughes, who again tried to define what it means to be black, the relationship of being black to the mainstream. This is a poem of Langston Hughes from the 1920s called "Theme for English B." In this poem he presents himself in the persona of a college student who has just been to class and gotten his assignment from his instructor.

The instructor said,

> *Go home and write*
> *a page tonight.*
> *And let that page come out of you—*
> *Then, it will be true.*

I wonder if it's that simple?
I am twenty-two, colored, born in Winston-Salem.
I went to school there, then Durham, then here
to this college on the hill above Harlem.
I am the only colored student in my class.
The steps from the hill lead down into Harlem
through a park, then I cross St. Nicholas,
Eighth Avenue, Seventh, and I come to the Y,
the Harlem Branch Y, where I take the elevator
up to my room, sit down, and write this page:

It's not easy to know what is true for you or me
at twenty-two, my age. But I guess I'm what
I feel and see and hear, Harlem, I hear you:
hear you, hear me—we two—you, me, talk on this page.
(I hear New York too.) Me—who?
Well, I like to eat, sleep, drink, and be in love.
I like to work, read, learn, and understand life.
I like a pipe for a Christmas present,
or records—Bessie, bop, or Bach.
I guess being colored doesn't make me NOT like
the same things other folks like who are other races.
So will my page be colored that I write?

Being me, it will not be white.
But it will be
a part of you, instructor.
You are white—
yet a part of me, as I am a part of you.
That's American.

Sometimes perhaps you don't want to be a part of me.
Nor do I often want to be a part of you.
But we are, that's true!
As I learn from you,
I guess you learn from me—
although you're older—and white—
and somewhat more free.

This is my page for English B.

It's an interesting poem because, again, it raises those questions of how do we define ourselves and why, and why would we possibly think that anyone who grows up in this society is not the beneficiary of the same culture? We were all here while it was all happening, so we share the same experience, even if we look at it from different perspectives. I want to read two more poems, one by Houston Baker, who, before he became a professor, was a radical poet. This is a poem that perfectly answers the "Theme for English B" and, indeed, shows what happens when we are unwilling to agree to the proposition that Langston Hughes provides there. So Houston A. Baker, Jr. writes in the 1970s:

No matter where you travel,
You still be Black,
You carry all your history
On your own damn back.

Your momma raised you proper
Your daddy caused you pain
You understand Beethoven,
But you still love Trane.

I guess that's how he got to be president of the Modern Language Association: he understood Beethoven. All of those issues are raised in that poem, and they are the same issues that were raised in 1772 by Phillis Wheatley and questioned by Joseph Seamon Cotter, Jr. How is it possible that you can question the membership of your fellow Americans in America? Regardless of what their subculture or distant national origin [is] or if they came here yesterday from someplace, they came for a reason and that was to be here.

One last poem, and I don't think this has anything to do with anything, but maybe it does. This is Al Young, who is one of the greatest African American writers alive today; he writes novels, poems, a tremendous series of essays, in which each essay is about a specific piece of music; he sits down and recalls the first time he ever heard, for instance, Elvis's "Blue Suede Shoes" or a piece by Rachmaninoff, and that's the basis of each essay. They are absolutely beautiful pieces of writing. This is a poem called "The Blues Don't Change."

> *"Now I'll tell you about the*
> *Blues. All Negroes like Blues.*
> *Why? Because they was born with*
> *the Blues. And now everybody*
> *have the Blues. Sometimes they*
> *don't know what it is."*
> —Leadbelly

And I was born with you, wasn't I, Blues?
Wombed with you, wounded, reared and forwarded
from address to address, stamped, stomped
and returned to sender by nobody else but you,
Blue Rider, writing me off every chance you
got, you mean old grudgeful-hearted, table-
turning demon, you, you sexy soul-sucking gem.

Blue diamond in the rough, you *are* forever.
You can't be outfoxed don't care how they cut
and smuggle and shine you on, you're like a
shadow, too dumb and stubborn and necessary
to let them turn you into what you ain't
with color or theory or powder or paint.

That's how you can stay in style without sticking
and not getting stuck. You know how to sting
where I can't scratch, and you move from frying
pan to skillet the same way you move people
to go to wiggling their bodies, juggling their
limbs, loosening that goose, upping their voices,
opening their pores, rolling their hips and lips.

They can shake their boodies but they can't shake *you.*

—July 3, 1997

GEOGRAPHIC DISTORTIONS: CULTURE, POLITICS, AND DIVERSITY

Victor Hernández Cruz

GUESS YOU KNOW WHO CHRISTOPHER COLUMBUS IS. IN SPANISH, IT IS Cristóbal Colón, and it has a lot more pitfalls. Christopher Columbus, Colón, was present in Granada, which was the last stronghold of the Arabs, the Moors, when they were in Spain for over seven hundred years. So when that ceremony to give the keys back to the Christians took place, he was in the audience, because of course he had been after Isabel to get her to finance a voyage he wanted to take to some unknown lands across the sea somewhere. So he got a translator, a converted Jew who was fluent in Arabic; I suppose this is the language that he thought he would more than likely run into, or something that would have those kinds of sounds. So they came with this translator to this part of the world, and at a certain point, in Cuba, he got off to greet the Cuban chieftain—I'll tell you his name within the context of the story. His name, or rather the name of Cuba, is *Cubanacán*. So Columbus brought his translator to greet the Taíno or Arawak chieftain, and the translator I suppose spoke Hebrew, Yiddish, and Arabic, to confront the man who was half nude there speaking in Arawak. Somewhere in this dialogue, the chieftain thought they were trying to ask him what land is this, so he said this is *Cubanacán*. Christopher Columbus heard "Genghis Khan." So the origins of our Latin America is based on a linguistic mistake. We are geographic distortions. We are Indians without India. Everyone is called Indian, even the Eskimos sometimes, all the native peoples in Argentina, when we know specifically that different people have different names for their places and different names to identify themselves. The first place to make this contact with the Spanish was the Caribbean; the first European development was Santo Domingo, and the second was the area of San Juan; Havana was the third, and then this notion of San Agustín in Florida. These were the beginnings of this new world. Everything was mispronounced, everything was based on this original linguistic mistake.

Puerto Rico, the country where I was born, became a territory of the United States after the Spanish American War; the United States gained

Guam, Cuba, parts of the Philippines, and Puerto Rico around 1898, and in 1917 we became U.S. citizens. Some time around 1910 they decided to change the language in the public schools from Spanish to English. That experiment totally collapsed; it was a mistake from the beginning. People were not going to school—not to say that there were any good schools at the time, in the mountain areas there was not much school to speak of—most people only went to school through maybe sixth grade. Finally, after they saw that it was a failure, that Spanish was already too intact, they had to change it back. Today we have English as a second language, which doesn't mean necessarily that people know English in Puerto Rico. Sometimes they have taken a survey and if a person knows just a few words in both languages they say that person is bilingual. They don't ask if that person can read or write in that language or can actually dialogue in that language, beyond "hello, how are you." As opposed to people who work in the hotels, who do know a certain amount of English. Our situation, having a relationship with the United States, has created something called *la guagua aérea*, which is this back-and-forth movement of Puerto Ricans who grow up in the United States and go back to the island, Puerto Ricans who have worked all their lives in the United States and go back to the island to retire. So we do speak more Spanish than other Latin American countries, because of that situation, because of the U.S. Postal Service being there, also because of many teachers who have gone there, teaching English, there has been a North American community, but it hasn't been enough of an impact to erase the Spanish language, which is still the predominant language in Puerto Rico; it is still the language which the writers from the island use.

Recently a funny thing happened. A woman named Rosario Ferré wrote a book called *The House on the Lagoon (La casa de la laguna)*; she is one of the major Puerto Rican writers. By publishing this book, which was written in English, she became the first major Puerto Rican writer to write a book directly in English. I'm not speaking here of the Puerto Rican writers in New York, that movement there called the Nuyorican writers, or the writing I have done, Puerto Ricans in the United States writing in English; we have lived here, we have lived the English, we have molded it to express our own feelings within it. Rosario Ferré did not have this experience. She did go to school for a few years in the United States, but her experience was native to the island. So it was interesting to see that happen. Recently, too, she wrote an article in the *New York Times* in which she went over for the independence movement; traditionally all Puerto Rican writers have been proindependence, pro-Spanish for the island, pro-Creole culture, pro–Puerto Rican culture over U.S. culture. She became

the first major writer to change; she said that she would in the next election vote for statehood. That became a very interesting thing. Her father
was Luis Ferré, who was the cement buyer on the island of Puerto Rico;
he was an industrialist and probably the richest man on the island. If you
have read *The House on the Lagoon* you know that some of the things she is
saying about living in a rich house with a lot of African servants down
below is more than likely a true account of her own family. And that
Dada she murders at the end is more than likely actually her father. The
impression you get from this book is that she would take a pro–Puerto
Rican independence stance, an antipatriarchal stance against the family of
her father. Many people are saying that she has in a sense come all the
way around and gone back to her social class, from the other opinions
she had. There are some others that write and publish to some extent, but
she is the only major Puerto Rican writer of the Spanish language who
has transferred over into writing directly in English. She thinks, she has
said in many interviews, it will give her a broader audience, because we
[the United States] are a country of almost four million people; the rest
of the Latin American continent, and Spain—I guess she wanted a broader
audience than that. She didn't do it for money; she has all the money she
wants from her father.

In my case, nine years ago when I went back to Puerto Rico, I didn't
just go to chase the climate, I went to get back into the language, to feel
the language, and to write back directly into that language. I always felt
there was something that I could not express in English, no matter what
Spanglish things and experiments I would try, no matter how much
Spanish or Caribbean flavor I would give the English, there was something that I could still not get out. I felt that I still had to go back and
recuperate the Spanish. Because I came to the United States at five and a
half or so, my first language of listening, of sound, and my first language
of speaking, was Spanish, I have always maintained that sense of rhythm,
the sound and the cadence of the Spanish language. And it is true that I
was able to go back to it, to capture the grammar, the usage, the writing.
Because English was my reading and writing language, what I went to
school in, but my first sound language was Spanish. So I have this strange
situation created, that I have an accent on both sides. In Puerto Rico, the
native speakers there, and in Latin America, they know that I have been
somewhere other than a Latin American country, that I have been outside. And the same thing in the United States; I can never get rid of my
accent, no matter how much oil I try to put on it. It is always divided,
immediately, right in half. I know there is a part of me, deep down in my

bones, that functions within this other language. And part of my process of writing has always been this translation, constant translation from one to another; that is my normal state of mind.

—June 29, 1998

SOME QUESTIONS
FOR JEROME ROTHENBERG

Anne Waldman, Laura Wright

You introduced the term ethnopoetics *in the sixties. Could you talk about what it meant at the time, and how the concept has (or has not) changed over the past forty-some years? What have been the responses to this kind of ethnography?*

When I was constructing *Technicians of the Sacred* in the 1960s, there was no word to cover what I and others thought we were doing. I already knew enough to understand that the sources of poetry on a global scale included areas that were then spoken of as "primitive" or "archaic," and that the further I went into it the more alternatives I discovered for what we could think of as poetry from our vantage point in the present. I think it was only when the work on *Technicians* was already completed that I began to use "ethnopoetics" as a term to cover what I was doing and what I was encouraging others to do as well. The first occasion was an invitation from George Quasha to prepare a selection from *Technicians* for *Stony Brook*, the journal of poetry and poetics that he was then publishing. To clarify my function as a contributing editor, we agreed on *ethnopoetics* as a proper designation, and that was, as far as I can recall, the first time that the word as such was used. The word itself, which had a kind of pseudoacademic sound, led me to imagine a collaborative project that would bring together poets and scholars in the attempt to uncover and to find new ways of presenting the largely oral and traditional poetry in a contemporary context. In the year after *Technicians,* there were already contacts with Stanley Diamond and David McAllester, but most importantly with Dennis Tedlock, which quickly got us into *Alcheringa,* as a "first journal of ethnopoetics." In the wake of that there was a rush of poets and scholars who came to join us, culminating in a first international symposium on ethnopoetics, 1975, at the University of Wisconsin in Milwaukee, and a second one a few years later at the University of Southern California. By then, too, the range of ethnopoetics had opened into Europe and contemporary North America, and on my own I was pushing also for an ethnopoetics of the book and writing, to set beside the earlier focus on orality and performance. If this represented a "movement" of some sort—even a *poetry* movement, since I always made sure to have poets at or near its center—it was short lived as such, as most such movements are, and the ongoing "project" never materialized much beyond *Alcheringa*. It did however embed itself in the poetry world over all, sometimes with poets to whom I was closely allied, at other times with poets from whom I was considerably more distanced. Its impact on ethnographers and anthropologists probably reached a high point in the 1990s, but there also it remains part of the landscape over all. As with much that I've been into in the past, it has remained a part of my own thinking, pervading big books like *Poems for the Millennium* and *A Book of the Book*, as well as my own poetry, where it remains a constant stream beneath the surface. Outside the United States it emerges from time to time in a context where it may sometimes appear as something new—my own poetics, say, as brought into Spanish by Heriberto Yépez, or into Brazilian Portuguese by Azougue Editorial in Rio, or Yves di Manno's first-time translation into French of *Technicians of the Sacred*, published by José Corti in 2008. More than my own, though, the "success" of ethnopoetics—if that's the proper word—is that the poetries in question have become, for many of us, an undisputed if unremarked part of our poetry and poetics over all.

Could you speak about the connections/lifelines for you, as a writer and as a performer, between poetry and song, poetry and ritual?

With both of these, song and ritual, poetry reaches its limits or finds its actual beginnings. From my own experience, I would hold to certain distinctions between these (song and ritual) and my own practice of poetry, while thinking back to those occasions when a merging seemed to be taking place. There is for most of us the sense of the poem as song and of the poet as a singer, where sound at least remains a dominant concern. At the same time, David Antin's attack, say, on a song-centered poetry and his exploration of a talk-centered one is also worth consideration, as is the absence of phonocentric poetry in deaf culture, where sight and gesture make up the difference. My own inclination, which is what ultimately counts for me, is toward song and music, while recognizing that to say so often lacks precision and may block recognition of what our art is really about or where it's really coming from. And remember that I'm saying this even though I became—much to my surprise—one of those poets who went all the way into the practice of song and music—on my own or in collaboration with various musicians. There is the same relation between poetry and ritual, waiting to trip us up or making us too absolute in describing the connection. Over the years I've been a witness to a range of traditional rituals, both as an observer and more rarely as a participant, and I've thought often of the relation between ritual and performance—or performance as we know it. In that sense it's easy for me to see a performance aspect to all the rituals I know—at least to all the religious or sacred ones—but not a ritual aspect to all performance. There are, however, times—and those are very meaningful for me—when I feel my own readings, my performances, crossing the line and taking on a kind of ritual quality, "a sacred action," as someone like André Breton, an atheist like me, had it for all the poetry he was then pursuing. I would have to say—for myself at least—that that's very rare, but when it happens, it's damn near overwhelming.

What is the role of poetry today? Has it changed in the past few decades? What about the "careerism" of poets? Has poetry changed how you live, in any fundamental or practical ways, in the world?

There's a strong implication here that "careerism" is connected to some kind of change in the role of poetry today, which makes this into something like a leading question. My own sense of it is that most poets from the literate past to the literate present have had some concern with "career" or "profession," though a word like *calling* might be more ennobling or enabling. *Careerism*, as such, implies something much more negative, if you think of it as the defining motivation or characteristic of the poets or artists in question. That it comes up as a topic here may have something to do with the way in which so much poetry has been increasingly positioned, and careerism, or something like careerism, encouraged by MFA programs and competitive awards and prizes—a proliferation of all of those compared to anything I knew of when I felt myself first driven into poetry. I can't say at what point careers as such came into it—or schools and programs in preparation for careers—but the negative result, the collateral damage, has been again to separate poetry from its sources in the numinous and, in the nonpredictive sense, the prophetic. If that has been key to what we want from poetry, its placement in a classroom or a workshop context will, under most circumstances, turn students and teachers, apprentices and masters, in much the opposite direction. Naropa in its early days may have been an exception to this, with a stress on the communal and on the poets—past and present—who gave themselves to poetry in a lingering Beat or quasireligious sense. As a life practice, then, poetry as it appeared here was a match and more for the surrounding Buddhist establishment—a way of life and thought. Or that at least was my first startled impression, circa 1976, a visit never forgotten and never repeated in quite that way.

ADDENDUM TO THE PRECEDING

At the time that I first came to Naropa I was on my way west, to end up eventually with a solid professorship at the University of California–San Diego. While I was never able to shape that institution—or any other, for that matter—in a way that corresponded to what I thought was possible for poetry or even for the teaching or transmission of poetry, I made a few stabs at it right from the start. The following, anyway, is a proposal from early 1979 that I came across recently and that still reflects my sense of what a course should or shouldn't be for those of us who get involved with it:

> [January 8, 1979] *It's my strong feeling that a creative writing program based on a generalized and repetitious critiquing of student work is relatively useless. I can, however, conceive of a program that would provide a grounding in what writers like myself have had to learn through an extended process of trial and error. To be worth the effort such a program should take into account (1) content: i.e., investigative procedures, use of data, and the ability to read and recycle previous writing; (2) social function: i.e., what has been the relation of poetry etc. to "society," and what may it be today and in the future; (3) a viable poetics incorporating knowledge of tools and materials on a broad basis (compositional modes including other-than-western, plus major twentieth-century techniques: collage; concrete, visual and typographical poetry; oral and sound poetry, etc.; (4) relation to, and intersection with, other arts; (5) performance, including a thorough grounding in oral poetry, where applicable; (6) technology of printing, book production, contemporary media, etc. The principal value of such a program is to encourage a questioning of preconceptions about writing and language ("a fight against the fascination which forms of expression have upon us"—Wittgenstein) rather than their reinforcement.*
>
> *Postscript. I would also recommend—at least for students whose concentration is "poetry"—some grounding in translation and linguistics, particularly in language systems outside of Indo-European.*

Something of this sort remains of interest to me, even and up to the present.

—Encinitas, California, and New York City
   September/October 2011

HORIZONS OF EXPECTATION:
PANEL ON PROSE TRANSLATION

Samuel R. Delany, Karen Tei Yamashita, Nina Zivančević

SAMUEL R. DELANY: It's hard for me to begin any sort of dialogue about the vagaries, possibilities, and wonders of translation without recalling an anecdote from the early days of computers, when the United States government was trying to reduce translation to a computer program, and its programmers were working diligently on a program to translate text from English to Chinese and back. After many months of work, the programmers finally announced that they had found it, so they presented the program to the powers that be to test it out, and someone suggested that they try out translating the old folk adage *out of sight, out of mind*. It was fed into the computer and someone said, now let's see what happens when we translate it back into English; from the printer emerged a little ribbon of paper on which was written *blind and crazy*.

The problems of translation range from the problems of translating within our own language to translating from other languages. And I like to see that not as two separate problems, but as something that exists on a gradient and that presupposes a view of languages themselves, not as separate streams with pieces of dry land in between, but rather a much more complicated marsh which has deep pools here and there, but the places in between are always sort of soggy. There is interchange at all stages between all stages of language. So that in one sense, translation is always a matter of paraphrase, paraphrase frequently from words you are not so familiar with to words that you are more familiar with. But again and again, as anybody starts to look at other languages learns, words in one language are frequently recalling words in another language; sometimes the meanings are very similar, and sometimes the meanings of words that are quite similar sounding are very different.

I'm going to start by asking the two panelists to talk a few minutes on their own about whatever aspects of translation or slogging around negotiating the great marsh of communication, the great marsh of language, what interests them about it. And then I'll go on to ask some questions of them both, and we can start a dialogue, and hopefully we can very quickly open it up into some kind of dialogue with you [the audience] as well—where you're asking questions, we're asking you questions, and we're all coming up with those particular clumps of language that we call answers, but we all know are really just provocations for further questions.

NINA ZIVANČEVIĆ: In order to discuss such a vast and complex subject as contemporary fiction as well as the problem of translating it—communicating the incommunicable, as French philosopher Jacques Derrida would have it—I decided to take a peek through a minimalist kaleidoscope and look at a tremendously varied and complex sample of Eastern European literature. This sample is discussed in detail in my course, When Writing Is Dangerous. It is always healthy for a writer as well as a literary critic or historian to take a step away from the body of literature that he or she is teaching and have a new look at it from a distance. This panel represents to me a "fresh look" at fiction from a distance. Speaking impressionistically, one may say that while the nineteenth century in Eastern Europe fiction had several K2s and Mount Everests: the titanic presences of Pushkin, Dostoyevksy, Tolstoy; the twentieth century had a number of entire mountain ranges, dense groups of fantastic though perhaps lesser-known peaks that are equally awesome in terms of their artistic talent and charismatic personalities. Some of the works of the twentieth century, such as Kafka's *Castle*, Pasternak's *Dr. Zhivago*, Bulgakov's *The Master and Margarita*, Nabokov's *The Gift*, can stand alongside and by no means in the shadow of Pushkin's poetry, Dostoyevsky's *Brothers Karamazov*, Tolstoy's *Anna Karenina*, the first family novel in Western literature. As before, however, the problem of translation is crucial. Just as Pushkin, arguably the central figure of the entire tradition, is less appreciated in the West because his poetic genius is difficult, if not impossible, to capture in another language, so too are the legacies of the great modernists and now postmodernists such as Osip Mandelstam, Joseph Brodsky, Milan Kundera, Václav Havel, or Eduard Limonov, exceedingly hard to pass on outside their specific linguistic contexts. Also important to realize in these connections is that the Russian and more generally Slavic literary tradition (that I come from) in the twentieth century grew up in a tight symbiotic embrace with some of the greatest theoretical and philological minds in the history of literary studies. As the Eastern European poets and writers speak out, there is actually a vast critical body behind them, because there were people (who emigrated eventually) such as Roman Jakobson, who came to the United States; the Russian formalists, Viktor Shklovsky, Boris Eichenbaum, Boris Tomashevsky, Yuri Tynianov; then the Prague School structuralists, Jan Mukařovský, Mikhail Bakhtin, Lydia Ginzburg, Juri Lotman and the Moscow-Tartu School of Semiotics, Boris Uspensky, Vyacheslav Ivanov, Vladimir Toporov. Here one might say, and not entirely polemically, if in previous centuries Russian culture was in a hurry to overtake the West, then in this century the West has been slowly learning what the Russians have already discovered, in certain aspects.

It is important to bear all these elements in mind while approaching the translation of an Eastern European work of fiction or literature at large: the differences in cultures, the presence of theoretical elements in works of fiction, as much as the so-called horizon of expectation. The horizon of expectation is a theoretical term coined by Hans-Georg Gadamer's student, Hans Robert Jauss, from the Constance school of philology and philosophy. This term explains the acceptability of a work of fiction presented in translation, that is, a language different from the original language in which it was written. The so-called horizon of expectation explains why one either was or was not ready to receive a certain work of literature which was a hit or a masterpiece in one language but perhaps had poor reception in the language of translation. Or the phenomenon can go both ways; we can have a work of fiction badly received in the original language in which it was written, such as Paul Auster's works in the United States, which, however, were magnificently received in France. There, he is more popular than Flaubert. Or we have the case of Charles Bukowksi, also extremely well received in Germany and elsewhere in Europe, who is, according to his United States publishers, somewhat less appreciated here.

There is an American saying, allegedly by Robert Frost, that poetry is something lost in the translation. There is a French dictum coined by Pierre Menard which says that translations are great and beautiful when unfaithful—"la belle infidèle." I would say as a person who has lived her entire life speaking six or seven languages at a time, or all of them at the same time, that the truth lies somewhere in between, between the beauty of the untranslatable work of art and the beauty of a worked-upon or altered translation. However, as a translator of Kathy Acker, Lynne Tillman, Allen Ginsberg, Anne Waldman, Alice Notley, John Giorno, Jerome Rothenberg, Octavio Paz, Jean Baudrillard, Julia Kristeva, Simone Weil, Paul Dumas, Miloš Crnjanski, Benedetti, Cortázar, Charles Bernstein, Robert Creeley, and others, and as a translatee into more than fifteen languages, I would say that translations are both possible and impossible to execute into any human language. What is often untranslatable, as Armand Schwerner used to say, is the music of the language or any extralinguistic quality of the language into which we are translating, even if we know perfectly both the language of reception and the language of departure. I gave up on translating my own work into different languages long ago. For the Oxford University Press anthology of East European verse, *Contemporary East European Poetry: An Anthology,* edited by Emery George, I sent my versions of my own poems in English to Charles Simic and I said, "Charles, you can sign your name beneath these translations. Just keep my original syntax and wording in English." And that's what happened, actually. Charles was really nice about it, he just changed articles; the most difficult thing for me as a Slavic speaker is to master articles, which we don't have in Slavic languages. So Charles Simic fixed the articles, fixed whatever was fixable. With the French translations, I did not know French well enough to write the original versions; it was much more difficult. My book *Recherche Philippe Sollers* is actually a version of *Inside and Out of Byzantium*—this is for linguists, it's an incredible case of writing a book in two languages. I wrote it sort of in a mixture of English and Serbo-Croatian, and the final version was looked over and worked on by Ken Jordan, so it is the American version of my Serbo-Croatian thought that found itself in *Inside and Out of Byzantium.* The book *Recherche Philippe Sollers* was a translation into French from this book, *Inside and Out of Byzantium,* and it was perfect because it was done by my spiritual double and lifelong friend Françoise Bouillot, who is a fine writer of her own, a sort of Susan Howe in French. We grew up together, and she knows in advance what I'm going to think and what I'm going to say. With my poetry it was much more difficult. I have written a piece in English, for example, a piece which talks about life between two cultures; that was about my trip to Egypt during the Gulf War. This piece is called *I Was This War Reporter in Egypt,* and it was literally untranslatable into French; it speaks about the translatability of cultures, extraterritorial communication between two civilizations, one from the East and one from the West.

Part of this had a lot to do with translation in general; it was really the translation of civilizations. The language comes after that.

KAREN YAMASHITA: I'm going to put a kink in this idea of translation to talk about the translation of ethnicity and the representation through those kinds of translations, and take a more parochial look at the English language. In thinking about this question of cross-language studies and international poetics, I've been thinking about the problems of globalization. Since the events of what we call 9/11, the consequences of globalization have become much more real to the mainstream public and consciousness. We associate globalization with the access and movement of capital and products and the connections to corporate structures; we think of globalization in terms of money. But also we think about it in relationship to the access and movement of culture, and we're very aware of this now, of belief and thinking. This globalization is enhanced or made possible by technology and the media. The result of this globalization has been the homogenization of culture across the globe, in particular the spread of American culture. The easiest example is Coca-Cola and McDonald's. You can get that anywhere in the world. But also the English language—this is in relationship to access to the internet, to CNN and BBC—knowing English is important. So with globalization we are aware of the disappearance of difference and the disappearance of the "native" and authenticity, which has quickly been consumed by the Discovery Channel and *National Geographic.*

So, what has language got to do with this? Obviously it's about communication through language and the translation of language and about the hegemony or the assumption of the privilege of the English language. The colonization of the world has pretty much been finished, in fact, through the assumption of language. From here of course the discussion can go in all sorts of directions. But I'd like to think about the ways to contest and complicate these assumptions of globalization and anglophonism, and throw in an idea about diaspora. Diaspora: normally we think of it with a large *D*, as defined by the Greek meaning, but also by its association with the Jewish Diaspora, in which people are forced into exile from [their] original home and have spread like seeds to destinations and locations across the earth. But lately we've seen that diaspora has a small *d*, and it's been applied to many other groups of people, in particular Africans and Asians. And we begin to think about the dispersal of these groups, who by consequences of slavery, of war and exile, of economic and political circumstances, have been forced to become exiles, refugees, immigrants, migrant labor, sex workers, prostitutes, and transnationals. Thinking about diaspora in this way interests me because it connects and complicates this idea of globalization, to move it away from just the idea of products and capital moving across the world, to also connect it to people, human beings and their cultures, histories, memories, and languages.

I have been thinking in particular of diaspora or the traveling of languages and narratives and stories, and the diaspora of imagination and memories, and the dynamics of languages as they travel and get recreated and changed. For instance, the creation of pidgin languages in new places; we see this in Hawaii but I can also claim that Japanese is now a kind of a pidgin language. Certainly with this there have been appropriations of culture and language along the way; but this appropriation can be seen to go both ways. There's a dynamic which both disempowers and empowers migrant people, in terms of language.

For the writer in this brave new world of globalization and diaspora, the question of our use of language and our associations to language is critical stuff. I imagine that our use of language entails considerations that are political and ethical. For example, what sort of English language are we creating? If we assume that language and thinking are tied, and that language is the way we organize our reality, and that language may change the way the world works or influence the way we are connected, how shall we use this English language? The need to consider language in this project of globalization is critical, considering the sloppy use of language, and thus thinking, of our current [as of 2001] leaders—laughable and pretty hard to stomach, often. What, indeed, does "homeland security" mean? How is it we can have a war on terrorism?

For my own project, I have over the years studied the immigration of the Japanese to Brazil. The population of the Japanese and their descendents in Brazil is the largest population of Japanese outside of Japan; it's larger than the community in the United States. It started in 1908, and in the 1920s large numbers of Japanese immigrated to Brazil. I'm also thinking about moving this conversation to the Pacific but as well to South America. Since 1990, however, there has been a return migration of Japanese Brazilians back to Japan to work in factories there. This has been because of the economic situation in Brazil. Currently there are some two hundred thousand Brazilians, most of them Japanese Brazilians, working as contract labor in factories in Japan. That's part of my project then: both looking at the Japanese immigration to Brazil and also looking at this return migration to Japan. Here in the United States, of course, we see many fronts of migration, which we recognize in particular from Mexico and Canada, South Asia, China, and the Philippines. The Philippines may be experiencing the largest diaspora of their people across the globe—it's really immense; they may be actually creating a diasporic community that's outside of the islands.

What happens to national borders, what happens to nation-states, national loyalties, and responsibilities of citizens in all this? Up to now we've been mostly concerned with how immigrant communities speak and are represented in the United States. I'm just talking about my projects with ethnic literature, with Japanese or Asian American literature. We've been concerned mostly with immigrants. But now these things are changing radically. We're beginning to talk about diasporic communities which are moving across the globe. How will these new migrants speak? They are bi- and trilingual people. How will these populations and movements be represented and how will they represent themselves and be self-empowered?

SD: I wanted to move on quickly to some general questions for everyone. But listening to what Nina and Karen said I found myself with a couple of thoughts. One is a kind of paradoxical situation that may be of interest to think about in a situation where we're talking about translations—which is that great literary languages, no matter what culture they come up in, the result of great literary languages is that immediately they produce pidgins, they produce pidgin languages right on top of them. Because to have a great literary language almost implies that some other culture acknowledges that, indeed, you have a great literary language. So immediately there becomes interest from other languages in your great literary language; and suddenly, for instance, the French start talking about "le weekend," as a direct result of English scholars being interested in Racine, because the English scholars also have their contemporary language.

Another notion that hits me in all of this is a notion that it's easy to trace back to two very different thinkers, one the Russian psychologist [Lev (Leon) Semyonovich] Vygotsky, and the other the English philosopher A. J. Ayer. That is the notion that Vygotsky puts across from studying children and how they learn; says Vygotsky, we don't learn to think first and then express it, we learn to talk first, and from learning to talk, *then* we learn how to think. Thought is internalized language; language is not expressed thought. Vygotsky came up with this notion in the first decade or so in the twentieth century, and in the 1920s the twenty-five-year-old A.J. Ayer probably independently came up with pretty much the same notion just from generalized introspection. This means that when we translate from language to language it is not a matter of going and finding some originary meaning that we all possess; we are always translating more or less of the context— the discourse that makes this perfectly arbitrary linguistic sign, as Saussure called it—we are translating some of the context that informs it with meaning. Where to cut off the context, where to stop bringing in more contextual information? If anything, the whole critical/philosophical movement represented by structuralism and deconstruction, that's what is at the base of all of that theorization. When can you actually say, we've got enough context at this point, we've got enough consideration of the rest of the discourse, *I know what you mean.* To say I know what you mean is always a leap and possibly a lie. It's a leap or a lie to allow the conversation to go on.

I have a few questions for our panelists today, since they have had a lot more direct experience with doing translation than I have; I am basically monolingual. I can read a bit in other languages, but I'm terrified of speaking in even languages that on paper I will say I kind of know.

Is there any difference between how you translate poetry and how you translate prose? Do they pose different problems for you as translators?

NZ: I may not be the best person to answer this question because I hardly make any difference between prose and poetry. If I say this, we could open a night-long discussion. However, first of all translation is a problem; I see it as a problem. If you are translating either so-called fiction or so-called poetry, the problem is always the same. The problem is big because you always feel in a way you are deceiving the original; you know in a way you are creating an independent work of art. As Hans-Georg Gadamer said, no matter how hard we try to translate a work of art, the original creation is always untranslatable. I think he mentioned this in his famous essay. If we start with this assumption that we are doing a job which is highly unrewarded already, then we arrive at this supposition that actually we will create something else. So we know we are starting from something that might be deceptive as such, but we may arrive at something which is equally wonderful, an equally great, independent work of art. If it's a question of what is fiction, what is poetry, then we are running in circles. But any great work of art, it could even be a newspaper ad if it is composed appropriately wonderfully, then it is equally difficult to translate. How do we translate a newspaper ad in the *New York Times*? It has all these extralinguistic, extracultural references—for instance, it is absolutely foreign for the French mentality that if you buy three bottles of Coke you get the fourth one free. We can translate this into the French language, it's linguistically possible, but then all the people would stand in front of that store wondering what it actually means, this fourth bottle of Coke. That's the problem; it's not a problem translating the literal meaning.

SD: I guess this is particularly apparent because so much of advertising is not selling just the product, it's selling a whole lifestyle along with it. The people who are the audience for the ad have different relationships to that lifestyle.

Karen, do you have any thoughts about the difference between translating prose and poetry?

KY: I don't think of myself as someone who translates languages, although I speak Portuguese fluently and I can get in trouble with Japanese. So the project for me is more the translation of culture and experience. And between poetry and fiction—I don't know.

[ANNE WALDMAN ASKS A QUESTION ABOUT A PROJECT]: The *Circle-K Cycles*, which is the book that came out of that project, is cross-genre, it's both nonfiction and fiction. But Coffee House decided to call it fiction, and I think they're right.

SD: Just an incident in the recent history of translation that I think is fascinating: The poet Richard Howard, who writes a very odd kind of poetry that is very much informed by history and research, which I think is not research just for the poem but he has the kind of mind that absorbs all this information; and very carefully written, almost to the point where some people would almost possibly find it constipated; nevertheless, one of the things that he also does is a great deal of translation. I discovered him first as a translator before I discovered him as a poet; he did a translation of André Gide's *L'immoraliste* which blew me away when I first read it; he also did the early translations of Michel Foucault, he did the original translations of *Madness and Civilization* and *The Birth of the Clinic*. He didn't do *The Order of Things*, but he did a sort of doctor job on *The Order of Things*, because the person who did that translation did such an appalling job that Athenaeum decided they couldn't use it, and they asked him to go over it and he did a clean-up job. Anyway, a couple of years ago a book hit the best-seller list, it was on the bottom of the *New York Times* best-seller list for about three months. What was the book? It was Stendhal's *The Charterhouse of Parma* in the new Modern Library edition. What's *The Charterhouse of Parma* doing on the bottom of the *New York Times* best-seller list? Well, it was translated by Richard Howard, and it's a remarkable work, it goes down like cotton candy. If you're going to read *The Charterhouse of Parma* . . .

NZ: It's a great book.

SD: Yes, it is a great book, and it may be a great translation; it's certainly a wonderfully readable translation. And the only reason I think it was on the best-seller list is because such a good job was done of the translation. No one expected it, [no one pushed it]—Random House does not think that way—this is a case of, purely because someone did a good job of the translation, it actually made a small dent in what we might call that bizarre culture that thinks of itself as central.

What works have been important to you in translation? Works that you first encountered in translation, perhaps, before you encountered the original. And if you eventually went from the translation back to the original, what was that experience like for you? Can you think of any specific examples, either one of you?

NZ: Yes, I have a very good example actually, of one of the greatest poets of all times, Rainer Maria Rilke. Rilke's work that I read first in Serbo-Croatian translation from German, which I can just barely read. However, when I came here to the United States I read Michael Hamburger's translation, and I was really happy that I had read another translation in Serbo-Croatian, because if I read Rilke for the first time in Hamburger's translation I would not have liked him. There are so many bright examples, it goes both ways, there are many brilliant translations I've read in the United States. There's a very good school of translators now coming from major universities, Yale, Harvard, Princeton, there are great schools of translation already established here. If I'm not mistaken, I especially think that the translators from Spanish into English are very skilled and capable of producing great translations, perhaps because Latin America is closer and there is more exchange.

SD: Karen, can you think of a translation that's meant a great deal to you that you then went back and read it in the original?

KY: No, but I can think of translations that made a difference to me. As I was going to Brazil there were two things I read, one by Claude Lévi-Strauss, *Tristes tropiques,* and I also read Gabriel García Márquez's *One Hundred Years of Solitude,* and that was an interesting introduction to Latin America before I reached it.

SD: Did you ever encounter Elizabeth Bishop's translation of *The Diary of "Helena Morley"* by Alice Brant? I've only read Bishop's translation.

KY: No. But I was thinking of a film that I saw early, *Orfeu Negro,* not knowing what it was all about at all. And then only after years of being immersed in the culture, being able to see it and understand it in Portuguese. Then seeing the new *Orfeu,* which is so inferior to the original, even though the Brazilians claim that the French *Orfeu* is not to their liking.

SD: For me it was a very standard one: Gustave Flaubert's *A Simple Heart, Un coeur simple,* which I fell in love with in the English translation, the good old Penguin edition, which I thought was just an amazing story; then when I finally got up nerve enough to look at the French and struggle through it, by the time I had struggled through it I realized, oh! it's a lot more amazing than I ever thought. It was quite a wonderful experience.

NZ: I would like to add something: A certain phenomenon that strikes me as amazing is not so much the bad examples of translations from one language into another, but the more blatant examples of writers of works of art that are not so important or significant, and then once translated they hit these, not really large audiences, but qualified audiences. For instance, I know that Stephen King is very important in France; when my students want to impress me they always say, "We read Stephen King," because I teach English as a second language. Then I have no heart to say anything but "Great," because they're reading; whatever makes them happy, just keep on reading. Actually I started exploring the phenomenon, and I realized that there are certain not totally capable translators, but the culture or climate, all these extralinguistic moments that make a translation possible and living in a certain readership.

KY: One writer I've been thinking about is Ha Jin, who is, well, I don't know what he is. He is a Chinese ex-patriot; he's here in the United States now and writing in English. He's influenced by Chekhov, he says, but his second language is English. It's interesting to look at his use and articulation of the English language. One of my friends said, is it a bad translation? I would disagree. But it's interesting, the kind of process that he's going through to make this transition to express the world of the Cultural Revolution in English. And yet, his work is banned in China.

SD: The phenomenon that Nina brings up—one thinks of the reputation of Edgar Allan Poe, of whom I think it was T. S. Elliot who said, the mark of bad taste is to like Edgar Allan Poe. Yet the French, starting with the Charles Baudelaire translations and going on with people like Paul Valéry, who is no intellectual slouch, [are] finding a real philosophy in works that we look down on and say they're unreadable, like *Eureka*. Or the fact that until fairly recently the most widely read American writer in the world was Jack London.

For a certain sort of speaker of foreign languages, such as I am, all translation is the translation of poetry, which may be the underside of what Nina was talking about originally, when there's no difference between prose and poetry. By that I mean, to translate anything, because my foreign languages are so bad, I have to pay the same kind of attention to any kind of text.

What are some of the problems, can you think of specific problems that you have encountered translating either for yourself, a piece of work that you are reading in another language, or a piece of work that you're working on a translation of?

NZ: When it comes to making a choice—I undertook this crazy project, which was far beyond my ability when I was in my early thirties. I was still in the United States, and I decided I would make an anthology of contemporary American poetry [in Serbian]. I started selecting poets I felt close to with my own poetics. And then I arrived at the problem of the actual translation of the actual work. My first impulse was to choose to translate something that was translatable from the poetries of respective poets, because every poet has his own poetry's poetry that cannot be translated. I remember also when I chose something from Anne Waldman's *Fast Speaking Woman;* I chose some parts from the book that were exclusively translatable, that could be rendered into my mother tongue, Serbo-Croatian. And then, it's true, I was not asking too many questions. When I was translating Kenneth Koch, for instance, he had asked me, how come you're not asking me any questions? Michel Deguy, the French translator of his work, was asking so many questions. I could relate to all these poems that I chose to translate. From Alice Notley's work there were difficult parts; from John Giorno's work, which is like sound poetry, it was very difficult—how do you translate sound? Musicality or music is certainly the most difficult thing to render into some other language. When it comes down to translating music from one language into another, we don't have to be in trouble, but we have to know the music of the language we are translating into.

KY: I guess I could talk about my experience with having people translate my work. I met the translator of my first book, *Through the Arc of the Rainforest*, in Japan. And I had the distinct impression he was blind; he was wearing dark glasses the entire time, inside. I was never really sure. The other thing is, he could not converse with me in English, at all. He had no oral knowledge of the language. I never corresponded with him. He never asked me any questions at all about that book, it just came out. Someone said it was a nice translation. I don't know. But I do remember working with a woman who was trying to translate the same text into Dutch. She was constantly in touch with me. She wanted to know things, like, what's *Mother Jones?* Those sort of cultural things she would not have known. And then it occurred to me, I really wondered what the Japanese did with *Mother Jones*. There's one section of the book which I had originally tried to write in Portuguese. Because it's conversational, it's on the phone, I thought I could do it. But after I finished what I felt to be the Portuguese chapter, my husband laughed hysterically at the whole thing—he's Brazilian—and I was so demoralized I threw it away. I wrote it again in English, translating from the Portuguese to English, and had someone more capable translate it into Portuguese for me.

SD: I've always had a feeling that—well I'm not a poet, I'm a prose writer, and, as I said, I don't think of myself as someone with any sort command of other languages, but on the other hand, I also thought, as a civilized member of the world, it behooves me every now and again, just for my own pleasure, to try and translate something. So there's a little poem by Friedrich Hölderlin, called *Hälfte des Lebens,* "Halfway through Life." It begins with some yellow pears and, full of wild roses, the land hangs down into the lake. It's two stanzas long, it's very short. And I was going along blithely doing my translation—it's got some swans who dip, or possibly plunge or dunk, their heads into the sobering sea, or at least that's what I thought. And I sent this to a friend of mine who is German, who objected to the "sobering sea." Because, the problem, she said, is that nothing in this poem does anything to anything else. So for the swans to dip their heads into the sobering sea, the sea would have to sober them. It's a *sober* sea, not a sobering sea. And this was quite an insight into this poem. This is a very static poem. And indeed, things don't do anything to anything, they just sit there side by side.

NZ: You are very brave; I would never dare translate Hölderlin.

SD: Of course! But little insights like that, I think, can be quite illuminating.

—June 11, 2001

CHORALIZING CULTURES

Eileen Myles

SOMEONE BROUGHT UP A QUESTION THE OTHER DAY ABOUT "PENE-TRATING the mainstream." I feel like all of us who have been writing for a while in various ways have penetrated the mainstream, but there are a lot of different ways of doing it, and you don't have to go in the front door. It reminds me of a friend, David Rattray, who died in 1993. He was a great friend, poet, translator, and a huge influence on my novel, *Cool for You*; his death figured in the book in some way. He was a very smart guy, and as he was dying he dropped many bits of information on me that just went right into my thought stream. One of the things he said that was really cool, and I couldn't get it into my novel somehow, was that heaven was a house and that often the holiest way to come in was through the basement—implying every bodily thing, blood, shit, but also just that message that there's not one sole approach. I'm thinking about the whole way that one operates as a writer and as a poet over time. The first time I ever came to Naropa, in 1979, I was sort of a young, constantly-getting-trashed lesbian with her girlfriend, and we came here and raised hell. We laughed at the Buddhism. Now I sit a bit. One of the things I've learned since I've been a bit of a Buddhist is that just as sitting is a practice, so is poetry. It released me from a whole bondage to the marketplace and to the meaning of my practice, that poetry is a practice that I do again and again and again, and it makes an order in my life; and that is the meaning, not getting in the front door. I'm not knocking pleasure and success, which I like and want, but as long as that keeps being the lure for my writing, the meaning falls out really quickly and I have to build myself up again. My hot image for the week is the shipwreck; water keeps being the solution I float my thoughts through. Imagine one's writing career being a procession of fragments and repetitions that you just keep floating out and floating out over time. Ultimately if heaven is a house, it gets in; I feel like one's work "gets in" in more ways than you know, and that's the pleasure, that's the success. You float a lot of stuff, you don't stop—and things happen.

I think of a good friend of mine, Roberto Bedoya, who is another person who has a way of saying things that stick; I remember him talking about the crisis in American politics since the 1960s or 1970s—Proposition 13 in California, the one about education, where it was suddenly determined who the public was or wasn't, and that money could be tagged rather than untagged. The thing he thought was so disturbing about that was that they changed the notion of the public, because the most important notion of the public in America is that the public is something you can't know. That notion is real and good, and as long as we can count on that there can be a free flow of information. A lot of the problems with the way literature is getting taught and distributed right now, what's problematic, is the corporate shape of it. The writing program creates a tunnel; the writing program can be a piece of the corporation. We homogenize the poem and the poet and the novel and the story and we shoot it right in—talk about penetrating the mainstream. It's like an injection. It's like an extruder. It works, but it doesn't work for me. I like the idea of the public being kind of a body that can be entered in a number of ways, and that's what's interesting. The weird metaphor I think of today is the poisoned shirt; every time I see a poisoned shirt in a movie, I think it's incredible that you can kill someone that way; you soak the shirt in cyanide, and then you put it on the body and it gets in. There is that kind of incredible allover penetration. But of course I think that's true and good, in terms of how information, if there is a body public, how does that get communicated to, and with, from the inside and the outside. I think it's a little bit like that poisoned shirt, though not so ghastly, necessarily. There are lots of holes, and we can use all of them, and do. I always think of the story about mainstream movies—I think there are odd reasons to be cheerful about how culture works today still— they talk about these big blockbuster summer films, and how they pump a huge amount of money into the first week, but the movie makes money on the second week, and the second week is word of mouth. The mouth is the body talking, you just can't stop it; there's something great about that.

I'm trying to imagine, I think I have to imagine, a utopic place of being heard, and hearing. I think these moments of being heard and hearing are like meals, that it's a crucial exchange, an even, often anonymous, exchange. Maybe when one thinks about being an artist today, part of the problem with that is thinking about being an individual artist, how in a certain way we have to lose control of our message, certainly when someone asks for a poem for a website—you don't get any money, the whole thing seems so blurry, and then eight million people might have read your poem. The possibilities for the unknown destination of any piece of writing or art are incredible right now and have to be embraced. Then again, they change our ideas about writing, copyright, fragmentation, the destination of our work. What that all brings into question, too, is who we are as a people, and I think that needs to get looked at differently too. I love a lot of what Robin Blaser has said about the irreparable and the twentieth century; if the twentieth century was just an exemplar of mass destruction, my fantasy about the twenty-first century is a possibility of mass knowing. That we as a people could, for starters, desire that. And how that occurs—*how that occurs?* There's a little square right here in my notes, and it's empty. It is some different way of thinking one by one of who we are and how art gets made.

I'm going to read a little piece that my friend David Rattray wrote. As I said, when he was dying he was kind of leaking all this great stuff, and he did leak me an image that I've grabbed onto a lot. What I'm thinking of is a chorus, but I'm thinking of a shattered chorus; in the same way that there are all those lovely quotes about how we're continuing other people and other people are continuing our work—what does that look like? I have many ideas of what that looks like. This is kind of a great picture:

For years I've pondered the conclusion of Albrecht Dürer's collection of images titled *The Triumph of Maximilian*. These pictures were commissioned, I think, by the emperor Maximilian in the 1520s, executed possibly by himself, possibly by his school. His work, which I have admired all my life, was published some years ago in a cheap reprint by Dover Books. It was out of print some time but it was a boon to the public, to people like myself. The part of it that attracts me is where the procession that forms the subject of this great work trails off or thins out from a great imperial progress to finally a straggling group of scouts, irregulars who are not under any visible military discipline but are simply foraging their way through the country. Somehow these final images rooted themselves in my mind. I have dreamt of creating a work that would trail off in the same way as *The Triumph of Maximilian*, from something grandiose and profound, profoundly unrecognizable as a group that was under a special kind of discipline or formative patterning. Of course the patterning in the Dürer work is very strong and very beautiful, but the ending no longer has anything to do with imperial triumph or with the values, I suppose, of organized culture of any civilization. I would add to this, these scouts did not in any way of their appearance resemble Quantrill's Rangers or any other similar raiders. A very notable aspect of their appearance is that they are not threatening, they do not look like a group of dangerous, evil fellows. The contrary—they look almost as if they might be harbingers of a future golden age or utopian state. They certainly do not look like cutthroats or bandits, they are perhaps pioneers of a new and different world. However, this point is left ambiguous, happily so. The whole scene is enveloped in mystery that I find magical when I consider this in the way that it trails off into a kind of organic shapelessness.

I guess I'm thinking about the idea of a discontinuous us-ness. When I think of the huddles that we do as poets or as homosexuals, as women and men, and the parts all fly apart. What chorus did you belong to? The notion of regrouping that you carry in your head doesn't necessarily carry—even the army, somebody mentioned recently, with their "be an army of one." As an illustration of something bad . . . I didn't think it was actually such a bad thing because I feel like the same notion is being tapped into. There's a Buddhist idea that when I write a poem it's not like I'm writing this poem for everybody; everybody is writing the poem. That one by one as artists, you carry a notion of us-ness when you create. And of course it's always true, when I write, when it turns on is when I feel anonymous, when I'm simply being used by something.

I've got a poem that does this in some kind of a—well, I'll let the poem talk. It's called "New Poem" [from *Maxfield Parrish*].

My lover came over my house
one afternoon—I was doing
a big mailing for a show—
the one before this. She
was crying and I was trying
to make her happy. I was
sitting on the floor in this
sand chair we bought to go
camping last summer. I
was sitting there counting all
the people in the zip code
one thousand three. Myra
announced she was leaving
and I started to do a
little dance from my
chair—I was making
faces and had paws

it was a little dog dance
I explained to her. It's
a little dog chorus line.
A show about a chorus
line of dogs. But dog
chorus lines are irregular.
They just wander all over
the city, stray dogs.
Related but not you
know doing anything in
sync, but shitting eating
pissing fucking just having
a dog life. That kind
of chorus. It's a
very modern art, the
dog chorus line and
I thought about all
the dogs on my lap I was
mailing my postcards to.
Eventually we got sick of
the shape of that kind
of dog chorus line. It
was true, but there's
so much of that, truth,
and it's so irregular so
we decided to make something
new—dogs in saddles,
dogs sprayed blue &
gilded, you know arranged
in galleries or groupings.
The irony of that kind
of product, an external
order, that's the joke,
despite the fact the
dogs are still roaming
around hungry &
hopeless, we're getting
very involved with
the new blue dogs
God, now we can decorate

them so many different
ways and we feel
so hopeless about
life, what can we
really do, so we
find another funny
way to arrange the
dogs, make a big
show, act as if
just for a second you
can have some kind of control,
and it is kind of funny, I
mean dogs aren't blue

This particular fragmented image keeps erupting in the weirdest places. A movie that I liked a lot was *My Best Friend's Wedding*. At the wedding, the whole kind of stumble into surrealism that occurs in mainstream movies where suddenly a strange uncle starts singing, "What do you get when you fall . . ." and then it starts hopping all over the movie in this odd way; it's kind of a break out of the narrative, and now it's happening in movies all over the place. Certainly some of you have seen *Moulin Rouge*, which I also think is kind of great. Again, what they do is they're always—and I bet some of you have had this as a joke in the past, if you've ever seen musicals, there's always that odd moment where you could break into song with your friend or your lover; I know these two girls who would only communicate through lines from Beatles songs, and they would do it for days, it was sick—but in *Moulin Rouge,* of course, they do it constantly, these 1980s songs, Elton John songs, and the thing that's really interesting is the audience, the audience goes nuts, the audience completes the chorus of this. I've never seen an audience in such a state of delight; every time they'd do a song people would clap and cheer and there was this odd way in which this movie that was using the most simplistic sampling techniques was hitting some buzzer of being included that people were desperate to have. Any time I see a piece of art that invites the audience to complete the work, there's some kind of odd choral buzzer getting hit, and I think that's almost a survival mechanism for us as artists, to somehow engage that thing. *A Knight's Tale* does it too, it's actually a great movie, it's Chaucer, and Chaucer himself is in it, but they have a jousting scene, and all the medieval folk are in there with their sticks and stuff, ready for the fight, and suddenly they break into song, "We will, we will rock you." It opens out the movie into farce and possibility, and it's great.

What I'm thinking is I came to the idea of being an artist out of a hope of individuation, and now I feel like my hope in being an artist is to find a way out of that, that almost the only valid way to approach it now is to deindividuate and create work that can be entered. Before one ever wrote, we all know there's a sort of sainthood ascribed to the person that gets to write; you tell someone you write and you're published and suddenly you're the wonderful person that gets to do the lucky thing, and we all know what hell our lives are. But it was that you would go into some private place and you would come out a star. What's strange is, it is a lonely job, but the occasion of sharing the work is communal always. And at this point in time that has to be utterly adrift. Could that be the end of what I have to say?

No, there are two more things I'm thinking about. One is somebody I've learned a lot from in various ways, a guy from San Francisco, Paul Haller, who is a Buddhist and a teacher. One of the things I heard him say once is that pattern is contact. I've bounced that around for a long time trying to figure out what the hell that means, but I'm thinking it's exactly this: that if we as artists participate in becoming commodified, individual artists, with this individual, special message that can be consumed in a comfortable, easy way, one by one, then nothing ever changes. But if the work itself participates in some kind of new patterning, then I think real contact can be made. I think the reason difficult things can't be consumed is because people's lives are so difficult, and they don't have slots or holes for difficult work. And somehow or other the challenge is to address that. So who is writing now? I can think of a time when I was sort of involved with two people, I was in a menage, and we all talked about who we wanted to be; I remember one of us thought that she felt like no one and then someone thought he would like to be someone and I thought, well, clearly I'm anyone. I think "anyone" is a great place to be writing from now. When some of us were hanging out last night at the bar we were talking about how forgiveness is easier to obtain than permission and talking about being young, if you wanted to do something you might as well just go rebel and do it and then get forgiven, rather than waiting until they gave you permission. But there's a certain way in which if anyone wanted it, permission to be anyone is endlessly available. As artists we may not think that's a worthy place to go, and yet it seems to me it's wildly powerful. What that means, I have to say, I do not know. But it's incredibly interesting to think about; there are many entries into that spot, and it invites a choralizing of culture that I think has to happen if we're to be heard. Because if we're not heard, our culture is only heading toward destruction. The ultimate direction of the corporate culture is continuous, continuous, continuous consciousness, and that only yields psychosis. So I think there's a massive healing possibility in making holes that fit anyone, and writing from that weird, empty, strange place.

—June 29, 2001

HIP-HOP CULTURE

Alexs Pate

'VE BEEN TRYING TO FIGURE OUT HOW TO TALK ABOUT WHAT I WANTED TO talk about today, which was innocence, and something else that I'm really interested in right now, which is rap and hip-hop, and how those two things work in relationship to the dominant narrative that we were talking about yesterday. At first I was going to choose one or the other; I didn't really want to sacrifice talking about one thing over the other, and I can't really do justice to either one in this time frame. So I think I'm going to just mess around with this for a little while and see where it goes.

I started thinking about innocence actually not long before, or during, the time I was here last year; I did a short lecture about it, I pieced together a lot of things that I had been working on that I thought related. Let me begin by saying it was the first Halloween of the new millennium. I was sitting in my house—I never go out on Halloween, I really don't understand Halloween; I depend on knowing exactly what's going on around me all the time as a black man in this country, I need to know who people are, I count on my ability to assess the intentions of the people in front of me. As I told my students this week, and I always tell anybody—most people know this, but some people don't—the oppressed always know more about the oppressor than the oppressor knows about the oppressed. Women know this and people of color know this. My knowledge of what I'm calling loosely "the oppressor" at this moment allows me to survive, this is how you survive. So on Halloween, people start putting on costumes, and who the hell are you? Then you find black people putting on costumes, which is weird to me—who are you trying to be? I just have a hard time with Halloween. And I'm a recluse anyway—most people wouldn't believe that about me, but in Minneapolis, I don't go out very much, I don't interact with people very much, mainly because I am trying to maintain an environment in which I am who I want to be, not who I am perceived as being. I made a short film with my friend David Mura, and in it there's a scene in which I simply say to him, I don't like it when the doorbell rings, I don't like it, I don't go to my front door, I *never* go to my front door. I just don't go to my front door.

In Minneapolis, where I live, it was a wonderfully mild fall night, a slight misty haze wrapped itself about the streets, streetlights muting their luminescence ever so gently. In my neighborhood there aren't enough children to hide from, trick-or-treaters, so I boldly kept my living room lights on even though I hadn't thought once about buying candy for any errant or misguided kids. I'm almost always ashamed to admit it, but Halloween scares me, not the iconographic element, not the idea of ghosts or goblins, or the simple revelry or horror that happens—I'm not fond of that, but that's not what frightens me. It's the level of abandon that people celebrate on this holiday. I understand the history of Halloween, and I understand for some people it has different meanings. But I'm talking about the way people in the United States, people in this society, celebrate Halloween. I live with the knowledge of a barely unspoken racial hierarchy, with black men at the bottom. Whether it's true or can be proven isn't important within the context of my life. I believe it. Consequently when I'm forced to be in environments which by their very design are meant to disguise reality, I get really nervous. But even at home, away from the deliberately disguised world of painted and masked revelers, I am usually not always at ease. Nagged, yes, nagged by the choice I made to try to be safe. A friend had called earlier asking if I'd like to join her for a drink. She wanted to be "out," see the masquerade parade for herself. She spoke of the devilment and the magic the night held, just to see people uninhibited. She didn't know that I depended on the inhibitions of people to feel safe, to soothe myself; so I didn't go. And while I went about my evening the Halloween of the new millennium embraced the partygoers. I couldn't help but think about something I'd written about Halloween in my novel *The Multicultiboho Sideshow*, when Ichabod says to the cop, "I'd almost forgotten Halloween. Halloween used to be a special day for a black boy like me. I got to put on a mask and go to white people's front doors demanding food and they gave it to me. They weren't nervous or scared or anything. In fact they'd say stuff like, my, aren't you a cute young man. Yeah, those were the days. On Halloween a black man could be a monster and still get paid. What happened to Halloween, lieutenant? I mean, young black boys can't do that now, can they? They'd probably be shot for banging on a white person's door nowadays."

Perhaps not long after I thought this in my head, three thousand miles away, in the cauldron we call Los Angeles, a gruesome situation was unfolding. Thirty-nine-year-old actor Anthony Duane Lee was hanging out with his friends at a masquerade party at a place called "the castle." It had been a party party, with a DJ, attended bar, a raucous, bacchanalian jam. People were in all manner of costumes; there were people dressed as nightstands, people dressed as animals, ghouls, but Anthony Lee had decided to dress simply in dark pants, a dark sweatshirt with the hood pulled up. I think he wanted to be a homeboy. But Lee was anything but a homeboy; a practicing Buddhist, Lee had appeared in the film *Liar Liar* and the television series *NYPD Blue*. For an African American man who was obviously striving to penetrate the pristine, too-white world of Hollywood, to pose as a thug reveals the self-confidence of someone who felt safe enough to posture without damaging his own reputation. Indeed this is all that is required of those folks bold enough to celebrate Halloween with outlandish disguises. But unbeknownst to Lee the LAPD had been called because the noise was so loud. The LAPD, enmeshed, it seems, in a perpetual morass of incompetence and outright racial hatred, approached the house from the back, and actually the two cops, a black man and his white female partner, shone their flashlights into the house from the back. Unfortunately, Lee was standing in one of the bedrooms near the rear of the house, and when he saw the beam of the flashlight through the glass, thinking it was somebody from the party playing, he turned and aimed his plastic replica of a semiautomatic pistol at the light. It was the last thing he'd ever do. Patrolman Hopper shot him nine times. *Nine* times. According to the police chief, he dismissed the idea of a racial motive, he said that yeah, Lee was black, but so was the officer who shot him, and that things happened so quickly that the officer had no option but to fire. The officer thought it was a real gun. I don't think you'd want an officer to die because he took an extra second to see if it was a plastic or a metal gun, would you? the police chief said. The guilt of Hopper, the police, was that he knew Lee was guilty. This is the dominant narrative. Because he could not disassociate his black face from that very fact. Indeed as a song by Jay-Z with R. Kelly, one of the rap songs, [says], Lee was guilty until proven innocent.

Frankly, one of things that attracts me to rap is this preoccupation with guilt, not innocence. A valorization of guilt, if you will. An immersion in guilt and in the consequences, the natural consequences of guilt and violence. In other words, if you listen to Biggie Smalls's "Life after Death," "Ready to Die," these are not single, individual pieces, poems, but rather entire compilations of poems that are simply premonitions of his own death. Tupac Shakur, in the same way, and there are many other examples of rap artists, poets really—I'm going to make that case a little later—who already see their death coming at them, mainly because the dominant narrative has already condemned them. So when people start talking about *narratives,* I get agitated in so many different ways in environments like this, small agitations that don't relate to the individual who's speaking the agitation, because the agitation is a narrative *they've* been told. It's a part of a history they—the way in which we gravitate back to Europe as the locus of all knowledge is ridiculous to me. Every time I hear someone quote Nietzsche I tremble. I tremble. Not because Nietzsche wasn't brilliant, but because he wasn't the singular brilliance, because there was an African brilliance, an Asian brilliance. There is brilliance, all over the world, and we don't know that. It's not a part of our consciousness, a part of our information base. And yet I am a part of that too—I constantly fall back to James Baldwin; I am as white as you . . . and you are as black as me. I recognize my whiteness; you won't recognize your blackness. I can't help that. But I can try to keep you honest; I can keep saying it to you, that you are as black as I am . . . maybe not nearly as black as I am, but your understanding of my culture intuitively and instinctively is there. You just deny it. Because you know what the narrative says about your ability to identify with that, and, if you do, what that means for you. This is why black people pass for white, or attempt to. And it's also why young white men and young white women often attempt to pass for black now. Because the rap narrative is a much better narrative. The hip-hop narrative is a much better narrative than a narrative we live under, believe it or not. I know what you hear about rap music, but it's not true. Hip-hop culture is rich, all-inviting, all-accepting. Yes, there's this really ugly element to it, but that is just because—well, I don't know why that is—because America is that way, because our education system is that way. These kids are not capable of displacing the hatred and the ugliness about gender, about sexuality, and many other things. The system doesn't educate them; their fathers are misogynists, their teachers are misogynists, they are homophobes, that's just the way it works. We have to change the system to change them. I don't fault these kids for feeling that way, I just make them feel guilty for feeling that way, for being that way. In the process of my teaching, I try to shame them into getting straight with themselves.

Anyway, in Jay-Z's album, this song he does is "Guilty until Proven Innocent," which is a recurrent theme in rap. And it's hard to ignore the fact that Lee, the black man who was shot, perhaps naively, oblivious to his proscribed label of outlaw, or worse still, defiant of it, was entrapped by his own lack of consciousness. Thus began my meditation on guilt and innocence. It's been with me since very near the beginning of my life, my silent partner so to speak. I found myself thinly haunted from within, under pursuit, hunted, I would find myself flinching every time I heard a siren, watched in stores, on the street—but why? And worse still, I understood it. I didn't know why, but I understood it fully. Could those two things be true? For an African American man they could: to not know why and to understand. Somehow it's been built into my consciousness that I deserved, demanded, perhaps even required such general and anonymous suspicion. It was O.K. I understood and accepted it as a necessary part of my capacity to survive in this society, the logical manifestation of W. E. B. Du Bois's idea of [the] double consciousness that governs much of the behavior of black Americans. I understood it. Slavery, racism, Jim Crow, night riders, white backlash, Confederate flags, all these things tell me I'm guilty, that I should behave, that I am being watched. But that all comes from outside of my body, it's all external. What did I believe about myself? What was the nature of my guilt, how did it manifest itself in my life, and why did I feel guilty in the first place, other than that I'd been taught to feel that way? Assuming that everyone who is initially placed into custody by the police has *not* committed a crime, why do black men in handcuffs appear more guilty than white ones? No. The question I mean to ask is why do black men in handcuffs *feel* more guilty than white men in handcuffs? For us to look into the rearview mirror and see a police car ten feet behind instigates an instinctive nervousness, even if we've done nothing wrong, *especially* if we've done nothing wrong; we begin preparing for what we know, for what we feel is inevitable; our date with destiny has come. White men or any other race of men may feel these same feelings, but the palpable uneasiness it gives to African American men, born out by the brutality of police and by the history of racism in this country, is overpowering. You can never escape it. It is, quite simply, a fact of life. It doesn't matter if you have a decent job and are a law-abiding citizen; there is a good chance that a sense of guilt is present nonetheless.

I want to switch, I think, over a little bit to the rap side of this equation. I recently asked a friend of mine, a trial attorney, what her definition of innocent was. Her reply stunned me a little. She said, you're innocent if they can't prove you did it. I looked at her, thinking this definition would never do. It's telling, as it relates to the judicial system, but it doesn't address the knowledge that I have as to the truth. By her definition if I pulled off the perfect crime or, as may have been the case in the O. J. Simpson trial, the prosecutors were inept, a verdict of innocent or not guilty may be the proper legal conclusion, but I would know what I did. I would still bear the burden of that guilt. No. I wanted a definition that would simply allow me to jettison the chains of blame that had been laid on me simply because I was born black and a man in this culture.

The first formal definition of innocent is "without guilt." This is easy to understand but difficult to talk about, because it's hard to talk about things that are defined by the absence of something else. Innocence is the absence of [guilt], so perhaps to reacquire innocence one must sort through the piles of guilt which are stored deep in the unused spaces of our souls, to identify and discard those which were not earned. One might simply decide to discard all guilt, start fresh in the world. I know a lot of people try to do this. And you might, if you were an African American man, wear your innocence like a brightly colored garment, majestically draped over your shoulder like so much kente cloth. This might work. I know black men who try to live this way. But one of the frustrations of this general and anonymous guilt that is placed on black men is that the color of your skin often preempts the articulation of innocence. In other words, before you can begin to articulate what type of person you are, in a culture that has already cast its guilty verdict on you, you must spend an extraordinary amount of time explaining what type of person you are *not*. I know black men who, in 2001, if they see a single white woman walking toward them on an otherwise empty street, will cross to the other side just to keep from threatening that woman. I know men who will cut a joke quicker, smile faster, or be over-the-top social because they don't want to be thought of as evil, angry, or full of rage—"nothin' to be afraid of here, I promise, I'm not an angry black man." That's what's being said. They are already compensating, fighting for what they think is in someone else's head, never to be seen as innocent, even without the requisite guilt. When a black man is sitting in a bar in the midst of a sea of white patrons, and the television flashes the latest gang murder, suddenly you have to not be that person on that screen, inside. Reacquiring innocence, for me, for men, for African American men, to me is a fundamental step in a kind of equalization of power. No matter what other powers we have, they are undermined by the assumption of our guilt, by ourselves and by the world around us. My concerns are these: Must I, as an African American man, accept the fact that I will forever feel guilty, even when I've done nothing wrong? Where does this guilt come from? How does one reacquire innocence? And once reacquired, is American capable of recognizing it?

So, this leads me, or articulates my walk, into hip-hop. As a poet I'm naturally gravitating to hip-hop. Moving to Minnesota from Philadelphia—believe me, before I left Philadelphia I was more hippy than hip-hop, more into rock, James Taylor even. I was tired of R&B; I had gone through my jazz phase, gone through my blues phase, knew all about black music, and I had sort of let it go. As soon as I got to Minnesota and its definitive whiteness, suddenly I wanted to know what the people I left behind were thinking. I consider myself an exile in Minnesota, just so you know. It's a self-imposed exile, which is one of the reasons I don't have to be out, because I've locked myself in this place on my own terms so I could write. I couldn't write in Philadelphia because it was too oppressive. Anyway, I don't think you can see all of this at home. Henry Louis Gates talks about this in *Figures in Black;* particularly for African American writers, moving away from home is one of the best ways to see home. I think it's true for all of us. Get away. Suddenly that guy down at the corner isn't an interesting old guy anymore, he's a creep. You think about it a little longer and realize he needs to be locked up. It takes time and distance, and your acuity becomes sharper. So I started listening to rap because rap is, as Chuck D says, a black person's CNN. You can learn so much because rap is not general, it's very specific. I'm talking about rap poetry, I'm not talking about Mystikal or Ludacris or what you might hear on the Top 40, although some of that is good poetry too. I'm talking about some of the stuff that doesn't stay out there very long, or, if it's out there, it's what is below the Top 40 level or even underground. A lot of my students have turned me on to a whole underground hip-hop world that is deep. And they are talking about political things, economics, vegetarianism, and now there is a new kind of growing movement of gay and lesbian rappers. The Geto Boys for example, or Bronx from KRS-One; you learn about Atlanta right now from Outkast or the whole Dirty South thing. You may not like it, you may not like the beat, but if you listen to the words it's telling you exactly what's going on *on that street corner.* It's specific. And you can't memorize rap . . . I'm getting ahead of myself. I give it literature status. The book I'm writing will probably be called *In the Heart of the Beat: The Poetry of Rap* [published as *In the Heart of the Beat: The Poetry of Rap,* 2009, Scarecrow Press]. And I'm doing lit crit on a hundred rap poems. Because my position is, in MFA schools now there is this rise of neoclassical poetry; I ascribe the genesis of that not to the natural resurgence of classical poetry, but to hip-hop, to the fact that hip-hop poets, rap poets, use iambic pentameter almost exclusively—well, not exclusively, because there's a lot of movement between iambic pentameter, tetrameter, and dimeter— and also the couplet form is a central part of hip-hop and rap. Rap. I've got to stop saying "hip-hop" because hip-hop is the culture; rap poetry is the words, and that's what I'm talking about. In fact in my classes in school, I don't want to talk about the music; the music is mostly regurgitated, refried, looped. These poets know that to engage a large number of people they go back to tried-and-true beats. James Brown, George Clinton, Sly Stone, this is easy. The music part of rap is easy. You don't like the music, you hear nothing. But if the beat is right, you're dead—if you like the beat and you want to dance . . . Rap has form. It uses rhythm, obviously; it uses all manifestations of language, metaphor, assonance, consonance, simile, incredible imagery, the narrative that is being developed, the storytelling capacity of some rappers—for instance a rapper like Slick Rick, one of the first great storytellers of rap, an amazing storyteller, better or as good as any storyteller you will ever sit in front of. You may not like the story he's telling, but his capacity to tell that story is great. I think Biggie Smalls was a great storyteller.

To me poetry is about a search for the truth, a way of reflecting truth back at the people who are it. This is certainly what has marked African American poetry. So I consider rap a new form of African American poetry, just as important as the work of black poets that came before. I teach a book called *The Black Poets,* and it begins with field hollers and slave chants. This is as close to rap as you can possibly get. And it predated Paul Laurence Dunbar, it led to that, it led to Phillis Wheatley and Lucy Terry, it led to Margaret and Alice Walker, it led to Nikki Giovanni and Sonia Sanchez. The continuum of African American history, which reaches all the way back to slavery and before, back to Africa, is continued with rap poetry. I make my point simply by saying, even in this illustrious and knowledgeable room, how many of you can name more than five living, American, publishing, male African American/black poets? Not rappers. I know some of us can do that, but I don't think many of us can. And if you're fourteen and you have an interest in language and words and you live in the 'hood, who are your role models? What are you going to do? How are you going to scrape up enough money to come to Naropa to learn how to write poetry? *You're not.* It's not even going to come into your con- sciousness. You want to be like *that guy.* If hip-hop is the culture, rap is the heart; within the heart is the beat, and riding on and carried by the beat are the words.

In every rap poem there exist at least two realities, that of the speaker and that of the listener. In rap the speaker always forces the listener to enter their reality. In order to fully enjoy it, you must accept the parameters that the speaker sets out for you. First and foremost you must understand the language. I realize that a rap poem with a dope beat can often make you not care whether you understand it or not, but in this work I'm not inter- ested in the beat. It is true of course that the beat is the lure, the open arms of hip-hop. For many the beat seduces, recalls the strength of the past; the beat of rap is often the air of a particular street corner, somebody's base- ment house party, or a moment of confrontation with some dude who stepped on somebody's else's shoes. It's the music of the past, as I've said: Sly Stone, James Brown. But it's what's said that matters to me. Perhaps the most important idea embodied by the language of rap, as it is in African American literature, is that language can reflect an oppositional position. Words spoken can oppose existing ideas, supplant them with new ones, and, perhaps more significantly, rap poets know that depending on the number of people listening, the speaker has the power. Rap poets confront the challenges of expression with the same devices and techniques poets have always used: metaphor, metonymy, synecdoche, alliteration, assonance, rhythm, and meaning. But the language, the actual words they use, are fluid, sometimes existing for only brief periods of time; the words transform in spelling, in sound, in meaning, meaning is fluid—the word *dope* for example has many meanings, from "idiot" to "cool"—and the reality of all those meanings can disappear at any moment so that they can't be memorized. This language changes like lightning, it is preslang; by the time it is slang it is no longer useful to the rap poet. So people who dabble in hip-hop culture always stumble over the language; they know they can't keep up, you have to be deep into it to stay up on it, but that's where the idea of coding comes in. Rap poets always provide a map, a context for the word, a space for the word to exist differently. They fashion a way to say the word *game*, for example, in such a way that you know they don't mean dodgeball. In order to fully break the code of a given rap poem, you have to first understand the context in which it came into being, who the speaker is. As Common would say, "Some say I'm too deep, I'm in too deep to sleep, through me Mohammed will forever speak." This line is coded so deeply, just as an example; not only is he saying of course he's smart, but he's so smart, and he's not going to back off of his purpose; his purpose is to convey issues and ideas that are being developed by Islam, for example, the black Muslims. And in this he provides even an allusion to a newspaper that they sell on the corner in New York City and in most big cities called *Mohammed Speaks*. If you don't know that you don't get that. "Some say I'm too deep, I'm in too deep to sleep, through me Mohammed will forever speak." Or even less depth—another thing he says is "under the Fubu is a guru." If you don't know Fubu, then you don't know what he's talking about. That's how fast the language moves.

—June 29, 2001

ARABIC POETICS & THE INTERNATIONAL LITERARY SCENE

Pierre Joris

[Note: this lecture took place September 19, 2001,
just over a week after September 11, 2001.]

IT IS GOOD TO BE HERE. I WAS PLEASED WHEN THE SKIES OPENED WIDER AND New York State receded . . . when I saw the wide-open spaces of this part of America, it felt as if a load started to lift off my shoulders for the first time since September 11—eight days that feel like a year. Obviously I have not sat down in these eight days to write out a lecture, so this is what the French would call a talk *à bâtons rompus,* a talk as a bundle of broken sticks, and no doubt the New York City events will wind their way through them.

First of all, I am pleased to be here because in my thinking through the events of the past week there are two people I tried to think with and through: they are Allen Ginsberg and William Burroughs. It was Allen who years ago taught me about the need, sometimes, to try to think or write through somebody else's mind. I think there was an occasion for this this past week, thinking through Allen's mind in terms of compassion, in terms of trying to see what one can do without anger, while trying to keep a compassionate mind. And of course Burroughs is extremely useful to think through exactly such catastrophic events; for me he has the most penetrating political mind of any writer of the second part of the twentieth century.

I was going to speak on the nomadic aspects of what I think of as the most adventurous poetry worldwide, but I am going to restrict myself, for reasons that are obvious, to an area & culture much in the news, much reviled while little known—though that should, exactly now, be studied deeply: Arab poetry and Arab culture. Maybe this brief talk can help in some small measure to widen our knowledge & appreciation of this culture, allowing us a wider view & deeper, & thus more sympathetic view, so that we do not fall into the kind of stupid "Bushisms" we have been assaulted by of late.

Last week at the New York state university where I work, SUNY Albany, we held teach-ins because most of my students are from New York City or

Long Island, and the events of September 11 were very rough on them. Most of these undergraduates don't have much knowledge of history—& thus also lack any way to think through & place such a catastrophic event. With this in mind, William Kennedy, the novelist & founder of the New York State Writers Institute at SUNY Albany, & I did a reading of sorts. Kennedy read from a historical book citing Truman's diaries of the moments before the atom bomb was dropped, followed by witness accounts from Hiroshima and Nagasaki. I read a text by the Palestinian poet Mahmoud Darwish, from a book called *Memory for Forgetfulness*, which is the memoir he kept during 1982 in Beirut, when Beirut was being shelled daily by Israel. This is from the opening pages of that book:

Out of one dream another dream is born . . .

—*Are you well? I mean are you alive?*

—*How did you know I was just this moment laying my head on your knee to sleep?*

—*Because you woke me up when you stirred in my belly. I knew then I was your coffin. Are you alive? Can you hear me?*

—*Does it happen much, that you are awakened from one dream by another, itself the interpretation of the dream?*

—*Here it is, happening to you and to me. Are you alive?*

—*Almost.*

—*And have the devils cast their spell on you?*

—*I don't know, but in time there's room for death.*

—*Don't die completely.*

—*I'll try not to.*

—*Don't die at all.*

—*I'll try not to.*

—*Tell me, when did it happen? I mean, when did we meet? When did we part?*

—*Thirteen years ago.*

—*Did we meet often?*

—*Twice: once in the rain, and again in the rain. The third time, we didn't meet at all. I went away and forgot you. A while ago I remembered. I remembered I'd forgotten you. I was dreaming.*

—*That also happens to me. I too was dreaming. I had your phone number from a Swedish friend who'd met you in Beirut. I wish you good night! Don't forget not to die. I still want you. And when you come back to life, I want you to call me. How the time flies! Thirteen years! No. It all happened last night. Good night!*

Three o'clock. Daybreak riding on fire. A nightmare coming from the sea. Roosters made of metal. Smoke. Metal preparing a feast for metal the master, and a dawn that flares up in all the senses before it breaks. A roaring that chases me out of bed and throws me into this narrow hallway. I want nothing, and I hope for nothing. I can't direct my limbs in this pandemonium. No time for caution, and no time for time. If I only knew—if I knew how to organize the crush of this death that keeps pouring forth. If only I knew how to liberate the screams held back in a body that no longer feels like mine from the sheer effort spent to save itself in this uninterrupted chaos of shells. "Enough!" "Enough!" I whisper to find out if I can still do anything that will guide me to myself and point to the abyss opening in six directions. I can't surrender to this fate, and I can't resist it. Steel that howls, only to have other steel bark back. The fever of metal is the song of this dawn.

Memory for Forgetfulness, published by the University of California Press, is a tremendous memoir by one of the great contemporary writers, Mahmoud Darwish. Some of his poetry has been translated.[1] If the early work is more profoundly and maybe essentially political in terms of creating a Palestinian identity in the midst of the disaster that befell his people, his later work expands to encompass wider cultural concerns, as he tries to write of & through the culture of the Mediterranean, & specifically its Arab contribution via the culture of al-Andalus. This is something we in the West know very little about, and that is definitely a major lack—& a shame.

A strong tradition of poetry is not only core to Arab culture—until the twentieth century it is the essential genre of literature—but tremendous in its achievements. On the plane over, when I had a quiet moment—I was looking around to make sure nobody was seeing it, I was afraid someone might call the marshal—I was reading a book that came in the mail a couple weeks ago called *Peaks of Yemen I Summon* by the anthropologist Steven Caton. It is an ethnopoetics study of Yemeni tribal poetry, clearly demonstrating—as do a number of other books I have read on this matter—that the role of poetry in tribal Yemeni society is still core to the society's sociopolitical dynamic. That is, all events that make up the weave of the social life, get vocalized & often realized through poems—be these marriages or wars. War, for instance, can get calmed down. War in such a tribal setting can often be faked, i.e., performed symbolically by verbal &/or gestural jousts, to some extent: this is not how we Westerners, weaned on the Lawrence of Arabia fiction, imagine things to be. Caton describes a tribal war situation where there was shooting indeed, and then people were asking him to bring them something. When he said, "How can I?" they answered, "Look, those shots missed by three feet, this is only a show, for honor—in half an hour we are going to talk." And they did so, through poems—improvised, yet very formal, poems. Nearly everything can be put into the form of a poem, making poems still a major form of political and social discourse.

This has been going on for a couple millennia. We have very famous poems from pre-Islamic times, the seven odes known as the *Mu'allaqat*, i.e., the "hanging ones," because they were supposedly stitched on cloth that was hung from the *Ka'ba*, the big black stone in Mecca. Later on, when the more pure religious elements took over, they replaced these hangings with verses from the Koran. Those seven odes are extremely complex poems—& I would have loved to see someone like Louis Zukofsky, maybe our greatest formal genius, do an extra section of "A" that would have brought something of this great work over into English via adaptation/translation of complex European forms. The *Mu'allaqat* are nearly untranslatable for us, because American poetry in this century, from Pound on, has worked at cutting away rhetorical blubber, something that was necessary to get us out of late nineteenth-century Victorian verse & find a language that was usable in our modernist age. But that kind of discursive rhetoric was a very important & central ingredient of those odes.

For centuries, classical Arab poetry worked on a very rich rhetorical level while at the same time being extremely formal. You have totally determined stress patterns, you have inimitable monorhyme structures that could stretch over one hundred lines and/or a whole ode, something we obviously cannot do in English. The translations that we have are mainly nineteenth-century British, i.e., colonial translations, and they are awful to our ears because they sound exactly like very bad late-Victorian or Tennysonian Orientalism. There is a huge job to be done in this field—to bring all of those major poems back into our present. At this point much, if not most, of this work is nearly untranslatable into English, because the language does not allow it, does not give permission—maybe because no great poet of Zukofskyan, formal abilities has bothered to go at it. Basil Bunting did a little in this direction, with his translation/adaptations of Persian work by Firdausi & Rudaki in what he called his "overdrafts." But most translations of this kind of work have been limp-languaged, fake-mystical things—vide the various versions of Rumi we are stuck with. In French, on the other hand, it has recently been shown that such rhetoric-based translations are still viable: a profoundly worked, complexly syntaxed, rhetorical translation of the *Mu'allaqat* was proposed by Jacques Berque, one of the greatest Maghrebi scholars of the twentieth century—born of French parents in North Africa, and dead just recently in France—who did a marvelous translation that kept the Arabic rhetoric in a very complex, but gorgeously written, French while transforming it into a syntactical structure so complex that it never falls into easy Hugolian rhetorical alexandrines.

I tried a number of years ago to translate one of the odes with the help of an Iraqi poet friend exiled to Algeria, where I was living & teaching at the time, because the Iraqi government wanted to hang him for being a member of the Communist party. When I began asking him about the *Mu'allaqat* and the pre-Islamic tradition of poetry, he said, "Oh, my father had a secondhand bookshop in Baghdad, filled with old scrolls and manuscripts. I know these poems—we all know them—by heart, the seven odes, and love to recite them, as that is the way they live again, they were oral poems made to be spoken or sung." I told Mohammed that I was really interested in Tarafa's ode, because Tarafa was, from what I had been able to glean, the wildest of those seven poets, and to me very Rimbaud-like—always walking on "the wild side," he was independent & a rebel against the state, and eventually arrested for insulting a king, who sent him on a treacherous mission where, caught, he was given the choice of how to die. He said, fill me with wine, then leave me in the sand, bleeding out through the holes you'll make in me like a water bag made of goat skin. And that's how he went, very young, in his twenties. His ode is gorgeous. With Mohammed's help we created an interlinear, very literal, version, which I then needed to fashion into a readable, contemporary poem in English. When I tried to work this out, the need to cut out the rhetoric made me try to pass the text through a Japanese mode, the haiku, or rather the renga, though one with a William Carlos Williams twist, namely his three-step lines, which indeed allowed me to cut away the rhetorical language-husks, leaving just the image kernels. In a way it is a totally unfaithful translation, but it was truly the only way that I could think of doing it and coming out with a viable poem.

Let me read you from this ode:

> *Khawla's abandoned campsite:*
>   *an old tattoo's fading glow*
>   *on the schist slopes of Thamad mountain.*

>   *Between brown lips her smile*
>   *mirrors marigolds unfolding in white sand*
>   *on a dew-wet dune*

the sun lent it its rays—black antinomy
                darkened her gums
        never touched a tooth.

If you look for me among the assembled sages
        you'll find me—you'll find me too
in the taverns where they sell wine.

                When late at night she sings for us
                        my illustrious companions' faces
                        light up like novas.

        Come off it! you who tell me
                not to fight & not to fuck,
                if

                        ever I did quit,
                could you offer me
                                immortality?

        As you cannot save me from death
let me offer death, right now, all
                        this hand can hold.

                I wouldn't give a damn
                        to know the hour of my death
                                if it weren't for these three:

        first—& quit bugging me about it—
                the pleasure of an old wine that
                        foams as soon as you add water

        then there is the call from someone in need:
                I come running, hunched over, a
tamarisk wolf sensing water

        & last but not least the joy in shortening a cloudy day
                laying a well-fleshed lady
                        under a firmly pitched tent.

I have spent my life generously drinking
            at its source. If death should come tomorrow
                whose throat would be parched?

    No matter how fast a man runs
            death is a long leash
                its other end firmly grasped

& the days will lay bare what you don't yet know
    & someone will refuse you bread
            someone will come

                            bringing news:
                    a traveler with no luggage
                        & no invitation.

Now this tradition of the ode, the *qacida,* as it is called in Arabic, is still alive today—is still seen as the foremost model of Arabic poetry, from or against which you have to write, even all the way through the twentieth century. You'll see it reemerge in the last poem I'll read by one of the great contemporary Algerian avant-gardist poets. Now, the critical-scholarly tradition, for good and bad, has also survived through the ages. In the eighth, ninth, & tenth centuries—the early centuries of Islamic culture—there were incredibly intelligent & fastidious scholars who wrote great treatises on poetics, often Aristotelian in inspiration, but often also improvements on Aristotle, with an interesting feel of modernity, in fact, in terms of elegance of classification and formalization. Those books have held sway over the centuries, and like Aristotle & Horace, are still read & studied today. In a way it was very difficult to break out of that mode— just as in the West until very recently, the core literary values were based on Aristotle, Horace, & Longinus.[2]

Unhappily, the West has been very negative about the Arab poetic traditions, either ignoring it totally or touting its supposed backwardness, even when glorifying, à la Lawrence—of Arabia, not D. H.—its antique achievements. An interesting story showing how far such denials & misconstructions can go, has to do with the European lyric tradition, which, as we have all learned from Pound and others, goes right back to the troubadours, in Provence, where the first lyric poems were composed. After a hundred years it disappeared, but before that Europeans had some epic writings, such as the Occitan *Cançon d'Antioquia* or the Old French *Chanson de Roland,* basically old tribal epic, i.e., a nasty or glorious world seen by males: I, boy, beat up on you, boy. But the lyric, the love song, comes from the troubadours. Since the Middle Ages, the root of the very word *troubadours,* our philologies have told us, comes from *trobar,* which means, they say, in Latin "to find." Now if you look *trobar* up in the etymological dictionary, it has a little star on it that means this is a suggested root, this is not a documented root of this word. If you ask any specialist in Arabic poetry, specifically in Arabic Spain, the Moorish kingdom, that root is in fact *tarab,* the Arabic word for "song." There is no question that that is where it came from. But even now, in 2001, philological discussions of this matter keep going on, with the best European—German & French & Spanish & English philologists—unable to tear themselves loose from what at base is cultural imperialism, namely their belief that there has to be European roots, an autochthonous European origin to lyric poetry & that it may—must—not come via Arabic song & poetry. But that is indeed where this lyrical tradition, that will also give us Dante & beyond, comes from.

If we now have a look at what is happening with Arabic poetry, a quick overview would suggest there was, belatedly, i.e., well after European modernism, the beginning of an Arab modernism. This can be linked to a specific group of poets in Beirut around the magazine *Shi'r*—which means poetry—namely, Yusuf al-Khal, Ounsi El Hage, Adonis, & a few more, who, indeed, read Eliot and a range of twentieth-century French poetry in the early 1950s. *The Waste Land*'s mythopoeic materials sent some of these poets back to their own mythopoeic past to look for inspiration & matters of spiritual rebirth, and also, via French modernism, forward to free verse experiments. Adonis, for example, originally Ali Ahmad Said, took his name from the ancient fertility god. These poets began breaking down the classical norms of Arabic poetry, as represented by the highly formal qacida structure. These experiments would eventually spread to other countries of the Mashreq.

But one more word on the idea of "belated": If you ask Adonis, it is the European modernism of the late nineteenth century—Baudelaire, urban poetry, Whitman, formal innovation, etc.—that is belated—from a wider, non-Eurocentric view of things. He points to the great Baghdadi poets & thinkers of the tenth and eleventh centuries, such as Abu Nuwas & Abu Tammam, or Omar Khayyam, & al-Rawandi and al-Razi, as thinkers & theoreticians, and to the nature of visionary experience by the Sufi mystics, to locate a modernist, i.e., urban, experimental in both form & content, antitraditional, sexually adventurous stance leading to "the emergence of new truths about man and the world—[which] is not only a criticism of the ancient but also a refutation of it."[3] It is still difficult for us to see this, or realize it, because again, somebody like Omar Khayyam has been killed over and over again by bad translation, giving us a kind of easy, new age-y Orientalism; on top of this we don't have the cultural context available, i.e., we lack the necessary information to be able to see the ways in which he & these other poets and thinkers were revolutionary.

Simultaneously, throughout the Arab world, you also have had & still have an ongoing, lively tradition of oral, demotic poetry of songs & proverbs & tales, also relatively formalized, as such literatures usually are. This, by the way, is one of the features of Arabic culture that fascinates me deeply: while in Europe, after Gutenberg, the oral tradition rather quickly died out; in the Arab world, both written & oral traditions have maintained themselves for two thousand years, enriching the one, the other in the process. So, even if the written tradition, after the Baghdadi modernism, suffered a setback in that the conservatives & reactionaries took over, & much of the production grew, if not stale, then repetitive, poetry stayed alive as the major form language arts took in the Arab world. As already mentioned, it is the *Shi'r* poets who "broke the heave," to quote EP [Ezra Pound]. They began writing—and here is something, when you read them, something to watch out for, the term, they call them prose poems, but it is not the Baudelairian & twentieth-century Euro-American prose poem set as a block of justified prose. The Arab prose poem can be freely all over the page with various line breaks; what makes it "prose" in the Arabic sense is that it simply does not follow the old forms, eschews the metrics, though it may even still rhyme at times. It is really what we would call free verse.

So indeed there is a very strong modernist movement that emerges in the 1950s from Beirut, as a center, but also from the wider Middle East. And this is very interesting to think about even now, when we are getting filled via our media with these images of a medieval, old world, where nothing is modern, we are shown these rural, backwards Arabs and told that in Afghanistan & elsewhere, all that they, the people, want is America, everybody wants America & its gadgets. Unhappily the disinformation about those parts of the world is rampant, & has only been made worse by the events in New York.

So there is a pitch here also for people who are here today—you're still young and have the memory to learn a language like Arabic. There is a huge amount of work to be done in terms of what needs to be brought in our language [English] from that language, or that needs to be done anew. Translation always needs to be done anew. In a way, every generation has to translate the major texts again for itself. When you have a situation like the one in relation to Arabic poetry, where you have two hundred years of bad translation, the job is even more urgent. Bad translation can kill a poet for a whole generation in a country or for a culture. Take a poet from any language you are not familiar with and read him or her in what a knowledgeable person could tell you is a bad translatation. For example, I recently came across someone advertised as a major Czech poet, so I got the one book translated; it might sound like bad Robert Pinksy, and I put the book down—that poet's work may never again be visible for me. So as a translator, there is a responsibility you have & should feel.

My own work in this area—except for Tarafa and some other work I have translated in collaboration with a native speaker, not my favorite method of translation, has been poetry from another center of Arabo-Berber culture, namely from the Maghreb, that is, Tunisia, Algeria, & Morocco. These countries gained independence in the early 1960s, & given the strictures of French colonialism it was forbidden to speak Arabic in whatever schools there were for the quote natives unquote. I remember people telling me how, as kids in grade school in Algeria in the 1950s, they would be fined the equivalent of a dime if, during a break, they were caught speaking Arabic, even among themselves. So you have several generations of poets for whom French was the available cultural language, who had to write in French, & who are writing brilliantly in French. There are a couple of beautiful texts in English by a Moroccan, Abdelkebir Khatibi. There is one translated called *Love in Two Languages,* that came out in the mid-1990s. Khatibi has this ideal vision that every poem should be written in two languages, at least, which of course speaks to me as a poet very much. Every poem should be written in all languages simultaneously. Here's how he puts this:

> Yes, I spoke, I grew up around the Only One and the Name, and the Book of my invisible god should have ended within me. Extravagant second thought that stays with me always. The idea imposes itself as I write it: every language should be bilingual! The asymmetry of body and language, of speech and writing—at the threshold of the untranslatable.

In Maghrebi literature we have a vast amount of interesting work. I could read for the next three hours . . . By the way, a magazine people should look at is called *Banipal,* an amazingly rich magazine of Arab literature that comes out of London. Its drawback—it translates poems both from Arabic and from French, so from Maghrebian and Mashreqian literatures—

some of its translators come from a rather more middle-of-the-road American or English tradition, so the poems wind up being closer to what we usually call confessional poetry, what we might call the Iowa tradition. So there are some translation problems to be kept in mind. But it is a very useful magazine if you want to find out what is being written now in the range of Arab countries.

I'm going to read a few extracts. Ounsi El Hage is one of the great 1950s poets, born in Lebanon in 1937, both poet & journalist. There is in fact a great tradition among Arab poets to be journalists and writers at the same time, and there is a great tradition of Arabic newspapers publishing poems. My first poems translated into Arabic appeared in *Al-Quds,* which is the Arabic daily published in London that goes into those Arabic countries that will let it in on a given day, because it is politically independent. The cultural editor is a Jordanian Bedouin poet, Amjad Nasser. It's wonderful to get the morning paper, and with it, as you unfold it, a whole page of poems. Again, this goes back to what I said earlier as to how poetry still is of core importance in this culture. Here is a poem by Ounsi El Hage, written in the 1960s. I'll read an extract, translated by Brandel France, from the long poem, "The Messenger with Her Hair Long to the Springs," a kind of reworking of the genesis story:

This is the story of the other side of creation
I discovered it, my eyes obscured
The path, my beloved,
Leads from her awaiting me
Leads from my return to her
This is the story of the other side of creation
Listen
Do not shoot the doors
The breakers bear the message to the wind
The wind to the trees
The trees to notebooks.
You, old men with homes, and you, young boys of the streets
Sit this very night in the presence of the lover.
You, who hurry about, did you really leave only to return?
Shatter the night for an instant
Come, gather round the one to testify.
Pray, my love, that I spread a feast, befitting their appetite.
Birds of the harvest season soar past
But your light does not recede, its hand before me still.

I am the collector of your echo's traces
Read me before they know me, then I will arrive early at the heart
This, in my twisted language, is your vision
This, in my thieving hands, is your treasure
This, from my row boat, is your sea, so watch over your sea from my boat,
your eyes the sails that protect me
You, who change life with crushing ignorance
You are the dependable one
You change life, effortless
With the nakedness of purity, to its passion alone do secrets yield
This is your story
The story of the other side of creation

Thinking of the old myths and stories, I wanted to read one, maybe two texts. A good friend puts out a magazine in Paris called *Arapoetica*. He is an Iraqi in exile for thirty years, the last of the great surrealists, a total wild man of poetry, called Abdel Kader El-Janabi. Here is the first text, translated by me, called "Against Ibn Arabi":

Here I am all alone, quarreling with the age, both feet kicking the jugs of Being. Night vibrates with a litany of shadowless reflections. From its window the Absolute in profile contemplates its confines: the celestial sounds propagate through the old pond where metal and loam, past and ends, bone and vocable come to slake their thirst. Mud explodes and consciousness sails against the current. In this immense opacity of contemplation where air is the anticipation of darkness, I see the singular rise in multiples from the bottom of the amphora and wait in the cold of the real to be smashed.

No need to step into a sea at the edge of which the prophets came to a halt, or crack open the world's safe, for man to be the knot of creation and keep in his hands the Seal of future treasures. Creative in each one of us, the spark, no longer hoping to unite with the fires of heaven, becomes flame, spark of itself, mother of all ignitions, new lands. A drop flees the ocean, becomes ocean. The universe holds out a hand to the ephemeral.

One of the great Moroccan poets who has a book out now is Abdellatif Laâbi.[4] He published one of the great avant-garde magazines, *Souffles*, from 1966 until 1972, which is on the web[5] now, for which he was arrested & jailed; he spent eight years in jail under the regime of King Hassan II for being a revolutionary threat. He has been in Paris since his release. I used one of his poems as an epigraph to one of my books. This poem goes:

I'm not the nomad
searches for the well
the sedentary has dug,
I drink little water
and walk
apart from the caravan.

I want to close by reading a poem—or an extract at least—by Habib Tengour, the Algerian poet, from one of his great works, which I published in translation as a chapbook called *Empedokles's Sandal*.[6] It presents itself *ab initio* in an astoundingly wide nomadicity: the author's name clearly locates him as an Arab, the title refers to a Greek philosopher situated in Italy, and the epigraph cites a nineteenth-century German poet, Friedrich Hölderlin. There is Poundian or post-Poundian modernity visibly at work here, confirmed by the poem itself, which reads as a modernist textual montage/collage of a wide-ranging array mixing the personal and the historical. The opening lines set the tone of contemporaneity, down to the slashes used to separate the word-shards. Then, paradoxically, the poem starts with the word *stop*. It took me awhile to realize that this is a reference to the classical ode motif of the atlal, the first stanza of the poem in which the poet stops his mount at the site of last year's campfire—and then realized that the whole of the very postmodern poem is ghosted by the structure of the most classical of Arab poems, the ghazal, or ode.[7] Here it is:

Traces/ Renown/ Shades/ Urns/ Life(s)/ Epoch/ Zenith
Lucid/ Strangely/ Suspended

Stop
a pause of short duration   the closed
space   compelled remembrances tears
they are not necessary
the dictionary tempers the banality of the stereotype
a nostalgia emerges in the description of the place

like a circumscribed exile
like the eye dimming after the junction

handicap of the code
unusual names at night fall
despite the invocation's depth
the usages intermingle on the asphalt
the trace vainly sought   there   effaced
it is visible
                    o heart you weaver
the times don't change that fast their duration
nor the embrace that follows where a soul deciphers itself
a proliferation of signs but
                              the loud voice the one
that unties the tongues and curbs the discourse
alas
        so many lethal traps on the way
the angels refuse to accompany us
the lights blink ostentatiously
the harangues lead us far from the encampment

This is the moment

to enter subreptitiously I go in
my purpose my utterance to open the door
to say under the dictation of a continuous effusion
to align a text without history
for a moment to enjoy the stopping
to reveal the splendor and brilliance of the vestiges
without giving in to the letter's subterfuges

Paris november rue Saint-Antoine Constantine
cité du 20 août Paris again
examine each of these addresses

a small light rift whips the clouds

Itinerary
of precise annotations the return therein
envisaged I know
the tracings the dwellings and the hunger
the hesitation to take to the road is real

renown by auction
victims interrogate who kills and reason

pomp makes sense only if sustained
a hollow word illusions
charisma is not a copyright trademark
danger metamorphoses the limbs
there is nothing to brag about today

the days have become flat right after the exchange
the rivers advance in error in the moonlight
I hesitated a long time before coming
what is man without the praise that precedes him

Thank you.

—September 19, 2001

1 By now (2013) there are many of Darwish's books of poetry available in English. Check out *A River Dies of Thirst, In the Presence of Absence, Journal of an Ordinary Grief, Why Did You Leave This Horse Alone?*, all published by Archipelago Books. Darwish died in 2008.

2 Some of this early Arabic—at least the Maghrebian material—has been reproduced in the "Invention of Prose" section of my (& Habib Tengour's) recent anthology *The University of California Book of North African Literature*, vol. 4.

3 Adonis, *An Introduction to Arab Poetics*, Saqi Books, London, 1990, p. 78.

4 Since 2001, there have been a number of books by Abdellatif Laâbi published in English translation.

5 The magazine is available on the web now, here: http://clicnet.swarthmore .edu/souffles/sommaire.html

6 Since then, a full volume of Tengour's work has come out: *Exile Is My Trade: A Habib Tengour Reader* edited, introduced, and translated by Pierre Joris (Black Widow Press).

7 Since then I have developed this insight into the essay "On the Nomadic Circulation of Contemporary Poetics between Europe, North America and the Maghreb," now gathered in the volume *Justifying the Margins: Essays 1990–2006* (Salt Books).

THE EVENT OF THE BORDER
Bhanu Kapil

WRITING *THE DIARY OF THE WOLF GIRLS OF MIDNAPURE,* I TRANS-posed the Colorado forest upon the jungle landscape of northeast India. Though I researched the sal trees of the Sundarbans, trees with silvery branches in the delta flats of the Ganges, I had never seen them. I set the silver with the dark brown/orange and alternating cream or black of the Ponderosa pine back behind our house on the Hogback Ridge, so that the afternoon light of the northern Rockies was really late morning, Orissa, my back to the horizon, 1929.

Michal Rovner, Israeli photographer and filmmaker, whose work I was introduced to by Melissa Buzzeo:

> You asked me what I try to achieve in my work. I think I often like to take two realities and to combine them together into one reality. For example, I take footage from Russia in a snowstorm and from Israel in the heat and put them together, and they work together seamlessly. There are often two or three realities in my work. There are often abstract figures at a border site that blurs and warps. The border in my own thinking is that site which is not set and then people cross it; the border instead as an event that happens when it is crossed. Think of the hundreds and thousands of movements of people crossing and recrossing the u.s.-Mexico border. It is perhaps these movements or moments of crossing that constitute or solidify the border, but these hundreds of thousands of movements, human and animal, are also what make a border blurry: a series of rough, overlapping arcs. The event of the border not as a memory or a des-tination but as something that is changing even as we speak about it. Even this speaking, even this reading, brightens the figure of the border, so much brightness that it deflects my vision right back.

In this sense I do not regard myself as a multicultural writer, i.e., some-one writing from a specific location at the margin facing toward the center it wants to claim. The question—What does it mean to write as a British Indian woman permanently resident in the United States?—implies a set position rather than a crossing mind. The question I love is this one: How can I translate migration into the work of the line, my work with narrative?

From the *Wolf Girls*, some notes on divination, memory, and writing practice:

> To make an emotion out of this loss of territory, make a fact out of it that was [is] separate to the events of my life. The book as an activity of fiction said yes, the life you have been describing is no longer possible. At the limit of her story, Kamala walked vertically, parallel to the perimeter, until she reached the outskirts of Calcutta.

To put it another way: What, for example, is the character's response to space or emptiness when the story fails? When a certain outcome loses its strength, what happens to the girl's peripheral vision, her chronology? What happens to her fate as a character, a set of orientations experienced as interoceptive sense perception, hypervigilance, a hesitant progression? I think of her as capable of double movement, a being engaged with the notion of territory and homelessness at all times.

When I look slightly away from this character, blurring my eyes, I see a person alternating between visible and invisible narratives rapidly. Sometimes this person cannot press or cross and is stalled. In this sense the movement is less migrant than someone for whom a migration is not possible. The image here that helped me to make sense of congestion and refusal as activities of prose writing was the report of Iraqi refugees at Calais, trying to cross to England in the Channel, a forward movement that is constantly rebuffed, full of agonies.

I am interested in these failed movements, full of longing, as gestures or failures of the narrative, but also as the language that arises at the point where flows are deflected; what happens when the person, jarred in a repetition at the border, unable to cross, begins to speak. The border is unintelligible.

Andrea Spain, Deleuzean feminist scholar: "Perhaps this is why I am less interested in the figure Gayatri Spivak describes as the abundantly speaking, traveling subaltern, than the problem child, the immigrant who, crossing into newness, cannot shake her grief, her sense of loss, a person mistrustful of the alternative language she is being offered with jubilance, the language of hybrid modernity."

Who is this immigrant? For so much of my writing it is the figure of my mother, who was diagnosed with schizophrenia in 1981. The doctor called me into his office—I was twelve—and explained that this was "cultural schizophrenia." I didn't understand this term until much later, reading Frantz Fanon, I came across the accounts of the high incidence of schizophrenia and mental illness in newly decolonized North African populations, especially the women who could not "purify" themselves of the memory of war. I am not sure why I am placing the word *purify* in speech marks, but looking back on my notes—reading Fanon—the word is underlined three times. My mother crossed the border from Pakistan to India in 1947 in one of the bloodier civil wars this planet has ever seen. As a child, my bedtime stories included, in one breath, a complex mix of fairy tales, Hindu epics of exile and demons, and extremely visual memories of what my mother had seen, concealed in a hay cart, as she crossed the border: women tied to trees, their wombs cut out.

This border keeps returning to my writing, not always as a visible subject, but, I want to say, as the qualities of storytelling. Six weeks ago I began work on the hay cart/fairy tale material, translated by Jin-Hee Chung into the gestures of Korean puppet theater. I met Jin Hee in the Allen Ginsberg Library [at Naropa University] one day. Our conversations converge or diminish at the point that we have to work on the ending of our performance. What if I say I want to write a healing narrative? It's sort of horrifying, as an experimental prose writer, to have this thought, in prose. How can I compress then unfold this soft-tissue memory, reverberations of a moment of history that created so many violent flows—the extensions of domestic violence, walls covered with blood in the London suburbs. You're imagining things, don't say these things, I can't bear it when you say these things. Decades beyond the colonial moment of rupture.

This is my meaning of the word *postcolonial*. Write backwards from the dissipated, exploded, violent body. Write the blows backwards until you make a real body. This movement of a body through space, how to reduce the pain of this body, the pain of a static, habitual, repeated movement—impact—is what I mean by healing. Not resolution, but a rewriting in neuromuscular terms of gesture. As the new gesture, which is often much more painful to experience than the habitual gesture to hold, is held, we breathe deeply, to nourish the new structures of fibers and nerve bundles and cells. If we breathe like this long enough, the specific human cultural form can become something else. It produces an intense fire. "Gather the bodies"—Antonin Artaud. But if the bodies belong to Hindus, then this gathering is not a gathering of bones, it is the harvesting of ash. Ash particles drifting in the air. I tasted them when I tipped my father's urn of ashes into the Ganges at Haridwar, vultures whirling above the ghats I stood on. Is prose

the sheer, tilted shelf of ash drifting on the river at the wrong time of day—
too early or too late to take a photograph?

> Leon Golub, interviewing Michal Rovner: "You reduce humans to a
> molecular kind of level and movement. They are in some kind of
> motion and it's a kind of molecular motion. Each individual is
> somehow involved in a kind of mass movement, a process of con-
> tinual migrations, of interruptions and regroupings and then migrat-
> ing once again."
> Michal Rovner: "*Migrating* is a good word."
> Leon Golub: "What is the relationship of the birds to human
> form, if any?"
> Michal Rovner: "They are another example of moving material."

I want to write this moving material, tracking it until it disappears.

—June 17, 2003

CULTURAL ACTIVISM:
WRITING UNDER THE NEW WORLD ORDER

Akilah Oliver, Joanne Kyger,
Anne Waldman, Eleni Sikelianos

ELENI SIKELIANOS [CHAIR]: There have been many events of the imagination that have changed the materials of the world: the velvet revolution in Czechoslovakia, inspired by Beat poetry and the Velvet Underground, in part; the poet Léopold Senghor becoming the first president in a newly liberated Senegal; the composer Míkis Theodorakis, exiled during the Greek junta, whose compositions with texts by poets like Yannis Ritsos and my great-grandfather [Angelos Sikelianos] became nodes of resistance; the Negritude movement in its implicit denunciations of colonialism, fueling political change; Chinese poets involved in Tiananmen Square and other resistances. We recently heard of Allison Hedge Coke presenting a five-page poem before the South Dakota Department of Game, Fish, and Parks, which incited a unanimous vote to acquire the contested Blood Run Burial Grounds and set it aside as a protected historical site.

I was struck once again last week by how many people cited finding a copy of *Howl* in a local hometown bookstore, an event that changed their lives. There is a long tradition of poets and writers active in their communities in all kinds of ways, and there is a long tradition of those poets and writers being persecuted, imprisoned, exiled, and murdered because of those activities. I think of Anna Akhmatova and friends committing her poem "Requiem" to memory. Of Osip Mandelstam saying to his wife, "What are you complaining about? Only in our country is poetry so respected people are even killed because of it," and then being sent to the work camps where he was to die. Of Charles Reznikoff's incredible poems of witness; of Salvadoran revolutionary Roque Dalton, executed May 10, 1975. Francis Ponge's work in resistance; Paul Celan's poetry of anguish; H.D.'s crucial *Trilogy*, which strives to redeem human history despite world wars. Sappho, exiled to Sicily, Lorca's body dumped in a ditch, Mayakovsky gone mad. Duo Duo and Bei Dao exiled, Nigerian Wole Soyinka arrested, Ken Saro-Wiwa hung by the state. Mahmoud Darwish,

Edmond Jabès, Adonis, Nâzim Hikmet, Neruda, Vallejo, Claribel Alegría, Ovid: all exiled. Walter Benjamin fleeing the Nazis; Baraka, Sanders, Waldman, Ginsberg subjected to tax audits; Burroughs, Ginsberg, Henry Miller, and many more subject to obscenity trials. Henry Dumas murdered by the police. Muriel Rukeyser's and Grace Paley's undying political work. Miguel Hernández's poems of starvation. Ralph Ellison's luminous treatise on black/white America.

What becomes clear is, while our writings might not be exclusively political, they can never be exclusively private either. For politics is a contaminant, a virus, as culture and language are viruses and are political. We have all been exposed; we are all susceptible. In these dark times of fanatical wars, diminishing ecological returns, the religious right worming its way into America's heart, it seems more crucial than ever to get busy.

There are many kinds of cultural activism one can take on, as evidenced in the wide array of activities our panelists have been involved in. And I'll introduce them and some of the ways they have been engaged.

Part of national treasure Joanne Kyger's work these past thirty-five years in Bolinas has been in getting to know one place intimately so that, as she said the other day, "No one can pull the wool over your eyes." It is probably hard for most of us to imagine how intimate one can get in a small town with no signs to it: getting involved over the course of those three and a half decades with local politics, editing local papers, observing the intricate phenomena of that place in her phenomenal poetry. As Joanne writes in her "Snapshot for Lew Welch," "look, look, look quickly." Earlier Joanne carried on another kind of cultural service, recording a slice of the goings-on of a poetic era in her *The Japan and India Journals*.

Akilah Oliver is a local force whose work has been manifold as a poet and performer. In the late 1980s she worked as a guest artist with the LAPD— not the LAPD you're probably thinking of, but the Los Angeles Poverty Department, a homeless theater troupe. She was a founding member of the multicultural, multibodied, postfeminist, provocative performance collective the Sacred Naked Nature Girls. With that group and in her book *The She Said Dialogues: Flesh Memory*, Akilah explores the cultural site of the physical and psychic body as threshhold, sacred locale, and battleground. Most recently she has been working on a series in honor of her most beautiful son, Oluchi McDonald, whose passing this fall has also inspired her to take on the infamous state of our health care system.

Our illustrious and sizzling Anne Waldman probably does more than any other living poet I know to keep the world safe for poetry: traveling around the world to give performances, organizing protests, teach-outs, founding schools and presses, spreading the news. Her most recent endeavors include the founding, with Ammiel Alcalay, of the Poetry is News coalition, which has been involved in several teach-ins and teach-outs in New York City, where she also took part in the Poems Not Fit for the White House event at Lincoln Center with Saul Williams, Death Jam, Arthur Miller, Sam Hamill, and others.

JOANNE KYGER: There is something from the British *Manchester Guardian* I have pinned to my politically active refrigerator that I read almost every day. It still holds true, though it's a few months old:

> We can resist the u.s. neither by military nor economic means, but we can resist it diplomatically. The only safe and sensible response to American power is a policy of non-cooperation. Britain and the rest of Europe should impede, at the diplomatic level, all u.s. attempts to act unilaterally. We should launch independent efforts to resolve the Iraq crisis and the Middle East conflict. And we should cross our fingers and hope that a combination of economic mismanagement, gangster capitalism, and excessive military spending will reduce America's power to the extent that it ceases to use the rest of the world as its doormat. Only when the u.s. can accept its role as a nation whose interests must be balanced with those of all other nations can we resume a friendship that was once, if briefly, founded upon the principles of justice.

It helps me to read things like that. It helps me to have a language that articulates inner frustrations and grumblings. This piece I wrote last week on June 16 was from the *San Francisco Chronicle,* which I think is an example of the language that is used that obfuscates and obscures a lot of our clarity of looking at the current world political situation: "While not all the information is true, the important thing is to have a good volume of it. It is the military's job to figure out which data are worth acting on." This was near Fallujah, on Operation Desert Scorpion: "There is a certain element we need to remove [from Iraq] for there to be peace and security." They are not talking about themselves, of course. "Thus the rationale for any opposition to remove"—to where?—"via a hidden, secret place." Called forgetfulness. This is the type of language one sees and hears every day in the media. After removal, silence. There is a lot of media hype and repeated sound bites that go on, and then, to the next thing: a lot of silence on Osama. What *were* the terms of surrender, for example, for Saddam

Hussein? Edward Said said that it was a deal with Russia, also Turkey and Libya. The fact that we hear nothing about that—and then there is Ken Lay, lying still, in case the White House finds his Rolodex card and sacrifices him to reelection. Every day since president George W. Bush was elected in 2001, one approaches the daily news with a "let's see what is the next, awful, dreadful thing the Bush administration has done to wreck the world and its people." They are simply incapable of doing anything right.

I listen every morning, to get through this, to Amy Goodman on *Democracy Now*; I read the local *San Francisco Chronicle* for what it has in terms of editorials; I listen to the BBC when it comes on our local radio station, and it goes on all night. During the "war" that was the only good reporting that went on, TV's CNN being sensationalized and unreal, most of the time a digital camera movie set. I read the *Guardian Weekly*, which covers pieces from English and French newspapers, and also the *New York Times* and the *Washington Post*. This gives a much-needed and better vision of what is happening here in the U.S. Every day I also connect on the computer to commondreams.org, which has articles from various newspaper sources; I read everything by Robert Fisk, Arundhati Roy; I watch and listen to Michael Moore, I listen and read Noam Chomsky.

So I inform myself as much as I can; I live in a small place, so that is what I can do. And I talk with other people. I add my presence to the bulk of people showing their democratic right to oppose policies they believe wrong through demonstration and parade—although at the last parade all I did was, with a friend, make posters under the apple tree in the back yard and take pictures of ourselves, but at least I have that as a recorded opposition. I obsess, I write poems; I have deep and dark dislike for the current people in power, I think they invented evil. I never used to hear about evil in the speech of diplomacy before. I gag when I hear the word *terror*. Then what? You start to get a little poisoned. Is it only rhetoric that has power? I was recently on a retreat in the Zen Mountain Monastery near Woodstock and the only news I was getting was the ticking of my own mind as I tried to sit still. I came out immediately refreshed. Like I had been through a long brainwash of two years, jerked around through terror and hate and weapons of mass destruction and color alerts—a dreadful, paralyzing embarrassment in front of the rest of the world, provided by the action and language of the current administration.

Bob Creeley, who came through Bolinas a few weeks ago, said, reassuringly, "There's a lot of other people out there, like you . . ." That was a heartfelt remark—because I was beginning to feel that a coup had happened, that we could never get enough money and power together to elect a government that cared about its people instead of its golf carts. The actor Peter Coyote recently published a letter he wrote to California Senator Barbara Boxer on voter fraud. He recently narrated a film called *Unprecedented*, which documented the illegal expunging of fifty-four thousand black and overwhelmingly Democratic voters from Florida, which you are all aware of, just before the 2000 presidential election. They interviewed the computer company that did the work, who realized their instructions would produce massive error. Recent elections in Nebraska, Alabama, and Georgia point to an ominous source, this is a quote from Peter Coyote, "corporate-programmed, computer-controlled, modem-capable voting machines recording and tabulating ballots." In other words, elections can be rigged. And the current fifty percent of those boycotting elections will swell to the majority. Privatization of the vote is tantamount to turning over the control of democracy to the corporate sector. Peter Coyote is an old activist involved with the 1960s Diggers, and very skilled in putting together the needs of people or as he would say, tribes, through acting, proclamations, theater, personal persuasion, and when he is worried now, I get worried. Is it possible to drop out anymore, is there any way to get away from this? No, there is not. You can get off the grid a little bit with small amounts of capital. But you have to be really morally responsive and articulate about the massive and heedless wrongs we see perpetuated upon the land and our ocean.

I live in a town of about two thousand and there are nine hundred registered voters; about four hundred voted in the last election we had, which was a rushed school bond due to the cutbacks that are happening in most states from the budget crisis. It lost by fourteen votes. So voting does and can count; elections are won and lost by just a handful of votes. That makes a big difference where I live, where we are concerned [with] whether we are going to have a big sewage treatment plant, or massively dredge the lagoon, or cut down all the eucalyptus trees because they are nonnative; these are the kind of things that people discuss on and on and over again. I've noticed that you can discuss something, and you get it to a point, then everybody seems to have a little bit of amnesia, so when it's voting time you have to do it all over again. It's a constant source of discussion, discussion and language. We have a local paper, it has a circulation of two hundred, and that is really the forum where a lot of this discussion goes on, and it can make a real difference in terms of what the federal government does to our location. The great and passionate writer from India, Arundhati Roy, says, "History has already happened. It is over and done with. All we can do is encourage what we love instead of destroying what we don't." And "Twenty-first-century market capitalism, American style, will implode from within because it is flawed. Too few people usurp too much power."

So, to close, all of the writers I've mentioned and the sources for reading are good, but all of our voices are needed. A practice of articulation is needed. One needs to experience the language of the political situation, the climate of the times. One can start to think, upon listening to the various media, that somehow you *are* the news, that it is real, that it is a part of you. I look around when I'm writing this particular piece; I look around and I'm sitting in a big patch of poison oak, watching a doe and her baby, two hundred yards from the Pacific Ocean. This is where I am physically. But mentally, and globally, via the media of various sorts, I become aware of "the news," but I am not the news. You can see or hear in a blink a statistic, a story, and feel it is a part of you, a common cause. But really what is happening to you is in your local air, and that is what you take care of.

AKILAH OLIVER: Hearing Joanne talk about the practice of articulation nicely brings me to this practice of articulation that is being shown. I'm concerned about graffiti art; I'm concerned about insurgent and visible absent bodies and how they articulate, how they write, how that changes the cultural landscape, how that investigates the cultural landscape, how it challenges it, how graffiti writing specifically is a form of cultural activism. The absent visible body, that is, the people who actually go out and write on walls, are both visible and invisible. In the act of writing they are not seen; what is seen is the result, the product; the bodies themselves are those absent visible bodies. Guerrilla tactics, those bodies strike, they retreat; in striking they change the landscape, they alter the public imagination, i.e., political space. They force a discourse that is outside of the script or outside of how those expected bodies are proscribed to speak. The techniques that inform the style of their writing are part of the discourse, though we don't necessarily see that discourse happening; it is an articulate conversation that the writers themselves, in crews or individually, have between themselves. When it comes out as code, how does it challenge how I see, how I read? How does it challenge the sacred space of advertising? What does it do when it invades the public imagination, whether we choose to read it or not? It still becomes part of our discourse. In trying to ignore it, it becomes a counterdiscourse.

I am calling the graffiti writers the phantom transient body, the phantom transient body that is a specter, again, the seen/not seen, and that is also the moving body, or that creates a nomadic discourse or language, a language that physically, if painted on trains, moves from one location to the other, hitching a ride on a freight; a language that positions itself on billboards, on the sides of walls, any public space that can contain it. Amanda Vitteri is a BA student who wrote an excellent thesis on graffiti art called "The Adjacent Light." I want to quote a bit from her thesis on this sense of the nomadic relationship between graffiti and the public, and the public imagination. She does an excellent job of setting up this idea of nomadic writing.

> Now having a sense of nomadology as an alternative way of looking at and using language, one returns to the contrast between how public space is viewed by the nomad and, similarly, the hip-hop movement, to that of the state, and how this difference may be significant. A basic example for comparing these differing views may be found in the ways in which shared public space will be occupied by the state versus how it would be occupied by the nomad.

In this analysis the nomad, the graffiti writer is also the nomad, that transient phantom body that appears, that strikes, that paints, that creates, that alters the public imagination and alters for convenience what could be called the state; complicating or troubling the position of the graffiti writer as the specter or the phantom, the absent writer or the absent author, is that we know very well that, in fact, this specter, this phantom *is* embodied. There is an author somewhere who actually makes this language. But the inability to locate the body is in itself another form of nomadic or insurgent or guerilla writing, it forces a different kind of articulation. If we can't identify the body, we can't attach an author to the language, how do we enter into discourse with it? How does that reshape how we think about writing as being something that is owned and authored, identifiable?

Though this public or this absent visible body may not be present, that is in the public imagination, it very much is speaking through a subject position. It very much is speaking from specific bodies, specific communities, specific aesthetic conceits, specific intents. In other words, graffiti is not random. The conversation that it incites is not random. My question is, is that a form of cultural activism? Is that a form of insurgency?

Those markets that are graffitied are the very same markets that are unsanctioned to the bodies who insist on appropriating that space, the space that is a hegemonic space for advertising, for political-speak, for other master discourses that this writing is not supposed to disrupt. That it finds itself on these very walls and very buildings, the very frames and structures that structure the political-cultural landscape—how does that disrupt? How does that change or challenge those landscapes? Graffiti in its production uses reiteration, repetition. The same tag name will be seen over and over again. You may see around Boulder "a-holes, assholes, a-holes, assholes" over and over again. What does reiteration, the actual naming—how does that become a cultural act? And the name is not necessarily owned by one located or locatable body. That name might be shared by several authors or taggers or writers who are all sharing Asshole or A-hole, which is the code of their crew. Is that a political statement in itself? Not that it's asshole, it could be anything. But is it a political statement to name on public property, to insert identity, to insert presence on specific public spaces or random public spaces?

If writing is an act of cultural activism, and it is concerned with the mode of naming as an active way of bringing into discourse that that really always has been named, has always possessed agency, has its own aesthetic of references, recognizes itself as both subject and agent, in other words, there is no margin. There are no minorities. That the minority, the marginalized, have always been visible and exist in full bloom, in full communities, but instead of cultural, active insurgency where the "margins" make themselves visible, not just in the margins or in a specific rhetoric, but in a very visible way.

If cultural activism, or if writing as cultural activism, is engaged and concerned with sociopolitical systems, then it is concerned with content as well as meaning. That is, meaning does not exist outside of codes and symbols and signifiers. Meaning is not accessible necessarily in graffiti writing. What does that mean? What is the level of interpretation I am seeing as I glance behind me and the images keep changing? If writing is more than just the level of meaning then it is also the level of signs and the level of code. As writers, when we concern ourselves with form, not just content, or we don't separate form from content, as graffiti writing doesn't, [and] the form in itself is a political forum, the content can contain anything on the level of meaning.

Graffiti is in a constant state of tension: it's illegal, it's vandalism, it distracts, it displaces, it appropriates cultural space. It's punishable by the law; in Boulder you can have your driver's license taken away. Big, bad things happen. In New York the trains that were used as canvases, that traveled from one borough to another all over the city, that were traveling canvasses that articulated speech that left its location and invaded other locations wherever the train went, lots of money was spent by the MTA to make trains that would reject paint, so that you can't paint on the trains.

So I guess to answer some of my own questions, in fact, graffiti does force a discourse with the state, it does force a discourse with the imagination, with the public imagination, or with the government entities that would proscribe who speaks, where, and how. It forces such a reaction that a new technology was developed to shut them up. That's the form, and that's part of the impact that graffiti has.

Is it guerilla warfare in its production? If I say yes, it is, then the choice of how, when, and where to paint is a part of that strategy that graffiti artists come up with. It is a form of direct action; it is a manifestation that upsets and redistributes the agreed-upon systems of public discourse. There is a community discourse, a story behind the artistic production of graffiti writing, that the authors, the graf artists, the writers themselves hold; there are mythologies and histories of individual writers. There is a subcommunity, an internal or hidden community, made entirely of writers, but that is not part of the public discourse. The ego is someplace else. The ego is not necessarily in the representation or in the production, what I see in front of me, but the ego is very much alive and embodied in the writers, in the myths, in the communities that form and inform and articulate what the message is, what the speech is.

As a form of engaged activism, graffiti will always force a response from the state in the same way that the act of writing will force a response. I am not going to say it doesn't matter what you say, just that you write, but it almost doesn't matter what you say anymore, just that you write and how you write and where you place that writing and what discourse that writing upsets or instigates or refashions.

ANNE WALDMAN: This is for Hakim Bey; this is an ongoing manifesto/investigation I'm calling "Is There Anyone Under That Burka," with due respect to women who choose to stay covered. Since the by-now mythic, tragic, biblical walls came tumbling down, I have been using that phrase somewhat euphemistically. For me it is to evoke the salient question of accountability, responsibility of the human realms, the citizen of planet realm's role as legislator, actor, arbiter, investigator, gadfly, seer, vocalizer in this matter and other matters of the polis so urgent upon us. What's really going on? We have all these euphemistic veils. One of the chants we had in a DC or New York rally, I think Alan Gilbert came up with it, was "Cheney is a quakin' in a secret location." What's underneath there? And also as gender commentary, it is perhaps enraging and enraged. And I ask it of myself: where do I as woman, female, position myself in these matters, as an activist, as a Buddhist, even? There is the wonderful sense in Buddhism, from the vow "Dharma gates are endless, I vow to enter every one of them," [of] what that means. That is kind of the basic vow that any space can be entered; you can have any conversation, you work with the enemy, you enter places you are not supposed to go. It's the sense of intervention, that you can work in that space, that risky space. It is not that you are just a gate-crasher or the uninvited thirteenth fairy or witch, ready to pass a spell. But you show up, you are awake, you are armed with your twin instruments of vision and with your third eye, imagination . . . imagination's other place, the interstice between this or that, for or against, that third place is where we can slip in and shed the burka.

So you can describe the charnel ground that was/is Ground Zero. These are just some of the events I've been involved with, actions and writing practices with others. Describe that charnel ground, the stories from the various fronts. I was with Ernesto Cardenal in Italy during the events of fall 2001, so I was able to interview him, and that brought into the mix stories of the situation in Nicaragua, with the Contras, that whole war and the endless karma of that, how still the various official bodies have not acknowledged the participation of the u.s. in criminal acts against that country. There is that kind of investigative writing.

Earlier, I have notes from a trip to North Vietnam, which was made as a kind of pilgrimage during what was the twenty-fifth anniversary of, what they call there, the American War. There are notes from a trip to Berlin, after being there when it was very clearly East and West Berlin, seeing that wall coming down and what it is like now. We have a wonderful former student of this program, the writer Josepha Conrad, who is actually living in that situation in reclaimed neighborhoods. There are recent trips to DC, where one observes SWAT teams within their matrixes, reloading.

So, invoking skillful means; the word in Sanskrit is *upaya*, which actually has a masculine connotation as separate from *prajna*, which is the feminine. The *prajna* is the atmosphere, the container, the womb. The *upaya* I would see as the performance, translation, crosscultural projects, editing, working in collaboration with projects such as I've mentioned. And the project here, a community of writers.

I also ask, in this ongoing discourse, the question of "is there anyone under that burka"—where are the women? I ask it of women writers: What are your boundaries, how far do you want to go in these militarized and demilitarized zones? How far can you go crossing a line? How far will you go? We see these wailing images, day after day, of women mourners. It's so powerful seeing these images of women from Iraq, Afghanistan, Palestine, Israel, women keening at the death of their martyr sons, the death of their children, howling at the skies. And then to evoke again that burka, that cloth, that towel, that sense of death shroud, and also that sense of hiddenness—

having that as an image. Where are we safe in this zone under the burka? How do we come out of it? Is it the place for this almost iconography of the woman as mourner, as weeper, tearing her hair, and how to transmute that? It's real, of course, it's totally real. But is that the only image out there?

What is hidden; what is revealed and why; what is the disguise of language, the guise and guile of language; why do women and others continue to be disempowered in "their" version of reality, "their" version of gender, "their" version of the body politic, "their" version of language? After all these liberations, gay liberation, black liberation, women's liberation—did we really ever have that? It's hard for some people in my generation to look at the work we were doing in the 1960s and really have to think about where we were offtrack or ontrack, or how "they" were working so much harder than we were; maybe we were having too much fun, writing too many poems, editing too many magazines. In any case, it's very disheartening, this lack; there is no remnant of any kind of public intelligentsia discourse in the bigger version of reality, what we would get on a screen or on the air. We do have wonderful Amy Goodman, Saint Amy, every morning; she is extraordinary, and you sometimes wonder why isn't there more of that. There still is this kind of discourse in parts of Europe. I've been fortunate to be privy to some of that in recent travels; it seems that more and more of these conferences and festivals I go to are engaging in political- and cultural-activist discourse and discussion, action and writing, composing statements that are then signed by representatives from all over the world. Writers from all over the world are formulating statements that then can be used by all of us.

But then thinking about how to reclaim that or invent it at this point. Also, compared to many oral cultures that wouldn't feel alive or right without their art and articulation, this need to tell the stories and put up its signs and its handprints on the cave walls, cavort with the animals and imitate their animalized spirit intensity. So what's lacking here? . . . a delight in the discourse.

Other images: the male terrorist disguised in [a] burka on an Israeli bus. The immortalized character in William Burroughs's version of the sinking of the Titanic, dressed as a woman, jumping into the lifeboat. Again, thinking about this image: what's under that burka, what does it signify? The guise of the feminine, cowardliness. I want to reclaim that image of woman as coward and also think about cross-dressing as a kind of ploy. Also another image that the skilled Balinese performer, now in her nineties, [Calon Arang], leading participants to the graveyard at dawn in a rite of passage to look death in the eye. Or María Sabina, whom Jerry Rothenberg invoked last week, the transducer, shaman, crossing a line through language and song in these all-night *veladas* or watches, so that one travels, mentally helped in her case by the *hongos*, the saint children, and flying on the phones and phonemes of language into other states of being . . . and other empathies, really, in that Bodhisattvic sense of return. "The wisdom is language," she says. Also, Arundhati Roy, whom Joanne has invoked, with salt on her tongue, diminutive of body, chiding at the gates.

We are looking at the question of woman as writer, reclamation of a certain kind of power, this idea that you are safe from her, she is under the burka. You still have that gaze. And in some cultures you can be stoned for looking a man in the eye. So how to reclaim the power of that gaze? To exist in one's own eyes. That is the praxis. And in the working of our own writing to exist in *its* eyes, in the eyes of our writing.

The revolutionary potential of everyday life as a writer: that seems to be the order of the day. And tithing our time. How many hours a week are you willing to spend in some kind of intervention or cultural reclamation activity? I know a lot of people here and in our extended community have been very busy on the internet and in lots of ways that one has been able to participate. Hakim Bey quotes the Red Queen's admonition to Alice: "Entertain six impossible ideas before breakfast." That's what I want to put out to you, here: entertain six impossible ideas before breakfast. There is also the idea of ten directions simultaneously, which is another command for the Bodhisattva—you have to manifest in ten directions simultaneously, all the time.

So we may live in this one world, this world of global capital, the world order, the world market, and it has somehow succeeded in being that, it has triumphed. And it tends to transform the world in its image, in its monoculture. Is the burka a holdout against that monoculture? We can shake off the burka or rest comfortably inside it, but isn't it getting hot in there? When you have two choices, always choose the third. Maybe that's the direction for your work. Always choose that third song.

—June 23, 2003

PUT FIRE ON THIS CRAZY WORLD:
AN INTERVIEW WITH NICOLE BROSSARD

Melissa Buzzeo,
Anne Waldman, Soma Feldmar

MELISSA BUZZEO: Your work is so much about a kind of architecture to me; about the making of space, space as the cohering form, a window of fluidity, trembling spaces, dissolving spaces, spaces that attach and detach as they are strained and held in different ways, against different contexts also. So could you talk toward the making of these kinds of structures? Do these spaces enter into each other? What exists inside and outside of positive structure?

NICOLE BROSSARD: That's a wonderful question. I don't know if I have all the answers because yes, indeed *space* is a vital word in my work. When I think of space I think of making the essential space for me to say what matters. It has been particularly important in regard to feminism, to feminist consciousness, to make that space, and widen and widen that space, so you can exist properly in the sense of going along with your values, with your fantasy as well, with your responsibilities, and with your desire and your writing in that space. Does the space change? It is always renewed, certainly, because I think my writing tends to keep opening different spaces for the subject to exist and resist everything that wants to get rid of it. Certainly space has to be related to the word *horizon*. I think that I need absolutely—when I think and when I exist and when I write— I need a horizon, I need the space in front of me to explore—to see in front of me, but mostly to explore. You have used the word *window*. The window is important, but only if it allows me to see the horizon. Without the horizon the window would be much less important. Some people will use as a metaphor the window or the door opening into another world. I keep sticking to the idea of horizon, which has to be related to the fact that I say that I see myself as an explorer in writing, not as a witness of reality. Really it's always to move forward and to move there: *l'inédit* [that which is unpublished]. Maybe it is naive on my part to think that I will always, that I can always, be into the *inédit*. But on the other hand, it might not be that naive, because I believe that everything is always virtual. We have seen this this week when talking about writing; we have been able to see the virtuality of language, all the possibilities of permutations. So you are never finished with anything in regard to language.

MB: So, is the horizon of your own making, or does it exist outside you and your texts?

NB: Well, it's a space that can represent desire, that can represent the future, that can represent a movement. It's essentially an open space. It's amusing because I often say when I am writing a novel that I'm just about to enter a little prison. In poetry, I feel the opening in front of me, because I'm always in the present tense. But when I write a novel, very often I have the impression that I am in a little prison and I will not be able to go out until I am finished with the project. When I say I am in a little prison, it is that the only horizon would be the cover of the novel once it's over. And every day I know I have to go to work in order to complete that novel. As with poetry, it's an eternal present; even though you can work on a poem for one month, six months, you are still in the present tense, you never leave that precious moment of the present tense when you are with the poetry. Maybe it would be different if I was writing some narrative poetry, but I am not.

ANNE WALDMAN: I want to ask about literal space, and some of the differences in the procedures for the novels and the poetry. Because you travel so much, and there are many places invoked in the work, are you grounded in one place when you're writing?

NB: When I write poetry, if I have time by myself, I certainly can write wherever I am. But in order to do that I need to be by myself, and I need to completely relax and enter that second state, that state of writing, of inspiration, that second state of consciousness in fact. As for the novel, I need my dictionaries, I need my books, I need my references. And I need to be focused completely. Of course if I travel, I will take some notes, but it will be only notes, sometimes a few good sentences that can fit into the novel. But most of the time for the novel, I need to be at home or surrounded by books and my dictionaries. For poetry, it's better if I am at home, but at the same time it can be everywhere. There is one very specific place where poetry is related to time and space, which is if I am close to the sea. If I have the sea in front of me this is very inspiring, but it's always a very dangerous place because it's about time, it's about space, it's about death, it's about people passing by, centuries passing by. So it's always a source of inspiration, but on the other hand it's always a difficult source of inspiration, half Zen and half related to the world of language and how we construct our hope and our desire in that world.

SOMA FELDMAR: I'm wondering how the horizon relates to what we had talked about in class, about silence, and the necessary aspect of silence, some aspect of silence to write. The other word that's coming up is *gravity,* that you were using in terms of writing against the gravity; and how the horizon and those aspects interact for you.

NB: I think certainly the horizon is related to silence, because the horizon brings us into a notion of immensity, of vastitude, and as long as we touch these dimensions, even time also, as I was mentioning—when we are in front of the ocean—it brings in a certain humility and a certain silence. Maybe then it's a—the word *game* would not be appropriate—*un jeu* between the horizon, which is really in front of us, and at the same time creating a new space so you can engage into a relation with silence. You let silence make its way through yourself. Silence is also comfortable, but at the same time very uncomfortable because it's silence—language. You need silence to write your poetry, but on the other hand if you fall too much on the side of silence then you say, why bother writing, because then you get into another dimension. I know that writing is definitely about desire; it is not about quietness and silence of the soul. Language is about fighting, is about desiring, is about movement of life. It's a big distraction compared to silence, which definitely brings us to the essential. And that's why yesterday I quoted Adrienne Rich when she said, "Language is not everything."

AW: I was just going to ask about silence in relation to feminism, and also the sense of body in relationship to the *jeu,* the horizon, the body, the space, what you were referring to as within—I wasn't in that part of the class . . .

NB: I've said that it is very strange for a feminist to be talking about silence, because women have been so much silenced. And of course in regard to women, silence seems to be imposed and therefore you have to fight to find the proper words, to make the contrary movement to the one I was talking about, when I meant, to let the silence come in to yourself. So, regarding the voice of women and their writing, what I mentioned was one specific zone of silence, which was related to the inavowable—*l'inavouble*—and most of the time would require a narrative about rape, or about incest, about violence against women. I would have also talked about another zone of silence which would be more related to *l'inexprimable*, the difficulty to express something, which it seems there is no word for, which would be extreme pain or extreme joy. But there are no words for that, so all your life you can keep looking to express ectasy, or to express extreme pain. But mostly regarding women, I think that we have to talk about the zone of silence in regard to *l'inavouable*, which is what women have been forced to live.

MB: I'd like to talk more about feminism and language. Do you think you could explicate the difference between the French term, *écriture de feminine*, and the term I understand is used in Montréal, which is *écriture au feminin*? And what would be also the term that could exist today or that would be possible for women writers? Or is it possible to have a term?

NB: *Écriture feminine* for me seems to be very simple. It would be the writing of a woman expressing herself from the perspective of a woman, from the perspective of her body. Because I think that we write also very much with our body, whether it be a female or male, lesbian or gay body, we do write with a very specific body. So when we say *l'écriture feminine*, it would be a woman telling about the experience of having a female body and living in a patriarchal society and living through that experience and telling us about it. That's one way to witness reality and the female body. *L'écriture au feminin* is something else because I see it as being the product of what the feminist consciousness is questioning, is affirming. So therefore *l'écriture au feminin* would require one to keep moving between genres, using poetry when you need it, using fragments of narrative if needed, writing a text, constructing a structure which is totally unknown but which is a literary structure. So *l'écriture au feminin* for me has been much more challenging and much more stimulating than *l'écriture feminine*, which is O.K., but it's just a way to witness about one obvious reality, there is no research in that writing. Whereas with *l'écriture au feminin*, there is a questioning, a disobedience as well, because of the constant movement among genres. I know that in Québec it's been very important, and I'd say, I don't know if it happens in a lot of literature, but for sure it has changed Québec literature. And it has somehow allowed a lot of men also to join in, in that kind of writing. So, this was mostly between 1974 and 1985. I think that now, because the feminist consciousness is not on the edge, it is not searching anymore for answers; now the writing is being done either in poetry or in novels or in essays. We have gone back to the more traditional space of the different genres. *L'écriture au féminin* was certainly very exciting from the point of view of feminism, of society, but any literary point of view as well. It was really women giving themselves the necessary tools to explore, experience, and talk about what they were and what they wanted to change as well.

MB: What was it about Montréal and the literary community—I know you worked a lot with Erin Mouré and Gail Scott—that allowed for that kind of thing to happen there in particular? It seems like it hasn't happened in many other places at the same time.

NB: In Québec it happened, I think, because we were at the center of two different feminist movements, the movement in the United States and the movement in France, which were totally different. In the United States you would have radical voices, and when I say that I think of the first voices, books published in the 1960s by Kate Millett, Shulamith Firestone, [Theresa Atkinson], Phyllis Chesler, Rita Mae Brown, really exploring and radical texts, which for me certainly were a great source of inspiration. On the other hand, you had also a very pragmatic feminist, which was not the feminist that would stimulate me, but nevertheless it was very important. And on the other hand, in France, you would have feminists, but feminists who would let other ideologies come first, like Marxism, psychoanalysis, and so on, because the weight of history was so strong on their shoulders. In Québec, the weight of history is not that important. The man we've been living with for centuries is a colonized man, so he had no economical, no political power. I often say that the only one who had power was the priest, and somehow the relation with women, the most tense relation that women had was with the priest, because he was the one making the decisions—to say you are going to have another child, you cannot use contraception. So it was a very specific situation, plus the fact that we were questioning, as a people, our identity, we were questioning the language. It was a very turbulent period and a revolutionary period. I often say that Québec feminism and Québec society grew together. Maybe feminism in Québec is forty years old and the nationalist movement might be forty-three—so we grew together, we went to school together, we created the institutions together. In terms of writing, if I think of myself for example, already I was writing in a formalist way, so by working with a feminist consciousness and lesbian emotion, I was able to connect all sorts of literary possibilities. At that time I was also directing a literary magazine, *La Barre du jour,* so it was easy for me to make space for women's voices in that magazine. Even though there were three other men directing the magazine, it was easy for me to say, let's make a special issue on women and the city, for example, or another issue, *le corps, les mots imaginaires,* the body, words, and the imaginary. That was quite new in Québec at that time, so part of our feminism was related to language and to the imaginary, not only to questioning the patriarchal institutions. That created a favorable space for literature and to discuss the patriarchal imagination and so on. I know that I have always tried to surround myself with women that I respect for their work, especially literary work. A little later after, it might have been around 1983, I surrounded myself with five other women who were writers, each of them very different—we were three mothers, three lesbians—so we were a good mixture. Our differences were very stimulating. Gail Scott was in that group, France Théoret, Louky Bersianik, who has written an incredible book called *L'Euguélionne,* which is a huge sort of feminist bible somehow. As for Erin, it's another story. Erin came much later; she was living in Calgary, so she was more related to Canadian feminists. I knew Erin as a writer, then she translated, with Robert Majzels, two of my books. That was a fantastic relationship, because it's wonderful when you have your poetry books translated by other poets. It's good when they are being translated by an official translator, but there's nothing better than to be translated by another poet. So Erin is not much more related to feminism in Québec, in regard to that group, which was called *la théorie un dimanche.* It was called that because we were meeting on Sundays, the first part with a lot of coffee and discussion, and then around two in the afternoon we would set the table and have food and wine. It was very interesting because the conversation would just change a little bit, though it remained all the time very stimulating, clever, and so on, but it would just change a little bit, and that little bit allowed us also to move into some confidences that were very appropriate for our discussion as well.

AW: You touched on it a little bit, but the sense of course in France, the burden of history and this context, and—it would seem that the movement in Québec was more literary, more out of poets and novelists in America, some of those women you mentioned, of course, but one doesn't think of them in this more literary context. So I'm curious about the language, the French in Québec, as related to the kind of theoretical language in France, and then the more, as you said, immediate, or activism, dynamic—in terms of, were there conscious moves in the language itself in which you—not that you formulated, I know some of your feminist critique—but, [were] formulating as a group? Did you feel that only you could understand each other, at some point, maybe in the beginning? Or was there a feeling of reflexivity, that you were actually doing something very different and original? Because in a way seeing it in those three places seems very unique.

NB: You mean with that group. Yes, well, with that particular group there was still enough energy to have that project of writing a book, but we would take our time. But it was already late, it was in the early 1980s, so that was very late for our books to necessarily change anything. But then we would be questioning what has become somehow of feminism, even in the 1980s we could ask that. Madonna was very popular, and we were questioning that kind of image also. So it was very different then, the texts written in the 1970s and the 1960s in the United States and for us in the 1970s. For example when I came to New York in 1973 or '74 with Luce Guilbeault, with whom I have done a film called *Some American Feminists*, we went to New York because there were films being made in Canada, but most of them were made on women as victims, victims living around the city and the suburbs. And we said, we would like to hear women who could explain to us the world in a much more challenging way. And in order to find these women, we had to go outside of Québec and outside of Canada. So we went to New York and interviewed Kate Millett, Betty Friedan, Rita Mae Brown, Margo Jefferson, and so on. But already the feminist movement was losing some of its momentum, even in 1973. As for France, there were the important texts, like by Luce Irigaray, *Speculum* and *Ce sexe qui n'en est pas un*, which were important to us; some texts by Hélène Cixous. But the problem was that Hélène Cixous and Julia Kristeva kept saying that they were not feminists, that they were interested in the feminine. The texts of Cixous were very brilliant, intelligent, sexy, erotic, everything—very challenging. But if we were to talk about feminism and try to find out what is patriarchy, how it works, what it does to us, what we can do to challenge that huge reality, then we would have to rely either on ourselves or on U.S. feminist books. Because I think that women like Phyllis Chesler, like Theresa Atkinson, went very far. You could use those models or not, but certainly they were a great source of inspiration. Kate Millett, Shulamith Firestone— and these women have paid also for these books. When the books came out, society said they were best sellers; but after, they were left alone, they were really punished for having written—

AW: —for transgressing . . .

NB: Absolutely. So I don't know if it answers your question . . .

MB: I wanted to ask about—this in line with your question more about Montréal—but also the city in the abstract. How does the city exist beside the imaginary in your work?

NB: I think that I have always been a very urban person, but the city is related to the patriarchal city, *la cité des hommes,* where the world is being constructed, through activities, through projects, through writing, etcetera. So I've always said that I was a rebellious girl, fighting. I prefer to remain in the city in order to fight patriarchy than to go to an island surrounded by beautiful women and wonderful women, but nevertheless not being able to change anything of what's happening in the city. And that's why I say *je suis une fille rebelle dans la cité.* Because it is in the city that I felt I could better combat patriarchy. When I mean "the city" I mean the written word, of course, because it is with the written word that laws are being made, that the imaginary is being constructed. So in that sense I talked about the city. Then of course I can talk about *my* city, which is Montréal, and of course we know that the cities are not really welcoming women when it's dark, because the cities are dangerous for women. But I've always occupied, in a very easy way, the city. I took that place, I made that place; I wanted to be a free person, a free woman, in the city. And in a certain way I've always felt that the city belonged to me, that I could move easily in it, knowing, of course, that it was not the same for every woman, but in my mind I was part of the city and it belonged to me, and I could intervene in the city.

Also about the city, I have to say that it is related also to my Québecitude, to the fact that I am a Québecois, in the sense that most of the writers of the generation that came before me were born in the country, and for a long time the city in the Québec mentality was a place of sin, of danger and sin. And I believe that it is my generation who first occupied, literarily, the notion of the city: city with lights twenty-four hours a day, city with freedom, city with movement, city with neon, city with *terrasses,* with alcohol of course. But to occupy the city—and then you have also to relate another dimension to the city, which is insisting on our *Americanité,* being American, belonging to the Americas. This was also a very important topic for the Québec imagination. So, you have shifting from the country, from the landscape, from the snow, into a more urban poetry. And related to that, the notion of our *Americanité,* which meant another freedom, freedom of movement all over the continent, and also feeling close to other cultures in the Americas, and constituting a part of our identity, in relation, certainly, to our ancestors from France—but nevertheless we insisted more on our *Americanité* than on our French roots.

So, about the city, in relation with the city, I wrote a novel titled *French Kiss,* which is now being reprinted in the *Blue Books.* French kiss: the notion of the tongue, the notion of language. The novel is the story of one woman in her car traveling through Sherbrooke Street, the longest street in Montréal, coming from the east to the west. It is, like most of my novels, a very weird novel, a very strange novel, which talks about language, about desire, about sexuality as well, and the city. The city is the big star of that novel: the French city—the French kiss, but the French city also. Because after the conquest, Montréal became an English city. And it rebecame a French place only really after the 1960s, after the independentist movement got stronger and stronger.

MB: In your essay in 2001, "The Giant Nature of Words and Silence around Identity," you write about the almost impossible desire to become a complete person in a patriarchal world. I wanted to know: what would real completeness look like in or outside of the city?

NB: But I don't understand, I wanted what—desire?

MB: You were talking about receiving a women's award and talking about the desire of women to become, as a kind of horizon, to become a complete person in a patriarchal world; this would be a desire to reach.

NB: For women to become the subject in a certain way. They are always in the margins, the feminine is always in the margins. For example, interesting philosophers in French, like Derrida, they were very much interested in the feminine, but no one cares about real women. Only feminists seem to be caring about real women. The desire for each woman indeed to become whatever she has to become, to use her own energy, her own power, her own capacities whatever they are, but not to be *reprimée*—repressed—that her own quality, whatever she has, that it's not repressed halfway; so society benefits only from half of women's energy, half of women's creativity. Yes, it's to create that space, not necessarily the horizon, but to create that space. And the feminist movement in some ways has created that space. When women got together, women would legitimize themselves and each other, would say O.K. go there, just do it, be whatever you want, but take a chance on yourself and risk whatever you need to risk, and we will do it also collectively. What has been so powerful also with the feminist movement is not only what it has achieved in transforming laws, in habits and traditions, but to make a space. And it is in that space that women had more chance to become integral, to find their integrity. As soon as that space gets smaller, women have to rely on themselves; they cannot benefit from the energy of that space or of that community. I have done an anthology of women poets in Québec, and you just see it when there is feminism in the air—women poets become audacious, they dare more, they become great lovers and they tell about their love; they are full of energy, and I believe that this energy is being given because of that feminist environment, that feminist space, even though at the beginning of the century it was the suffragettes, but nevertheless that was important. And then after that it seems that the space narrows, and then they either have to be included in a very traditional society, as it happened in Québec, or they are on their own. Then the second wave of feminism came in Québec, and that was incredible, the creativity of women. Many wrote, published, and I think it has transformed what Québec literature looks like today, definitely. Now we talk less and less about feminism, and I see the younger women coming back to a certain solitude, losing some audacity, because that space where you can be audacious and take risks is taken for granted but is not inhabited in a certain way. It's also very interesting to see whom women are addressing in their poetry. At the beginning of the century, women were addressing God, and then they were addressing Men, capital M, then they were addressing, in the feminist period, they were addressing also their lovers, which was quite audacious, and they were addressing also other women, each other, for the first time. Then that period of feminism stopped and they were on their own. It took until the early 1960s for women to be isolated subjects, good poets, but isolated. Everyone was talking about Québec or French Canadian poetry at that time, but people were only thinking about men—even though, I have to say, we have two very important women poets, Anne Hébert and Rina Lasnier, so these women were very respected. It was only in the 1960s that we would see women constructing their own work, *leur oeuvre;* and then feminism came and everything was changed, many women started to talk. And that same energy brought by feminism transformed, I believe, our literature.

Now the young women talk about a certain solitude; they don't seem to be great lovers, because they don't talk much about love. But there is that phenomenon they use very often, the "you," but it's not "you" the *alterité,* it is a reverberated you, a narcissistic you, which is very efficacious in the poem, but it tells of a very strange situation, that the only other is "you," is not a real other, as if there was not a real *alterité* on which you could construct a relation.

AW: A lack of desire?

NB: I think it is not expressed, actually, by the young women poets. Yes. I think there is less and less use of sexuality or eroticism in the texts, presently. I don't know if it's because it is taken for granted, but I guess that [in] every generation, normally, people fall in love and write a lot about that, no matter how it is expressed, no matter how erotic it can be or not be. Among the young women we would find some young, I would say, architects, women that—possibly they are at the beginning of a renewal, I believe, of poetry in Québec. But it will take five, maybe ten years to really see the results of that.

AW: A question about the political power structure in Québec: Perhaps, as you say, these victories are taken for granted, and so you can explore the influence of language for language's sake or some kind of stepping outside dualities of relation? I was curious about the contemporary political strictures, whether you feel any. Is there support for the writing that people do in Québec?

NB: There are not that many people who are politically involved in their writing. But there is one which is particularly interesting, Hélène Monette. Her writing has for its concern the society we live in now in 2004, the new liberalism society, globalization, also the attitude of men, she will question. So altogether she is protesting, in a very intelligent, sometimes humorous tone, this society. If I think of others, their writing is much more focused on themselves as individuals. The writing is good, but if we are trying to understand a pattern of what's going on, it is much more the result of individualism. On the other hand, if we look at it in terms of Québec poetry, Québec literature, we can think of a possible renewal. Because this generation of women who are, let's say, twenty-five, seem to have recognized also the grandmother of feminism; whereas the women who are forty, forty-five, for example, rejected the symbolic mother of feminism, and they were also a generation that was writing in a sort of vacuum in a certain way. It was difficult for them to find themselves, who they were, because the parents, the mothers and the fathers, were so strong and were taking so much space in Québec literature or Québec society, that somehow they evolved; but they didn't have the real tools to evolve, because they could not be worse than we were in our writing when we were evolving. So they could not be scandalous, because we were so scandalous, and so they were in a sort of vacuum. But the younger generation and especially the young women—well, and young men—are more individual, singular, so we are reading the specific poems of this person or that person. But I have to say that now there are new magazines coming out, and I think that if women don't pay attention, the boys will be back. In a very smooth—*ça se fait tout naturellement*—in a smooth way, because they are aware. I think women are very strong in Québec. Every day you hear a radio program or study saying how poor little boys are going to school, they cannot learn anymore because the girls are so good, and so now we should prepare society to help those little boys. We have to be careful because I can see it coming in magazines.

AW: Do you also feel that some experimental conditions continue in these younger writers, if they're working more out of their own self, more isolated?

NB: You are asking me this question now, so I would have to say, I believe that there is a renewal of experimentation in writing, in literature, which is being made by the young men. That's why I say the boys are coming back. But for women, I don't see any kind of relation with experimentation. If you had asked me the question one year ago or two years ago, I would say that in Québec, formalism has been important, if you think of *La Barre du jour*, if you think of my work and others' work, but it has never followed the same continuity as I see in the United States, whether in New York or San Francisco, and as I see it also in Toronto and Calgary and B.C. We have fallen into what we call *la lisibilité*—easily readable texts, more and more narcissistic. I believe that there is a renewal that will come through a sort of formalism or experimentation with language. But that is being done by young men. That's why I say if I think of the magazines of new writing, then women have to be very careful, because they won't be there, or they will be, as in the past, the girlfriend of—. It's being done in a very smooth way. Because I don't think we have given ourselves some institutions that were very effective in the United States and Canada, which were women's studies, gender studies. In Québec yes, there are some courses, but it never really developed. And I believe that women's studies, comparative studies, gay and lesbian studies have been very ineffective in at least offering a possibility of continuity. It is through the institution that somehow you can assume a continuity.

MB: This is sort of related to what you were just talking about, maybe a possible way for these young women writers to go from the individual to the outside, in a way that I see you doing very textually in your work. I've always thought that you've had a kind of swollen language. Perhaps this comes from a slowing down of each word. I'm reminded of the image you projected the other night at your reading of the Lee Miller lips by Man Ray; and I can see your words as lips, open, the before-speech and the after-speech all encountered and held, a loosening gesture opening that offers a kind of arrival that's emptied out to the reader. Words slipping through lips that are not quite together and not quite apart and so addressing in a totally different way. Does this swelling or immediacy in some way make dialogue with others more possible? Even word to word, sentence to sentence within your own texts, but also the reader and other writers or other parts of the city. This kind of pressing or nearness because of a swelling that would go into other places, a reach that comes out of simply being, but located.

NB: I have to tell you that I have a problem with the question, understanding the question. When you use the word *swollen*, what do you mean by that?

MB: When a thing swells—

NB: *Enfler*—But you mean it's reaching—

AW: Not in a pejorative sense.

MB: No, not at all; full and also leaving space, it's almost like it swells and enlarges with so much desire or so much reach but a reach that's a circumference, it's not—that's one thing. Plenitude, but also making a space for emptiness inside this swollenness, which is different from the boys.

NB: Your question is, if you translate it . . .

MB: Does this make dialogue more possible? With your texts, inside, and outside the text.

NB: I hope it does make the dialogue possible. Because I think in my texts, even though some of my sentences have been very radical, I believe that there has always been an open space for dialogue in my texts. Even though sometimes the text, or the sentence, seems to be closed on itself because it's an affirmation and I dare you to receive it, or you can question it, and I've always been open to that. As, for example, the example that I was giving yesterday, when I use a "we" some women say well, maybe it's not all women that would like to be included in that "we." And I say, who cares? It doesn't matter; what's important is to try to say that, and those that want to jump in the "we" and join the "we," jump in, and the others who won't, well it's natural that they might not want to join that collective we, which is always in movement and in transformation.

It is interesting also to see how things are going in the course of the life of a writer, with very powerful moments, like questioning patriarchy for me was an important moment. There were two pages that I was writing on somehow. On one page I was questioning patriarchy, how it's functioning, what it does to women, how it is depriving us of our subjectivity, our energy, our creativity; and the other page was written through the utopian lesbian desire, that beautiful energy. So I was able to move forward because I had two pages on which I was writing, and on which I was exchanging the energy. That was a very important moment in my writing life, and my writing was changing formally. I would say that there were more curves coming into my writing; coming into the writing of a book of poems called *Lovhers*, for example, it's different from *Le Centre Blanc, The White Center*. But I am also the writer of *The White Center*, which is the place of silence, which is the Zen place, I am also that writer, but at the same time I am also the writer, *la fille en combat*, the girl in combat in the city. Both of them are working when I'm writing. And recently, I would have liked to read this text in English but it's not translated yet, it's a ten-page text called *"C'est étrange,"* "It's So Strange." It starts with, "Why would we say that the eyes of someone are frightful, it's so strange." Then there are different situations in the world we live in, whether it's the prostitution of young girls, or the young males in Africa who are killing each other, boys of ten years old who have access to arms, who are forced sometimes to be soldiers. *C'est étrange*, that green rabbit, so relating to art, the genetic rabbit. So the text goes like that; there's talk about the pope, it's a very political text, and I felt absolutely the need to write that text, because there comes a moment where you think, "in what world am I living?" We don't notice the changes because they are everyday, very, very small. Five years later—and they are not only very small but very numerous—so you can not pay attention to all the little changes while the world is changing. Suddenly you wake up and you notice that your relation to time, to space, to your friends, to your own desire has changed. Because we are like civil servants of our life; we take notes all the time, we have to negotiate, to go to the bank, to take care of our health, we have to take care of so many things. The system has changed in such a way that we are spending most of our time trying to organize our life, because of those numerous little changes that are being done by the system. At the same time it is accompanied by the fact that we have absolutely no memory of what was said by a politician two years ago, and people don't think, they just vote for what has been said yesterday or maybe tomorrow morning. So, why am I saying that? I'm saying that, yes, I am still the same writer that wrote *Le Centre Blanc* and *Suite logique*, who wrote *Lovhers* and *Langues obscures*, which is a little book of poems in which I question the use of the "I"—*le chien de l'âme* I called it, the dog of the soul, the "I" being the dog of our soul—and I say because of that kind of narcissism that I have noticed also in poetry, and I know in poetry you cannot do anything without that dog of the soul—he's watching all the time, he's there all the time—but nevertheless you cannot only focus on your little self. It's always the same person who is writing those texts, but I've noticed that this writer has been using more and more frequently the word *silence*, since 1998.

AW: "*C'est étrange*" was written when?

NB: It was written last November, and then I read it at the Voices of America and there was a great response to that text. Every time I've read it people have responded, because there is a need somehow to hear about politics, politics and the way changes are being made, all the changes we are going through.

AW: Those are the scientific, the genetic issues. I read about an adult child dying, and the investment of the family to collect his sperm so that they could propagate the family lineage. They were actually getting the sperm off a corpse, this kind of awful necrophilia. And you feel this more and more, this kind of necrophilia is going on in many, many levels of our reality, culture, existence. It made me suddenly see how out of control, a certain kind of narcissim, I don't know if I want to use the word *ethic*—

NB: We have completely stretched the limits of ethics, the meaning, and usually people do that for power and mostly for profit, profit is the key word. Everything has become a commodity, and you have to wonder what it means to be a human being today, where our humanity has gone. Because this is something we have certainly taken for granted in the last four or five centuries, but it's slipping away. As soon as you—*la société marchande*—where human genes are being manipulated, not only manipulated but also genes are, information at the end is being sold. Then, what is a human being, where are we in that? We are living a sort of *désert noir,* when you are, it's not despair, it's not knowing where to go, you've lost your *points de repère,* your points of reference. And acknowledging, certainly, the fact that we are moving from one civilization into another one, not knowing what's the other one; we know we are moving from humanism into something else, but what is it? And when are we going to say no, we don't want humanity to go further, or are we going to go further, further, further, and become the cyborg? We won't be there to check on that, but certainly we are moving through the cyborg; it's not fun at all.

SF: This has been great. It's bringing up a lot of things for me. I've been really involved in reading and thinking about Robin Blaser's work recently, and some of what you're saying, just because a lot of the words and ideas in my head are in relationship with him, and there's a lot that's coming into context here. In your talking about where we are now as a culture and a civilization and also about things that are going on politically, economically, culturally that are very problematic for human beings in terms of the genes and the manipulation and commodification, and in the silence lecture that you delivered—I'm not sure when you delivered it—in the conference?—you read it to our class—

NB: . . . 1997 or 1998 maybe later . . .

SF: You said [that] within words we earn our humanity. Something that I'm really working on in my own writing is, sort of moved over from Robin Blaser and some of his concepts, how do you write protest poetry and keep it poetry, keep it poetic? And within those words find the humanity in this nowhere place that our culture is? I'm really curious about what your relationship is to the actual, to language as an other, and how that works in the identity and the humanity and the culture.

NB: How you write the political poem, somehow, or your protest, or how you put into poetry your lucidity and the consciousness you have of what's happening politically and economically and culturally. I think that you have to rely on the energy, the specific moment, in order to go [to] a moment of the subject. Like when I wrote that text which has for a title "C'est étrange," it came to a point where I said, I cannot pretend that I'm going just to write my own poetry; I have to get involved in questioning what I feel, what I've read, what I understand of this new world we are moving in. I think it's a good poem, but I think that what might make it a good poem is the fact that I inscribe myself as a subject. In the beginning I also inscribe a philosopher in the text by that question, why would we say that the eyes of someone are frightful.

AW: Not frightening?

NB: *Pourquoi dirons-nous que les yeux de quelqu'un sont effrayants.* Are frightful.

AW: The eyes of someone scare you?

NB: Yes, so I start with a problematic philosophical question. And then I move by how strange it is, and I describe for two or three paragraphs. Then it gets philosophical again, and there is that little sentence which says, "give me a match." And it keeps moving because you don't know if you need the match to see more clearly, or if you need the match to make fire . . . And the text keeps moving with the inscription of philosophical questions, and the "I" is there. The last paragraph is, "You are always saying to me please, get out of your solitude, but I cannot, when I look at the sky I cannot." And so the subject comes back, and I say, no, I cannot. Then the last sentence is, "give me a match, it's so dark in our humanity." So, all the time you don't know if you need the match to put fire on this crazy world, or if you need it simply to see your way.

. . . *courir la lumette,* which would be "to go out and have fun," which was a very old expression from the seventeenth century, but no one would know about that expression.

AW: . . . in Québec . . .

NB: I don't know if that answers your question. A political text somehow, for it to be working, needs, I believe, an inscription, it needs to be thoughtful, and somehow needs the inscription of an "I" which will say, I'm furious, I'm not that neutral, I'm not writing about that because I'm neutral; also an "I" which is not only angry but an "I" which is somehow in despair in front of that political situation. This is where the "I" and the "we" encounter, as I was explaining yesterday; if I say "I," everyone understands "we," and if I say "we," everyone understands "I." I think that would be the answer, maybe, to the question about the political text. When you use your "I," that "I" has a lot of chance to be understood as a "we" with the intensity of the emotion. Of course we are dealing with words, but somehow I strongly believe that we put in the word a certain energy that the reader or the listener really catches. This is the subliminal part of the writing. But I don't think we cannot, we *do* not, avoid the reading of that energy when we are reading a text. I've found that very often people will give prizes to some books because they have read the subliminal energy. You recognize that this is a great book because not only of what is being said, how it is being said, but you recognize someone who's really breathing their life into that text. But this you recognize only in a subliminal way.

SF: I think, for me, that's the difference between language that is purely a political text and poetic language that encompasses a political environment or a political agenda. It's the breathing of the life into it and having the language maintain some of the actual experience, rather than just a propaganda or an in-your-face kind of thing. There's a lot more life involved in it.

NB: You have been perfectly right. [laughter]

SF: Does anybody have anything that's really up there right now?

AW: I was reading this in the middle of the night [*Baroque at Dawn*] and was struck by, in this and especially the novels, the sense of you as an international citizen, with many cultural references. I know it's particular to the story and the characters and so on, but to come upon Linda Ronstadt, you know, her songs . . . Your writing exists in a landscape that beautifully includes these kinds of references that are not cheapening in a way, they're subtle and they become just part of the landscape of a particular setting or atmosphere or scene or encounter. I'm curious about your approach to that kind of material: is it just natural to you, or is there an intentionality in the way you use cultural artifact?

NB: It can be natural, but I think there is a certain intentionality. For example, after I had written *Mauve Desert*, which is my nature—hot place, desert, it connects to the nostalgia and the melancholia of the country-western culture and so on—I wanted to go up on the contrary. So what appears here is the sea, another horizontal field but this time not the desert, the absolute contrary, water, the sea. I'm naturally inclined to go to the south, where it's warm, where it's hot. And in my most recent novel, called *Hier, Yesterday,* I have chosen, just to contradict myself, to go north, to go to a place where I have not been with some of the characters, to go to Stockholm. But it is not right now, because Descartes, the French philosopher, died in Stockholm.

He had been invited by Queen Christina; she wanted him to explain to her about emotions and things like that, so he was invited there, and of course it was cold as hell, and finally he died in Stockholm.

AW: That's referenced in the novel?

NB: Yes. But the story is referred to through a Swedish immigrant living in Saskatoon, in Canada—

SF: And you're going to Norway—

NB: So it's a woman who's always telling women immigrants from Stockholm, from Sweden, and who's always repeating to her daughter that story of Descartes dying in Stockholm. Her daughter likes to play theater in the field, so Descartes becomes one of her characters. There is one of the popes that you will find in Francis Bacon's *Tableaux,* and so on. It's intertwined, cultural elements, which somehow are all coherent in relation to the questions I ask myself. Like in *Baroque at Dawn,* I went to Rimouski; I inscribe very often my Québec; I went to Rimouski, close to the river where they have a program on oceanography. I would get more information, then look for other information. But I always inscribe it in Québec, whether in Montréal, in Rimouski; the last novel is in Québec, because it is a woman novelist coming from Saskatchewan who always comes to Québec city to finish her novels. And she encounters the narrator of the book and so on. So, Québec is inscribed, then we can move to Stockholm, we can even move to Istanbul, we can move to Venice, we keep moving all the time because the culture is like that, it's everywhere. But in *Baroque at Dawn,* the problem will be that one woman writer, one woman artist, and one oceanographer will go on a boat, because the oceanographer wants those two women to produce a book. But the problem is that they'll never really have a chance to look at the sea because they are both put in the library, there's a library on the boat, and then they'll be put to work, because they'll have to watch the reality through virtual reality.

AW: You said that at one point, it'll all be done through virtual reality, all their information . . .

NB: Yes, and in that book I question also the fact that we have seemed to enter an eternal present; we seem to be just *enjambé,* walking over a present tense, then we come back.

AW: Like amnesia.

NB: *Exactement.* The main character says, what's happening, because all my life I have promoted existing in the present tense, because it is a very privileged and precious feeling to exist in the present tense with all of what we are living at full speed, in our mind and in our senses. And she says, well now it's the whole society who seems to be living all the time in the present tense, and it seems to be urging us very much because we don't have any more memory, we don't have any more emotion, we only have sensation. So this, *Baroque at Dawn,* is really a book of starting to understand what was going on but not being able to name it properly. I had to write the novel in order to understand or get closer to those feelings. Sometimes it might seem like science fiction, which was not my intention, but we are living in a certain science fiction. When a grandmother gives birth to her daughter's child, isn't that science fiction? That's one example, there are so many. So to answer your question—

AW: I'm curious also about the title—

NB: *Baroque d'aube.* Well, the word *baroque* is important in the sense also that, well, it goes so fast that maybe five years, ten years ago, we were entering a sort of baroque time, where we put in all details or we are overdoing it, inscribing it, adding a lot of information on our space, on our minds. We are designing with so many little details, that's why I used the word *baroque.* And dawn is an important theme for me also, which you find in *Mauve Desert,* but it's been there all the time. Horizon and dawn. Probably I am a person who keeps hoping no matter what [laughs]. Dawn, which is symbolically full of hope, and the horizon, which could be also a great symbol of hope. Probably even though no matter what I know, no matter what I understand, I still keep hoping till the last minute.

AW: Even looking out the window . . .

MB: I feel like we've been talking so much about kinds of passages, and you are somebody who has made so many passages, in your work and in your life. I wondered if you could talk about how can we speak to or write to, or toward, a passage that is not yet present in ourselves?

SF: What came to mind was your hearing *border* as *passage,* so if you're on one side of the border—I don't know if this is close to what you're talking about—but if you're on one side of the border and there's a passage in the future, but you're not there yet? Is that kind of a passage in yourself that's not there? I'm just trying to understand your question.

MB: There seems to be, it's so much about a language passage, a passage is made out of language. But how do you start it, where you can see it in the future or you feel the desire to make this kind of language passage, which is also like a mouth, when it doesn't exist inside yourself in any way?

NB: If you desire a passage, normally it's in yourself. For example, if you desire a passage that will bring you to your next novel, obviously you have first the intuition that you're about to make a new passage. And gradually that intuition becomes more and more important, and then requires you to organize your mind and prepare, with the desire, because at first it is a desire, something that you don't understand. And because you don't understand it, it will take maybe one year or two; and then you will not be able to escape it, you will proceed and you will start writing that novel—not having all the information of what will happen, but you know that you are ready to put words on the page. And with the first pages that you will be writing, then you will take your swing, your *rélance* to go forward, and by rereading yourself all the time, every day, you will keep moving into the novel. And a certain design will appear, certain images will appear, and I believe strongly that we cannot escape the coherence and the logic of the world we want to create. Everything gets put together by the end of the novel. There is a logic and you cannot escape it. It's good if you think about it, but somehow things will take place, because things that will take place are already somewhere in the structure of your mind. You won't be able to avoid those structures—that is your way of seeing reality, of designing your emotions in a reality, or translating them. And as Anne said, there is a passage that obviously we would like to avoid, which is the passage from life to death. For me there's nothing much to say about that except that sentence that came to my mind in English: "I can push that away like a mother in the future." Sometimes sentences come to me directly in English, even though I'm thinking in French, suddenly, and that one came. Yes, a very strange sentence. So if there are passages that are not in our minds, of course we don't think about them. As soon as they get in our minds, then we will manage to make them come out in language, articulate them in language, and in a book ultimately. What form will it take, poetry or narrative, it is up to you somehow, what you feel will be the most appropriate.

AW: . . . follow the pattern of your energy, psychophysical energy around whatever that project will be . . .

NB: I think so.

AW: You seem to have explored that in so many genres . . .

NB: *Il faut se fait confiance* . . . you have to make yourself confident. We cannot fight all the time and organize all the time the reality. You have to make yourself confident that one project will take its own shape at the proper moment. I do strongly believe in that. Nevertheless you still have to work on yourself, not to get lazy, not to quit, and still be able to enjoy the little moments of life, every moment of life, enjoy simply being alive. I think that our senses do provide us with a lot of pleasure, simply our senses in a very banal way, plus the pleasure that we get from transforming, from imagining, from creative thoughts. In that sense I'm a very optimistic person, because I like being alive. Some people have to learn that, because they've been wounded so very young that it takes almost their whole life to recuperate from that wound. Probably I got *une piqûre* of the positive—I really believe that imagining and creative thoughts give energy to us, and we share that with other people that, in turn, give us more energy. It's a vicious circle, but a good one.

—June 11, 2004

WHAT IS THE LIGHT?: REFLECTIONS ON OTHER WORLDS

Mónica de la Torre

6/21: What makes other worlds be *other*? Who traces the line, and with what certainty? It's all a matter of distance: the farther away you are from the other, the easier it is to see it as a distinct entity.

6/22: I tend to feel rather uncomfortable when I'm around people who show no apparent signs of struggling when articulating a thought. At different moments I've thought that clear diction equals clear ideas, and that consequently, snarled expression is only the result of trying to communicate muddled thoughts. Underlying this belief are two assumptions: that articulating an idea is nothing but translating a thought into words, and that language and thought are synonymous with the enunciation. Yet can the thinking process take place in something other than language? And what about liars, what about intentionally trying to eliminate sharpness in language so as to manipulate people? All roads lead to politics.

6/23: There's a question that Gerardo Deniz asks in the poem "Parable," which I translated into English, that fellow poet/translator Clayton Eshleman felt inspired to answer in a poem of his own: "Do you know, dimwit, what 500 consecutive brutalities end up sounding like?" To me, this poem has always been about high-flown poetry. However, my fellow's response refers to a list of American atrocities, including Abu Ghraib. Problem is, the original question in Spanish is "*¿sabes, imbécil, cómo acaban sonando 500 severidades consecutivas?*" Severities and brutalities are not synonyms, and if not for the sake of sound and colloquialism, I don't remember the logic underlying my choice. "*Severidades*" result from excessive rigor, and "brutalities" from lack of it. It's only in their cruelty that they coincide. It doesn't seem coincidental, however, that from this *terrain vague* stems poetry.

6/24: A night ago I was with friends who were talking about curating an exhibition in Milan a few years ago that included the works of a woman whom they described as a militant Native American artist. One night they were all out at a bar when the artist broke into tears, because no one had ever spoken to her like they had been doing; she was always treated differently, was always *the other*. I asked what they had been talking about that made her cry. Not much, they said, basically what we've been talking about here for the last hour.

6/27: I went to an electronic music performance in which a video of a building at night was all the audience could see, since the musician was behind a screen. Among other things, the piece seemed to be alluding to voyeurism and narrative disclosure. To convey desire and the presence of an elusive world, all that was needed was light in a random series of windows. Inevitable not to ponder the relationship between what was heard and what was seen: if music is the building, what is the light?

6/13: Yesterday's entry reminds me of a poem by Alberto Caeiro, one of Pessoa's alter egos:

> To see the fields and the river
> It isn't enough to open the window.
> To see the trees and the flowers
> It isn't enough not to be blind.
> It is also necessary to have no philosophy.
> With philosophy there are no trees, just ideas.
> There is only each one of us, like a cave.
> There is only a shut window, and the whole world outside,
> And a dream of what could be seen if the window were opened,
> Which is never what is seen when the window is opened.

> —*Fernando Pessoa & Co.*, edited and translated by Richard Zenith

6/29 and 7/3: In the essay "The Task of the Translator," Walter Benjamin sees translation as a site in which the kinship of languages becomes manifest. This kinship doesn't become apparent when a work has not been translated and translation is not meant to be invisible. Despite what booksellers might think, no work in translation is supposed to sound as if it had been written in the target language, for if the presence of the language of the original is obliterated, the purpose of translation is lost. Benjamin argues that all languages aspire to be pure language, and that this can only be glimpsed when languages are set against one another. Reading João Cabrol de Melo

Neto it dawned on me that in Spanish and Portuguese a common metonymy for a living being is that it's made of flesh and bones, as opposed to the English flesh and blood.

6/30: Last night I watched Herzog's *The Enigma of Kaspar Hauser*. At some point Kaspar realizes that he had never dreamt when speechless and in captivity. As if language could be the matter of dreams. The story of Bruno S., the untrained outcast who plays Kaspar, is not that different from the character's one. As a boy his mother had brutalized him so that he developed a speech impediment. She put him in an institution from which he escaped, and after this he kept being imprisoned and consequently fleeing. His brilliant performance earned him the respect he'd never gotten from society. The irony is, he was playing himself.

7/2: I find the following definition of noise in information theory quite provocative. "Noise is any undesirable signal in the transmission of a message," Abraham Moles, *Information Theory and Esthetic Perception*, as quoted in the essay "Rough Music, Futurism, and Postpunk Industrial Noise Bands" by Mary Russo and Daniel Warner in *Audio Culture: Readings in Modern Music*, edited by Christoph Cox and Daniel Warner. Examples: crackling in a radio transmission, a tear in the page of a book. When one begins by saying "*In* the end of the day" and realizes that the right preposition ought to be "at" and then repeats the correct phrase "at the end of the day," one is making noise. To learn to speak a language other than one's own is to make noise. The transition from one world to another is inevitably noisy, unless it is smooth, which would prove that the *other world* isn't really a different one. A phrase I heard the other day, "so-and-so is a riot," has just acquired an entirely different meaning.

7/4: A common notion is that poetry itself is another world. Does the poet enunciate a poem that is part of a discourse that relates to everyday reality? Does he write a text that could be enunciated in a different reality, but that isn't in our own? Is a poem a script for what could be said in another world? If a poem is a bridge, to where does it lead?

7/5: I heard about a collaborative book, entitled *JFK*, by Dennis Adams and the French artist Laurent Malone. The artists walked from Adams's loft in downtown Manhattan to JFK International Airport, and as they did this, they took photographs of their trip, back to back. With each step, one took a picture of something seen ahead, another a photograph of something seen behind. The project brilliantly speaks of traveling, of translation. Literally, though, the gaze is split even if the artists inhabit the same landscape. Somehow this project shuns the possibility of contemplating what's ahead and what's behind at the same time. I believe in this possibility, as in the existence of parallel universes.

7/1: Myths about bilingualism: "Bilinguals have to translate from their weaker to their stronger language." As if one were stronger than the other. In fact, "the majority of bilinguals can think in either of their two languages. They do not, as some monolinguals assume, think in one language only and immediately translate into the other language when necessary." Hence the learning process is parallel, nonhierarchical. Another myth: "Bilingualism is a charming exception, but monolingualism is of course the rule." ("Myths about Bilingualism," on the website http://www.hethelp.no/) Specialists find enough reasons to believe that over half the world's population is bilingual.

7/7: Fernando Pessoa agreed with Whitman's "I contain multitudes," and took this notion so literally that from his imagination he culled nearly sixty-nine personas besides the main four heteronyms with which he penned his body of work. Yet he might have had trouble with the first-person pronoun in this statement, since, predictably, he refused to believe in identity. For him, it was nothing but a construct whose mechanisms could easily serve to undermine its very foundation: that is, if a real identity is built the same way as a fictional one, why deprive oneself of multiplicity?

7/8: Yesterday morning a series of bombs exploded in London's tube and a double-decker bus during rush hour. I prepare myself: the thought of dying unexpectedly in a public place for the next few days or weeks or perhaps even months will intermittently come to me when riding the subway, crossing a bridge or a tunnel . . . Can't help but find it infuriating that this unfortunate event makes me empathize so much with Londoners.

7/14: Infuriating because it is not right that I do not feel equally empathetic when I read the news today. Twenty-seven children died in Baghdad when a car bomb exploded near the place where they had gathered to receive the candy and toys that American soldiers were handing out. I'm horrified, certainly, but can't feel empathy. It's as if they knew that, and here I go again, speaking of *us* and them again.

The OED defines empathy as "the power of mentally identifying with (and so fully comprehending) a person or object of contemplation."

I heard a linguist being interviewed on the radio. He discusses the notion of "language as self-image." The words in a language say as much about a society as the words *not* in it. Think about a language in which personal pronouns are not differentiated.

—July 17, 2005

THE DELUGE:
CONTEMPORARY VIETNAMESE POETRY

Linh Dinh

BEFORE WE START, I'D LIKE TO GIVE YOU A BACKGROUND ON VIET-namese poetry, the context in which this kind of poetry has been written. The thing about Vietnam is that the oral tradition was very much alive until fairly recently. And it's still alive. I would say that most Vietnamese over forty know at least a dozen of these folk poems. I've translated a lot of these folk poems because I'm very drawn to them; they are very earthy, they can be very raunchy, and they deal with everything, all aspects of life. One thing I don't like about the folk poems is the rhythm. It's a popular form and it's passed from mouth to mouth, and its music tends to be fairly predictable, usually six-eight form. This six-eight form is fine in itself, it's just that when you hear it so much it becomes part of how you hear language, and it permeates every kind of writing in Vietnam. So the writers I'm most interested in who are writing poems right now are the ones who slice up this rhythm. Consequently a lot of them are not read by the general public. The public reads these poems and they say they don't sound like poems, because they don't hear that rhythm. Just to give you a taste of that rhythm I'm going to read three folk poems in the original language. You can hear the singsong rhythm.

Gà tơ xào với mướp già.
Vợ hai mươi mốt, chồng đã sáu mươi.
Ra đường, chiều em cười.
Rằng hai ông cháu kết đôi vợ chồng.
Đêm nằm, tưởng cái gối bông,
Giật mình gối phải râu chồng nằm bên.
Sụt sùi tủi phận hôn duyên,
Oán cha, trách mẹ tham tiền bán con.

Young hen stir-fried with old loofah.

Wife twenty-one, husband sixty.
On the streets, women joke, girls giggle.
Granddad, granddaughter, a married pair.
At night, a cotton-stuffed pillow I'm hugging
Turns out to be my bearded husband.
Sniffling, I feel sorry for myself, curse my fate,
Curse my greedy parents who sold their daughter.

Đôi ta như thể con tằm,
Cùng ăm một lá, cùng nằm một nong.

The two of us are like a pair of silkworms,
Eating the same leaves, lying in the same basket.

Văn chữ nghĩa bề bề,
Thần lồn ám ảnh cũng mê mẩn ngời.

Inundated with books, he is
Still haunted by the vagina.

That sense of humor—actually they go farther than what you find in the official poetry. There are many examples of that. These are things people tell each other as they're drinking, talking, joking around.

So, to bring things to the present: Tran Vang Sao, Khe Iem, Nguyễn Quốc Chánh, Lynh Bacardi, Miên Dáng, and Phan Nhiên Hạo are the poets we're going to get a glimpse of today. Most matured at the end of the War, most of them have published since the end of the War. The social context they came out of is the aftermath of the War.

The oldest poet is Tran Vang Sao, and I'm going to talk a little bit about him because the trajectory of his life is interesting. That's not his real name. Vang Sao means "yellow star." He was a city person and he joined the National Liberation Front and went to the jungles to fight. So he changed his name to Yellow Star, meaning the communist, the North Vietnamese flag at the time, which is now the national flag. He got injured and was removed to the north, and I think at some point he became so disillusioned that he started writing poems that were fairly critical, although he kept his name. The government has given him a really hard time; they raided his house and took his poems away.

I'm going to read one poem by him. In the poem he's talking about hunger, and in this sense it's literal, but there's a sense of humor to it too.

Actually, before I start the poem I'm going to quote from two other poets talking about hunger in postwar Vietnam. Phan Nhiên Hạo, whom you'll meet later, went to univeristy in the 1980s. He had this to say: "I was hungry all the time. All the students living in the dormitories were really walking skeletons. Most of the time you could think of nothing else but food."

And Nguyen Quốc Chánh had this to say: "Before 1975 our family grew sugar cane. Then my father was intimidated into giving much of his land to the government. They would have taken it away anyway. It didn't take long for the entire country to become destitute. We would eat this yellow sorghum imported from India, which tasted really rubbery, for months at a time. And once a week we had to hear some idiot stuttering and lisping his way through a lecture about the glories of Marxism."

This kind of bitterness informs much of the new poetry, the poetry that I find most interesting.

This is Tran Vang Sao and the poem is called "I Get to Eat Meat":

I let myself imagine a day when I get to eat meat
I laugh and talk cheerfully
a piece of meat with a hunk of fat
                    slips down my throat
my two eyes are wide open
I squat on the floor and
            a plate with lots of meat in front of my face
long stalks of green onion floating
                    in grease
hand holding chopsticks mouth chewing
the sun blazing through the leaves
an afternoon in summer with no wind

I wake up and scratch my neck
the river water is salty
I go to the end of the alley to smoke a cigarette
then say out loud to myself
it will thunderstorm this evening bringing cool weather

The next poet is Khe Iem. He is of Tran Vang Sao's generation, born in

1946. He escaped Vietnam by boat and stayed in a Malaysian refugee camp for a year before coming to the United States. In the United States he lived in Los Angeles and he was a Domino's Pizza deliveryman. I'm giving you these details because this is how—I love these guys because of the fact that they go on, in spite of everything. Anyway, he managed to start a poetry journal that up till two years ago he was still running. Khe Iem is interesting to me also because he started out such an interesting poet and editor, and somewhere along the way I think he just went wrong because he got really involved with the New Formalists. He became infected with this sort of American disease; it's not something that was happening in Vietnam. He became so militant about the New Formalism that he started translating a bunch of these people, the least interesting American poetry, and lecturing people about it constantly. So at some point I thought, wow, this is very dangerous, because he is in charge of the poetry magazine most Vietnamese poets were reading, and the ones in Vietnam didn't know what was really happening here. So for this guy to keep going on about the New Formalist movement sort of distorted what was happening here. And people inside Vietnam would think that's really what's happenin' here, maybe that's the only thing happening here. So at one point I came out and in an interview I just said, listen, this is nonsense. Because so much is happening, there are so many strains here, and I'm sorry but I don't know why Khe Iem is doing this. Since then we've stopped talking, he got so angry with me. I think he's lost his mind. He has a New Formalist website, in Vietnamese of course, with all these New Formalist poems, really hectoring people to write New Formalist poems. On the website there's also an FAQ, with questions like "Why are there people who attack New Formalism?" And his answer will be something like, "Well, whenever there's something really radical, people react. These people are going to be left behind and they'll regret it."

So I'm going to read the poem from him that I really love, this is maybe from the mid-1980s:

Doubt

tears
sun rise
(sun-risen tears)

atmospheric song
wind corrupting
bitter memories

haggling with century about wretchedness
inverted voice, crying buds
tender O familiar heart out in plain
amid thatched roof rain and fire, moon kiss

past washed
to hear hair mist whispering beyond lip is river
flowing abandoned

sitting wild beast
hung dried ragged
nibbling on verdict issuing from source

From Khe Iem we'll move on to Nguyễn Quốc Chánh, who is still in
Vietnam. When I returned to Vietnam in '99, most of the poets I met were
not that interesting because they were sort of intimidated from writing anything that might get them in trouble. Chánh stood out because of his fear-
lessness. He would say anything in any context. You'd find some people
would be very guarded in any kind of public situation, including a café,
they wouldn't say certain things, but Chánh was just constantly talking.
Even his friends were worried about him, saying maybe you shouldn't be
so open, you don't know who's at the table.

In the early 1990s there was a brief moment when people were able to
publish more risqué material, and Chánh's first book of poems came out of
that time. It was greeted with a lot of hostility in the newspapers, which
are government controlled. The book is called *Night of the Rising Sun,* and one
review called Chánh's book "a cemetery of the spirit and of the body.
There's nothing left for a person to look for or to lean on. This book can
only lead man toward madness, irresponsibility, obliviousness toward the
present, humans and objects. The lofty and the abject, the real and the fake,
right and wrong, virtues and cruelties are here mixed together in a slimy,
disgusting blob." Another review stated that this writer will end up burnt
by the fire that he is messing with.

This is from a recent interview in which Chánh talks about himself:
"I was born in a dull place, Bạc Liêu, into a dull family, went to dull
schools not worth mentioning, with dull teachers not worth mentioning.
And now, although I live in the brilliant and chaotic city, Saigon, I have
no alternative but to become a dull person. And I have to take antistress
pills every day."

Low Pressure System

The thumb stops breathing.
There is a sound of a dropped glass.
Needles piercing the ear.

I see water gushing from hollows in the wall.
(The house's artery is broken.)

Water is drowning the word mouth.
A character cannot escape the death of a wet book.
Our character is tattooed: Small. Weak. Wicked. Shell.

Words stepping on each other trying to remove themselves from literariness.
They float blue on the water.
Individual corpses sink to compete with bricks and shards of glass.

The remaining fingers have headaches and runny noses.
Memory stands then sits stringing pieces of intestines around a hole.

I hear cries of a newborn.
A fish crawls out from a bloody hollow.
The woman closes her thighs and a corpse is covered up.

A laugh crawls in wiggly lines across a cheek.
Look into the thumb.
Sperms reborn in the flow of sap animating the wild grass and flowers.

After the bee season the flowers and grass are plowed up shredded and
     burnt.
The grass regrows and the sperms open their eyes.
(Even if the land is mortgaged joint ventured or sold to another.)

The hunt is a thousand years old.
A distance only blind eyes can perceive.
Its concentrated flavor cannot be tasted by anyone besides the moss-covered
tongues of turtles.

I hear wild laughs from a circus mixed with the rhythmic prayer for
     the release of

the souls of many female nuns.
(They are performing a circus for another world?)

A low-pressure system on the hill seeps into the body.
Termites dig up dirt inside bones.
Nests grow from the ground to resemble artistic graves.

I carry a cemetery inside my body.
A fist missing a finger.

I'm scheduled to give a reading with Chánh and I'm still crossing my fingers that they will let him out. Vietnam is such a corrupt place that with the proper amount of money, you can just about do anything. So if you want a passport to leave the country, you've got to know the right people to pay. The last e-mail I got from him said everything is still on schedule. It will be his first trip to the West and it will do him a lot of good.

The next poet is sort of influenced by Chánh, but she has her own thing going. Lynh Bacardi—that's obviously not her real name. She was born in eighty-one, lives in Saigon, and works as a typist and a translator of children's literature. She is a fifth-grade dropout. She has worked as a vendor of cakes and lottery tickets. I first encountered her poems online, and I was amazed by the energy, the weirdness of these poems. About a month ago she had this to say in an interview. It echoes what Chánh was saying, and this is a general sentiment: "I studied many things I did not want to study, memorized many things I did not want to memorize; did not get to study things I wanted to know more about. I have not been out of the country. Walking in circles, I look down then up. Thanks to the internet, the mouth of the well has become wider although the bottom is still narrow."

There's a Vietnamese proverb about a frog sitting on the bottom of a well who thinks that's the whole universe. She's referring to that.

This poem is called "Shrink & Stretch":

today waking up speaking like an opportunistic death rim. I cry buzzingly a scrawny milk cow. missing the last grasping chance. mother sits counting money inside a jar brimming with black water. a hot line for polluted spirits. outside all living things are in mourning clothes and trampling on each other to reach heaven. I uncouth a building built with virginal blood. feigning an orgasmic moan. sunlight high above weeping inundating the streets. men who become bloodless when overburdened. the obese rain flows hotly.

I'm pregnant with coins reeking a burning smell. a mother selling her flow keeping the cultural flow for her brood. needle marks wilting along with each vein. numbly I chew the cheery invoice. the ulcerated mouth teaches civilization to its children. I give birth to well-off swindlers. a tiny body running after a beer can recklessly tilting. drooling at leftover food inside the eyes. bad nerves jamming the buddha's miracles. a shivering fairy guffawing up a pack of lice. today all ideas upset the stomach. a look loaded with the code of one who defecates often. hey little girl laughing savagely a prurient pain. let's wear the voice of the opportunistic death rim. I carry your shadow into a coffin bought with a bitter tongue. headstrong words trading blows with each other. stepping on red coals I walk spellbound. budding pubic hairs dying of old age. at midnight laughs and cries grind down the city. the malnourished timid whirlwind. I sold my ass seven times the first time. pay back with a bout of lovemaking without joy. woke up the next morning with a blood-smeared death rim. virginal blood more precious than living blood. a mother laughing baring her teeth inside a jar brimming with black water. I drape my skirt over lumpy heads encrusted with woven spider shit. now my male member festers.

We have two more poets. The next one is Miên Dáng. She was born in Dà Nẵng in 1974, came to the U.S. in 1989, and now lives in Tampa, where she works as a manicurist. It's interesting how these people are spread out around the world but they stay together through the internet and their love of poetry. Miên Dáng is also partially deaf. She studies with monks, two Burmese monks, but her poems seem, I don't know, not very serene. That's what I like about her, the fact that she has a different side of her.

This first one is called "Laugh":

Abandon yourself
The window bar decanters the slanting sunlight
Shape of a creature that knows how to sulk
Urgent howls of crazy love talks
Curse in the filthiest language
Let's try to kiss each other
I borrow the soft parts of the lips
To reconstruct a ravaged face
Rotating upward the pupils
Roots like tangled lightning elongate

Reddened the cruel dawn
Doddering love's black magic
Killer pupils
Doubts then modesty
On pale pink cheeks
The skin has become musty here
In panic the river licks the bank
Joy erupts
And who are you?
I save for you grief on round breasts
How can I wait?
And what would I be?
What's repulsive hidden deep inside the uterus
I want to pierce shame into you
And what would we be?
I want to see you laugh
A trembling puppet bursting
A hand on shrunken testicles
Opening wide the flat chest
Flash frozen the self-absorbed lonely substance
To escape raggedness by stripping naked
Tickle and laugh
Laugh!

One more by Miên Dáng, "Can't Speak Yet":

Extending the color of sunshine,
He touches the blue shadow of the sky.
The sharp tip of pregnancy
Seduces
A flipped jaw.
Existence drifts completely the soul,
Frothing an ape dream.
Carousing.
The subconscious warps the other side of the face.
Cruelty crowds passion into a corner,
Rams the body as the flame rises.
A short nerve
Softens the water.
Calamity ridicules:

Let's pierce to pieces the illusion!
Appearance bares its back whispering.
The hand not black enough for the heart of night.
Cannot speak now.
Striving for meaning at the end,
In a cattle state,
Stretched out the wet eye . . .

I'd been translating so many of these poets, and at one point I realized I should try to compile them into proper books so they could each have their own space, so they're not all mixed up with each other. The first poet I managed to do that with is Phan Nhiên Hạo, the last poet today. The book is coming out probably in November, it's called *Night Fish and Charlie Parker.* Hạo was born in 1967. He immigrated to the United States in 1991 and now lives in Los Angeles, where he works as a librarian at UCLA. Because he lives here and got a degree from UCLA, his influences are different than the others you've heard so far. Even in Vietnam he had a head start on exposure to Western literature. From an interview, he explains:

It was very hard to find good books in Vietnam after 1975. Fortunately I had an uncle who managed to keep a very good library. I grew up reading a lot of translated literature, especially French and later on Russian. I enjoyed the French existentialists very much, a couple in particular. At a very deep level, existentialism has influenced the way I look at life. I quickly realized however that its writing style was not what I wanted to follow. Existentialism showed me the beauty of man's loneliness and made me rely on my own inner strength. This strong belief in the essential isolation of man has helped me cope with the isolated life of an immigrant in the U.S. Without this foundation I must have already killed myself several times.

And then he went on about his exposure to American literature:

Being educated in Vietnam, where the highly cultivated literature of the French had been the model for so long, it was difficult for me to accept at first the 'no ideas but in things' plain speech writing style of much of American literature. Over the years however I have developed a passion for this low-key literature. I feel much more healthy as a writer now, although the isolation of life in this country is unbearable at times.

It's funny, he attributes his isolation to being an immigrant, but I think that's the natural state of everyone, of most people here, at least the ones I know.

Here are three poems of Phan Nhiên Hạo:

Night's Dawn

Those are the invited secrets
in the middle of the night toward dawn
you tap the face of the clock with a hammer
the ceiling fan rotates beneath the moon
breathing in the smells of the city the way it was

There is another way to step out of
the blinding roars
of the poisonous night
but you rejected it
the ceiling fan and the flowers shed their petals
dawn repeats:
homicide
and a child eaten by dogs

There is another way to stop
halfway between two asphyxiations
but still you swim toward the sea
toward the secrets of the kelp.

Night, Fish, and Charlie Parker

Night negotiating a plastic spoon
on a table littered with fish bones
all the illusions have been picked clean
Charlie Parker, a piece of bread not yet moldy
a black ocean and black notes
a few million years, a few small changes
at the bend in the road on the horizon
grows a strong type of tree
the black cat is in labor
gives birth to a few blue eggs.

Night in the South

A ringing phone on the carpet
a child is calling from the womb
night in the South
women open their doors to flirt
O spittle
the kind of germs belonging to wicked souls
returning to a cultured city
only to see ducks and chickens pecking on graves
shards of stars
encrusted in the deep dark horizon
the blue ocean and the monkish jellyfish
slackers are lining up
to buy cups of ice cream and a dripping night in the South
I walk on my hands
I drive seventy miles on the side of a mountain
the precipice is below
O the women, the jellyfish and the rosy cheeks
standing on the sidewalk with legs festively spread
all I have is jazz jazz jazz

and lots of gasoline in my bloody abyss.

AUDIENCE MEMBER: It seems like a connecting factor for a lot of these poets is the internet and a love of poetry. Do you know of any sort of community, whether online or in print, that reaches into other Southeast Asian languages or immigrant populations? Particularly countries like the Philippines that have had a lot of American influence also, where English is a language that's commonly used. Are there any sort of dialects that you know of?

LINH DINH: I don't know. I can talk more about the Vietnamese websites, the particulars of these websites. One website updates every day, so the energy is always there. People look forward to reading it. I read it in the morning, because they update it in the morning, but in Vietnam that would be at night. So people would turn to it like a newspaper. Every day there are new translations and new poetry. I don't know of any American website that does that. I think it's very exciting. The problem is how to maintain quality; usually you have three or four new pieces a day, so some days it's not so great. Actually I think it influences how people are writing too, because they can respond to each other's poems and see it online—instead of your typical journal where you wait six months or a year to see it.

AUDIENCE MEMBER: I was struck by the, for lack of a better term, image-based, almost surrealist threads that ran through a lot of the poems that you read. I was wondering if you could talk about influences in, or for, Vietnamese poetry to get to that point.

LD: I'm glad you asked that, because it's very important to point that out—why there's so much surrealism. First off, they were allowed to be translated. The surrealists were Communists, so there was no problem translating them, although their poetics has nothing to do with Socialist realism—that was more the official line. So their books were available. Another book that was very influential was *One Hundred Years of Solitude,* because Márquez was also a Communist. So the censors would say, this guy's a Communist so this is O.K. Really the work is not Communist writing. Also, surrealism is a way to talk indirectly and not get in trouble. Really these censors are not that bright. They read stuff like this and don't know what the hell's going on. But there's a danger in that too—you can get too convoluted and too weird. I think the government also encourages a kind of soft surrealism. Some of the official poets also write in a kind of vaguely surrealist style without any political or deeper connotations. One guy I like to ridicule all the time always brings ghosts into his poems, so he gives it a "mystical" kind of feel, but it's really nonsense. In one poem the ghost could be a cow—all these things are talking and floating around . . . And he's the official poet, or one of them.

MICHAEL DAVIDSON: The previous questioner asked the question I wanted to ask, which is something about predecessors. You started out by talking about this folk tradition, but I'm wondering about a classical tradition which all of the writers would be directly responding to.

LD: The so-called national poem is thirty-four hundred lines or something; it's the story of a prostitute. A lot of people have problems with this poem because of its values, like sacrifice and resignation, so this poem has been debated on forever. But that's the poem that is always held up as the Vietnamese masterpiece. Another problem I have with it is that its plot was borrowed from a Chinese text. I think people keep returning to this poem because of its language, it's fresh. It was written in 1817, but the Vietnamese in it is very rich and very beautiful. So the language is great, the story is not so great—it's a woman who sacrificed herself to save her father. A lot of people have pointed out—why do we want to have a poem about a prostitute be our national poem? The Vietnamese language now is written in the alphabet; this poem is written in the native script, which is no longer in use; hardly anyone knows it anymore. Another poet who has a lot of influence is Ho Xuân Hu'o'ng. She wrote a lot of raunchy poems. John Balaban translates some of these poems. I have a problem with John's versions because on the cover he has a bare-breasted woman next to a gong or something, and I think, *come on*. But it's more complex than that; you could build her up as a woman ahead of her time—she was early nineteenth century, late eighteenth century—you could build her up as a bold, sexually aggressive woman. But most of those poems were probably not written by her. I would say none of them were written by her, because the only book that was compiled of this body of poetry, the only surviving book, is a century later. During that gap so many texts . . . One book might have seventy poems, another book might have fifty, another book might have forty, and there are all these arguments about which ones are authentic. I think they belong more properly to the folk tradition. So we should talk about the Ho Xuân Hu'o'ng tradition, rather than—what I'm trying to say is, it's fine that the peasants liked the idea of a sexually aggressive and dirty-talking woman, it's great. The folk poems are like that anyway. But many of these poems are probably written by men too, and what do you make of that?

These are held up as the two—Truyen Kieu is the first one and then Ho Xuân Hu'o'ng—they are like the Whitman and the Dickinson of Vietnam.

AUDIENCE MEMBER: I was wondering about the relationship between Vietnamese culture and sexuality—a lot of the poems are dealing pretty intensely with sexuality. I was wondering if it was due possibly to some sexual repression in the past or whether it's a pretty free culture in terms of sexual expression?

LD: I think with the material on the web, since there are no censors, it's gotten to be very aggressively sexual, by men and by women. One new group of poets, these guys are in their midtwenties, call themselves M'o Miệng, which means "open mouth." They are getting a lot of attention now, they are the most sexual people; I think they're influenced by rap music. When I first encountered the Open Mouth guys I liked it, because I liked the defiance in their work. In Vietnam people live with their parents for too long, because of economics or tradition; some people never leave their parents. The parents are such an oppressive presence in the Vietnamese psyche. So when I encountered these very young guys in their early twenties writing very aggressively, writing kind of belligerent poems, I applauded. I know these kids. Then at a certain point I realized something is not quite right; the rap thing and the misogyny in there is something I cringe at. But what can I do? I almost regret some of the statements I've made in interviews endorsing these people. But I endorse also the female writers who write very aggressively. I think it's a trend right now. They're basically punks, these kids are punks, male and female. There's room for that for now. It's good because it's overthrowing the elders, like saying, fuck you, get out of my face.

AUDIENCE MEMBER: You might have already touched on this. Because of the restricting government in the past in Vietnam, I'm not sure about the situation today—when poets would immigrate to other countries, did you notice a difference in their expression of poetry? And were there new restrictions in being an immigrant in a new country?

LD: You definitely see changes. For example, in syntax. Phạm Thị Hoài is a novelist living in Berlin, and you can see her sentence structure is not how things used to be. Her German is influencing her Vietnamese. I find that very exciting. Definitely. And her reading—I can see Arno Schmidt in her writing. If she wasn't in Germany that would not have happened. We are all reinjecting into the Vietnamese language what we take from the host culture, and that's very healthy.

Maybe some of the issues that are affecting me here, I'm also dragging back. My experience as a minority person here is also going back into my work. Maybe that's a form of restriction? The effects of living in the host culture and the new problems you encounter.

AUDIENCE MEMBER: Are there any debates concerning language between the people who are not in Vietnam and the writers still working in Vietnam? For instance with other languages, especially Spanish, writers who are abroad are sometimes criticized by writers who stay in Mexico, because they think the language has been to some degree corrupted and they're not speaking "pure" Spanish anymore and not writing it, and they're maybe too open to outside influences. So I was wondering if there was any kind of debate between the writers in Vietnam and the writers abroad.

LD: What I find most interesting is some of the most corrupted writers are in Vietnam. They are more enthralled by English, so they tend to throw in

English more. When I write in Vietnamese I never use English, so I'm purer than them. They'll throw in English words all over the place, some of them that is, not all of them, because they think it's cool. I don't need to do that. I think there's also a tension; the ones in Vietnam look at the ones from the outside with a kind of—most of us get along pretty well, but I'm sure some of them probably resent the fact that we are outside, for many reasons. They would like to dismiss us as not relevant. Some of them who come here are treated very well by the Vietnamese community, and then they go back and they never mention who they met, they just dismiss us, they block us out. I think some of that is pure cowardice, because they don't want to get in trouble with the government. There are a number of people who don't acknowledge Vietnamese writing overseas at all, and I think most of that has to do with politics, but some of that could be just personal. For whatever reason they don't want to acknowledge us. I was talking to a man recently from Hanoi who said some people told him that what I write is not even poetry, because it sounds so flat. Maybe that's the critique: my Vietnamese sounds so odd to some of these people's ears. Isn't that the whole purpose of it? We've got the pure stuff, let's mix it up, let's pollute it up.

—July 20, 2005

LOVE AND POLITICS

Judith Malina and Hanon Reznikov

HANON REZNIKOV: JUDITH LIKES ME TO TALK FIRST [LAUGHS]. I'VE only been at this for thirty-odd years; I met The Living Theatre in 1968 and started working with them soon after. Judith had begun seventeen years before that; in 1951, the first productions of The Living Theatre opened in New York, though Judith and Julian Beck had been preparing them for years. They had hoped to open in 1949 in a space on Wooster Street in Manhattan, but it was closed down as a front for prostitution before they could even open. The authorities just couldn't believe that anybody could actually be opening a theater space in that neighborhood, which later became SoHo. It's a gargantuan enterprise, opening a new theater in the city. There's a poem I wrote about it that we'd like to read to you to begin. It's called "Why The Living Theatre is Returning to New York":

because the people in charge haven't got a clue
because we're all tired of waiting
because we deserve better
because we're all fallen angels and we're on our way home
because it's all so boring
because it's too easy for us in Europe
because this is where we grew up
because we want to recapture New York from the Americans
because sex is coming back
because there isn't a lot of time left
because we need new peace strategies to foil the bloodthirsty bastards
because it's cold outside
because the winds are blowing hard
because the earth is about to shake off the human species like a
    bad cold
because civilization is still a new idea
because Americans believe that anything is possible

because New York is it, man
because of the estuary
because of the little paper cup of coleslaw they serve with the
    sandwich
because of al sharpton
because of george bush
because we are still vulnerable
because regime change begins at home
because the europeans think they know it all, anyway
because no man is an island, but Manhattan is
because the west side rules
because of slaughter on tenth avenue
because we have to
because all the secrets are out
because we feel guilty about being away so much of the time
because nobody should be president
because some knuckleheads are giving anarchists a bad name again
because it's expensive, darling
because we want to make it so hot
because midtown needs a not-so-temporary autonomous zone
because of the death penalty
because millions ride unchallenged underground
because we've been around so long that no one remembers
because the revolution isn't a movie that was shown in 1968
because the beautiful nonviolent anarchist revolution needs a new
    york chapter
because the i.w.w. needs a new meeting place
because the poets always have a home with us
because for us, it's all music
because the whole thing is a dance
because political isn't enough
because the spiritual is so difficult
because as far as anybody can tell, god is absent
because satan is lurking in every invoice
because the angels are tired of los angeles
because there's no time like the present
because of Hiroshima, still
because my grandparents were killed by a hit-and-run driver in
    Coney Island
because people think nothing really matters

because the suspense is driving us crazy
because it's a no-win situation
because god expects it of us
because we have sinned
because repentance isn't enough
because we know thousands of wonderful people in New York
     and three in Rocchetta Ligure
because the Morgan Library is closed until 2006
because it's hard to really care about the movies
because of magnetic forces
because psychology is not what it's really about
because Marx was right about a lot of things
because if we didn't exist, they'd have to invent us
because otherwise . . .
because Brooklyn was annexed against its will
because Staten Island is another matter
because the World Trade Center is gone
because we're all suspects
because Allen's dead, and Jackson, too
because Anne Waldman lives, and Ferlinghetti
because the Statue of Liberty is still French
because America is lying to itself again
because not even a three-party system will save us
because of the real-estate interests
because of the improvements
because we are making a life for ourselves
because women have it almost figured out
because gay is queer like us
because no one knows where to put the garbage
because the cats are talking to the dogs
because in heaven they teach you to gamble
because there is no straight path
because metaphors can be lethal
because experiment is difficult and decision dangerous
because of the protection racket
because we have a home in the genome
because we're all dying to make a living
because the score is tied
because the end is unknown
because of all the human energy

because Emma Goldman left debts
because of the movement in the streets
because the UN replaced a slaughterhouse
because of the chatter
because we're in trouble
we're back

JUDITH MALINA: My first thought is that I really can't tell you the story of fifty years of work in an hour, that's not possible. So much has happened to us. We've been very lucky and had very rich, full experiences, some magnificent, some miserable, but over a wide range of years a wide range of experiences that I'd like to tell you about. And I will touch on some of the things that occur to me at the moment. I think it might be best to speak first about some of the origins, since most of us here are here because we are in some sort of formation, to become something, to move toward something. So I wanted to talk about some of the origins of The Living Theatre.

It's such a long story; I was destined for my fate. By "destined" I don't mean anything spooky, I mean that my parents decided. My mother was a young actress when she was still doing her studies in Germany, and her idol was the avant-garde theater director Erwin Piscator, who was a very interesting part of all of modern theater, of all of modernism, what we're trying to do, all of us here. Not everyone has heard of Erwin Piscator, but everyone has heard of his close collaborator Bertolt Brecht. Between Brecht as writer and Piscator as director, together they really invented the modern political theater. Piscator made a great splash in the Weimar Republic and was considered the white hope of futurist theater. The year I was born he directed *Hoppla, wir leben!* his great masterpiece, and Schiller's *Robbers*. I was born at that point—my mother wanted to be an actress, but then I was born because she met a young rabbi, a very radical, forward-looking, modernist rabbi, but a rabbi at that time still in the German army—he had to get out of that, and at that time it was unthinkable that a woman could be both an actress and the wife of a rabbi. It was just not imaginable, even to very modern people. Today of course we've gone a little further and you can be a rabbi and an actress and it's fine; there are such people and god bless them. But my mother thought that was impossible, my parents thought that was impossible, and they decided before I was born that my mother would give up her theater career and that I would be, as it were, a surrogate for her and would possibly even work with Piscator someday. As history had it, terrible times fell on Germany and my parents left early in 1929, when I was a babe in arms, and came to New York. Piscator stayed a while in Germany, but arrived in New York in time for me to graduate high school just as he had an interesting theater school going, and I got to study with him.

Piscator was very important in the whole history of modern theater, and my going to him was a very important moment in my life. I'm thinking a lot about that, because I'm writing a book about Piscator and his work in New York. He taught us two basic principles that I'd like to bring up here, because I can't tell you the whole story of Piscator, nor the whole story of The Living Theatre. I came away from the school with two important ideas. One was Piscator's and Brecht's concept of total theater. Piscator has written about total theater; for him it meant extending the possibility of theatrical means, mostly by technology but also by audience communication, which he dreamt of but never did. That waited for us to do. He dreamt about audience contact, but he didn't do it. He did, however, create an entirely new form of theater that used films, projections, sound, moving scenery; if he were alive today, he would be working with lasers. It was very important research in extending the possibility of theater. All his life he dreamed about also doing a lot of audience participation, but he never got to do it; he was always a little timid about it. It's a sad story, but an important one, and one that I think all modern theater today has overcome. We've stepped out into the audience, as have hundreds of other groups of theater experimenters. In the evolution of our work, the concept of total theater was very important, and I want to add that today modern theater has taken the concept of total theater into a much wider field and to mean something much broader that what Piscator ever dreamt of. Total theater in a way means that everything is theater. Obviously this [lecture] is theater because you would be the audience and we would be performing, but everything, everywhere I am is theater; if I walk on the street it's theater, because where I am is theater. We have learned now in modern theater that we can do theater anywhere. We do site-specific things in public parks, in hospitals, in stores—guerilla theater against the store owners, knowledge or desire in political situations; in an elevator in an apartment house I've seen theater performed. So total theater has come to mean very much more. But it also means, in a way, that theater is total and that we are total theater. That is, that any moment of intercourse I have with you, any moment is already theatrical, because it has certain theatrical elements. But what does that mean? Does that mean that if everything is theater that nothing is theater, because everything is theater? No, it doesn't mean that at all. Because theater is also a place of a higher consciousness. That is, if I'm an actor and I'm standing backstage talking informally to another actor, saying, let's have a coffee after the show, I hear my cue, something happens. I step out into the playing space or on the stage and I'm different. Not because I'm playing some other character, but I'm different because I look at my fellow actor differently now, I feel the presence of the audience around me in a different way than I felt the people around me before. I get to a higher level of consciousness when I'm on stage, everybody does; you're just not functioning in the same way. When we say everything should be theater, I mean we should all get to the higher level and stay there. That's the utopian dream, to get to that higher space.

So then theater is everything, is everywhere; but Piscator taught us another principle outside of total theater, which consists of the presence of the performer and the presence of the other people around in terms of why we're here. That is, Piscator said, if you want to stand here in the middle or on top of a platform or in front of a bunch of people and say to them, now listen to me, be quiet and listen to me, to what I have to say, watch me, or in some situations the light is on me and you're in the dark, pay attention to me—we have no real right to do that unless we have something to say to those people. If I just get up in front of you and I say, you listen to me, I'm charming, I'm a delight, I can make you laugh, I can make you cry, look how wonderfully my voice works, I move like an angel—that's egotistical bullshit. It's everything we want to get rid of. And yet it's the basis of much of our theater. Much of our theater depends on these lovely personalities we all admire. I watch them on TV too and say, wow—what Robin Williams can do. It's not what it's about to make theater, to stand up there and be admired. The only reason you could possibly have for saying to people, shhh, listen to me, is because you're burning to say something, because you've got something you've got to communicate. If you don't communicate it, that's a tragedy, but you're trying to communicate something and it has to be something more than that you're charming or that you're admirable or that you look nice. Therefore, Piscator said, you have to have a commitment. He wanted everybody in every production to have a commitment. He felt it was important for the stagehand to have a commitment, for the lighting people to have a commitment, and for everybody to work collectively on that commitment.

When I came around after many years to creating a theater, after having studied with Piscator and hopefully having taken in those two principles of total theater and of commitment, Julian Beck and I were talking about what kind of a theater to make, how to make theater, what it meant, and what was our commitment. We gathered around us a group of like-minded artists and we created The Living Theatre. That was in 1947. In 1947 we registered The Living Theatre and I've been working at the same job ever since. That's a long time to work at one job, but it has been a very rich experience because we've never ceased to make certain basic explorations: how to bring about a political vision by poetical means, how to use the poetry of the theater in order to strengthen a certain very specific political ideal. We are almost all anarchists, pacifists, vegetarians, feminists. Certainly these ideals include the concept of peaceful anarchism, the concept of changing our world from a political, hierarchical, punitive society into another society—everybody would like to live in a better society, everybody wants to live in a society without war and without poverty, but if you take those things to their logical conclusion, if you say peace and liberty, everybody says hooray; if you say pacifism and anarchism, everybody runs out of the room. We're afraid to be free and we know why we're afraid, there's good reason for it, but art is there to strengthen our hope that we can live the way we really want to live. And, in fact, we can, and we've been working at it by various means of theatrical experiment for lo these many years.

First, in New York, we explored the European writers because when we started in 1947, when Julian Beck and I began to discuss The Living Theatre, a lot was happening in Europe; there were some great playwrights working in Europe at that time, and there were very few in the United States. We began with the work of making poetic theater, and we thought we had to, in some way, hide the political aspect and sugarcoat the pill. But as we moved from the 1940s into the 1950s and 1960s, it became clearer and clearer that the pill was the thing and the sugar coating was a lot of shit. So we came closer and closer to a more nitty-gritty political commitment, so that we could, in some way, say in one way or another all our work has tried to inspire people to the possibility of, and the hope for, the beautiful, nonviolent, anarchist revolution. We're still working on that, and we will continue to work on that.

The second part of our history is one of journeying across the world, partly because we've had great problems in New York City—actually we've had five theaters closed by various authorities over the years, and now we're building one we hope will last forever, at least for our lives. At that point, in the midsixties, we began an enormous tour; I think we played in every country in Europe except Norway—nothing against Norway, it just so happened. We played in hundreds of cities and we played in six languages, and in some way we will continue to do that, though we'll be based here, and continue to make our major experiments of which perhaps the most important is trying to find ways in which to integrate and activate the audience—

not just to make them clap and sing, that's easy, but to create theatrical situations in which they can act, speak, perform, change the ideas that have been presented, refute them, overthrow them, bring new ideas—that is, in which we can have an actively thinking, participatory audience. We have worked on this for many years; we continue to work on it, and we will continue to work on it. Hanon is going to tell you some of the many ways in which we've explored this vast field. Maybe he'll talk about *Paradise* as the epitome of that?

HR: The times being what they are, *empowerment* is an important term we think about when we look at what we're doing. That's why, when Judith talks about having learned from Piscator that you have to have something to say to justify making theater, the workshops that we do have become an important part of our work over the years. We do a lot of them, all over the world; we're doing one here, right now, with a wonderful bunch of people; they're all writers, but they're wonderful actors too. For us, the purpose of a workshop is to create a situation where people are given this premise that if you're interested in making theater, you have to determine what it is you want to say. So we insist that the group define—the form of our work is that, along with some training exercises, we're essentially engaged in creating a piece together, an actor-collective creation, and we insist that the participants define what it is they want the piece to be about. That whole process is an important political and psychological hurdle to get past in order to reap some benefits in terms of feeling empowered in dealing with your reality.

In this day and age it seems to me that it doesn't make a whole lot of sense to bother doing theater if you really just want to present your vision of the world. You can incise your vision into somebody's brain better through video and film than you can through theater. But theater has this unique possibility of bringing people together, live, in a space. We work with a lot of young people, too, and I find that there's an enormous thirst for that direct contact, because for these generations that have grown up with computers, all experience is somehow mediated by one screen or another; there's the computer screen that gives you access to the internet, and the TV screen and the movie screen—very little goes on between people that doesn't pass through a screen at this point in history. So there's a real desire for direct human contact, and the theater offers unique possibilities for that. That keeps our feet in the water of the theater, feeling the attraction of that possibility. And, more importantly, the possibility of using that aspect of the encounter as a political tool, as a social model, and creating plays in which the audience has an active responsibility, has a role. It's a tricky business, getting the audience to participate. We've been at it for many years, and I feel we've just barely scratched the surface of finding creative ways for people to participate. The most interesting ones are the ones where the outcome of the performance is determined by the choices the audience makes. I'll give you some examples of ways we've tried to accomplish this. When we did our version of *Prometheus* in the 1970s, we first confronted the audience—we created this in Italy, performing in these big, fancy opera houses with reserved seats—the house would come in and they would find the thirteen actors who were performing in this ensemble chained, bound by ropes and chains to the seats, which were numbered, sold seats that people had tickets for. People wandered around; we had given the ushers strict instructions not to give it away, and we weren't allowed to talk to them, we could only look at these audience members imploringly and wait until they figured out, which ultimately they did, that until they liberated these actors, nothing else was going to happen. That was a concrete lesson. In the same play we worked with two other forms of participation. In the first act we told the classical story of Prometheus. Julian Beck wrote the script, and in the second act he retold the story as the story of the Russian Revolution, where Prometheus becomes the anarchist movement and Zeus becomes Lenin and Io becomes Emma Goldman traveling through Russia. I played Prometheus, Judith played Io, Julian Beck was Zeus. And in this second act, when we were telling the story of the Russian Revolution, Lenin got up on stage and narrated and decided we were going to restage the taking of the Winter Palace in the manner of the great Russian director Nicolai Evreinov, who staged these mass spectacles in the years following the revolution in which they would, on the site of the Winter Palace itself, get thousands of people to reenact the taking of the Winter Palace; it was a theatrical event. So we decided to incorporate this into this version of Prometheus, and we had a rehearsal in the middle of the play for twenty minutes, where Julian cast people in the house as different roles in the Russian Revolution and they came to work with various members of the cast, who rehearsed them in the scenes they were about to play that would enable them to take the Winter Palace; the anarchists crawled under the seats and the Bolsheviks stormed the palace, etcetera. That was a very effective device, especially when it came to the end and the final red tape was cut and the palace was taken, and everyone sang the "Internationale" and Lenin said, "Thank you very much, you can take your seats now. We don't need you." Then we moved on in the third act to yet another form of participation, which was, it being a play about Prometheus, the classical symbol of an imprisoned figure, we invited the audience to walk with us to the nearest prison—surprisingly it was never terribly far—and to do a silent meditation outside the prison on the end of punishment. A good part of the audience would accompany us, and we would stand there for a half hour meditating on getting past this phase of human history.

Let me say parenthetically: I'm optimistic. First of all, pessimism is cheap; I think most people know that—it's easy and it's not very interesting. Optimism is hard, but it's challenging, and I feel there is reason to be optimistic. I have a kind of scientific, evolutionary perspective; Judith met and corrupted me in 1968, I was a biophysics major at Yale, and—look at me now. The point is that I think this experiment we call civilization is extraordinarily young; it's only six thousand years of written history and basically six thousand years of large, urban settlements with more than a few families trying to live together, and when you think of the fact that people live a hundred years and always have, six thousand years represents no more than the life span of sixty one-hundred-year-old people; all of history is no longer than the lifetime of sixty people who lived a hundred years each. When you think of it that way it's astounding, it's nothing—how could we have hoped to have worked out all the problems of billions of people living harmoniously together in the lifetime of sixty people? We need a little more time. Maybe if we act like children it's because chronologically we still are. But right now we're children who are playing with guns, and this is a dangerous business, so we've got to be careful.

Moving with this notion that progress is possible, we're working on exploring further ways of using the theater to communicate this. Other examples of these experiments we're making include a play I wrote a few years ago called *Anarchia*. There's a moment in the play when rocks are thrown at the audience; they are papier-mâché, they don't hurt, but they look real, and they've got messages wrapped around them. So individual audience members find them on the floor and find these messages, which come from characters in the play. They'll say, "This is Ted, I'm a character in the play, and I need to tell you that at a point later on in the evening there's going to be a terrorist attack on stage and I'm going to die in this attack unless you save my life. This is no joke. Now, if you want to save my life, here's what you have to do," and then he gives the instructions of what cues to listen for, where to go, and what kind of action to take to save the life of this character in the play. It varied from evening to evening; some people would take up the challenge and others wouldn't. So the play was constructed with multiple endings depending on who survived at the end of the play, which was determined by the audience's choice. That was a particularly effective way of getting them involved on a responsible level, where the characters' lives and deaths depended on their choice and their willingness or reluctance to intervene.

More recently, after the Soviet Union fell and everybody decided that capitalism was the only game in town, we figured we'd better get a serious look at that phenomenon, to understand what might lie beyond it. In looking for source material, I came upon the remarkable work of a French historian, Fernand Braudel; he wrote a remarkable two-volume history of the Mediterranean and the era of Philip ii, and more relevant to our project, a three-volume work called *Capitalism and Material Life, 1400–1800, Civilisation matérielle, economie et capitalisme, XVe–XVIIIe siècle,* an enormous wealth of primary material about what was going on in this period from 1400 to 1800, when the modern economic system took shape. I created a play telling this story, that spans these four hundred years, and we decided to tell it as the story of thirteen people who lived through these centuries of economic change and who represent all the people of the world. There is the Empress of China; there is a Mayan slave of the Aztecs who betrays the Aztecs to the Spanish conquistadores; there is a French nun who flees the convent and becomes a prostitute in Istanbul; there is an Indian beggar who eventually makes it to England and gets a job in a factory; and these people's lives change by virtue of the changing economic circumstances. We created this rather wonderful play, it's one of my favorites of our work, and wondered how we were going to involve the audience in this one. Finally we hit upon the idea that we created a real stock market, and we printed up stock certificates for each of the thirteen characters, and at various intervals during the play the actors went out into the audience and sold these stocks for real money with the audience's understanding that the values of the shares would change depending on what happened in the play, and at the end they could turn them in and they might lose or they might win money. They sold hundreds of these shares; it worked extraordinarily well. And in the end people got this very direct lesson. First of all, people [were] watching the play with an investment in what was going on on a level that you don't ordinarily see in the theater, and then finally they got to see at the end that that's the way the system works. You can win a lot, you can lose a lot—but you can only win at the expense of somebody else losing, which is the problem with the system, and one of the reasons we have to be a little more creative. That's why these people gathered together here, you, the poets, people for whom imagination is a primary value, are so important to what needs to happen next in history.

JM: I want to add two things about our work. One of the things we've done for the past twelve years is a street play, which continues to be performed, whether some of us are in Europe or not, pretty much regularly in the middle of Times Square—because that is the center of our city, and it should be done in the center of every city. Every time that there's an execution in the United States, we do a play called *Not in My Name*, since executions are always committed in the name of the people, and we protest against that. We get into the middle of the city and we do a little play about the actual person that is about to be killed somewhere at the hour of their execution. Ideally the play begins when they are still alive. They are somewhere in Texas or Tennessee, offed in the middle of the play. We then say now we have to reverse the cycle of violence, how are we going to do that? We are in the middle of Times Square, there is no invited audience, it's whoever stops, and we decide the thing to do is to determine right now, here and now, to take the first step to reverse the cycle of violence. We say, "I'll start with myself," and that's good, but it is not enough. We have to do one thing more. And we turn to the people standing around and we say, "I'm going to start with you." We pick somebody, and we do something that's taboo in Times Square: we touch somebody we've never met. You're not supposed to go up and touch people you don't know in Times Square. We touch somebody and we say, "I'm going to reverse the cycle of violence, starting with you. I'm going to say to you, 'I swear to you that I will never kill you'; now, could you promise me the same? Yes?" Then we declare a victory for the first step toward the cycle of violence being reversed, because obviously the first step of reversing the cycle of violence is to have trusted each other: to give trust to each other, to be able to trust each other. Of course they don't always say yes, they say all sorts of things; we're standing in Times Square, it's their turf, not our turf, and they can say anything; they can say, fuck off; they can say something funny; they can giggle. But we are trying to say that here we are able to do this one step. And then we say in chorus, "Now I could never bomb a city because I swore I wouldn't kill you. I could never fire into a crowd because I swore I wouldn't kill you," in order to emphasize the personal responsibility in something like the abolition of the death penalty, that it is our personal responsibility and it depends on a personal trust and trustworthiness and loving kindness that we can hopefully give each other. We've been doing that for twelve years now, and we haven't gotten busted yet; we expect to any minute, but so far it has worked.

The other thing I want to talk to you about is pessimism. Hanon has already spoken about how banal pessimism is. We all read the papers and see the news, and it is sickening. Certainly everybody here has had moments, if not more than that, of pessimistic feelings about where things are going and what is happening. I am, in The Living Theatre, one of the few who has managed to keep up a kind of optimistic view through lots of changing political scenes. Optimism is a great strengthener, a great fortifier, and a good thing if we can find it. I want to talk about where I found it recently. I have found the best theater and the best optimism in the big street demonstrations against the G8, against the World Trade Organization, against the Republican National Convention. I have seen two hundred thousand people marching and two hundred different kinds of theater groups, some of whom didn't think they were theater groups; they were chanting and drumming, they had big puppets, each one trying in some way to communicate the importance of their commitment as they marched down the street. Our first experience was in Genoa with a large group of people. Since this was about the economy, we did a formation of bodies that went down the street reciting Allen Ginsberg's "Moloch," which seemed appropriate. Other groups, with other people, were doing other things. What was most meaningful to me was that there was a group ahead of us and a group behind us that we got to know, because unfortunately the police got crazy and killed some poor boy down at the other end of the demonstration, Carlo Giuliani was offed by the police, and so the parade stopped. We had a chance to do our piece a couple of times, as did the people in front of us and the people behind us. The people in front of us were the Madres de Plaza de Mayo, the mothers of the *desaparecidos* in Argentina, very beautiful, holy, and tragical. Behind us was a float with a bunch of Berlin transvestites in all their glory, with pearls and tinsel and screaming queens. It was very wild; they were asking for their liberation. What was beautiful about it to me was that this group of solemn, bereaved mothers and that group of screaming queens knew exactly why the other people were there, were in sympathy with them, and felt solidarity with them. For me, that's a movement. What I think we need today, and what I'm hoping to see again, is the strength of a kind of movement that many of us have lived through, a time when there's a tremendous amount of action for political optimism. We need that optimism now.

—July 26, 2005

NOTE: In May of 2011, just before her eighty-fifth birthday, Judith, Tom, and Brad finally brought The Living Theatre to Norway.

WHAT'S POETRY TO YOU?

Cecilia Vicuña

WANTED TO TELL YOU ABOUT CHILE. WHEN YOU LOOK AT CHILE TODAY FROM a satellite, Chile stands out from the rest of South America because you can see two huge rivers, rivers that are so large that you can see from the stratosphere. One is the river of shit that Chile has put into the ocean without any water treatment. And the second one is the pollution that comes from the copper mines. You know.

Chile is a mineral land that is being made by the volcanoes pushing up from under the ocean. The Mapuche people of Chile call this "spirit of fire" that is coming and spewing magma from under, they call it Pillán. And Pillán, as far as I'm concerned, is the spirit of poetry, because it is not a volcano, but something that's behind and under pushing the volcanoes.

I wanted to begin with the copper, because this is how my life really began. I want to take you to how Chile was when I was a young girl . . . *before* the military coup. Because it was copper that ultimately infuriated Henry Kissinger and Richard Nixon. And it was on account of this copper that Chile was destroyed and so many of my friends and family were killed.

I think what infuriated them, brutally, was a number of things. We are talking of the 1970s, at the time that the Chilean people, I believe, were the first people to choose, democratically, a Socialist president: Salvador Allende. I was a young girl then. And I think the phrase that condenses what we were going through is this phrase that in Spanish goes like this: *Ahora somos dueños*—now we own ourselves. That owning ourselves became, in Allende's view, owning back the copper.

When the copper was nationalized from American companies, that was a little too much. Kissinger and Nixon started to conspire, to try to turn the Chilean military, who had been democratic and peaceful for one hundred and fifty years, respecting the constitution, telling them, "This is not right. This is not real democracy." Because they are numb. So eventually they conspired and did a military coup.

But going back to the owning ourselves: you can imagine what it was being in a place where you could own yourself. That meant that you could imagine things. It meant that your thoughts could connect to the land. The land is not a physical thing. It is a feeling that includes everything and everyone in it. *Mapu*, we say in Mapuche. Mapuche is the people of the land. But *mapu*, *wenumapu*, is the land of the sky, which is not a land at all. Or *n'eyen mapu*, that's air, not a land at all, but the land of air.

So, what kind of land is the land? Is it our togetherness perhaps? It is looking at ourselves and choosing collectively. Look at that word: *collectively*. It means to choose together what we are. Something happens to and with you when the way you imagine, your imagination, is at work with that collective. Something happens to the poetry that emerges from that force.

I want to tell you why I made a film. I had never heard of poetry readings when I was a young girl. I grew up writing poetry before I knew there was something called poetry. My mama knew that something was wrong with me from the start. So she would always be providing me little papers. And she always tells this story like I could be a baby! . . . you know, and could be drawing so she could say, "Come on! It's time for lunch." And I could hardly speak and I could say, "*Estoy pintando,*" "I'm drawing!" So that tells you the drawing comes before the writing. But I was drawing my thoughts into the paper.

Later, I am maybe twenty years old, and I'd been writing all my life, and somebody invites me to do a reading. I arrive in this reading with my tribe. I had invented a *tribu,* that was not a tribe, no, that was why it was called *tribu.* This was just friends who had gathered around; each one that came into contact with me at the time, my boyfriend included, was contaminated instantly with this disease. Everyone started to write poetry. So when I was invited, I would show up with all my tribe. There were just six of us boys and girls.

This was our first poetry reading. We arrive at the Museum of Fine Arts in Santiago and there were five thousand people there. Five thousand people! So, somehow, we don't have time to think. We don't have time to do anything. We're suddenly in front of a mic. So, I became. And my poems at the time were *dirty* as can be, and my girlfriends' *dirtier* than me, and my boyfriend's even *dirtier;* everybody was just so overly dirty. And so we read this outrageous and uncensored poetry, and the result is that the people started, this five thousand people, when we were done, start shouting, "*Más! Más poesía! Más poesía!*" "More poetry, more poetry!"

So, you know, *what* is poetry?

I think it was the desire, who knows, of dead people asking for more of that thing going on then. In any case, I thought if poetry is what Novalis says [is], "the original religion of mankind," of *my* kind, I almost said, it must be true. Or it may not be true. The only way I can do it is through research.

I made a film with this question: what is poetry? At the time, I only had access to a telephone. So I pick up the phone book and started with A. I pretended to be a researcher from the Universidad de Chile, and I could call on anybody who answered the phone and I could say, "Hello, this is a research from the Universidad de Chile. Can you please tell me, ¿qué es para Ud. la poesía? And I got all kinds of responses: "Fuck you! I don't have time for this shit! Pa!" You know. And something else; for example, the maid would answer and she would say, "No. You want la señora, the owner, the patrona, the lady of the house." And I would say, "No, no, no, no, no! I want you. I want you." "But me? Why me? I cannot say this." And I would finally settle her into speech. And it was from such a person that I got the most incredible answer. She would say, "Well, if you really want to know, this is what poetry is for me." I figured she was an Indian, because when she spoke of the land and of the river, I immediately started to get these images from the south of Chile. She would say that when she was not forced to work, she could escape into the river and would lie face down into the edge of the river to have her tummy feel the river. That is what poetry was for her.

I didn't tape these conversations, I just wrote and wrote and wrote and wrote and I got pages and pages and pages after only about fifteen people; and then I got tired and stopped, I didn't do any more research. Then many, many years go by and I am back in Bogotá. Back, I say, because when the military coup happened in Chile, I was studying in London. And I am in Bogotá living as an exile and again a sort of group of people is gathering around these thoughts, these kind of ways of going about the questions.

CHRISTINE FOX: I'm wondering, what is poetry to you?

CV: [laughs] If I knew I wouldn't write it, would I? I mean, we write it for the purpose of finding out. I don't know. And I like not knowing. All my training is to get to the point of not knowing.

ANNE WALDMAN: Maybe you could talk a little more about living in exile and, because this has come up as a theme throughout, the situation with our Pan-American culture now, the idea of inclusion, exclusion, censorship, articulation, the kind of euphemism of the public language, and our job as writers. Just how are you seeing things now and what could we learn from this, your own experience?

CV: *Exile* is, I think, one of the deepest words. I was in London on the day of the military coup in Chile, and what I felt that day is that, by this act,

Chile had been exiled from itself. So, it was not I who was in exile, but *Chile* who had become in exile of itself. And I could see that this was the case when I finally had the guts to go back and Chile was still under the dictatorship.

Chile was a place where, in spite of it being a semi-Catholic country and all of those things, there was an incredible freedom when I grew up. I was personally not brought up as a Catholic girl, so we would go around naked, we could play incredible, erotic games . . . as kids. And all kinds of workings on a continual basis. Then all of Chile disappeared, instantly.

So the exile became an exile of itself. And I think, in the culture of fear that we live in now, every single person is in exile from its true potential, its true possibility, of being.

So, even though I am away from Chile, that is a sort of superficial kind of exile. The real exile is from the soul, is from the heart, is from our connection to each other, to language itself. I instinctively understood that. And, therefore, I tried to find that I feel very happy anywhere I am, because there is no possibility of going back.

The entire earth is our earth, and the earth is exiled from its earth-ness. The water is exiled from its water-ness and so forth. *Exile* means "out of." Exit and exile. So everybody is *out of* this life force, therefore the life force is out too. The shamans say that even the medicinal plants are sick, so this being out, this disconnect, is what's killing us.

AW: How do we work with that knowing, that kind of displacement? It is so tragic and deeply haunting.

CV: Nobody knows the answer. We know how to quest. We know how to ask. If we can find our questions and our desire, that's what I teach, the art of desiring. To desire is to shine, so if we consider our deepest desires and we shine *with* them, this being *with* this pain, inside this pain, is the only true speech. Coming to and from that grief, that pain. That's where joy is to be found, only there, in that depth.

AW: It's very powerful and helpful. I guess there's still an urge to try to remedy the sense of this reversal of realities that's upon us, the projection of this version of the world, which seems unnecessary and wrong. It's the kind of thing that makes you feel crazy, because you know and experience a reality; it's like being a child and you're told, "No, no, that's not your experience. That's not really how it is. This isn't true." You're constantly in this cognitive dissonant, schizophrenic state. So that your mental powers, your energy has to be even stronger. We have to work harder in a reality where even the idea of empathy, compassion becomes more and more extinct and in exile.

CV: Yes, exactly. What I feel about that is that it is a question of the body and the heart. The Chinese and the Quechua people have only one word for consciousness: *heart/mind*. I don't know if you are aware that there is all this new research, there is a new science called something like neurocardiology. They have discovered that, in reality, there is a brain in the heart? And it is a brain that has deeper knowledge and better knowledge than this one. So the ancient Chinese and the ancient Quechua word, *sonqo*, is actually a better representation of where that knowledge and that guidance is going to come from . . . from that thing that is beating down there.

AW: And in Buddhist terminology it is *boddhichita*, this same kind of heart-mind.

CV: And that heart/mind *is* compassion, it can only be compassion.

AUDIENCE MEMBER: I felt, as I'm sure many people did, a surge of anger and grief in the United States's role in destroying Chile. And I was wondering, how have you dealt with that in a way that hasn't let that kind of anger destroy you; and have you ever gone through a period of just feeling anger?

CV: Yes, the main thing with that—and this is the old woman speaking after a lifetime—I think in reality, one of the first things that I wrote when the military coup happened is that however much Kissinger and the CIA conspired, they could never have done it without the collaboration of the Chilean military. So what is the point of blaming the u.s.? The u.s. were defending their so-called interests. The point, the real point, is *why* are we doing these things to ourselves? *Where* is this hatred coming from? There is no point in blaming somebody else. It's coming from within yourself. And only when you have that realization, and you can begin by having acceptance and compassion for your own anger, that that energy begins to dissipate. And then everything changes.

The energy of anger, if you look at it in Spanish, the word is *ira*, like you have in English, *ire* . . . it's the same root as *sacred*. So there is something sacred about this ire, that is sacred as long as you learn from it to understand your own force, the life force within you that can always turn to waste. If you use it or turn it against the other, that is against life, that's against the life force. That is, I think, the primary principle of this whole thing.

So, it is easy to feel angry against the u.s., but I think people all over the world don't feel angry with the u.s. They feel puzzled and angry at the fact that Americans are not claiming their democracy. *Why* are Americans passive, letting these freedoms and this democracy slip away? I think that is sacred ire, because everybody is in danger of that, not just the u.s.

—July 28, 2005

TELLING STORIES

Samuel R. Delany, Hoa Nguyen, Meredith Quartermain, James Thomas Stevens

SAMUEL R. DELANY: By way of introduction, some years ago on the little motto board of a church on Central Park West that I used to pass on the bus every day, someone had put the statement "the world is made up not of atoms but of stories." This quote had been attributed to Muriel Rukeyser. It is an interesting thing to think about—when you think that really the atomic theory is itself just a complicated story, you realize just how true that is. If we bracket for a moment the complicated relationship of stories to truth, you have lots to think about.

HOA NGUYEN: My journey through story and narrative is what I'm going to be talking about. Like so many journeys this one is a bit circuitous, going from one extreme to another and then finding a middle way. My early poems were your typical narrative lyric poems, informed by my scattered and mostly uninformed readings, which included random Emily Dickinson and Sylvia Plath—two models of women poets, incidentally, that I found a bit distressing when looking at them as models for life as a woman poet. The poems I wrote then brought experience, emotion, and memory to the foreground in a typical lyric, narrative fashion. In one poem by Joanne Kyger, she writes, "I am so tired of memory as content." Similarly, at the time, I felt likewise dissatisfied with the mode that I was engaged in, this narrative, confessional modality; it felt limiting and somehow inauthentic to the experience I was trying to relate. I was fortunate enough at this time to begin my formal studies at New College of California with Tom Clark, Lyn Hejinian, Gloria Frym, David Meltzer, among others, and in 1995 here at Naropa, I spent a summer writing with Joanne Kyger, Harryette Mullen. I shared my poetry with Jack Collom informally, and he made a very useful remark at this time, noticing how often I'd use words like *blood, stone,* and *bone.* To be honest, at the time I felt slightly chastened by his comment, but I knew it illuminated a failure in my poems that I knew existed. I think what I was after by using these words was mythic language, trying to get at the expansiveness of myth by using those words, but making the mistake of memory as content.

In 2001 I was preparing for the birth of my first child, and wanting my labor to be as undisturbed from medical interventions as possible, I furiously studied natural birth. And I found the most useful information to be reading birth stories. So I read all these stories written by mothers. Since birth is so various, every birth is unique in its conditions, I literally read hundreds of birth stories to get a sense of what natural birth could be; I think I read every natural birth story online at the time. That exercise completely changed my relationship to narrative. I could see deeply and maybe for the first time the essential in story, an essential information. So my poems changed again.

Charles Olson wrote once, "I would be an historian, as Herodotus was, looking for oneself for the evidence of what was said." My interest in poetry turned to narrative, to what was said, and seeking ways in which poetry could be useful, contain information, and to connect to the mythic. Seeing that myth is a kind of history, a ready frame of reference that can connect human events or moments in time to a myth or archetype, which could expand it and give it dimension, depth, and context. It seems to me in the United States we are so bereft of that old literary myth, and also cut off from our own histories. What we are left with are corporate images and electronic spectacles, that televised events and characters on TV seem more real to us than we seem to each other.

I'm hoping that I'm going to read two useful poems to end my piece of this conversation. This little book, *Red Juice,* came out in 2005. The note on the first poem in the book references the herb nettles, which is a weed that grows abundantly in waste areas. "Nettles are used as a liver and blood tonic and support the endocrine system, cleansing and nourishing the glands. It is high in minerals, especially iron and calcium, and many vitamins. To make an infusion, put a handful of dried nettles in a widemouth jar and add just-boiled filtered water. Cover and steep for four hours or overnight. Strain and drink." This is the poem that goes with that note:

Up Nursing

Up nursing   then make tea
The word war is far

"Furry" says my boy
about the cat

I think anthrax
and small pox vax

Pour hot water on dried nettles
Filter more water for the kettle

Why try
to revive the lyric

The second poem I'll read from this book has a reference to the fertility awareness method. The reference is to mucus, which is cervical mucus. "Using the fertility awareness method, or FAM, not to be confused with the rhythm method, women can track changes in cervical mucus among other indicators as a means of conceiving or preventing pregnancy, thereby avoiding synthetic hormones, barrier methods that rely on petrochemicals, or surgery."

The Earth Is in Me

The earth is in me
I am old
and clay   nameless
"grass" with tiny yellow flowers

More mucus this morning to feed warm sperm

The Earth is capable and heals you
You have friends among the weeds
Reddish "sugar ants" next to the mugwort

I had this idea
stubbornly
    Dog still barking

Write something "new" about the national tragedy

MEREDITH QUARTERMAIN: My title for this little talk is "Historical Surrealism and How I Got to It." The panel topic we received asked us to think about the questions of mythologies and cultural traditions, and whether these are reinvented in postmodern forms. The short answer is that the artist who does not develop his own sense of appropriate form ends up a cultural fashion victim. That was not my wording, but it is true—you have got to rethink form. Every generation has to do that. Otherwise, the cultural fashion victim, according to Walter Benjamin, produces a socially minded, bourgeois program for literature: "A bad poem on springtime, filled to bursting with metaphors," singing of the "finer future of our children and grandchildren" who live angelically in a world where everyone imagines themselves rich and free, when in fact they are nothing of the sort. His essay on surrealism calls for "mistrust in the fate of literature, mistrust in the fate of freedom, mistrust in the fate of European humanity, but three times mistrust in all reconciliation: between classes, between nations, between individuals" [*Reflections*, pg. 190–191].

Postmodernism concerns the debunking of master narratives, showing how the normal is actually produced by specific power imbalances and specific historical conditions. Today every aspect of human experience is Walmart-ized, everything prepackaged, digitalized; all you do is push buttons. You get the latest CD, the latest cool jeans, the latest cool drug. But what is pushing your buttons? What is making you a little button machine to circulate dollars into powerful pockets? If you don't want to be a little button machine operated by Walmart, Microsoft, Nestlé, Shell, et al, you must question and disrupt the norms, the rationalisms, the ideologies that push your buttons.

My work looks at place, specifically Vancouver City on the west coast of Canada. When I started writing about it, I wanted a way to break through the surface of normalness in a city street, some way to disrupt this unquestioned presence of colonial skyscrapers on aboriginal land. History became the way to do that. History is the most important story that must be told and reinvented and retold again and again, not some bland notion of textbook history, but all the various histories of all the stakeholders.

Ezra Pound's *Cantos* gave me a way to collage many texts and voices into poems, using material from a range of historical records. Canto 33, for example, is a mix of letters from Thomas Jefferson or John Adams, statements from Karl Marx, numerical facts, and statements from various politicians and congressional records. He includes prohibitions from the British Factory Act, which was trying to stop child labor, and puts beside them factory-owner propaganda against the Factory Act, all of it plunked down in separate chunks. You can see that in the layout of the poem, each verse-paragraph is a separate chunk of some kind of verbatim text that he's pasted in. The pieces are carefully arranged to be sharply discordant but at the same time bound together rhythmically. It is a canto—a song—but it is made out of chunks of research, verbatim. For me it was one of the most exciting things to discover this.

Pound was practicing montage, the pasting together of fragments. Writing at about the same time as these cantos, Benjamin, in "The Author as Producer," advocated montage as the chief means of resistance. Interruption is key. Interrupt the apparatus of art, the apparatus of education, the apparatus of social power, which maintains the status quo, keeping others as other, keeping workers in Mexico or China earning pennies making things their bosses sell for megabucks, keeping billions poisoned by industrial pollution, billions without medical care. Interruptions are a way of reinventing the smooth stories that keep othering others, and a way of reinventing the form in which we see things.

In the 1920s and 1930s, surrealism was very much in the forefront of avant-garde and resistance writing. Writers challenged realistic conventions and norms by invoking surreality, in which logical rationalism was only one small part. They sought to free experience from the cage of rationalism and record unfettered other thought processes that make up our consciousness. The subject-predicate logic of the complete sentence was impotent for this, it was powerless to get that across. Surreality included dream reality, with its rifts and surprises; it included the reality of the subconscious revealed by Freud. Fragmented and cross-pollinated language gave access to surreality. In his essay "Surrealism," Benjamin remarked that the city itself is the most dreamed-of object. He came to see the "arcades, winter gardens, panoramas, factories, wax museums, casinos, [and] railway stations" of Paris as "dream houses of the collective" [*Arcades Project*, pg. 406]—crystallizations of our unconscious desires and assumptions, power structures, and so forth. Studying these collective dreams, Benjamin wrote, "allows us to recognize the sea on which we navigate and the shore from which we push off" [*Arcades Project*, pg. 391].

For me, writing about the city became an exploration of the city's unconscious, the dream houses of western colonial capitalist states. My methods involved montage of historical records, archival research, and direct observation of streets and buildings, as well as fractured sentences, seeking to reopen the experience of my city, to lift that experience out of middle-class material assumptions. I came to think of these juxtapositions as historical surrealism.

Like many cities, few streets in Vancouver are named after women. I found just a couple. In the city archives I researched one of them, Frances Street, a small backstreet named after Sister Frances, who started the city's first general hospital in its poorest area. My poem contrasts her street, the street she walked, with the streets walked by her contemporaries—the British Columbia coal barons Robert and James Dunsmuir, who were multimillionaires at the time that they were paying their workers a couple of dollars a day. Of course they got a great big, impressive downtown street named after them.

The poem includes collaged and crosscut fragments of description of current businesses on the street; historical figures that the neighboring streets were named after—Vernon Drive was one of them, and Victoria Drive, named after Queen Victoria; descriptions of heritage buildings; commands from the Heritage Act; politicians behind the Crimean War; Florence Nightingale's work in the Crimean War—Sister Frances followed in the footsteps of Nightingale; letters from Sister Frances; treatises on smallpox; and wages and conditions of coal miners in the Dunsmuir mines.

Here's the opening of the poem:

Frances Street

how many have walked it?

boxed against coastal mountains
Loyale Automotive, Winner Sportswear, New Profession Collision
    six blocks—
real-estate-man slash Land Commissioner

Forbes George Vernon's
    up to Queen Vicky's drive

                                                            the

columned porches and clapboard,

    classic   1905

        Sister Frances at St. Luke's
                                                torn down for
Turbocharger Service Centre,
                            Pacific Plating Bumper
Exchange & Custom Chroming

        no person shall destroy desecrate deface
        no person shall demolish a building or structure
    the façade

the unsolved eastern question

Lord Aberdeen, 4th Earl of,
needed a hell of a lot of men
for Russell and Palmerston's war
    can't have Russkis owning Bethlehem

    maybe it's just one army or another
we're writing for the sky
to read like fungus writes
    maps for us we think its blindness

    diggers in Dunsmuir's pits

$1.20 a ton

2700 pounds on his scales
    or maybe a dollar if he thought coal was slumping

and he wasn't gonna make his $8 a ton profit
    $3.00 a day, if he didn't cut you for rock
buy your powder from the Company
pay your own helper
no pay for bracing tunnels

funny how Mine Inspectors never found
the Right Honourable Robert or the Right Honourable James
Dunsmuir

at fault
    the Act—whose act?
said miners were responsible
for the gas at Wellington's No. 6
    she'd pop from sparks off the hammers
    working on their bellies to breathe
it was miners, the Act said, made her blow—
they brought out brothers cooked to crackling
it was miners
killed 11 in 1881, 65 in 1884, 23 in 1887,
150 in 1888, 75, then 55 in 1901

JAMES THOMAS STEVENS: I have a love/hate relationship with stories. Coming from an oral tradition culture, Kanien'kehá:ka, or Mohawk, as most people say of the Haudenosaunee or Iroquois Confederacy, I have grown very used to hearing people use story in a denigrating or patronizing way, writing things off as "well, that's just an old Indian story." Being that these stories were not written down and they varied from time to time, when non-Indians did take it upon themselves to check up on us and see how we were maintaining our culture, they were often discredited and discounted, even as American intellectuals such as Benjamin Franklin were noting the accuracy with which Iroquois women could recite the Great Law of Peace, or Gayanashagowa, over hundreds of years. As early as the 1930s anthropologists such as Elsie Clews Parsons were discrediting entire tribes and writing them off as lost causes due to the fact that their stories collected earlier had changed with the time. They had adapted. This is also the great strength of America's indigenous peoples. A major element of the oral tradition is change. Even in the naming of trees, the names of trees are not fixed but fluid, and as nature changes, as trees change in their reaction to nature. And although we are supposed to ignore this global warming, the day before I left Buffalo, New York, two tornadoes touched down on the New York State throughway east of Buffalo. I think we may need to start changing some names of things as our world changes.

Stories must change to create relevancy, just as the cultural signifiers of any given age change. What good would it do to today's youth to explain patience by example of the skill needed in the buffalo hunt, or of the slow process involved in the making of wampum, shell beads? Stories can remain while the basic layers may change. It is a kind of synthesis of the old and the new which I strive for in my own work. To do this I often write in a parallel structure and find that works best for me; where I can honor the traditional while exposing its relevance to me as a mixed-blood, two-spirited Native in the twenty-first century. An example of this would be the poem "Canoe Song," derived from a simple, rhythmic song designed to sing in keeping pace while paddling a canoe. I could easily write off the traditional song as useless since I don't often find myself paddling along in a canoe, rather driving away in a Subaru Forester. What the song did make me consider was the strong eddy, the ebb and flow of other personalities, that I must daily ford my way through. The poem and others in the series are written in a three-tiered, parallel structure, beginning with the Mohawk, followed by a literal translation, and ending with my own "sui translation" as I ended up calling them—"sui" in that I didn't want people to mistake it and think this isn't really translated exactly—that's why I do put in the literal translation—

but also the sui translation is the one that is written purely for myself, to make sense of and connect with that old song or old poem. The literal translation, I have to say, is not literal in a sense that to write literally we would have to take apart each of our words. I used to do this when I was an undergraduate; I began writing by writing in Mohawk and then taking apart the actual word. People were talking about how influenced I had been by the Language poets, but at the time I didn't know who they were. It was just how our language is constructed. For example, a simple word *yakohsatens*, which translates into "horse"—that word actually has three parts. *Yakohsatens* means "the that thing side by side." People were trying to figure out how "the that aside" can mean "horse"? When Iroquois people first saw horses, they were tied next to each other pulling a cart, so it was this animal that was always side by side with itself. So there is a choice, translating: Do I write "horse" and lose the image that we have traditionally? Do I translate a word as "bicycle," or "that thing that gives your ass a ride," which is what it really means? We have those questions in translation.

I'll read two of the poems so you can hear the structure. I love reading poems in Mohawk, and they are very short songs. The first will be the "Canoe Song" that I mentioned, which is to keep pace; the second is the "Mosquito Song." It is something you sing when the mosquitos are annoying you and you are talking to them about how annoying they are. You will hear the Mohawk first, then you will hear the literal translation, then the sui translation. The thing that I like about reading in Mohawk is I have an obsession with filling a place with the language that has never been heard in it before and leaving that language there, in the same way when I travel— I was in Petra, Jordan, last fall, and I picked up a stone and left it in Dunkirk, New York, and I'll take a stone from Dunkirk, New York, and leave it Sweden when I go this summer. Someday there will be very confused anthropologists and geologists.

Canoe Song

Teiohonwa:ka ne'ni kahonwe:ia.
Kon'tatieshon iohnekotatie.
Wakkawehatie. Wakkawehatie.

The canoe is very fast. It is mine
All day I hit the water
I paddle along. I paddle along

I am the hull—rapid against your stream.
Birch beneath the ribs
    circumnavigating your body
Endless propeller of my arm
    as it circles to find the flow
I move this way against you.
I move this way.

Mosquito Song

Okariata:ne tahohotharatie.
Tahsakohraria:ne ne tsi niho:ten.
Ne se aonha:a thorihwaka:ion.
Ne se aonha:a thorihwaka:ion.

The mosquito is bringing a message.
He comes to tell us how poor he is.
In truth, he is repetitive
and brings the same old message.

A voice returns
    to tell these things.
Of unencumbered arms.

Returns to remind me
    in truth   —   I am alone.
Sleeping through the din
    of solitude's stinging messenger.

That *Mohawk Samoa* book that was mentioned—I was in Hawaii teaching
a class in Juliana Spahr's workshop and met the Samoan poet Caroline
Sinavaiana. In talking with her over dinner, I realized I was thinking of her as
one of my Mohawk aunts who had passed away, and thinking how similar
our cultures were. I had proposed sending some of those translations to her,
to have her respond to the Mohawk poems, and she sent me Samoan songs
she translated and I responded to them, so that book is a collaborative piece.
    Later in my life, upon the passing of my father due to a brain tumor, I
turned to the ways of the Iroquois people again and remembered how
strong our stories were in helping us to deal with life itself, and the relevance of the condolence ceremony hit home. The grieving community in

Iroquois culture is thought of as a grieving wife, and all the elements of grieving are addressed as the *orenda*, or the life spirit of the community, has been lessened by the death of one. These elements are addressed and cleared away, elements like the failure to recognize the sun passing overhead, the stoppages of the throats and ears, the placement of the heart. In rewriting these fifteen parts of the ceremony, originally devised by the grieving Aiionwatha, whose daughters had been killed by the evil Atotárho with his hair of snakes, the ceremony proved just as effective for me today as it did for the death of Aiionwatha's daughters.

It is not only traditional Native American oral tradition, legend, and allegory that I look to when I write, but also the written word of those who have followed, both Native and non-Native. I am wholly in love with the text, be it the writings of the Jesuit relations in the seventeenth century or the letters of our most famous chief, Joseph Brant. I believe that splicing in older texts not only allows the opportunity for some very little-known writing to come to light again, as well as the beauty of its style, but it also shows the marked difference in thinking between indigenous and non-Native peoples. Often non-Native writings about Natives tell more about white-think than they do about the people they seek to describe.

My most recent undertaking involved hours of research at the American Antiquarian Society in Worcester, Massachusetts, reading through children's alphabet primers used at the Christian schools that sprang up in the eighteenth century for Indian children. I was amazed at the propaganda involved in such simple alphabet lessons, especially against the Catholic Church—above anything else they did not want Indians to become Catholics. But then I was less amazed later in the day when I happened to flip by a *Fox News* broadcast and realized how much propaganda surrounds us constantly. The coupling of these sources, along with letters written by Chief Brant, who went to London, and a recent trip I had taken there myself that coincided with the Tube bombings, led to my *Alphabets of Letters, a New Primer for the Use of Native or Confused Americans*. One of the quotes I found when I was doing that research, that I began an essay with, was [from] George Washington; when he led his campaign to wipe out the Iroquois in New York State, [he] made the statement, "The future success of our country relies upon the amount of terror which we can inflict." Our stories are all around and intermingling, and they do not die when they adapt, but like a healthy tree they grow new limbs, and they may be renamed.

—June 2006

MOVING ACROSS LANGUAGES, BORDERS, AND CULTURES

Heriberto Yépez, Myung Mi Kim, C. S. Giscombe, Sherwin Bitsui

HERIBERTO YÉPEZ: I have mixed feelings about translation as I have about . . . everything, basically. Writing, for me, is about the disclosure of contradictions. Obviously that comes from my biography and also from my geography. One of the main contradictions that runs throughout my work is translation. I have two ways of approaching and understanding translation. One is to love it and do it a lot. I have translated the poetry and prose of Jerome Rothenberg, a good amount of it, and also from the Portuguese, from what you call the New American poets, from that period, and also poetics from the concrete Brazilian movement, and some scattered materials like William Blake's "Fragments," into Spanish. I like to translate. I learn a lot translating; we transform ourselves, translating. The other part of me, which is more critical of what I do—and I know that involves what other people do, also, I have come to discover—asks, why do we translate? I think psychohistorically it has to do with trying to dominate the other, trying to absorb the other. As Oswald de Andrade, Brazilian poet and philosopher, said, it is a sort of anthropophagy—how to eat the other in a sacred way, to ingest the totem. Our civilization depends on eating others. We disguise that as a good enterprise, as communicating between cultures; we suggest a lot of Judeo-Christian beliefs behind this—I do this, I'm not criticizing you, I'm talking about me. There is a lot of imperialism; if writing is, as we know, imperialistic in nature, translation is more clearly imperialistic. How to gather the other. If we are still hunters, how we hunt, and how the ways we hunt become fixed, and that is how capitalism arises, once the hunting methods get stuck and repeated. One of the ways we hunt in a fixed manner is translating. Why do dominant cultures translate so much? It is the same as gathering oil. Counterculture has a lot to do with eating the other, this imperialism by other means.

So when we understand translation we need to understand translation also in that context, in the context of a not-so-innocent and a not-so-good way to see ourselves. Because as writers, as translators, we mostly see ourselves as missionaries, as Christs. We need to get over that, which is, I think, the most difficult part of writing, losing your own *imago* as a messianic figure. Translation has a lot to do with this. It has a lot to do, also, with suspending your own risk of emptiness and building something from emptiness, so you start to translate others. Translation has also a lot to do with how you renounce the risk of your own work, to make yourself a figure of service to others, which is just projection. We choose to translate whatever we identify with, but we don't want to recognize ourselves there, yet.

Writing can be a gathering, imperialism, stopping time and making it space. American literature is all about that, postmodern and modern American literature is all about transforming space into time. It is clear in Gertrude Stein and Charles Olson, they even say it explicitly. So that is a problem, how to follow writing and stop it as a space, or keep it transforming into what now I am calling time. If we do that, processes such as translation are left behind. What we must do as writers is to transform languages, not to transform a language into a dominant language, that has a lot of myths and beliefs in it, lies, that this language has a meaning, that I can get across a meaning and put it here. That is the old paradigm about writing, and translation mostly works with that paradigm.

This may sound like—pfff. So what to do next? And I am not sure. I am just becoming aware of what happens in writing, what happens in translation. So translation must maybe be exchanged for learning the other language, the language you want to replace with your own, with a whole set of myths behind that action. And maybe keep your research in that language you got interested in and write in it, for example. Or transform your own language, be active in your own context, and the fixed space which your language is now—liberate it through the teachings you hunted and got from the other language.

MYUNG MI KIM: "A Study of Six in Six." This is a provisional title, and the only reason I am even mentioning it is that I hope it serves as a glimpse into what I'm up to; a study of six in six, meaning I am using the actual words of the panel, and the title and the six that I am referring to are these six words: *translation moving across borders, languages, cultures.* I am going to try to address those words in the six or so minutes that I have allotted. This gives you a frame, a form, it gives you a little bit of the motivation, how quickly I think I will be moving, but why I feel like I need to hit at least some part of each of these words, so that we can promote the conversation between the panelists and you, the audience, and the readers, all of you collectively.

By mentioning the title, I am already starting in a state of translation, that is, I am beginning in a place without designation. I'm looking at translation, rather than this notion of one to one, a kind of proportion and equivalence, moving from one to another—what I'd like to question here is the twoness of the thing. Can we crack it open and invite in a kind of plurality and a multiplicity? Not even a multiplicity, but the very act of pluralizing, multiplying. For every noun that I catch myself saying today, I immediately want to convert it into some kind of verb, and I hope you will do that as well. In other words, I am operating between genres. This is a panel; that is usually an institutional format, there are talking heads at the front of the room; and what I am trying to release here is using convention, using form, but translating it. So I am already arriving here in a state of translation, between discourses, between formats, between occasion—formality/informality, written/spoken, fragment/whole. The thing that is being presented: there is this weird idea when you are working with translation that there is *an* original, a fixed point in language, in time, in history, the original, the problem of the origin. What I am trying to enact here is that as I am presenting there is already an elaboration taking place, so can I begin to put this somehow into this public space, this public discourse? So that as I present there is already an elaboration, which is already being further elaborated by the fact that there are all of us here. How can we get all those parts to function on behalf of what I think translation is, which is the site of something under transfer. If you really look at the word *translation, trans* as in "across"—which I will be talking about, as it is one of the six words—and *latus,* which is the root [and means "side"], as in transferred—pay some attention to that notion of translation as transfer. Of course the minute you say "translation" you are thinking trans-nation, trans-culture, trans-form, trans-port, trans-modify, trans-mit, trans-pose, trans-figure, trans-locate, transmute, trans-mutate, trans-gress. We could do this all afternoon. This problem of origin and the problem of equivalence—if I do nothing else I would like to propose the question of how immediate for you, as writers and readers of literature, is that connection between first and second and the demand of equivalence. So much of what I think language can do is distort and distend that expectation of equivalence, of meaning, of sense. To be somehow transmutated between one condition and the next is what I hope we can keep in the forefront as we talk.

Moving. It's a wonderful word in this context, because it stages for me a couple of different concerns. One, history is always on the roam. Similarly, working at some kind of analogous angle from the notion of the fixed origin, I think there is an opportunity here to rethink history as a fixity, a fixed continuum, a chronology, a linear shape onto which we hang experience, shared experience, and notions of collectivity. I would like to propose here that history is always on the roam; it is always remaking and reconfiguring itself. So the notion of moving through time, through immediate location, past, and a sense of futurity and of becoming, I also understand as part of what I am calling the translative condition. In moving in time and in history, in thinking and perception, there is this suddenly emergent. To be translated, or to be in a condition of translation or under translation, is in some sense to be able to pay attention to the suddenly emergent, the thing for which there is no name, the ungraspable.

Across: it's a pesky preposition, isn't it? Think of all the prepositions you know; they are all problematic because they try to fix one thing to another. That is their job, that is their function. But it would be a great exercise for all of you to think about all the prepositions you are friendly with and really try to figure out what they do. Why are they there? Why do they exist, grammatically? What are they serving in terms of the kind of taxonomical work that we are asking them to do, and that they commit on us even if we don't want them to do that to us. So, *across*. A problem, because it implies directionality: from what to what? Again, reproducing the problem of dominance and subjugation, one language to the next—who is the colonizer, who is being colonized. *Across,* by implying from where to where and a directionality, kicks up this question of placement. Look at all your prepositions; they will tell you a lot about where you are situated in relation to another object/person/thing/time/feeling.

Border. Big, juicy, impossible word. Especially because there has been so much theorizing about it in the last several decades. Everyone in the room has some kind of take, personal, as in, based on one's own story, to maybe the most theoretical discourse you've been exposed to around the notion of border. We can't rehearse all of that here. But I will simply mention some concepts I think will help elaborate how we might talk about border today. And I'll include something that might open up this notion of the mix, or the graft, or the border zone, or an *other* tongue, or one of the earlier moments of this kind of iteration, the notion of double consciousness, from W. E. B. DuBois, or notions of hybridity, the notion of heterogeneity, the notion of multivalence. Then we get into this counting effect—is it bilingual? Is it multilingual? Is it polylingual? Or, no, let's say heteroglossia. This clearly puts into some kind of evidence the useful struggle, and sometimes not-so-useful struggle, we have had with conceptions and practices of the border. What I would like to leave you with on the notion of border is rather than limit, border as boundary, border as boundary from which something begins to be presenced. Not border as a stopping point, but rather border as the occasion from which, or out of which, something can begin to be presenced.

I think I have two seconds left for *language*. Here I simply want to propose: how is it possible to think of language unhooked from its normal job as something that advances the ideology of a nation? Language bound to nation, soil, and citizenship—that way of conceiving and practicing language and what that has to do with the kind of political process of domination, subjugation, exclusion. In relation to that my question for all of us would be: how is it possible to think of language as an event in time and space, in history, in perception and affect, that has to do with attending to not how it organizes experience, how it normatizes, how it standardizes and regularizes how we come into speech and how we come into thinking, but where the event of language includes anything from silence to speaking to hearing to writing to saying to not saying?

Culture. Well, here we are, returned to the motherlode for the week, cultural activism. I will leave you with a question: what is the activism in cultural activism? As I have been attempting to suggest, activism is not a fixed, monologic state. But if one can think of the potential, the radical potential of the poem, it is the radical potential of language to activate the space of the unpositioned, the untried, and the as yet unavailable to the social-historical index.

C. S. GISCOMBE: My thoughts about translation are in some ways typical, in some ways very scattered. We, as Americans, need to know other languages and that way leave our content and self-referential lives, our fat lives, and that way get to the truly dangerous—and I mean that very seriously—pluralism that has been mentioned before. What attitudes might come in this *other* literature, with going along in someone else's economy, immersing oneself in that, giving ourselves up into that and recording it? How might these challenge our cultural mores? How might we be ruined by books, and ruin others in turn? The former mayor of New York City, Jimmy Walker, once famously said, "No girl is ever ruined by a book." But that's not true. Go back even earlier, to Frederick Douglass's relationship with the Auld family. Douglass was a slave who wrote three autobiographies, that somewhat contradicted one another in the way that a good autobiography should do. He reports in the first of those on his relationship with the Auld family, a family in Baltimore which owned him. Sophia Auld was teaching Douglass to read as kind of a curiosity, but her husband objected, saying, [per Douglass] "learning would spoil the best nigger in the world. Now," he said, "if you teach that nigger how to read, there would be no keeping him, it would forever unfit him to be a slave." *Spoiled. Ruined.* The same verbs.

I am running a workshop this week called "Traveling, Thinking, Writing." We have been reading some prose pieces by poets Michael Ondaatje and Audre Lorde; from Michael Ondaatje's book *Running in the Family*, about Sri Lanka, and Lorde's book *Zami*, about North America, Grenada, New York, Mexico. Travel writing is huge as a topic, and it necessarily includes stuff like slave narratives, records of military conquests, journals of exploration. But travel writing is attractive as well to people who are not slaves, not generals, not explorers. It is Ondaatje and Lorde that I think both speak to the crux of the matter here in terms of the problematics of travel writing, which is a both sexy and wide-open genre. I think that there are two kinds—however dumb and crude binaries are—there are two kinds of travel writing. On one hand you have the traffic and sightseeing landscape and exoticism, and on the other you have the consciousness of meeting the other and what that might mean, however messy. That will occur at some cost to you, as a travel writer, and—one hopes, assumes, plans for—at some cost to the reader as well. It seems to me that in the second way, conscious, thoughtful travel could be the thing that Theodore Roethke described poetry as being, that is, the long journey out of the self.

What I might propose is a couple of open questions. First among these is, how do you reference the other in your work? I bring this up to suggest that there are maybe a hundred ways in which we as Westerners do this, that is reference the other, every day. And if we can catch fifty of them, we are doing pretty well. Writing as Westerners, as Americans, we evoke the other for local color or for the subliminal, metaphoric effect that the subaltern's presence might provide, how the presence of a figure with no agency might enhance the Western speaker's own. The black writer Clarence Major wryly answers this in his long poem about Venice, about old Europe, "Surfaces and Masks," by evoking the image of a cultivated Negro in a country where one does not expect to find him available and speaking many languages, causing one to feel ignorant. The point here is that referencing the other as consciously as possible is something that we ought to be doing. Another question which comes up often, I heard it in the margins today, is what do you call "them," whoever "them" is. What do you call them in your writing? I would like to use that question as the occasion to posit a bigger question beyond that. When you bring up the "them" in your writing, how do you use the naming issue, that whole messy naming issue, to complicate and work to destabilize the status quo, if that is what you are interested in, and I am very interested in that, the unstated high position of the West, of here, of whiteness. These strike me as being issues in translation, widely defined—representation, translation, consciousness, it's all in the same rowboat.

Pavla Jonssonová referenced gypsies the other day, those perpetually marginal travelers that we are still taught to watch out for. They are travelers with no agency; the brother must have left home without his American Express card. Think of the good old racist verbs: to gyp or to jew. Who can get etymological on gypsy? I heard somebody say "Egyptians." Yes. It's from Middle English; gypsies were thought to have come from Egypt. Africans. That is a name in the West with much derogatory baggage. Gypsy; African; it's all there. If poetic language unsettles things and makes revolution possible by making the message strange, then the conscious traveler will necessarily return here with gifts that are unexpected, strange themselves, telling of wonders. To put crudely, such travel is a way of confronting stereotypes and neat little xenophobias. The French—oh, they are haughty. Jamaica—Jamaica is dangerous. Jamaicans love that ganja. Jamaicans love catering to the wishes of American visitors. As my friend the poet Billy Joe Harris said, "Neatness, madam, has nothing to do with the truth. The truth is quite messy, like a wind-blown room."

I have been fortunate in my life, in that I have been able to encounter the mess that travel is, and that travel has become an important site for me. Wang Ping said that this ridiculous fence the u.s. is building is there, in place, to keep *us* in place. It seems to me that subject position is a huge part of conscious travel writing, and that an important part to the subject position is on the far side of that fence, an important part of who we are. Who I am is over there, where I'm not supposed to go. If you put a beer or two into me I will yammer on about Canada and the black and white loyalists who fought against George Washington and then went to Nova Scotia, had good lives there, and are still there. That's something appropriate to think about for the Fourth of July. But this afternoon, let me tell you a brief story of my arrival in Vaduz, the capital of Liechtenstein. We were in Europe, my wife, my baby daughter, and I, and we had just a few days so we figured we would go to a really small country. And I've always had a thing for Liechtenstein. So we took the train from France to Sargans, Switzerland, and then the bus into downtown Vaduz. It was a rainy Sunday night. The hotel was full, but I argued with the hotelkeeper in my Hochschule Universität Deutsch and a room was found, and in a matter of moments I was downstairs in the hotel restaurant eating sauerbraten, drinking a glass of beer, happy as a clam. But that's the consumer being victorious. That's me using language to get something I wanted, using language to procure something. Of greater and longer-lasting interest to me is the incident on the way to the hotel. We were walking in the rain, it was a mile off, a car stopped and backed up, a door swung open, and a ride was offered, which we took. My daughter was only one year old, she was in a backpack. "Are you from Africa?" the man said in English. "No," I said, "I'm from the United States," and asked where he was from. "I am Turkish," he said. He was a dishwasher at a different hotel than the one we were going to. He and I talked briefly. We talked about work. He let us out; we wished each other well, and I did do well that evening at the hotel, and I did well also in that I read some about *Gastarbeiters,* something I knew a little bit about from Dušan Makavejev's movie *Montenegro.* I was lucky enough as a traveler from a rich country to fall in briefly with a marginal traveler, to go along with him in his car in the German-speaking world—and remember that English ain't nothin' but an archipelago off of German—and to be brought up to speed vis à vis the complexity of my own identity, at once American and "colored"—in a way that many black Americans are not lucky enough to be aware of. Like I say in my course blurb: travel is a complex, redefining event. I was redefined that evening in Vaduz.

SHERWIN BITSUI: When I was starting college, I had just gotten out of high school, and I grew up on the reservation; every morning and every evening I would cross the border, I would cross a physical, cultural, linguistic border. I felt like, as I crossed that border, people did different things in the city—it wasn't even a city, it was a small, one-main-street town called Holbrook—and I carried that border within me throughout my whole life; I carry it with me today. I don't know who empowered that border; I don't know if I keep fanning the flames or if I keep it alive inside me because that is my origin, that is my place. I speak both languages—I speak Navajo and I also speak English. In Navajo we call the language Diné bizaad.

This notion of always having to cross is certainly part of my own work, it is part of the consciousness of many Native people in this country. Our languages are the languages of this land, they are the languages that have been sculpted by the land. They are thousands of years old, they are sometimes continuous, and a lot of them are discontinuing as we speak.

One time I was actually walking, I had just got out of class at the community college in Holbrook and I was walking up the steps toward the dorm carrying my books on my back. It was a February or March morning. As I was walking I heard a voice, and the voice said, [in Navajo—"Good afternoon, where are you going?"]. I was kind of shaken. I looked around on both sides of me and I thought, am I hearing voices? Then there was a man watering the grass, who had got up and was looking at me; he was a white guy, an older white guy, so I was really confused because he spoke so well. He started talking to me in Navajo. The whole conversation we had was in Navajo. He said, ["Where are you from?"] and I started talking to him in Navajo without even thinking about it. ["I grew up in Greasewood," he said. "My father was a trading post man."] So he lived in Greasewood all his life. I don't know why it was shocking that this guy talked to me in my own language. Maybe because it's not shocking to the general white population to see me talk in English; but it was shocking for me that somebody of a different culture knew my own language. It was very pleasing. He reminded me of my grandfather. Then maybe five or six years later I had a reading on the other side of the reservation, in Farmington. I gave my reading and again I heard that voice ["Yeah yeah, thank you for speaking"] from the audience. I looked around and in a sea of Navajos I saw this older white guy waving at me. I guess he didn't remember that it was me he had spoken to five years before. Here he was at my poetry reading, sitting with his wife, who said, ["I am Navajo, I am one of you"]. This was all about disembodiment of language, this idea of what kind of power, what kind of breadth language gives you. Language itself does not necessarily belong to a certain people. Language is organic, language flows, language is a source of life.

In Navajo we have the concept of *saad*. I was interviewing a lot of Navajo poets for a class I taught, and I kept saying what is your inspiration, where do your poems come from? All of them eventually came back to language, they came back to *saad*, story, song; *hane'* is also story and song. This notion of always seeking equivalence between the cultures, of always trying to negotiate between the oppressors and the oppressed—I think it would be very important for non-Native speakers, nonindigenous speakers of this country, to learn and understand some of those concepts. I am very hopeful. I am an idealist in this sense. If you can understand a certain mountain range, if you can understand a certain story that has been handed down over generations, really understand those words and what they mean, what the concept is behind the word, the spatial and spiritual significance of that place, maybe it wouldn't be so easy for somebody just to plow it down, or maybe it wouldn't be so easy for somebody to sell off the rock for asphalt to be made into freeways. Maybe people would think differently about destroying this piece of place and building houses on it. English is sort of an important language—it is able to make everything into objects; it is able to cruise over the land and put it into acres. I think idealistically that it is necessary, wherever you live, to try to learn the local, indigenous names of places and what is the significance of that word. If you go to the East Coast all the rivers are eastern Native words, and does anybody ever think twice about that? *Cuk Şon*: it's not Tucson. *Cuk Şon* is the Tohono O'odham word meaning "this place." All of these words in this country are derived from indigenous words. This country has been lived upon for thousands of years. There is a tendency to create over and to mask over. Maybe in the languages of this place, where people have lived for thousands of years, maybe there is some way we can learn from that process.

—July 3, 2007

I AM BOTH. I AM NEITHER.

Michelle Naka Pierce

WHEN I ATTENDED THE FUNERAL OF MY MOTHER'S BEST FRIEND, there was something about the service that made it feel artificial—or at least somewhat surreal. It might have been my own anxiety about funerals and death, or that the priest kept mispronouncing Hatsumi's name, or that all of the eulogies were in English, even when given by Japanese friends. I wondered if these were the words her friends wanted to say. I questioned if they could truly express their feelings and emotions using English, when in the past, their conversations with her were almost always spoken in their first language or a combination of Japanese and English. I couldn't help but think about how language sometimes fails, how it isn't quite adequate in certain situations. Just before the service ended, everyone stood in line to receive communion while my mother played a recording of Hatsumi singing *shigin,* a traditional Japanese poem sung a cappella. My mother had been her sensei for twenty years, and in that instance, I understood nothing—and everything—in that song. Hatsumi's voice filled the room. It created a pocket of space where two cultures could exist simultaneously. For a brief moment, I found not logical understanding, but perhaps some kind of intricate clarity.

For Rosmarie Waldrop, "the function of [writing] is to waste excess energy," a concept she borrows from George Bataille's notion where "the living organism . . . receives in principle more energy than it needs to maintain life." I believe that for texts to live, whether they are poems or prose pieces or cross-genre endeavors, they must create their own existence, rather than solely retell an experience or just convey a particular and singular "message." And in order for texts to create their own existence, they must "mean" something. However, when I say "mean," I am not after logical or complete understanding—that kind of comprehension has a way of reducing the text to a so-called superficial "shared experience." Had I tried to explain the funeral, I might have only said that I felt sad, that I felt loss. But as Frank O'Hara writes, "There should be / so much more"—not of understanding, but of complexity in the way that life is complex. There's not a simple way to explain anyone's life, and oftentimes I do not understand my own, but of course, it still means something. Perhaps the "excess" energy could be used for the organism's/text's growth, the kind that makes a reader react and respond, as I did with Hatsumi's singing. The complexity I speak of often comes with contradiction. We need the ability to hold contradictory ideas at the same time while continuing to function. Similarly in music, there is counterpoint—two or more melodies played simultaneously. Writing that stimulates this energy has the ability to hold contradictory ideas by using counterpoint, by applying two or more genres, discourses, contexts, or forms to exist and mean, creating apparent incongruity. To show the complexity of the moment, these texts that try to carve their own existence, not replicate experience, create confusion, perhaps, but also offer a complex narration—one that depends on the reader. They reject closure, to borrow Lyn Hejinian's language. And in their moments of existence, they do not adhere to one genre's perfunctory rules. They cross the boundaries. They become hybrid.

What does it mean to be hybrid? According to Brian Stross, the hybrid has concrete origins: "In Latin the *hibrida* was the offspring of a (female) domestic sow and a (male) wild boar. The semantic range of the word hybrid has expanded in more recent times to include the offspring of . . . mating . . . . any two unlike animals or plants," which depends in part on the idea of the hybrid vigor or heterosis, that is, the capacity for growth. He cites the mule and certain strains of maize as examples—a certain necessity arises and to meet that need, two plants or animals are crossbred. But how can the concept of hybrid vigor be used in writing? Hybrid or cross-genre work is sometimes criticized, called gimmicky or experimental for its own sake. So how can writers pay attention to the initial gesture that urges them to explore the spaces in between or, as Kass Fleisher says, enact a critique of social categories?

Part of that initial gesture rests in a space somewhere between the writer and the reader. Hybrid texts are inextricably the link, the agent between the two. The writer creates the text, but for the text "to be resolved," as Michael Palmer refers to it, "calls for a dwelling" in the text: "the reader is an active part of the meaning"; "the reader completes the circuit." There is a nebulous relationship between reader and writer and between writer and language. Each individual brings experience, knowledge, and instinct to the page to find meaning, to find resolution. The same is true in the relationship that the writer has with language. When we write, do we offer readers an opportunity to inhabit words and find something for themselves to react and respond to? If so, does the hybrid text then become, not a reflection of the writer alone, but also a reflection of the reader? A reflection of language itself? Again, I am discussing a complex reflection that comes with a resolution that may be perplexing. In some cases, there may not even be any resolution because resolution is part of that need to simplify, to say that a word can only mean one thing. Daniel Schacter, when writing on memory and the brain, argues that "only bits and pieces of incoming data are represented in memory. These retained fragments of experience in turn provide a basis for reconstructing a past event, much as a paleontologist is able to reconstruct a dinosaur from fragments of bone." So could meaning perhaps be constructed the way that memory is constructed? In fragments, based on retrieval cues and encoding processes, retained differently for different people. Hélène Cixious writes: "All biographies like all autobiographies like all narratives tell one story in place of another story." In a way, she suggests it is difficult to provide that complexity in writing. Although the hybrid insists that we make the attempt and use all that we have available to us—various forms, languages, contexts, genres—to tell multiple narratives simultaneously.

Homi Bhabha, however, reminds us that hybridity "is not a third term that resolves the tension between two cultures." We cannot examine the funeral—nor the use of English and Japanese—through a binary lens. While the two cultures momentarily interconnect, the tension between the two does not resolve. Gertrude Stein forwards that each word should be laid down next to another and given equal weight. Neither paint nor word is in service to the object or narrative. And as such, one culture is not in service to the other. The hybrid carves out a new space to grapple with the tensions that arise to diminish the phenomenon of one story being told in place of another. As Michael Palmer expresses, the "question of how language means is continually an open one."

So when we say *hybrid*, it points in many directions and crosses boundaries. It speaks to our cultural existence. It reflects the danger in categorization. It worries about appropriation. It denigrates us with pejorative connotations like mutt, mongrel, half-breed. It marks limits and erases. It "waste[s] excess energy," while at the same time, providing space for new growth.

I am a hybrid text: both and neither.

—July 2007

POEMAAZU (POEMERS)
AND TORANRANRANZUREESHONZU
(TRANSLATIONS)

Sawako Nakayasu

'M RIDING A TRAIN IN [TOKYO] WITH SOME FRIENDS, SOME OLD, SOME NEW. When asked what kind of writing I do, I say that it's mostly poetry, and she says—*So you're a poemer?*—well, sure.

A less charming mistake: I am younger than I am now, and have yet to start talking about poetry in *Japaniizu* [Japanese] or with my family. I am in San Diego and the poet [Hiromi Ito] comes to read, and later I am on the phone with my mother, telling her about this poet I just saw read. The Japanese word for poetry is *shi*—and I attach a suffix that means "one who does," much like that woman who called me a poemer. I just met a Japanese *shisha,* I blurt out. Silence. "You mean, you met a *shijin,*" she corrects me. A *shisha* is one who does death, or, a dead person. Death—*shi*—is a homonym with poetry—*shi*. And the poet I had met was certainly not dead.

So—thinking about some *midoru guroundo* [middle ground] *purosesuzu* [processes] ma·ni·fes·ta·tions—how to get to "poemer" without killing off the poet. Expaaaaaaaaaansive translaaaaaaaaation versus mister misty mistranslation. Migration and immigration of people versus, or in parallel to, that of literature. Foreignization versus domestication—to use Lawrence Venuti's terms.

With regards to both humans and to literary texts: migration, immigration, displacement, can be voluntary . . . or not. Translations are traditionally instigated by the translator, which helps translation theorists and critics like Venuti speak of an "ethnocentric reduction of the foreign text to dominant cultural values in English." Venuti proposes working against what he calls the invisible translator, who produces a fluent, transparent, easy-to-read translation that conceals this ethnocentric violence and creates a text that is palatable to the target audience—or rather, the dominant culture within the target language.

Venuti is a proponent of foreignization—akin to an immigration model that does not ask one to let go of one's cultural difference—the salad bowl as opposed to the melting pot of American demographics. His question: "What would happen if a translator tried to redirect the process of domestication by choosing foreign texts that deviated from transparent discourse and by translating them so as to signal their linguistic and cultural differences? Would this effort establish more democratic cultural exchanges? Would it change domestic values? Or would it mean banishment to the fringes of Anglo-American culture?"

His suggestion resonates with what Steven Taylor was saying the other day, regarding the parallels between the modes of economic activity and modes of artistic activity. Or, Carole Maso: "If we joyfully violate the language contract, might that not make us braver, stronger, more capable of breaking other oppressive contracts?"

Often the writer of the original text, if they are alive and have some knowledge or interest in the target language, will express opinions about the work and become a collaborator in the process. In the case of Takashi Hiraide, there were times when I realized that he wanted his text to integrate more fully into English-language literature, that there were textual elements that I thought I would keep and re-create in English, and he was insisting against it so that his book would not mark itself as a foreigner in the fields of English-language literature. The production of the book involved some negotiation, too, as Hiraide was initially against a bilingual production—which again would mark the book as foreign. In the end we made a book that performed both cultural conventions of book formatting all at once—if you start on the English side, the pages open to the left, but then if you look at the other side, what would normally be the back cover of our books, you have the front cover of the Japanese side, with the pages opening to the right. This means that the two versions of the book end, or meet, in the middle of the book—and here we find a lightning bolt, which is what we find in the center of the walnut of the book's title.

So—a suggestion, or perhaps a point of interest, anyway, if one were a traveler in Translationland, is if we removed the translator altogether. Instead of the forced migration of literature, at the mercy of some imperialist, monological, hegemonic Translator—I'm not saying we all are, but let's just say . . . how about, then, voluntary immigration; this voluntary migrant text is, I believe, a relative of Pierre Joris's concept of a Nomad Poet, or a Noet, as he calls it.

One example I have of this is 関口涼子 [Ryoko Sekiguchi], a Japanese poet living in France, who translates her own work into French, though it was first written in Japanese. Some of this in recent years has been subsequently getting translated by others into English.

In 2006 we, with Belladonna and Litmus, brought four female Japanese poets to New York for a festival, a few days of readings and talks, which included a book publication featuring their work in bilingual format, along with an essay by each. In it, Sekiguchi writes about self-translation.

To me it's arguable whether one finds this applicable only to self-translation, or if it can and should apply to translation in general, but she says: "One must consider that a subordinate translation is not being made, but that two versions with the same status are; the chronologically later text can exert an influence upon the already existent text."

Again, thinking about immigration and that question, "where are you from?"—as if the place, the language one learned first, means the most and is the way in which one should be identified, or defined. Anne Tardos yesterday: "When I was five, we left France for Hungary, where my father was from; and at twelve, we moved to Austria, where my mother was from; at twenty-one, I came to New York, where I am from."

So this points toward the dismantling of a certain hierarchy, one that places *that which comes first*—one's first language, or the original version of a text—above those which come later—second, third, fourth languages, translations, and also, readings and performances of texts.

To continue quoting Sekiguchi: "The very idea of an 'original text' subsisting through the displacement of one language into another is therefore put into question in the change of language being written. And the intention is to put the classic distinction between language of departure and language of arrival [source, target] into question, since the text itself is nothing but a particular and infinite instance." She then discusses the strangeness we perceive in translation and the assumption that the strangeness comes from the originating language. "The point of departure text is not the source and departure itself is repeatable, origin and originals are multipliable. The original text then appears as persistent repetitions through the displacement of languages which react to and reveal the originals."

And: "One would also be wrong in considering this text multiplication as something quantitative or productive, since in creating two versions with the same status, nothing is 'added' to something else, rather the myth of an original text is removed, is eliminated from one of the versions."

In this essay, Sekiguchi is referring strictly to translation and self-translation, but I would like to extend these thoughts now into the realm of performed writing, and the performance of translated writing, as yet another kind of translation, one which has similar issues regarding "original" versus "subservient" versions. And then I'd like to, while I'm at it, toss in some thoughts about interpretation, which links one arm to translation, and the other arm to performance and improvisation.

It must have been four years ago, when the Republican convention was going on in New York and I was in an office job in Tokyo, and the president of the organization was watching Bush as he was broadcast live, with simultaneous interpretation into Japanese. This may be one of the reasons I got fired from that job, but as I was passing by, I couldn't help but stay and watch, and listen to the way the interpreter, invisible on the screen, was communicating not only the actual words coming out of Bush's mouth, but also the exaggerated dramatics of his voice, the rising intonation, and I was hearing this Japanese woman *do* George Bush, in real time, in Japanese, as a woman. The improvisatory nature of interpretation encouraged the interpreter to include other aspects of language beyond meaning—the sound, rhythm, and cadence, which so often get lost in literary translations.

Since then, I've been exploring other divergent modes of translation, including hybrid forms that are both translation *and* interpretation, or somewhere in between. When Bill Berkson came to Tokyo, we had him do a reading at the art school where I was teaching. Some of his poems we had done fairly decent translations of, but some were closer to sketches, and we hit upon a range of reading strategies, with a combination of improvised-or-not translations and interpretations and reconfigurations as I stood and read beside him. It's only too bad that Bill didn't know enough Japanese to see what was happening with his own work . . . but in any case it seemed an apt way to present work to a Japanese audience with varying English comprehension levels.

Or, other takes on it—my own work gained a multilingual, interpretive aspect in reading it aloud, partly because when my first book was published, I was living in Japan. I had opportunities to read and perform, but what to do with a completely English-language text, when in a foreign-language environment? And I began to see this as a self-translation of sorts as well, to be reading, or performing, my own work. It also helps that part of my influences are in music, the kind in which a written score is performed, or interpreted, or translated, by performers. Being both the composer and the performer of the same piece of writing meant that the composition didn't always come first, but that I could re-compose as I performed.

Finally—Cole Swensen once framed multilingual writing as the *opposite* of translation, as sort of a *refusal* to translate—an acknowledgment of the impossibility of translation, by throwing all the languages in together. I think this is one way to look at it, but my preference is to put all of it—

translation, self-translation, interpretation, performance, multilingual writing—on a continuum, with multiple vectors, to be sure, where texts might gain and acquire aesthetic values, problematics, local and global contexts, as they translate, get translated, and migrate through both "particular" *and* "infinite" instances.

—July 8, 2008

WORKS CITED:

Lawrence Venuti, *The Translator's Invisibility: A History of Translation* (New York and London: Routledge, 1995).

Ryoko Sekiguchi, "Self-Translation: Or the Artifice of Constraint" in *Four From Japan* (New York: Litmus Press/Belladonna Books, 2006).

Carole Maso, *Break Every Rule* (Berkeley: Counterpoint, 2000).

PIERCING THE WALLS

Margaret Randall

THE GREAT WALL OF CHINA, THE BERLIN WALL, THE WALL ISRAEL IS building to contain the Palestinians, or the wall between Mexico and the United States—currently advancing in blustering increments of hate across our southern border. Sometimes called curtains: as in Iron Curtain, Bamboo Curtain, or *el Telón de Azúcar,* Sugar Curtain—the term some Cubans use to describe the isolation of their island this many years after successfully rejecting foreign domination. Diplomatic, trade and military blockades, misinformation and lies, fear, abuse and prejudice: all make barricades effective for the walls' builders while dangerous and isolating for those kept in or out.

The kidnapping and sale of human beings, the slave ships of the Middle Passage and germ-infested blankets of the white man's wars against Native peoples—tragedies all, some reaching the definition of genocide—have become metaphors as well, separating the experience of the ravaged from the perpetrator's crime. This difference splits cultural roots, shaping the histories of the conquerors and those of the conquered in ways that may never heal. Slave labor, devastation of families, removal from ancestral lands, including those where family members are buried, forced marches, stock reduction: despite the fact that some of us descend from one of these histories and some from another, Empire's version of them all is what informs our consciousness. No accident, of course. Silencing, itself, is a wall as well as a weapon.

Now, through necessary historical rectification, we can understand how those human auction blocks and germ-infested blankets in effect represented walls between the colonizers and the colonized—and successive generations of their progeny. Atrocity always requires silence. Fear and a fabricated shame make silence possible. The Armenian Holocaust is still the subject of reluctant mention today; almost a century beyond its perpetration, few are able or willing to speak of its horrors. Recently Turkey and Armenia renewed efforts to heal this wound between their nations. Progress remains hesitant at best. Once such events pass into a biased historical record, ignorance and attitudes of trivialization, disregard, and fear of difference reinforce the distortion of memory.

Poets, writers, artists, scholars, and thinkers everywhere are called upon to retrieve this memory, break these silences.

Hitler's concentration camps, where six million Jews and thousands of Communists, Roma, homosexuals, and others deemed "imperfect" met barbaric death, remain the iconic symbol of twentieth-century criminality; one that continues to set the horrific standard and also, sadly, has sometimes been used as an excuse for later crimes. I think of those Jews who migrated to Israel, where they hoped to find a safe haven even as they grabbed territory and established new boundaries that ravaged their brother and sister Palestinians, for whom that land is also sacred and who have lived upon it for centuries.

As I began writing these notes I came upon an April 15, 2008, article from the Associated Press. It tells the story of Marek Edelman, then the only survivor among the four commanders of the 1943 Warsaw Ghetto uprising. Now he too is gone. Two hundred and twenty scrappy, poorly armed boys and girls, between the ages of thirteen and twenty-two, resisted the Nazi army determined to exterminate an entire Jewish ghetto of four hundred thousand.

Before he died, Edelman told this story: "I remember them all, not too many to remember their faces, their names. When you were responsible for the lives of some sixty thousand people, you don't abandon their memory." By his annual remembrance, sixty-five years later he continued to give lie to the repeated claim that the Jewish people didn't resist. His was one in a growing fabric of memory strands that helped to decimate walls of forgetting. Memory—preserving it, placing it front and center, honoring it so those who are born when everyone who participated in a precious moment are gone—may be the best resistance against the erection of walls.

Despite repeated pleas that these travesties must never be allowed to happen again, Cambodia's Killing Fields, Ireland's Catholics and Protestants set against each other for generations, two decades of Latin American Dirty Wars, and the contrived rage pitting Rwanda's Hutus against Tutsis are but three examples of subsequent crimes against humanity—and I limit myself to those in the twentieth century.

Fear and mistrust make the strongest walls of all. Walls that keep out and walls that contain, spawning a hatred that diminishes those on both sides. Silence, cowardice, and conformity keep the walls standing. Our challenge is to pierce these structures, give voice to memory, revive and reignite history. A single voice may inspire a chorus.

Colonialism and neocolonialism's arbitrary divisions create walls of unimaginable profit, pathos, and loss: Koreans separated by the imposition of their country's division into North and South, Vietnamese for so many years kept apart at the seventeenth parallel. In 1974, just six months before the Vietnamese victory, I traveled to North Vietnam. I was one of only nine foreigners in that country at the time. My guide was a middle-aged woman who had been active in the resistance in the south and at the moment of division was on a mission in the north. As we walked across the bridge leading to the liberated zone of Quảng Trị, we held hands. Tears spilled from her usually stoic eyes. It was the first time in twenty years that she would set foot in the south, where her only daughter had remained in 1954. She knew we would be nowhere near where she last saw her daughter, couldn't even know if she was still alive—all communication had been cut. But the symbolic closeness was enough to shatter her proud composure.

Today this tragedy is repeated among Cubans living on the island and their family members who emigrated; between immigrants from a dozen Latin American countries whose labor is needed in the United States but whose families are not welcomed here. Immigration reform remains a thorny issue for both u.s. political parties through a succession of administrations.

Surely one of the great ironies of the late twentieth and early twenty-first century is the enormity of migration: not walls but their opposite. Literally millions of displaced, homeless, hungry people walk toward a diminishing hope: Guatemalan families escaping hundreds of razed villages, the Lost Boys of Sudan, pitiful parades of refugees from Darfur, and other scenes of unrelenting violence. My generation retains images of those displaced by World War ii, as well as the knowledge that those European refugees were ultimately cared for by international organizations and most eventually returned to their homes. Today's migrants exist in numbers too vast for any organizational solution. They will likely die or remain in camps for the duration.

The partition of India and Pakistan. Kashmir's high-altitude pain. Today's Iraqi borders, drawn by men in European seats of power, ignorant and unconcerned about how their maps would affect peoples with shared cultural roots, language, customs, family, and desire. Today we have learned at least some of those divisions can actually be traced to mistakes: a simple misunderstanding here, a bit of drunken carelessness there. Error piled upon arrogance in a brutal history of violence and manipulation. Walls drawn on documents of conquest and erasing the everyday memories of people on the ground.

And of course one of the scenarios that claims our agonized attention today: the u.s. invasion and occupation of Iraq, years now and ongoing. It may be the most horrendous example of a war based on lies, denial—unpopular even in the country of its perpetrators. To date it has cost more than a million Iraqi and some five thousand u.s. lives—to say nothing of those tens of thousands more on both sides who have been uprooted, displaced, impoverished, traumatized, and often turned into helpless killers. More than any previous such travesty, the u.s. war in Iraq exemplifies the will of a few having their criminal way despite all manner of protest. Here we witness a wall of arrogance we have yet to effectively pierce. The u.s. invasion and occupation of Afghanistan is of increasing concern as well, eight years old now and rising, front and center as the mainstream press abandons Iraq.

Right here, inside our own country, we have a gnawing example of devastation, forced migration, ineptitude, and lack of official regard. I am speaking, of course, about the victims of Hurricanes Katrina, Rita, and Ike, many of whom years after those storms hit have given up on their government's broken promises, insurance company denials, or anyone's apology. Surely the wall that separates the impoverished, and mostly black, parishes of New Orleans from its upper-class neighborhoods is obvious to anyone who cares to look. It is a wall constructed of disdain, abandonment, failure to come to the aid of a dying people, fallacious mischaracterization, and scams perpetrated by government agencies and the private sector alike. And it is a wall that did not result from the damage of those storms but preceded them by generations. It goes back to the racist attitudes and policies that kept a poor, mostly black population in the low-lying areas while the wealthier whites remained safe on higher ground.

Today these walls still stand. Inadequately repaired levees are incapable of resisting a Category 3 hurricane. New Orleans survivors remain separated and scattered throughout the country; the city has been reshaped to favor a whiter, wealthier population; block upon block of rotting houses are still boarded up, and historic neighborhoods remain uninhabitable. The Bush administration turned its back on our country's Gulf Coast while at the same time having the gall to single out Burma's dictators as unresponsive to their people's needs when violent storms assailed that country. Obama's discourse has been better, but to date no real solution for the peoples of the Gulf Coast has been forthcoming.

Our prisons are also real and metaphorical walls that daily destroy the integrity of our society. More people per capita are incarcerated in this country than in any other, and the percentages of our various social groups are heavily weighted on the side of the poor and people of color. Building and running new prisons is one of our fastest-growing industries. Rehabilitation is a sham.

All these walls are traced on maps, which shift with new national splits and occupations but basically continue to reflect Empire's vision. Maps, since their inception, have been used as tools of misrepresentation, disparagement, denigration, and conquest, erecting arbitrary walls in conquest's wake. Chellis Glendinning tells us that "empire originates in the perception of place" and "maps are the tools of that perception." In her profoundly moving book *Off the Map*, she analyzes some of the ways in which she and all of us receive not simply a neutral education but one designed to reproduce "the perception, thinking and body language of a citizen of empire."[2] In 1569 the Flemish cartographer Gerardus Mercator published the first modern *mapa mundi*, detailing the world as it was then known: the entire round sphere with poles and the equator, depicting oceans, land masses, and all the different countries in relation to one another. The first European explorations of the New World had been undertaken not too many years before. Empires, striking out in the name of God and greed, and voracious of further possession, wanted to document their holdings and what they might yet claim. This map is still used in most classrooms, international institutions, and news reports today. The only changes that have been made respond to further national redistribution emerging as various countries fight for primacy, winning here, losing there.

Mercator saw the world from his sixteenth-century, Eurocentric perspective, one in which the era's science, mathematics, politics, even the capabilities of its machinery of knowledge reproduction, determined the cartographer's designation. Guided by longitude and latitude, he stretched lines to create equidistant divisions, such that the farther one got from the equator, the more distorted the lines became.

Mercator placed Europe at his map's center. The north became larger, the south smaller. Europe ended up being much more prominent than it is, and the United States, for example, appears larger than Brazil, which, in reality, covers many more square miles. What we refer to as the Third World—dependent nations of mostly dark-skinned peoples—all appear smaller and less significant than the nations engaged in their conquest. Way up in the Arctic north, the land mass appears thirty-six times its actual size. There is no acknowledgment of this. The distortion takes up residence in our worldview, affecting how we understand *what is*. Herein are the roots of the North's designation of a global South.

Of course a sphere represented on a flat piece of paper cannot but contain distortion. This is understandable, and in an ideologically just world might be easily explained, even remedied. Our world wasn't rooted in justice back in Mercator's time, and it isn't today. The problem with Mercator's map, more than the false dimensions of each country or continent, is the relationship between those areas portrayed as falsely large and those shown as unrealistically small. This proportional misrepresentation creates and maintains walls that invade our thinking, the way we see ourselves and others, propitiating an arrogant sense of entitlement in those whose countries are represented as oversized.

Even when an alternate cartography has developed—the Peters Projection and several others come to mind—Mercator's colonialist imaging defines our world. It continues to keep in place our overarching walls. Who, after all, defines what is up? As Arab American cultural critic Edward Said has written, "Today's empire is the global economy."[3] Today, when we speak of globalization, we are speaking of the logical consequences of the geopolitical, economic, and social vision Mercator gave us almost half a millennium ago. Its world image is imprinted on our DNA.

Beyond borders, our whole understanding of a living earth—and the human-provoked climate change that threatens life as we know it—can be traced to this same greed-based view of weather and accountability, or lack thereof. Unimagined advances in technology abet this view. Misrepresentation and misunderstanding are as close as the Hollywood blockbuster, nearest television screen, school curriculum, computer, cell phone, website, blog: cyberspace's whole ever-expanding web. We depend, among other elements, on our human heart, a creative sensibility, courageous scholarship, and the poet's primal voice to pierce the walls, recover or redesign possibility, redirect technology, nourish—indeed save—life.

I do not want to talk about these geopolitical walls without speaking as well of the more intimate walls constructed within families, social and religious bodies, and between generations, by unacknowledged greed, power inequality, and abuse. The wall between the patriarchal, self-serving, and power-crazed adult, who victimizes the helpless child through incest or other forms of abuse, is one that may last a lifetime. The husband who abuses his wife, parents who mistreat their children, clergymen who take advantage of their parishioners: these so-called personal assaults mirror the walls between nations, imposed by invasion and occupation. And those more publicly acknowledged walls, in turn, mirror those kept within the hidden crevices of family and community. Such walls are more alike than is generally understood. The line supposedly separating the intimate from the public or global is more permeable than we imagine. And the same courageous voice may pierce both.

Walls can be deceptive. Because time is not always linear, and no building material is entirely immune to the penetration of the human spirit or body's cellular memory, walls can be eroded by memory retrieval or disintegrate beneath the weight of need. We can tear them down and raise them up in unexpected ways and within the creative spaces we ourselves design. Communication of one sort or another can be traced to the very origins of life. Poetry, the most distilled and richest form of communication, crosses a magical line, entering a field where astonishment lives. It is charged with causing our bodies to tremble; our minds explode. It can reveal what has been hidden, retrieve balance, safeguard justice, inspire peace. Today, especially, it is a remedy to be taken seriously.

An opposing image to that of the wall—real or metaphorical—might be that of the road, path, or bridge. Talking stick or singing wire. Troubadour. Carrier pigeon. Whispered message. "From my mouth to God's ear."

Through centuries before our era, the Silk Road—splitting as it headed north or south—carried ideas and sensibilities, as well as goods for barter or trade, through precisely those parts of our world being ravaged by imperialist greed today: Afghanistan, Lebanon, the Sahara and Syrian deserts, Levant, and ancient Constantinople. Place names still salty on our lips: Persia, Mesopotamia, the Indian subcontinent. Five thousand miles of traders, merchants, pilgrims, monks, soldiers, nomads, and urban dwellers pushed forward in a constant movement of enrichment and exchange. At Petra, the Nabataens offered the sustenance of water in exchange for implements, rare metals, and spices; the arrangement built an empire that didn't require violence to consolidate its power.

Much earlier, the Bering Straits became a road for migrations of ancient peoples moving south. It is interesting to consider for a moment that nomadic peoples neither defended privacy of place nor competed for power. Walls did not yet exist. There were the stone roads along which runners carried fish from the sea to the Inca highlands of Peru. Food and messages. And roads that extended life and its creative force, like those broad, straight avenues moving out in the four directions from Chaco Canyon in New Mexico, linking outlier communities to the Great Houses our ancestral Puebloans inhabited from the eleventh to thirteenth centuries. Roads that connect. Pathways of energy and knowledge.

Pathways of wisdom, arcs and continuums of connection. Literature, mathematics, science, music, and spirituality. Books endemic to every culture, written and read in every language. Figures chipped into rock, painted in alcoves spanning millennia. Images we cannot decipher but whose power rivets us nonetheless, often signaling pathways back to ourselves. Lines forming figures or designs visible only from the sky: Peru's Nazca lines and the crop circles of northern Europe. And natural clefts and faults in the earth's crust, like the rift that splits Africa from south to north, continental divides that part waters and send rivers flowing in opposite directions, seaways that guided the peoples of the South Pacific, with only stars and wind for maps.

Today's examples may be more virtual than real: cyberspace information highways, by which we are instantly linked to people thousands of miles away, can send and receive words and images, rally idea and action, exhortation and lament. These electronic pathways propel us forward. I want to believe we can use the ever-evolving technology for life instead of death, that cyberspace may one day bring us closer together rather than broaden the gulf between rich and poor—the One Laptop Per Child initiative is an important start. But I am also aware of the danger implicit in the control of these technologies. Who owns cyberspace? We must continue to nurture some of the slower, more tactile and human means of communication as well. A meditative stillness. A hand on the shoulder. A slow caress. Faster is not always better. More is so very often less.

Our words, our poems, are bridges linking memory to energy, the natural elements to our waving hands, revelation to a mind burdened by noise and lies, a piercing streak of light to a heart in trouble. Connection embraces, engenders, propagates. The bridge may be electronic, spoken, or embossed upon the page with the oldest printing method known. Slowing down is always an option. "No ideas but in things," as the great William Carlos Williams observed, and although the line might seem to privilege product over process, I believe the poet was asking us to look at the places where object, idea, and use converge—and how.

I urge us to navigate and look past the roadblocks those who would control us place in our way, to explore our authentic experience in the development of a language that risks, embraces, and propels; in designing actions that put people before profit and redress social wrongs. I urge us to resist and reject the cooptation of language bombarding us daily through a sold-out, corporate media, rigged "scientific studies," lying commercials, and the empty verbiage that passes for public discourse. Even the academy is not immune to these distortions; often, because it has become so dependent upon Empire for recognition and funding, it may in fact perpetrate them.

One of Empire's most devious and implacable weapons is memory erasure. As it robs us of our histories, it fills our minds with seductive images, inserting us into a dangerous program in which we become the malleable pawns the system requires to consolidate its concentration of power. In this way we are coerced into acting against our own best interests. Memory is erased by false stories, by social manipulation, and by battering, even by incessant noise. Today's proliferation of noise—its sheer decimal volume—drowns out the voice within, the doubts, the alternative choices. We must learn the difference between power and empowerment.

Recent years have seen a great deal of important work in the area of memory. Oral history has developed as a genre in which the protagonists of events have been able to tell their own stories. And so certain histories have been rewritten, although their accessibility too often follows the fad of the moment. Language outside the mainstream is sometimes honored, like stream of consciousness or automatic writing, black English, Spanglish, hip-hop, dream. Feminist therapy has encouraged the retrieval of sexual and other abuse memories, helping many women and some men to begin their journey to healing. These, too, are vital pathways, piercing walls. This work has also opened us to the reality of cellular memory, making possible certain stunning connections.

I have found particularly relevant the idea that the invasion of a woman's or child's body by someone in a position of power, and the invasion of a small country by a larger, more powerful one, have a great deal in common. Both are rooted in the need to conquer. Both make use of violence and coerce through lies and manipulation. Both provoke strikingly similar damage in their victims. Only the scale is different.

In the years following the American war in Vietnam, more veterans took their own lives than died in combat. The wars in Iraq and Afghanistan—the so-called wars on terror—are already producing overwhelming numbers of men and women doomed by post-traumatic stress disorder (PTSD). The suicide statistics have intentionally been covered up, but the numbers beginning to emerge are staggering. An increase in domestic violence is another result of sending people off to kill and then expecting them to readapt when they come home. A recent report tells us two out of every five U.S. military personnel fighting or returned from these wars suffer a crippling form of PTSD.

During my generation, some of us have sought change and empowerment in political revolution. In the years immediately following the 1989–1990 disintegration of the Socialist bloc, many of us suffered a collective depression. Our very identities seemed in jeopardy. But our goal of an equitable division of power remains just, and many of our gains continue to shape us today, or to establish standards to which we may continue to aspire. We must resist the urge to see nothing but failure in the fact that we did not achieve our goals.

We did make the mistake of believing economic justice would bring with it all other forms of justice; that race and gender equality—respect for difference—would be achieved once the class war was won. Because we weren't able to braid the rights of women, people of color, and other relegated groups in the struggle for a better society, many of the old equations continued to plague us. The sexually "different," the mentally and physically othered, weren't considered at all. Power essentially passed from one dominant group to another, accompanying varying degrees of—always partial—social change.

Some of us looked to feminism, a philosophical stance that goes quite a bit further in speaking to us about the nature of power itself. Feminism, at its root, is a new way of looking at power and a practice that stresses empowerment. But almost everywhere, patriarchy defines traditional roles, and it has not been difficult for the capitalist system to distort and denigrate feminist ideologies. The notion that feminism is dead, or that this is a "postfeminist" era, is one more of Empire's inventions to keep us submissive. And the idea that feminism is a reflection of bourgeois conditioning that can divide the working class is an invention of certain quasi-revolutionary movements, used to keep their male leaders in power. A feminist analysis of power divisions is absolutely necessary to the creation of new forms of struggle.

But we need more.

Some have given up entirely on the more secular philosophies and turned to a variety of spiritual practices for clues to effecting change in our communities and ourselves. Positive values exist in a number of these, but the hierarchical structures of most religious configurations also tend to perpetuate power inequalities, to privilege stagnant constructs, and dull the individual's capacity to question and explore. I believe one of the greatest dangers in today's world is the explosion of religious dogma put forth as policy. The fundamentalist stratum in every one of the world's major religions distorts and threatens healthy relationships between individuals, family members, communities, and nations. Today, Christianity and Islam, in particular, are locked in a holy war of terror and annihilation. Walls rise ever higher.

Still, there is more than the science story. The Hopi story. The Navajo story. A thousand different stories in which peoples of every culture bring themselves from their beginnings and take themselves home. I walk across a desert landscape listening for the song of the canyon wren.

Recognition of, and respect for, difference is key. Empire's troubling race, class, and gender issues would not exist if we could see each person and group as a unique part of a healthy and creative whole. Patriarchy, greed, xenophobia, white supremacy and other forms of racism, heterosexism, and capitalism construct the walls of fear that make this so difficult. It is up to us to break down the walls—in our lives, our relationships, and our work.

I want to close by speaking of several initiatives aimed at building bridges where walls once stood. One of these has risen from the ruins of one of the starkest divisions in modern history: the splitting in two of Europe, symbolized and embodied by the Berlin Wall. It's been twenty years since it came down, not because Ronald Reagan pompously demanded, "Mr. Gorbechev, tear down this wall!" but because peoples throughout Berlin and all of Europe were ready to pierce it. We all know the subsequent history: thousands of joyous family reunions followed by the slow and painful reintegration of two very different social systems. Less well known, outside the immediate vicinity, is the effort to turn the once-barren and militarily controlled strip between East and West into a place of conservation and regeneration, one that stands as a model for what may one day be possible in other places where walls now divide: between the two Koreas, along the u.s.-Mexican border, and between Israel and Palestine, to name just three.

Dr. Kai Frobel, a German ornithologist and conservationist, grew up in the shadow of the Iron Curtain. From the small West German village of Hassenberg, he lived only about four hundred yards from the Bavarian border with the East. Between the two heavily fortified fences was the heavily mined "death strip." From his teenage years Frobel was an avid birder, uninterested in politics. He could not have imagined the fall of the Soviet Union nor a future removal of the restrictions that kept peoples separated but proved no obstacle to birds. As Frobel grew and observed, he took stock of an interesting phenomenon. Along that part of the strip not kept barren by militarization, something astonishing was happening. During the Wall's thirty-seven-year existence, off-limits to industrial farming with its poisonous fertilizers, a wide swatch of land gradually became a paradise for threatened species of birds, mammals, insects, and plants. Life was flowering in the shadow of separation and death.

Bird-lovers on both sides of the Wall began to make contact with each other. Change came and in December of 1989, only a month after the Wall came down, conservationists on both sides met to hammer out a plan that would lead to the creation of Europe's largest and longest permanent nature reserve. The green belt now stretches along the length of the former Iron Curtain from the Baltic to Bavaria's borders with the Czech Republic. Frobel says, "The aim is to turn the Iron Curtain's entire 4,250-mile length—extending from the Arctic to the Black Sea—into what is already being called the Central European Green Belt."[4]

Others are building innovative bridges along our southern border with Mexico. Sound sculptor Glenn Weyant has embarked upon what he calls the Anta Project. In southern Arizona he has been playing the fence with a cello bow, holding a contact mic to the vibrating construction material, and now has several hours of four-track sound that conveys the memory of division humanized by one man's creativity. In Southern California priests and ministers offer communion wafers through the chain-link fence. Members of families split by cruel immigration policy can sometimes be seen playing volleyball with a low section of the wall as their "net." And numerous photographers are documenting the travesty and resistance along what poet and philosopher Gloria Anzaldúa called *una herida abierta,* an open wound. Vision, courage, and creativity are required to make these transformational statements.[5]

Nation-states have mostly failed in their attempts to heal divisions, stop climate change, end war, or save the earth. Margaret Mead famously said, "Never doubt that a small group of thoughtful, committed people could change the world. Indeed, it is the only thing that ever has." Let us join the Frobels and Weyants to imagine our walls into gardens, habitats, and connection.

—2008
for my son, Gregory

NOTE: This essay was first published in *First Laugh: Essays 2000–2009* (University of Nebraska Press, 2011). It was based on a talk given at Naropa in June 2008.

1 Based on the keynote for "Dueling Eagles: A Seminar on U.S.-Mexico Border Issues" at the University of Oklahoma, Norman, Oklahoma, November 2, 2009. Rewrite and expansion of an earlier talk given at Naropa University in Boulder, Colorado, in June 2008.

2 Chellis Glendinning, *Off the Map* (Gabriola Island, B.C., Canada: New Society Publishers, 2002).

3 Edward Said, *Culture and Imperialism* (New York: Vintage, 1993), 5–6.

4 "From Iron Curtain to Green Belt: How life came to the death strip," by Tony Paterson, *Independent*, May 17, 2009.

5 For a more detailed description of the Anta Project, go to www.sonicanta.com. For articles on Friendship Park, between Tijuana and San Diego, where Sunday communion took place before the Department of Homeland Security stopped the practice, see NPR on February 9, 2009, among other sources. *National Geographic* and many individual photographers have published border images.

SAVORING DEATH IN MEXICO

Alberto Ruy-Sánchez
(translated by Rhonda Dahl Buchanan)

T HE FIRST TIME I WAS GIVEN A SUGAR SKULL WITH MY NAME ACROSS THE forehead, I was absolutely enthralled. I must have been four years old, almost five, because my great-grandmother had just passed away about that time, and they had made a sugar skull for her with her name inscribed on it, PAULA. They placed it by her photograph on the nightstand in the bedroom that had been hers. I remember my grandmother removing the vase of withered flowers and placing the sweet confection with the macabre smile in front of the serene image of her mother.

I had just begun to read, and spelling out those names was just another game for me. And I clearly remember that instead of thinking I was dead, like my great-grandmother, I believed that Paula, "the Big Mama," had become a little girl. Of course dying means you are no longer present, but it also means receiving toys and sweets, like the ones they gave me and my cousins. Skeletal toys to eat. And ever since then, I have embraced the idea that death, along with pain, leaves a sweet taste in the mouth.

The next day, after devouring my own skeleton, I wanted more, and asked if I could eat my great-grandmother's skull.

"No, that belongs to her," was the categorical response. No one in the house believed that she would return at night to eat it, yet everyone acted as if she really would come back.

No one forced me to believe, but they did expect me to act as if I did. It was like a game we played all the time and it really was fun. The dead allow us to pretend things happen, whether they do or not. This was the powerful feeling that came over me. And much later, I would learn that it is part of the baroque culture in which everything seems to be and not be at the same time, where language and reality always possess more than one level and one meaning.

In response to my insistent pleas to eat my great-grandmother's skull, my mother gave in and took me to the market where they were sold, and that was a true revelation for me: hundreds, thousands of sugar skulls.

Coffins, sheep, cadavers filled with chocolate, paper skeletons, miniature fake food, baskets, tombs the color of pistachio and crimson, canary yellow, and sky blue: colors of the pastry shop. And soft, fresh bread of the dead, proudly displaying femurs drawn with honey. Like a new, immense, and ephemeral toy store offering wheels of fortune, wooden theaters in which death dances, and buses brimming with skeletons.

Among the flowers, there reigned supreme a yellow, nearly orange, flower, the color of fire, with petals so thin and dry they almost seemed like paper: the marigold, the flower of the dead called *cempasúchitl*. They are sold in bouquets, by the bucket, or in paper bags, or just the petals for creating a little path to lead the dead to their offering.

"All this is for the Day of the Dead," they explained to me.

"For their special day? Like their birthday party?"

"That's right."

It is a strange party where the guests of honor are not present but receive gifts, where everyone awaits their arrival but knows that they will not come. Like my aunt, who always waited for her husband who never returned, and spoke of him as if he had never left. And everyone played along knowing that she knew that we knew. To die is to go away suddenly, leaving everyone waiting for an impossible return, organizing parties for someone who will never come.

That display of skeletons and delectable smiles was placed appropriately next to the fruits of the season. Both were meant to be enjoyed while they lasted. And my eyes lingered on everything, savoring the wonder of it all. What I saw was not a hell of suffering skeletons, like those seen in church in the paintings of the Final Judgment Day, the ones explained in great detail on Sundays by a solemn priest pointing a menacing finger. Nor did they resemble a paradise of puffy floating clouds with frightened angels and men in white beards gazing upward, toward a void.

It was the essence of this life, of the marketplace and the kitchen, of flowers and fruits, of a party without judgmental priests. A worldly spectacle in which all the senses are invited to take part in the sweet game of death, in the creation of excessive, carnivalesque representations that are delirious, pleasant, and absolutely whimsical, but also ritual in nature. A popular baroque ritual re-created in every house of my neighborhood by each family who remembers their loved ones in their own way. Festive Day of the Dead toys enter the houses, each a banquet of delightful flavors and colors.

Although I was vaguely aware of how strange and disturbing this carnival of sensations can be for others, it would be many years later that I experienced this firsthand, when I gave the children of some French friends a handcrafted wooden theater with skeletons that danced at the turn of a handle, a typical Mexican toy given in November, something I considered to be a naive Mexican version of the very European "Dance of Death." The parents of my French friends were absolutely horrified, and took the gesture as an offensive expression of serious poor taste. The same reaction, according to some witnesses, that Leon Trotsky experienced in 1938 when Diego Rivera, his host in Mexico, gave him a sugar skull inscribed with the name Joseph Stalin. Trotsky asked one of his assistants to remove it from his sight, considering the gesture an uncouth affront that further weakened their already fragile relationship. The image of Rivera, laughing, with sugar skull in hand, consolidated the opinion his guest had formed of him, that of a crude savage.

Although the handmade confection of twisted sugar, shaped according to one's whim or molded into skulls, animals, or coffins, is made in many parts of Mexico, the best place to find it is in the *alfeñique* market at the gates of Toluca, about forty-five minutes from Mexico City, during the last week of October and the first of November. The word *alfeñique* comes from the Hispano-Arabic word *al-fanid*, which refers to very thin and twisted noodles made of sugar, a form of Arabic pastry brought to America by the first Spaniards. At first it was made in the monasteries and convents, but eventually it became a popular handmade craft.

In his *Diary of a Voyage to New Spain*, published in 1763, Francisco de Ajofrín tells us:

> Shortly before All Souls Day, they sell thousands of figurines of baby lambs and rams made of sugar, which they call offerings and give as presents to the boys and girls of the neighborhood. Coffins, tombs, and thousands of figurines of the dead are also sold. Priests and friars of all religions and courtly bishops gather for the splendid fair under the gates of the grand marketplace, where the competition between men and women selling their wares the evening of All Saints Day is incredible. . . . All these figures and tiny creatures, and other larger objects are made by lepers with great pride and at a very low price. And if orders are placed, they ask for payment in advance (a practice familiar to many officials in America), and either they do not make them, therefore losing about as much as they earn, or they make them poorly. Late and expensive, it's enough to try one's patience.

The nineteenth century ushered in a growing eagerness for modernity among the Mexican elite. Educated men who referred to themselves as "scientists" governed and attempted to impose a new and tempered rationalism over the baroque rituals of death. It is logical to cry when one suffers. The contrary is irrational. The excessive forms were viewed as superficial manifestations of dreadful taste, vulgar forms with no place in modern civilization.

Thus in 1882, Tomás de Cuéllar, a Mexican writer, diplomat, and member of the Royal Academy, deplored the practices he considered the "remains of barbarism" and moral deficiency. "And the skulls of the tomb," lamented Cuéllar, "are made into toys so that later the children may celebrate the death of their father with laughter." He writes that authentic pain is the complete opposite of sugar:

> Is perhaps the painful memory of a father, of a mother, of a dead child, what leads one to consume those tons of peanuts and sweets? Physiologically, the appetite is lost with great pain. What happens to that very authentic deep pain that not only delights in the palate on the 2nd of November, but transforms the pleasures of the tongue into a feast of gluttony? . . . At this time of the year Mexico reveals its unique nature to the philosopher and foreigner, an original trait that unfortunately reflects poorly on our culture. . . . And those feelings, that pain and sorrow? Will all these flowers of the soul end up like the *cempasúchitl,* the ugliest and most ordinary of flowers? . . . It is heartwrenching that there exists something sadder than death: the joy and indifference of the living.

Cuéllar's indignation for what he considers irrational and unnatural emotions is still alive today at the beginning of the twenty-first century, shared primarily by those Mexicans who strive to be modern: Americanized economists who judge humanity in terms of economics. These new "scientists" who govern us view the excess of colorful cultural forms as superstitions and backwardness, especially those that are popular expressions. For many of them, they are only "primitive superstitions," vestiges of premodern Mexico, an historical and populist burden for the golden dream of economic progress they treasure.

Paradoxically, the more the desire for pure modernity grows (not unlike the Protestant dream upon which the United States was founded and described so elaborately by Max Weber in his classic book *The Protestant Ethic and the Spirit of Capitalism*), the more grows the myth, forged much earlier but reaffirmed in the twentieth century, that the Mexican enjoys a privileged relationship with death and laughs at it.

In 1932, Sergei Eisenstein, a Russian who loved all things Mexican, photographed himself holding his sugar skull. And in the final scenes of his unfinished movie *Long Live Mexico,* he filmed Death dancing, disguised as a young boy wearing a tropical carnival mask that he removes at the end, revealing his face to modernity.

Antimyth and myth go hand in hand perhaps because the aseptic and rational dream is as mythical as what it strives to negate. Interestingly, the idea of an independent and modern nation emerged from the hand of a dark-skinned Virgin. In order to free themselves from a monarchy, the fathers of Mexican independence petitioned a pope to declare that the American territory was so special that God had granted it what He had never done for any other land: a *mestiza* Virgin. And thus the fusion of Indian and European blood would create the myth of color for this young nation.

In fact, the rich indigenous diversity of Mexico converges in the cult of the Virgin of Guadalupe, which combines all the syncretisms and rituals of ethnic fusion, so much so that in the seventeenth century, Sor Juana Inés de la Cruz invented a literary form known as the *ensaladilla,* or "little salad," verses that consisted of a chorus of diverse indigenous, African, and Criolla voices, celebrating their diversity in a unanimous chant to the Virgin.

Indeed, something similar occurs with the rituals of death that, like tequila and the mariachi, form part of the vernacular spoken and understood in all of the regions of this nation of mythical homogeneity, an idea that Alfonso Alfaro explains in an essay published in Volume 27 of *Artes de México.*

Based on the nationalistic myth of a nation that embraces death, the smiling skulls and Day of the Dead altars abound in the very same Mexican cities that ironically strive to be more modern. And more and more frequently one sees in such public places as offices and museums, but also in the homes of the middle class, refined versions of the colorful altars to the dead with sugar skulls, decorative cut paper over tablecloths, photographs of the recently departed, and offerings of food and beverages.

Nevertheless, a visit to some of the small and large Mexican towns that celebrate the Day of the Dead in the ancient way will confirm that the smiling skull is not always present. Often what replaces the mythical laughter at death is a ritual serenity. This serves as a reminder that the country is a melting pot of mortuary diversity in which there does not exist a mythical homogeneity of "the Mexican," that literary character ingeniously reinvented by Octavio Paz in *The Labyrinth of Solitude* (as Alfonso Alfaro mentions in his indispensable essay "Death Without Skulls."

Octavio Paz examines the Day of the Dead through the concept of the "fiesta":

The Mexican does not seek amusement: he seeks to escape from himself, to leap over the wall of solitude that confines him during the rest of the year. All are possessed by violence and frenzy. Their souls explode like the colors and voices and emotions. Do they forget themselves and show their true faces? Nobody knows. The important thing is to go out, open a way, get drunk on noise, people, colors. Mexico is celebrating a fiesta. And this fiesta, shot through with lightning and delirium, is the brilliant reverse to our silence and apathy, our reticence and gloom.

Later Paz writes: "The word death is not pronounced in New York, in Paris, in London, because it burns the lips. The Mexican, in contrast, is familiar with death, jokes about it, caresses it, sleeps with it, celebrates it; it is one of his favorite toys and his most steadfast love." In spite of Octavio Paz's attempt to understand the complex and paradoxical nature of the phenomenon without simplifying it, he actually reinforced the mythical idea in one sentence that he wrote: "The Mexican mocks death."

A significant example that negates the myth that all Mexicans laugh at death occurs in San Gabriel Chilac. I have had the good fortune of experiencing its rituals several times. Its relative distance from the capital of the State of Puebla has protected it from mass tourism that assaults, for example, the island of Janitzio in the region of Michoacán on the Day of the Dead.

In his *Adventures in Mexico,* which begins in 1937, Gutierre Tibón, a writer of Italian Mexican descent, describes briefly his visit to that corner of Puebla in 1961:

I was in a cemetery that I believe is unique in Mexico and perhaps in the world. I still have engraved in my retinas a nearly unreal vision of color, beauty, and human tenderness. [. . .] A canopy made of emerald green banana leaves, or small green reeds, or black and purple fabric, is erected above each grave, providing shade for the offerings: the bread of the dead placed in straw baskets called *tenates,* bowls filled with *mole,* bananas, oranges, and flowers, everything extremely fresh, displayed with grace and abundance. The *cempasúchiles,* marigolds with their yellow-orange color contrast with the bloodred of a velvety flower they call *moco de pavo,* or foxtail amaranth. The virginal white lilies provide a stark contrast as do the purple gladiolas and the blue ground cover we call "cloak of the Virgin," which seems to have waited to flower that very morning. Candle flames flicker softly among the offerings and flowers, one candle for every loved one who is remembered. The families sit or kneel before the canopies, everyone praying, from the grandfather down to the children. Organs are placed among the tombs, and people sing and pray in perfect Spanish, or in clearly pronounced Latin, although among themselves they speak *Nahuatl,* the melodious dialect of ancient Mexico. [. . .] The atmosphere in the cemetery of Chilac, is not one of joy or sadness, but rather peace, serenity.

One notable inhabitant of San Gabriel Chilac, don César Cariño, tells us that the ritual for the dead, the preparation of the offering, begins when the seeds are sown: "In the first days of July, the seeds should be planted in the earth so that they may reach their splendor on the Day of the Dead. Along with the seeds of other seasonal plants, the seeds for the colored corn to make the *atole* are sown, and those of the *cempasúchitl,* or marigolds, the Aztec flower of the dead." According to don César, the ancient ones begin by reciting *intelnaimíquiz* in Nahuatl, a ceremonial expression that serves as an invitation to prepare the offering to give thanks for the lives enjoyed by those who have passed on.

On October 28 they go to the cemetery with flowers, candles, and offerings to "the unfortunate dead," that is, the souls of the dead who have no family or died without last rites, or by accident, or far from their home. Then they begin constructing canopies made of reeds, blankets, or plastic to place over the tombs. "Some tombs are whitewashed," explains don César, "like the immaculate soul who will come to visit us in these days." Then everything continues in the homes of each family, where as much attention is given to the preparations for the special meal as the selection of objects for the offerings.

Many years after the visit of Gutierre Tibón, nearly a half century ago, that serene atmosphere remains. Thanks to the friends of friends who receive us in Chilac, we have witnessed the other dimensions of the ritual. To begin with, what happens in the cemetery is the climax of the celebration, most certainly, a glorious culmination experienced by all. Beforehand, the heart of the ritual takes place in each house. It is interesting to note that even the architecture of the houses functions as a central shared space for displaying the altars and their offerings to the dead. Often a wing of the house around the patio is reserved for the altar and another for rooms in which the family lives. In smaller houses nearly everything is removed to make room for the altars. From the thirtieth and thirty-first of October, one may go from house to house to see the offerings. The festivities continue in the houses in anticipation of that last night of October, when the dead come to visit the family. In some houses chairs with the names of the distant visitors are placed in front or to the side of the altar. Their photographs serve as the centerpiece of the arrangements and deep, straw baskets hold offerings of bread and fruit wrapped in purple paper. If the loved one smoked, they also include his favorite brand of cigarettes and a glass of his favorite liquor, with the bottle next to it, "in case he wants more." I went inside a house where a television set was turned on, playing a tape of the loved one's favorite shows and programs and a new movie they thought he might enjoy.

The windows are adorned with *papel picado*, decorative cut paper, and the candles cast a light on the scene that is unlike that of any other day. *Copal* emits smoke perfuming the room. A woman sings a mourning chant as she lights the coals of her small grill: "Life is born full of death, just as this fire is born, and the smoke of the *copal* rises here like your soul on its way to heaven." The floral arrangements fill every space and adhere to a specific code of colors and forms. Sometimes baskets of offerings fill the space. The exceptional touch given to each detail, perceived by all the senses, envelopes the daily ritual in a poignant aura. In the past, banana leaves served as tablecloths, which are now made of paper or bright color-ful plastic. Banana leaves were also used to wrap the food and keep it fresh. Perhaps out of nostalgia for the banana leaves they now use green plastic.

The relatives, friends, neighbors, customers, and colleagues arrive to honor the dead. They bring flowers, or large and small offerings, or simply the gift of their presence as they come to pay their respects. Huge quanti-ties of food are prepared in the house to offer something to eat and drink to each visitor, and something for them to take with them: tamales, bread, or the hot corn beverage *atole,* because the visitor can never refuse an offering. As the hours pass, the altar dedicated to the departed one becomes filled with objects, which the family arranges according to a code that reflects the preferences of the palate and whims of the loved one, as well as his place in society.

They welcome us in the home of a woman who had passed away a few months before, and we notice the huge pile of offerings. They explain to us that for those who recently died, from the third of November on, their altar is called "new offering" and everyone arrives with special gifts, such as the handmade candles called "adorned wax," which are always associated with the "souls in Purgatory." The idea is to help the dead woman on her jour-ney to heaven and make her feel especially honored during her first visit home to the family.

This woman was a well-known citizen of the town, the owner of a phar-macy. Her daughters explain to us in great detail every step of the ritual.

Everything begins long before, with the death of the person who is now being remembered. The wake for her body was held in that very same chapel where today she receives offerings. According to the customs of the village, whenever someone dies, this ritual allows intimate friends and family to gather and renew the ties that bind them to the family of the deceased, and also provides the opportunity for small and large quarrels to be reconciled, and in fact, those who have had some conflict with the family during the year may come forward to make amends. The family in mourning must open the door to anyone who generously brings an offering, a gesture that cannot be rejected. And someone in the family must keep track of whoever comes during the night because the next morning, with the help of family and close friends, they must take breakfast to the house of each person who came to make an offering to their mother.

In this way, the ritual of the dead becomes a way of wiping the slate clean and erasing arguments and conflicts that are capable of loosening the social ties, weaving them together again and restoring the town's collective network. The excess of offerings and food is an indispensable aspect of this ritual, which adheres completely to an economic concept that pedantic scholars would call premodern and anthropologists would consider the economy of potlach, or consumption.

Its function is related to the idea of an apparently gratuitous act, *el don*, the gift, as described by Marcel Mauss in his *Essai sur le don*: a ritualistic excess whose function is not linked to practical savings but to an apparent extravagance with symbolic meanings that generates a profound moral reciprocity and impacts the entire social group, and the aesthetic dimension of that society as well. Mauss writes in 1925:

> Fortunately not everything in our societies can be classified exclusively in terms of selling and buying. [. . .] It is only our Western societies that quite recently turned man into an economic animal. But we are not yet all animals of the same species. In both lower and upper classes pure irrational expenditure is in current practice. [. . .] A significant part of our moral fiber and our life is influenced by the sphere of the *don,* or gift, blending obligation and freedom. [. . .] These phenomena are at once legal, economic, religious, aesthetic, morphological and so on. [. . .] The dances performed, the songs and shows, the dramatic representations, the objects made, used, decorated, polished, amassed and transmitted with affection, received with joy, given away in triumph, the feasts in which everyone participates—all these, the food, objects

and services, are the source of aesthetic emotions as well as emotions aroused by interest.

Thanks to its celebration of the dead, the town of Chilac lives an intense economy of exchange, of offering and receiving as a form of revitalized civility, one that encourages a profoundly civic life as well as civilization itself. Tonight, on the eve of the Day of the Dead, when everyone symbolically awaits the visit of their loved one, it is as if they hold a wake for them again. And it is the departed one who bestows upon them the opportunity to strengthen the social fabric. Families that have been torn apart reunite. Those who have moved away return because it is All Soul's Day. And the dead convene to be celebrated at the fiesta. And for this very reason they receive gifts as well. "It is in the nature of food to be shared"; says Marcel Mauss, "to fail to give others a part is to 'kill its essence,' to destroy it for oneself and for others. [. . .] Avarice interrupts the action of food which, when properly treated, is always productive of more."

A large part of the ritual that grants meaning to the social life of so many people takes place not only in the cemetery, but in those houses that have what seems to be an unused room or extravagant space for erecting an altar to pay tribute to their departed loved ones.

The day after the departed and the living friends of the deceased (who are our friends) have been welcomed in the home, the offerings, candles, visits, and prayers move on to the cemetery. The social circles widen and one can clearly see how the social ties binding the immediate family reach out to the extended family, some of whom live nearby, and the concentric circle keeps expanding until it embraces the entire town, incorporating members of each of its families, including the emigrants who have returned and the distant relatives who have come to visit. The home, with its family altar, has become a public square for the living and the dead, a colorful entity of tombs and relatives who have gathered for the same reason: to share their abundance and renew their existence as a distinct and unique community.

The cemetery has already been cleaned, employing that other institution of the economy of communal giving and excess: the *tequio*, the voluntary obligation to work at least one day of the week for the benefit of the community. In addition to family members who care for the tombs of their loved ones, others volunteer to work, some constructing structures over the graves, while others build stunning temporary refuges out of sticks and palms, or sheets and very brightly hued canvases. The offerings are placed directly over the mound of earth. Women skilled in the art of mourning and prayers offer their services from tomb to tomb. Musical groups, mariachis and soloists, do the same. The conglomeration of graves becomes a veritable labyrinth that leads us from one source of wonder to another. The smoke from the incense and *copals* floats above the yellow flowers. Some women wear their best traditional blouses with embroidered flowers, an offering on the body that delights the eyes of those who gaze upon them. Families go around visiting each other, curious to see what the others have created, sharing and lending a hand at times. New crosses are erected. Some tombs reflect the custom of placing a smaller cross each year on the grave, as many as ten. I am intrigued by two adjacent tombs that have the same name on their crosses, as if one body could be buried in two graves at the same time. I ask if they belong to two different people with the same name and they explain to me that the family owns two tombs but because everyone is healthy and there are less departed ones in the family than graves, instead of piling all the crosses on one tomb, they spread them out over two, affirming, "It looks so much prettier this way." The excessive aesthetic value is more important than the logical rationale of a poor modern man like myself, who would never dream of using two tombs for one dead man.

For themselves and for the dead, the living eat the food that their loved ones enjoyed. Some dishes are extremely ritual, such as *mole de cadera*, the end product of a ritual slaughter of thousands of goats beheaded on a single day near Tehuacán, a few weeks before the festivities. To prepare them for death, these goats do not drink water for months, grazing instead on aromatic plants whose aroma and flavor permeate their flesh.

The special dishes they prepare provide much more than food: a leap of the body toward the exceptional that lies beyond our reach. The *tamayálotli*, an enormous pumpkin prepared with white cheese, rises like fire in the mouth. The *potzintámatli*, a tamale made with beans and wrapped in *zacate* leaves, is baked in a special oven that is heated only for this community festival. Accompanying the corn tortillas are an enormous variety of wheat breads, whose ingredients include the fermented sap of the maguey plant, milk, brown sugar cane, or lard. And then there is the unique flavor of the *cuitlacoche*, that black fungus that grows on corn and, as many say, tastes like the earth. Much like the description in this verse by José Gorostiza:

Death tastes of earth
anguish of gall
Of honey I savor
this dying by drops. (*Death Without End*)

"This food calls for such extraordinary preparations," says don César Cariño, "that it is the greatest testimony of our loyalty and gratitude toward the holy souls, whose return on the Day of the Dead sets in motion this parade of excess."

Once again we return to the cemetery, where food is consumed in abundance and the grave is transformed into the family table. Liquor flows in excess, cleansing and reviving the sleeping soul, and facilitating conversations with the dead. Everyone remembers their faces, their favorite songs, their favorite food, and to assure they are not forgotten, photographs that had been displayed in the house are placed on the graves. The living and the dead eat face to face and also sing, so they tell me, because the dead live on in those who still have a mouth to sing, and together they harmonize and sing the departed one's favorite songs.

And some of those outsiders, like myself, commit that modern rite of religious tourism and take a photograph. In Chilac no one minds if their picture is taken. It is part of the festival and the exchange of offerings that are given and received. The principle of reciprocity is so deeply rooted that as soon as I request permission to photograph the family and their tomb, they consent and immediately ask me to join them and have my picture taken with them, with their camera, next to the tomb that I like so much. And with great pride they explain to me the origin behind each offering. They insist on taking my picture next to the photograph of their loved one, explaining that they wish to extend to me the same interest that I have shown in them. Then they ask me how we celebrate our dearly departed in that place where I come from. They share with me stories and the bread, which moments before adorned the tomb, as well as tequila and coffee "to wash it down."

I realize that each family grave is a kind of text in which an expansive social net is woven together and secured by the knots of generosity that unite the family and impart a sense of belonging in this world. The children are initiated, as am I, in the festive reading of the tombs. Two girls, who are a little older than the others, recite for me the symbolism of the flowers, the crosses, and the food. And once again they tell me how, why, and for whom each item is placed. Their interpretations vary, each one adding or taking away something. It is an evolving text in constant transformation, each image suggesting a thousand things. But at the same time, it is an encrypted mirror of the family that reflects the living as well as the dead.

The funeral art of Chilac is popular and naïve, but also ethnographically conceptual. Indeed it is an aesthetic code in which at times individual creativity breaks the rules, similar to what happens during Carnival, and in doing so, restores order in another way, sometimes establishing new norms, new ways of expressing death that others, the majority, imitate, for better or worse.

Between carnivalesque transgression and moribund repetition, we eat and drink with the dead, tightening our bonds. And thus, elaborately and serenely, we come to the realization that we are all in the process of dying. In fact they say that the deceased is merely "one step ahead of us." The mirror facing us. We perceive life as an endless death.

This is precisely the theme of a long, amazing poem, one of the greatest works of Mexican literature, which its author, José Gorostiza, entitled *Death Without End*. My experiences in Chilac have offered me a new way of understanding that text. I had read it before and had attempted to decipher its powerful metaphors, like many others have, from a modern perspective that contemplates death and life, the passage of time, and the existence of a god who controls us and is the embodiment of life and death.

After visiting Chilac and reading it again with eyes that had witnessed a baroque celebration, it became apparent to me that *Death Without End* was a poetic offering, a flower that can be read in different ways, an encoded composition whose meaning extends in different directions. Gorostiza says that "poetry, as it penetrates the word, dismantles it, opening it like a rosebud to its many shades of meaning." Now that the word has become a prisoner of the connotations that are normally attributed to it, poetry frees the word, releasing a multitude of meanings. "Poetry is for me," says Gorostiza, "an exploration of the quintessential—love, life, death, God—that unfolds in the attempt to disrobe language, stripping it in such a way that it becomes more transparent, allowing one to see these essences hidden within." He goes on to refine his definition: "Poetry is a kind of contemplation, a house of mirrors in which words, placed next to each other, reflect one another in infinite ways and then find meaning in a world of pure images in which the poet unleashes the hidden powers of man and establishes contact with that entity or force that lies beyond."

Throughout the poem, images emerge that seem to have come from a town like Chilac or from that very place that remains engraved on my retinas:

While we keenly revel in
this good, unknowing candor,
this eager innocence of spirit
that sets itself to dream by day
and dreams the mildewed yesterdays,
the ancient absent rose,

and tomorrow's promised fruit,
opaque as the back of a mirror
which consults the depth of the image it holds,
only to draw from it at last
another mirror in reply. [. . .]
The flower hoists its colors
water in the field.
Oh, what wares
Of winged perfume! [. . .]
The road, the fence, the chestnut trees, to die
a needless, early death, but beautiful,
enter at its urging
the torment of their own images
and in the middle of the garden, beneath the clouds,
spare lesson of poetry,
install a dazzling hell.

In the end, the poem changes its tone two more times, first by evoking a popular childhood game in which someone with symbolic powers tries to enter the circle of children holding hands. "Knock, knock? Who's there? The Devil." This passage serves to imbue the ending with a carnivalesque feeling. The game establishes a theatrical dimension that had been missing in the poem. And it shatters the tone of the entire poem with a very vernacular expression that boldly taunts death:

From my sleepless eyes
my death lies in ambush,
waylays me, woos me
with its languid eye.
Come along,
little wench of the frozen blush
Come along,
let's go to the Devil!

I am fascinated by one particular photograph among the many that are displayed on the tombs in Chilac. It is old and yellowed: the portrait of a little boy surrounded by flowers, dressed like an angel, with open, vacant eyes, a bouquet of flowers in hands that can no longer hold anything, flowers that would fall, no doubt, with the slightest draft of air. His parents and godparents stand around him.

"He is our little angel," an old woman explains to me with enthusiasm. "He died and we buried him without crying for him so that he would go straight to heaven and not have to return to wipe away our tears."

"And how could you bury him without crying?," I ask, thinking that that perhaps there can be nothing as terrible as the death of a son.

"We played children's games: The Spanking, Sandal-Whacking, and the Pinching Game, and we danced, and hired mariachis to play."

I notice that all the games mentioned are rough, and call for hitting and hurting someone. "If it hurts on the inside, it needs to hurt on the outside. That's just the way life is, and death too. It's hard on us, but we don't cry so we don't cause any harm to our little angel."

The photograph belongs to a visual genre that until recently had no name. They used to call them "photos of little angels" or "burial of little angels." Some time ago, in 1992, I was asked to publish a special issue on the topic in *Artes de México,* the editorial house that I direct. The issue posed quite a few difficulties, beginning with the challenge of finding a name for this unique, enigmatic, and ritualistic art. Then I remembered a few verses of *Death Without End* by Gorostiza:

To last as long as a gratuitous,
premature, albeit beautiful death" [. . .]
"To reach embittered age with silence and,
smiling, the sweet repose of child death
that rapes a far beyond of scattering birds.

That is how we came up with the name. The ritual art of *muerte niña,* "child death." The expression is now used in art history, museums, and galleries, as if the concept that describes the activity of painting and photographing recently deceased children had already existed.

The second obstacle we encountered was that very little had been published about this phenomenon. We found only one essay on the topic by the art historian Gutierre Aceves, whom we quickly contracted to oversee the edition of this issue. In the town of Ameca in the state of Jalisco, he had discovered a collection of poignant photographs, dating from about the end of the nineteenth century to the beginning of the twentieth. At a time when infant mortality was high, the photographer soon replaced the painter of this traditional art form. Although photography became the principle medium of the genre, it remained a subject of painting treated by many renowned artists. Frida Khalo painted *El difuntito Dima Rosas a los tres años* ("The Deceased Dima Rosas Aged Three") in 1937; Juan Soriano has several paintings; Arturo Rivera; Chucho Reyes; Gabriel Fernández Ledesma with his famous *Coloquio de la niña y la muerte* ("Colloquy between Girl and Death"); Olga Costa; and Lucía Maya, among others.

The genre has been practiced since the period of the viceroyalty. In a portrait from 1760, a very elegantly dressed boy, the son of the mayor of Guadalajara, is pictured as a Phillipian priest, but with a floral headdress like those crowning the heads of nuns in their funeral portraits.

In the nineteenth century, they began to create portraits of children standing and playing, often picturing them at an older age, as if they had enjoyed a longer life. It was an attempt to remove all cruelty from the genre and any hint of necrophilia. And so modernity invents children who are really sons and daughters of desire, of a delirious attempt to deny death. This sterile notion was a reflection of the times and allowed families to preserve the memory of the absent child and to display a "more rational" portrait whose presence in the home would not produce intense suffering.

For the cover of that issue of *Artes de México,* we selected a portrait made in 1805 of a wealthy child whose rare beauty distinguished him from all the other "little angels," because they had dressed him like an archangel, adorning him with pearls, feathers, and intricate brocade fabrics.

The impact of the publication of *The Ritual Art of Child Death* was so resounding that many young painters adopted the theme, often informing their paintings with the ancient images. Some conceptual artists actually searched for infant cadavers in the morgue of Mexico City or that of Guadalajara, a perpetual source of inspiration for contemporary Mexican art. And on an escalator in the airport of Madrid, I saw a person carrying under his arm some reproductions of deceased children taken from our magazine. A Chilean artist had given the images his own personal touch and his dealer was taking them to be exhibited at the ARCO art fair.

It is important to note that even though there were few essays on the topic, we did find an abundance of poems, songs, and stories. One of the essential qualities of literature, especially poetry, is the ability to delve into dimensions of life that other genres do not penetrate, or at least not with the same intensity. Poetry is a scalpel that explores life more deeply, teaching us lessons that only verses can reveal. And the same can be said about certain stories and novels. According to Milan Kundera, this is the one and only reason that the novel has survived.

We discovered strange and moving coincidences that linked literature and painting in peculiar ways. Juan Soriano had painted a deceased girl in 1938, after, as he told me, he had witnessed the entire ritual. He had been on vacation in Alvarado, in the state of Veracruz, and when this young girl died, he and all his friends went to the house, where she had been laid out in an extraordinary way. The image left such an indelible mark on his imagination that he felt the uncontrollable urge to paint her. A girl with cotton in her nostrils, her hands intertwined and twisted like flowers in pain. Surrounding her, more flowers on the verge of losing their petals, and many expressive hands, like echoes of the flowers, or vice versa. We were able to find a photograph of the painting in the Museum of Philadelphia, and while we awaited its arrival, we learned that the writer, Josefina Vincens (who is as sparing with her words as Rulfo and no less brilliant), had that painting in her house at one time and had established an intense relationship with the girl. The painting inspired Vincens to write a story that almost no one had read, "Petrita, la niña viva" (translated as "Petrita" for *Artes de México*), in which the author suggests that the girl cannot die as long as she remains obsessed by her. The story and painting were united for the first time in our magazine. Another contemporary artist, Arturo Rivera, created a painting based on a heartrending tale by Carlos Navarrete, an author and anthropologist of Guatemalan and Mexican heritage, who wrote about a country boy whose habit of eating dirt cost him his life. These are only a few of the interrelated texts and images from the issue that I could mention. The task remains to compile those that were generated from that publication. It would be fascinating to study how those baroque vestiges relate to present and future conceptual art that, to some extent, reflects the same demands.

The theme of death in Mexican art and literature has a thousand faces that are often quite astounding. Death continues to provoke powerful gestures, fortuitous encounters of select images, and words elaborately constructed from a tangible reality that forms part of a complex dimension of human existence, one that perhaps can only be expressed with utmost conviction in a baroque manner that engages all the senses. Art whose poetics, as Gorostiza says, are founded on the search for the essences of life, one of which is the dark side of the mirror that at times reveals its true colors: death.

—July 2009

WORKS CITED:

Ajofrín, Francisco de. *Diario de viaje a la Nueva España.*

El arte ritual de la muerte niña. Artes de México 15 (1998).

Cariño, César. San Gabriel Chilac.

Cuéllar, Tomás de.

Gorostiza, José. *Death Without End.* Trans. Laura Villaseñor. Austin: University of Texas Press, 1969. Trans. of *Muerte sin fin.* 1939.

Mauss, Marcel. *The Gift: Forms and Functions of Exchange in Archaic Societies.* Trans. Ian Cunnison. (Glencoe, Illinois: The Free Press, 1954). Trans. of *Essai sur le don, forme archaïque de l'échange.* 1925.

Paz, Octavio. *The Labyrinth of Solitude.* Trans. Lysander Kemp. New York: Grove Press, 1985.

Tibón, Gutierre. "San Gabriel Chilac." *Serenidad ritual. Artes de México* 62 (2002): 34–35.

ABOUT *TODAY*

Bei Dao
(translated by Perry Link)

W INTER 1978. A SNOWFALL COVERED BEIJING. IN THE EASTERN suburbs a little hamlet of only a few families looked across a dirty rivulet toward the embassy district of the capital. Not quite an agricultural village, but not part of the city either, it was a sort of blind spot in the stifling control system. One of the huts in the village had its windows covered with ragged cloths. Under a dim lamp, seven young adults were bustling around a rickety mimeograph machine. I was one of them. After three days and three nights, we came out with *Today,* the first unofficial literary publication to appear in China since the Communist Party took power in 1949. We bicycled to a restaurant in the city and raised cups in a silent toast.

The next day I went with two friends to paste the fruits of our labor up on walls in the city. We changed the numbers on our bicycle license plates in an effort to mislead the police. On December 23, 1978, *Today* could be read outside several government offices and publishing houses, on university campuses, and in Tiananmen Square. We wanted to know how people would react to our works, so we went back later to mix in with the crowds who huddled around them. The poems, in particular, were of a kind that no one had seen in public for thirty years. The response was stronger than we had imagined it would be.

The original impetus for *Today* came in the late 1960s. That was when Mao Zedong, during his Great Proletarian Cultural Revolution, sought to quell rebellion in the cities by sending high school students to the countryside for "reeducation by the poor and (middle) peasants." His results, though, were quite the opposite of what he intended. To young Red Guards, the fall from the heights of society to its depths was a jolt; they were, moreover, severely disillusioned to find a huge disparity between the rosy Maoist language about "people's communes" and the harsh realities of village life. They turned to books in search of truth, and to writing as a means to express their perplexity. Each winter, during the agricultural off-season, some of them returned to Beijing, where they exchanged books and writings, and formed underground cultural salons.

I can still remember how excited I was, at age twenty, to read the poems of Shi Zhi (literally, "Forefinger"). He started writing in 1967, and must count as the founder of the New Poetry movement that unfolded over the next thirty years. His poems were the first to break with the political didacticism with which we had all grown up, and the first, as well, to express the bewilderment of the Red Guard generation. His fresh images and lilting cadences had an intoxicating effect on young people, who spread his poems widely in hand-copied form. Many years later when I met Forefinger, he had gone insane. He passed his days shuttling between home and the hospital.

I took up writing poetry after reading Forefinger's. I was a construction worker at the time, assigned to an electricity-generating plant about two hundred miles outside Beijing. It was an isolated environment, and I needed some form of release for the inner malaise I felt. At the time, probably because of Mao Zedong's poetry, there was a fad for writing poems in the ancient styles that Mao favored. Nearly everybody, it seemed, could recite a few Mao poems. I, too, wrote a few ancient-style poems, but soon found that their formal requirements made it hard to express anything more complex than nostalgia or the parting of friends.

I knew that writing was a forbidden game, which could even cost one's life. But prohibition only sweetened the appeal. At the construction site, I lived in a dormitory with a few dozen others. In the middle of the night, surrounded by a medley of snores, I would read and write under a table lamp that I had fashioned from a straw hat. Later the Propaganda Team at the construction site drafted me to work on a photography exhibit, and a darkroom built to my specifications became my cherished hideout. Heavy window shades blocked off the outside world; I finally had my own study, and in just a few months I was able to finish a short novel in addition to some poems.

My friend Zhao Yifan, a collector of underground literary works, was arrested. The police confiscated every scrap of his papers they could find, including my poems and novel. I was ordered back to my original worksite for supervised labor. I began to say good-bye to friends, to entrust them with my letters and manuscripts, and to prepare myself for prison whenever the moment might arrive. In the middle of the night the sound of trucks rolling past would startle me awake and leave me unable to reenter sleep. The wait was long and difficult, but in the end the feared event never arrived. Only much later did I learn what had happened: the police could not make heads or tails of my poems. They consulted experts from the Literature Research Institute, who also were baffled. Finally the experts came out with a ruling: the poems had been plagiarized from the West. This judgment saved me. Those were also the days of the banned book. Books were seldom seen in public places. We used to sneak into closed libraries to steal books, or sift through recycle centers in search of them, or borrow them from other people who were rummaging just as we were. The phrase *pao shu*, "running around for books," entered our vocabulary; to find a good book you had to run everywhere, had to be patient and persistent, had to negotiate, to promise, to reciprocate.

The material one reads in youth can be decisive for the rest of one's life. At first we read omnivorously, hungry for any scrap we might find. But later we grew picky. We set our hearts on the "yellow-covered books." These were a set of about one hundred volumes of literature from the modern West and from the "thaw" period in the literature from Eastern Europe. They were meant for the eyes of high officials only, and thus had very small print runs and tight restrictions on circulation. Still, in the turmoil of the Cultural Revolution, they leaked down to the general populace. Among the underground cultural salons in Beijing, they became the objects of serious treasure hunts. Whenever a group managed to lay its hand on one of these books—sometimes for a negotiated period of only a few days—the group members would draw up a tight schedule for sharing the book around the clock. Reading time was more precious than food or sleep. My friends and I used to take pills that we knew would make us ill so that we could get sick leave—that is, reading time—from work.

For underground writers, the yellow-covered books not only opened new vistas for spiritual refuge but exemplified a literary form that was radically different from the official Socialist realism. It was called, at the time, the "Translation Style." Certain Chinese writers, including the best poets of the latter 1940s—Mu Dan, Yuan Kejia, Chen Jingrong, Zheng Min, and others trying to write creatively under the new political guidelines—had turned instead to work on the translation and research of foreign literature. The "translation style" of Chinese that they created became, for my generation, a vehicle for expressing creative impulses and seeking new linguistic horizons.

In the autumn of 1978, a power struggle at the top of the Communist Party led to a temporary relaxation of controls on cultural expression. Underground writing in journals like *Today* could appear in the open, where, together with unofficial artwork and photography, it posed a major new challenge to official discourse. *Today* published mostly poetry, introducing the work of Mang Ke, Gu Cheng, Duo Duo, Shu Ting, Yan Li, Yang

Lian, Jiang He, and other important poets. Our printing equipment was primitive and our "editorial office" little more than a hand-labor workshop. But quite a few young people pitched in. In two years we produced nine magazine issues and four books.

We also organized some literary events. Regular monthly sessions to discuss our recent work attracted a large number of university students. In the spring of 1979, and once again in the fall, we sponsored outdoor poetry readings in Beijing's Yuyuantan Park. Chen Kaige, who later directed well-known films such as *Yellow Earth* and *Farewell, My Concubine,* at that time was still a student at the Beijing Film Academy. He participated in some of our readings. The police supervised closely, perhaps puzzled that nearly a thousand people could listen so intently to our obscure poetic lines.

The Communist Party's brief flirtation with democracy passed quickly, however. Deng Xiaoping soon ordered the arrest of Wei Jingsheng and other democracy activists. When *Today* was forced to close in December 1980, the authorities expected me to write a "self-criticism" about my involvement with the disgraced journal. I had just returned from my honeymoon in Qingdao (Shandong Province), and decided not to do the self-criticism. I was suspended from my job "for reflection." One evening, as I was returning home, a friend darted from behind a tree to tell me he had a reliable report that my name was on an arrest list. Should I flee? My then wife and I talked deep into the night, and finally decided to stay put but watch closely. Before long the political winds shifted again, and once again I felt I was a lucky survivor.

Today was closed down, but many of its poems began to appear in the official literary magazines under the general name of "Misty poetry" (*meng-long shi*). A nationwide controversy about Misty poetry raged for many years. Official critics denounced it as if it were a pestilence or wild beast, but their fulminations served only to deepen reader interest. Young readers who had felt stifled by official language found in it new air to breathe. There was a spell during which virtually everybody on college campuses was writing poetry, joining poetry clubs, or putting out poetry collections. This lasted through much of the 1980s, until the society-wide rage for commercialism again pushed poetry to the margins.

Eventually *Today* itself became a kind of cloud that hung over a new generation of poets. "The third generation," as they have been called, differ from the *Today* poets because they have grown up after the Cultural Revolution and have enjoyed good educations. To some extent they have been able to lay down the burdens of history, to look more directly at present realities, and to write, as it were, in minor as well as major chords.

Important poets in this group include Bai Hua, Zhang Zao, Xi Chuan, Ouyang Jianghe, Song Lin, Zhai Yongming, Han Dong, and Zhang Zhen. Many are from Sichuan. Many, too, have become my friends. We have found that what we share in poetry well exceeds our differences.

In 1990, a year after the guns sounded in Tiananmen Square, a group of Chinese writers met in Oslo, Norway, and decided to revive *Today*. Publication resumed and has continued until now. The thirty-year history of *Today*—from its birth, to its death, to its rebirth—can be viewed as a metaphor for the vitality of all of China's contemporary poetry, whose genies will not go back into their bottles.

—July 2009

GREAT DIVIDES AND COMMON GROUND
(From a panel on "projects")

Dolores Dorantes, Jen Hofer

DOLORES DORANTES: [speaks in Spanish, as Jen Hofer interprets] My project is fairly simple. It is titled *Leer la ciudad (To Read the City)*. I live on the border in Ciudad Juárez, where a war is currently happening. The project takes place via both texts and photographs, and women from the community in general are called to participate. The idea is to record what is happening in a city that is experiencing a war, a city that is destroyed and reconstructed constantly, and to find some way to capture the various structures, both architectural and linguistic, that are disappearing moment by moment, that are being replaced by new structures. Oddly, what I miss most from the desert, and what the war has completely eradicated, is the silence. Silence has ceased to exist. And silence in the desert is unique. The other aspect of war that I have become conscious of is that there is no such thing as an equal war. All wars are different. So you cannot ever tell someone what it is like in the moment of living or experiencing a war. The moment of experiencing it becomes a different thing, it is something else for people in different places. This war is different from other wars, for example, in Guatemala or in Afghanistan. Basically that is the project.

[question from audience about how this is affecting the women]

The project does not exist to make the rest of the world sensitive to or conscious of what is happening in our small world. Really, what happens in our world is happening everywhere in the world. The project exists so that women who are not conscious of the importance of language and of writing are able to take ownership over those tools in some way. So that they will become conscious that writing is a right, for them to take ownership over writing so that they can take ownership over themselves. To cause, or encourage, them to become conscious of their own thinking, not to be overwhelmed, especially by fear, or by terror, which absolutely exists, not just among women but really in the community in general. That fear might begin to be released and to flow in a different direction.

To speak concretely of some examples of the work that we have done, we are working with women who have never written anything, perhaps, other than maybe a shopping list. When they start to write, even their very physical way of being in the world changes.

When I say "we" I mean the Mexico City–based nonprofit activist organization of which I am the Juárez site director, called DEMAC, Documentación y Estudios de Mujeres [Women's Studies and Documentation]. My work there, at the most basic level, is to give the texts written by these women to the association, so that they can continue to move the projects forward.

To give another concrete example, there is a building in Ciudad Juárez that is a hotel; the sign on it says *Aremar, are* of sand and *mar* of sea, but read backwards it is *Ramera,* which means "whore" or "bitch." That is where the project originates in inviting people to *leer la ciudad,* to read the city, that we might read our city and see a different message by looking at the ads and the publicity that are all around us.

JEN HOFER: Given that this panel is called Projects, part of what I want to do is try to link, perhaps only harmonically or via reverberations, a range of different strands and modes of practice in my own current thinking and living, which is very much in flux. I want to begin by talking about the gift economy and the ways that we, as artists and as beings in the world, can effect shifts in the language of commerce and the economy of exchange in terms of how we engage our work with the world. I do publish perfect-bound books with autonomous, small-press projects, and I'm really excited to support their endeavors and for them to support my endeavors. I am excited about spaces like independent bookstores, Small Press Distribution, spdbooks.org. But I also feel like as a writer—and particularly since there is relatively little interest in purchasing books of poetry, which I actually think is sort of o.k.—I make tiny handmade books at my kitchen table and I give them away for free. This is from the opening letter to my latest tiny book, called *Trouble:*

Dear Reader,

I've been having some trouble lately. Lately, like for a couple of years. I've been talking to people about this trouble a lot recently, so if you're one of those people and you're reading this and hoping not to hear the same old kvetching from me, feel free to skip this introduction and dive into the book—or better yet, go outside and take a bike ride to an unfamiliar neighborhood.

My trouble. I think of it as the "I hate poetry" trouble. Except it's not really "I hate poetry," it's something else. Because if poetry were to cease to exist—I mean especially the poetry of any of the numerous poets or prose writers whose writing thrills and inspires and challenges and energizes and politicizes me—I'd feel bereft. But lately I'm not sure if I would feel bereft if my own poetry ceased to exist. Perhaps this means my vision of what matters most—and what mattering looks like—is shifting, and I'm flailing to catch up. Perhaps this means that my poetry is becoming something other than it has been. And perhaps this is a good thing. Perhaps.

Much of my trouble is tangled up in ideas about public practice and usefully subversive interventions into institutionalized and legislated spaces (which would be pretty much all spaces, far as I can tell). Ideas about wanting to contribute something concrete and legible and real (does this word mean anything to you? I sure hope so!) toward constructing a more livable, joyous, just, and humane world for more people. Ideas about unlearning systems of privilege and permission, dismantling structures organized around inequity and competition and perceived or enforced scarcity. I know that artistic and poetic practice can decisively and radically reconfigure our perception and our ways of understanding what we perceive. I believe that the work of cultural production is part of the work of transformation or transmutation or re-navigation—of change, in a word—and I believe it is part of the work of building alliances and activating communities. Insofar as art-making invites us to understand how much we do not understand, how much more there is to encounter in the world than what we can access in our immediate surroundings, art instigates a space of listening that is antithetical to the posturing, disrespect, and brutality that continually re-enact and reinforce the status quo. And yet I continue to feel largely doubtful as to whether my own practice is enough. Or rather, I know that it is not enough. But I have not yet discovered or invented what else I can do that might be.

So now I want to bring up some questions that arose in Dolores's and my first workshop session yesterday. These are questions that were propelled by the students' wonderful inquisitiveness and criticality around some of the work we were reading. We came out of yesterday's session with a bunch of incredible writing and these three questions: What is writing supposed to do for us or give us? or what are we supposed to do with it?

How might discomfort be useful or necessary? What might be useful about feeling "othered" by a word or mode of using language?

I want to focus a bit on that last idea about being othered by a word or mode of using language. I want to talk very briefly about some of what I have been doing in my life. As a translator I see myself as a literary activist. I am interested in making it very real for people that there are amazing, exciting, mindblowing works that are being created in other languages that we are not accessing because "the greats" are so much more readily translated than emerging or unconventional contemporary writers. As an interpreter, I have been doing a lot of social justice interpreting and noticing how much even well-intentioned organizations who want to create space for English speakers and non-English speakers to converse sometimes end up remarginalizing those who don't have access to the dominant language. I have been trying to think creatively about how we can create multilingual structures, rather than structures where English is the dominant language and everyone who doesn't speak English gets to sit in the corner and be talked at by an interpreter. One of the things I think about a lot is how much resistance there is when there is a community meeting and the main speaker is presenting in Spanish and the monolingual non-Spanish speakers need to wear the interpreting equipment, how uncomfortable they are with that, yet it's totally fine [with them] if nondominant language speakers have to do that. I like to think about what is possible when we bring up those sorts of questions. I also think a lot about who we are able to listen to, how to make it physically and palpably real that there is *something else* we might want to listen to, other than what we can easily access in our immediate proximity.

Also, as a person who reads as "white," regardless of what my ethnic background may be, I have done a lot of thinking about white privilege, and for those of us who read as white and don't want that privilege—we have it whether we want it or not. What can we do *concretely* to dismantle the systems and structures that give us that privilege? Or what can nonqueer people do *concretely* to dismantle the structures of power and privilege that marginalize queer people? I feel like one of the things that I can start to do—although I am not enacting it at this moment—is to be more of a listener than a talker.

—June 29, 2010

HOW TO BE AN EASTERN EUROPEAN POET IN AMERIKA
(Written for the panel
Diasporas of Writing Cultures: Live & Virtual)

Ana Božičević

A S SOON AS I BEGAN TO THINK ABOUT THE DIASPORA ON THE ONE hand and the internet on the other, and then the mashing together of the two hands, it was clear to me that this coupling was not going to be uncomplicated. Coming from a more cosmopolitan place, where the human dispersal inherent in "diaspora" is trade-related and not trauma-related, and where unfettered access to the internet—to the new book of Google that came out of the West—is assumed, their relationship might be, at least on the surface, less complicated, more openly productive—more *utopian* in the best sense of the word. But for me, coming to the in-between place of diaspora from the in-between location where East meets Europe—it wasn't. And since we are in the week of Haraway's ironic manifesto, and manifesto hovers between discourse and action, I wrote an ironic sorta-manifesto for you today so that I may play chaos's advocate a little bit, and begin to convey why exactly I am ever-so-gently mad when I read, for instance, Homi Bhabha's writing on diaspora, and when this word is used in the vocabulary of healing and the internet. And I give you this manifesto even as I actively engage in just the sort of generative diasporic healing I am about to refuse to uncomplicate: I am translating via web a book by a Serbian poet I've never met, Zvonko Karanović, a man of the clan with which my clan had been at war. And yet.

‹Engage manifesto›:
How to be a Balkan poet in Amerika in the age of the interweb.
You will be straight. Lean, like a gymnast. Stain yourself right off with a nostalgia for the infinite. Make even your use of the web a vintage gesture, like you're wearing a jetpack. Twitter: I'm standing in a barnyard, and it's my soul that's atwitter, for I don't even own a TV. Be ur-post.

Leave your words simple. The accent shall be the only ripple on your vocab's sheen. Use "of" a lot: son of the sun. The Amerikan soul longs for the basic relational arrow of "of." Everything's a tender quip, pop-ref, allegorical:

but *you* use pop-ref only to sign the soul. Make the Lyric a password to all your apps. When you blog about New York, compare it to a mountain in the mist. Make your transparent *langue* the screen: wear a white bonnet onto which an anarchic archaic stream is projected. Be pagan.

In the natural world of Amerika, there's a great longing for gods who peek from every stream and tuft of heather to be named. They proclaim their values and names on the web. The One God flies over their country on an AirBus. Their language is Wild Western, the tongue of civ-in-the-making. These are your folk: you'll play the missing link between the Greek and German, the Many and One, with the softness of a Fyodor, a Ninotchka: unthreatening almost-Euro portal to the Other. You'll be of the West, but not.

There's a story where you're from: "Fisherman Palunko and His Wife." Palunko marries an orphan girl sent to save him from solitude. They live in a cottage by the sea, in the socialist world of ur-objects that are always recycled without the need for that word to exist. They hunt and gather, and one day they have a son. There's only one problem: the wife's a storyteller, and in time Palunko grows hungry for the capitalist courts from her tales of the Sea-King, a fabuloso ruler of an undersea Amerika. Obsessed, he takes his family on a search for this kingdom; when, weary, they fall asleep by the seashore, their son, the baby, is stolen. In her sorrow, the wife falls mute. None of this touches Palunko. Obsessed, he leaves the childless, mute wife in search of Amerika.

Let's stop here for a second. This childless, mute wife: make *her* your vessel, portal to Amerika. This is the path of the devotchka: radically unavailable with a sheen of available, always half-imagined, pre/post-digital, -historical, -verbal. In the story of Palunko, when the wife grows mute, she develops the talent of talking to animals. Since you must *never* tell tales about Amerika in the tongue of Amerikan humans for fear of deportation, it's best if you learn the language of animals. So write about the chickens. Tap into the technology of the barnyard. Be the connector between the species who are the guardians of the ark of the West. The techno-heavy West longs for a new-ancient technology to carry it out of its story's matrix. Engage this dream, and call it "new." Call it an online community. Like the surrealist lady-scientists in the paintings of Remedios Varo, be Amerika's link to the ancient technology of magic.

And there is magic in technology. The magic of talking to familiars. The magic is to speak to the familiar. Save Amerikan poetry from its free fall into affectless space. Use Twitter like a daily thing, Facebook like the lady's album: by gesturing to the olden, the barnyard, Wild West/East, you're growing a connective tissue, like a good diaspora should, in the gap between the horses of cultures-genders-genres. Make like a good scar!

Meanwhile, at the court of the Sea-King . . . there's much excitement: the fisherman Palunko made it. An artificial light illumines the marble-columned sea floor above which the sea towers like a space-dome. Enchanted with the technologies of capitalism, Palunko dances and cart-wheels, and is chosen for the Sea-King's jester. In this undersea world, everything is upside down: the homegrown lettuce he ate in his cottage is considered an organic delicacy, while the spoils of capitalist technology Palunko longed for are commonplace. For a while Palunko revels in the wealth of the undersea supermarkets. And then, in an hour or a day—he's jetlagged, so—he spots, in the cradle by the Sea-King's side, a baby. In a flash he recognizes his stolen son. The child is now a prince. Palunko is stunned silent. And now Palunko learns the first lesson of being a noncitizen artist in capitalism: to partake in the wealth, on some subjects remain silent. Particularly on the subject of open trauma. Palunko bows his head and becomes his son's servant to stay close to the boy.

You must *also* learn to make without appearing to speak. When you get an e-mail from the *Nation* challenging its readers with the question "how would you reinvent capitalism?" at threat of deportation don't mention the word *revolution*. Filter your socialist childhood through a vintage sepia. Remember, the essence you channel is the promise of war, the trauma you were local to, but must never more than hint at: no one wants to *see* the blood. They just want to hear its rush. Your domain's the pure moment just before battle: the excitement of the soldier surrounded by beautiful girls, the turn-on of the sentimental promise of suffering—never the actual economy of suffering. I hope you have remembered to be straight.

Meanwhile, back in the homeland, Palunko's mute wife seeks council with the animals. She bargains with a giant bird, snake, bee, and reaches the Sea-King's court. Through exchange and bargain, subterfuge and alle-gorical gesture—she babysits baby snakes, tells each monster she meets she is only searching for two fish, not her family—she extracts Palunko and child from the kingdom of wealth on a fishing hook, and they set off for home. There is a high-speed chase scene. And here the wise woman again proves her mettle: she fashions a sail from her rag and a mast from her sewing needle, and the family flees their pursuers. To be a Balkan poet in Amerika in the age of the interweb, you will master technology like it was the magic of household, myth, and barnyard. Like Palunko's wife, never quite describe what it is you seek.

‹Disengage manifesto›

So, what do I seek? Palunko and wife complete their diasporic return home.

The narrative anticapitalist, hetero paradise and the firstborn are restored. So are their voices: at the end of the story, a two-prong flute sings the tale of Palunko and wife. Healing and song have occurred at the site of trauma, just like the essentialist feminist myth said they would. The family are Oprah ready. But what if they had come home to find a billboard on their house for an adult superstore? What if there was no house waiting? If the wife only found her missing on Facebook many years later? On Facebook, first comes recognition, then the longing resumes. I want to believe in the utopian economy of the internet. The opening it offers is real, and the desire it triggers is real. But it would have been easier to post this online somewhere. I'm terrified speaking here in front of you, and I think that's good.

I go on Facebook and I register the faces of my friends, but I don't see them. I read their words, but I don't hear them. As a writer I should be accustomed to this, but I'm not. I'm still here, not there with them. And when I travel there, mostly it doesn't feel real. This trauma that, after countless productive internet exchanges, after work translated and books published through the power of the byte, still sits there like an undeployed program—this is the place where I've got to be tender, where I've got to build. But why must we build after trauma? Isn't a hybrid also a traitor structure, just another kind? What is "after trauma" anyway? This country is at war. There's no out of this in.

At the bottom of some diasporas is blood spilt. So why should the scar tissue of diaspora serve a purpose? Maybe I would prefer to create—not even *a* nothing—but just nothing, talk to no one. Maybe I'd like to light a fire. Maybe I'm not socialized for this sort of panel. It's polite to talk about the liminal hybrid of the interstice, like Borges writing down Pliny's descriptions of monsters in a neat little book, *The Book of Imaginary Beings*, printed and translated 'round the global economies. But when "here be monsters" at the edge of maps, do they sit at bookstores blogging? Online poetics discussions and remote-controlled missiles are launched right this second all over the world. What I mean is, since the virtual's real, things can get real dirty and painful on the outskirts. What I'd really like is to get real.

—June 2011

THE QUESTION IS HOW TO INTERROGATE THE REMAINS

Eleni Sikelianos

JUST RETURNED FROM TWO COUNTRIES IN WHICH ARCHIVES CARRY IMPORtant things for poets and writers. Cambodia's civil war, instigated by the secret bombings ordered by Kissinger, led to one of the most brutal regimes in history, a purge that fed on its own people, killing up to 3.5 million Cambodians, half the population. In that regime, intellectuals, artists, and teachers were eliminated, so that the system of handing on knowledge, including of literary life, has been severely crippled. Every single person I met was touched in some way by Pol Pot's terror, whether it was uncles who had been killed, as in the case of our embassy contact, or almost an entire family wiped out, as in the case of the woman who guided us through the genocide museum, housed in one of Pol Pot's prisons from which inmates were escorted to the Killing Fields.

In Vietnam, intellectual and literary life has remained vital, and of vital interest to a large public, though the writers there have had to manage through a system of censorship and suppression of archive and memory.

In both countries, I spoke of Charles Reznikoff, Lorine Niedecker, and C. D. Wright's work, of their inscriptions via the archives of genocide, geological time, and contemporary history, in Wright's case, the u.s. prisons.

Reznikoff, who was trained as a lawyer, once said, "I didn't invent the world, but I felt it."

He worked with the Nuremberg Trial documents to record individual human lives in a human-borne catastrophe of such enormous scale that we lose all perspective or possibility of comprehension. He worked with court records and briefings in legal cases from the turn of the century in America to reckon with the violence that attended our transition to an industrialized society.

Reznikoff, like many poets, often focuses on the micro to make real the macro.

"The most valuable traces are the ones that were not intended for our information." —Paul Ricoeur

What is the relation between archive and vision?

In Reznikoff, line break creates much of the emotion of the work.

For me, in family histories or elsewhere, the imagination organizes the evidence in various ways, blocking material against material, form against form, creating texture and palpability—see Waldman's *Iovis*, say, as it documents male energy. The imagination inserts itself and expands the real.

Investigation also provides relief from the limiting, all-consuming space, the self, and inscribes the self into a larger world.

What interests me particularly is the infection, the mutual infestation between the lyric and the document, the imagination and the artifact.

A poem is a fact, wherever it lies.

—Summer 2012

WORDS, QUOTES, QUESTIONS, IN AND AROUND AND ALL OVER "THE FIELD"

Anselm Hollo

ET'S BEGIN WITH QUOTES: QUOTES. FORTY-ODD YEARS AGO, I WAS intrigued by the way Lee Harwood, the English poet, a friend in the late fifties and early sixties—and, even though we have not seen each other for many a year, certainly still a friend and valued fellow worker—I was intrigued by the way Lee used quotation marks in his poems: they did not seem to indicate any recognizable quotations from other sources, but had been inserted there to indicate shifts of tone, often gently ironic, in what was being said. What was being said, *was* being said, but with a lesser or simply different degree of certainty, or emphasis, or what we then still used to call "sincerity." Later, quite recently in fact, Alice Notley expanded the use of quotation marks in *The Descent of Alette* in a similar manner, but also to present, represent, a *multitude* of voices within the narrative. So, it seems appropriate to start with two quotes from brilliant but also quite down-to-earth thinkers of the first third of the just-past century:

"Whenever anyone says anything he is indulging in theories."
—Alfred Korzybski, in *Science and Sanity,* 1933.

And:

"Do not forget that a poem, even though it is composed in the language of information, is not used in the language-game of giving information."
—Ludwig Wittgenstein, in his posthumously published notes or *Zettel.*

In a recent—well, this past Tuesday—informal talk on the poet Ted Berrigan, I quoted from Ron Padgett's memoir titled, simply, *Ted*—a passage in which he describes Berrigan's first enthusiastic encounter with the theories of the dynamic Polish count and pioneer of modern semantics: "The book (*Science and Sanity*) hit Ted like a thunderbolt. Korzybski's ideas were simple and reasonable, but couched in incredibly turgid prose." Let me interject here that those boys hadn't seen nuthin yet, in terms of the turgidity of later theoretical discourse! Back to Ron: "The basic idea was: 'The word is not the thing.' The word democracy is not the same thing as democracy itself; the word love is not love, it is a word. Abstract words are particularly dangerous. When people mistake the word for the thing, they get confused (neurotic), and all sorts of problems ensue. We lie to ourselves, friends become enemies, countries get crazy and go to war, etc. The realist does not confuse the word and the thing. This 'realistic' use of language appealed to Ted enormously. He somehow related it to the words orange and sardines in Frank O'Hara's poem 'Why I Am Not a Painter.'"

Why I Am Not a Painter

I am not a painter, I am a poet.
Why? I think I would rather be
a painter, but I am not. Well,

for instance, Mike Goldberg
is starting a painting. I drop in.
"Sit down and have a drink" he
says. I drink; we drink. I look
up. "You have SARDINES in it."
"Yes, it needed something there."
"Oh," I go and the days go by
and I drop in again. The painting
is going on, and I go, and the days
go by. I drop in. The painting is
finished. "Where's SARDINES?"
All that's left is just
letters. "It was too much," Mike says.

But me? One day I am thinking of
a color: orange. I write a line
about orange. Pretty soon it is a
whole page of words, not lines.
Then another page. There should be
so much more, not of orange, of

words, of how terrible orange is
and life. Days go by. It is even in
prose, I am a real poet. My poem
is finished and I haven't mentioned
orange yet. It's twelve poems, I call
it ORANGES. And one day in a gallery
I see Mike's painting, called SARDINES.

In essence, Korzybski states that words have no intrinsic meanings. They evoke meanings in us. The specific meanings they evoke in us depends on the context in which the word is used as well as the experiences of the evaluator.

But that is not all there is to these oranges and sardines. In his groundbreaking work on language, Korzybski's contemporary, the linguist Ferdinand de Saussure, introduced the notion of the arbitrariness of the sign. Since that recognition has played a large part—still does—in any late twentieth-/early twenty-first-century writer's awareness, I will try to summarize what it "means."

Historically, language has essentially been considered to be a naming process: things—including imaginary things—were provided with words or signs to denote them. Early grammarians—and religionists—assumed that there was—or that there "had to be"—some necessary connection between word and thing, name and object. Saussure challenged that notion by pointing out the radically different names given to things in different languages. For example: Latin *arbor*, English *tree*, and German *Baum* denote the same "thing" we see out there. Latin *equus*, English *horse*, German *Pferd*—likewise. There is no a priori—fundamental, "God-given"—connection between the word and the thing. If words stood for preexisting concepts, they would all have exact equivalents. But: different languages divide the world up in different ways.

Saussure differentiates between the *sign*, which is the totality of the sound/image, or *signifier*, along with what it denotes, *the signified*, and these two component parts must be considered separately. Signs are defined by their difference from each other in the *network of signs*, which is the signifying system. While the individual sign is arbitrary, there is an important sense in which the signifying system as a whole is not. Meaning is socially produced and operates by convention. Thus the social construction of the signifying system is intimately related to the social formation itself. This has important consequences for the relationship between language and ideology— the sum of the ways in which people both live and represent to themselves their relationship to the conditions of their existence. Ideology is inscribed in signifying practices, through discourses, myths, and representations of the way "things are," or of what "goes without saying." Expressions which inscribe gender relations are an excellent example of this.

In her essay "The Word As Such: L-A-N-G-U-A-G-E Poetry in the Eighties," Marjorie Perloff cites Maurice Blanchot's explanation of the crisis of referentiality and the slippage of meaning in the fact that words are "monsters with two faces, one being reality, physical presence, and the other meaning, ideal absence." Carla Harryman says in a recent typically impish text that "words *are* things," and Charles Bernstein speaks of "the fact of wordness" but goes on to explain that in this context "fact" does not indicate primarily referentiality or representation, does not mean, as it would, he says, to a poet like Charles Olson, "'perception' onto a given world" as "a unified field" but rather "onto the language through which the world is constituted."

I do not know if, or if at all, William Burroughs was familiar with de Saussure's work, but he is on record as a frequent quoter of Korzybski's maxim "the map is not the territory" and his "those who rule the symbols rule us." In an essay titled "The Genealogy of Postmodernism: Contemporary American Poetry," contemporary literary critic Albert Gelpi says that "the poetry of the Cold War period set out the defining features of postmodernism before critics introduced the term," and among those features he lists "a questioning of language as a medium of perception and communication" and "a shift from hypostatizing poetry as a completed work to investigating it as an inconclusive process of provisional improvisation."

A little side trip here, improvisation: poet John Ashbery writes, in a tribute to the painter Fairfield Porter, "This is perhaps the lesson of painting: that there are no rules for anything, no ideas in art, just objects and materials that combine, like people, in somewhat mysterious ways; that we are left with our spontaneity, and that life itself is a series of improvisations during the course of which it is possible to improve on oneself, but never to the point where one doesn't have to improvise." Having touched, briefly, on improvisation in an earlier talk—its analogs in jazz as well as painting and writing—I want to dwell a little longer on the "questioning of language as a medium of perception and communication" that Gelpi cites, with particular reference to postmodern writing.

In a panel hosted by the Poetry Society of America at Cooper Union a year ago, on the fifteenth of March, 2000, with the subject line: "Poetry Criticism: What Is It For?" critic and essayist Marjorie Perloff paraphrased my initial quote from Wittgenstein: "do not forget that a poem, even though it's published in the language of information, is not used in the language game of giving information." She went on to say:

> That's a crucial statement because so much of what passes for poetry, and what's discussed in poetry reviewing, is just information, and that means that last year's information is very dull. You get very tired of it. I'm thinking of writing an essay about this, called "The Lost Boys." In the 1960s we had poets like Galway Kinnell, James Wright, Robert Bly. These were the big poets, male poets, of the period. They wrote a certain kind of poem. Then they became unfashionable. If I talk about them to my students, especially in the case of James Wright, who's dead, they don't even know who they are: "Who's James Wright?" They were replaced by other people who actually write in a very similar way. They were just younger so they can get away with it. And lately they've been replaced by— and I'll get *trampled on* for saying this, but I'll say it, I'll be brave— they get replaced by minority poets who also write exactly the same way. In other words, if you read a poem by Garrett Hongo, let's say, it's not so different from the poems of James Wright a generation ago, but no one reads the earlier poets anymore simply because they're a generation old. But if it's always really the same poem, then what's really the point? It's not that I believe in any kind of direct progress model, but I do think that poetry has to have something to do with the culture in which it's being written. It must, and that's why I have, I guess, a peculiar reaction to a certain kind of nature poetry, let's say, or poetry that just seems not to take into account how we live today, and what it is we do ("How to live, what to do" as Wallace Stevens writes). . . . If you believe in poetic language, if you believe that the limits of my language are the limits of my world (which I do), that poetry is the language art and that you can't say it any other way, then those things become very important— whether you have a poet who can really present something that could not be said another way, whatever that thing is, and the richer the better.

It is significant that Perloff mentions Kinnell, Bly, and the late James Wright as the "big boys" of the sixties—they certainly were that, in terms of what Charles Bernstein has named the "official verse culture," the one created and maintained over several generations by a relatively small group of mostly Manhattan-based Ivy League graduates with "access" to publication venues like the *New Yorker* and the "uptown," "quality" publishing houses—even though the latter have become comparatively unimportant franchises of the corporate global entertainment industry. The "oppositional" writing culture's big boys of the period were, of course, Allen Ginsberg, Charles Olson, William Burroughs, Hubert Selby, Jr. It is also, to my mind, significant that she pinpoints those "hegemonic" figures as *still* being considered workable models for, and by, emerging minority writers. And this may be the place to insert a little-known instance of irreverent literary sabotage.

In 1993, Random House published a handsome chapbook of a poem read by Maya Angelou at the inauguration of William Jefferson Clinton on the twentieth of January of that year. Its title is *On the Pulse of Morning*. On the front cover above this title, which is lettered in gold, we read the likewise gold-lettered legend "The Inaugural Poem."

Also in 1993, Geoffrey Young's fine, small press the Figures published an equally elegant chapbook, imitating the "inaugural poem" format, titled *On the Pumice of Morons: The Unaugural Poem*. Its coauthors, Clark Coolidge and Larry Fagin, used the N+7 method first suggested by the French OULIPO group as a tool for the creation of new texts from old: for every noun in the old text, you substitute a noun located seven entries "down" from it in the dictionary . . . and I have to say that the result, in this case, supports Perloff's stance in regard to "last year's information."

Here is a brief sampling, the first and last stanzas of both poems:

(Angelou)

A Rock, A River, A Tree

Hosts to species long since departed,
Marked the mastodon,
The dinosaur, who left dried tokens
Of their sojourn here
On our planet floor,
Any broad alarm of their hastening doom
Is lost in the gloom of dust and ages.

(Coolidge/Fagin)

A Rock Crystal, A Roach, A Tree of Heaven
Hosiery to spectroheliographs long since departed,
Marked the masterwork,

The dingle, who left dried toile
Of its Soho here
On our plank flopover,
Any broad alabaster of their hastening doppelganger
Is lost in the gloss of duress and agglomeration.

(Angelou)

Here on the pulse of this new day
You may have the grace to look up and out
And into your sister's eyes,
And into your brother's face,
Your country,
And say simply
Very simply
With hope—
Good morning.

(Coolidge/Fagin)

Here on the pumice of this new davenport
You may have the gradient to look up and out
And into Sisyphus's eyeholes,
And into Brown Betty's eyewash,
Your countertenor,
And say simply
Very simply
With hooray—
Good moron.

Now, this could, of course, seem horribly offensive, even given the fact that Random House sold thousands of copies of *On the Pulse* and the entire edition of *On the Pumice* consisted of only three hundred copies; an act of vandalism committed by two privileged white guys, on a work written in heartfelt sincerity by a respected minority poet. But, line by line, the "unaugural" version provides more surprises and perhaps even more astute political commentary than the inaugural one—granted that "inaugural poems" are a thankless genre, and our newly *appointed* president wisely did not commission one from . . . well, *whom* would he have commissioned it from?

On the other hand, it is a demonstration of the gulf that has opened up, in the last forty years or so, between both authors and readers of the "official" and "un-or-less-official" versions of belles lettres. It also demonstrates the plain fact that there is not *an* audience, *one* audience, for any writing, including writing that aspires to a level of art, but many audiences, ranging from the inexperienced—let's say, persons who have not read much—to the experienced—persons who have read a great deal.

Discussing "high art" and "popular culture" in 1972—twenty-nine years ago—Samuel R. Delany, the brilliant Afro-American writer of works that consciously attempt to bridge the ever-widening gap between those two regions, wrote the following:

> In the United States today, we have nearly 225 million people. Perhaps eighty percent are literate, which gives us a literate field of 180 million from which we can cull both our audience and our poets—a field fifty times as large as the field of Great Britain in 1818 [when, according to Delany, there were "out of a field of four hundred thousand . . . six poets of major interest and fourteen of varying minor interest."]. . . . It is not unreasonable to suppose that . . . . today there are fifty times six major poets (about three hundred) and fifty times fourteen (about seven hundred) of merit and interest in America today.

Delany then quotes poet Dick Allen's statement in *Poetry-Chicago* that "there are well over a thousand fine poets working in America today," and continues:

> I am, as I said, an avid poetry reader, and my own reading for pleasure certainly bears those figures out, even though I doubt I read ten percent of what is published. Certainly, somewhat more than half of what I read is bad. This still leaves a staggering amount of incredibly fine work—most by people whom I have never heard of before, and, after I've read another fifty books of poetry, whose names I will not be able to recall without a trip to the bookshelves or the cartons in the closet. . . . Barring a fantastic decrease in population and/or literacy, no one person will ever be familiar with the scope of American poetry again. Nor can anybody be familiar with more than a fraction of the best of it—unless he or she makes that an eight-hour-a-day job, and even then it is doubtful. . . . There are hundred on hundreds on hundreds of American poets. Hundreds among them

are good. One critic cannot even be *acquainted* with their complete work, much less have studied it thoroughly. And I suspect one can find analogs of this situation with the novel, the theater, the dance.

Considering the population increase of the U.S. in the last twenty-nine years, Delany's figures need to be upgraded. The 2001–2002 edition of the *Directory of American Poets and Fiction Writers,* and I quote from its preface, "contains information on 4,142 poets, 1,884 fiction writers and 1,273 poets and fiction writers. Some additional poets and fiction writers are also listed as performance poets." It should be noted that this directory is by no means comprehensive: since its main use is as a periodically updated contact address book, many writers prefer not to be listed in it.

So, there being "hundreds on hundreds on hundreds" of us, to use Delany's phrase, and since no one could ever keep up with all of our output—what about the "canon" or even "canons"?

The standard definition of that word, by the way, is "a rule, principle or law, especially in the Christian Church, relating only to the Church and its members"; the specialized definition: "all the writings or other works known to be by a particular person"; it can also refer to "a Christian priest, often one who works in a cathedral." But in 1874, a philologist, Mr. Sayce, uses "canon" in "canons of taste and polite literature."

The successors of the nineteenth century's "philologists," our present-day literary theorists—while no doubt working under the constraints indicated by Delany's daunting statistics—do still use the term, mostly in a negative sense, as in "the Western" or "European" "canon." By many of our Lit Crit and Theory mandarins, this set of "Great Works" is considered bad, hegemonic, phallologocentric, the legacy of a culture of oppression and exploitation. However, and thankfully, total unanimity does not reign on this subject.

In an interesting, openly polemical tome published in 1998, *Literature Lost: Social Agendas and the Corruption of the Humanities,* author John M. Ellis writes: "In a comparatively short time, academic literary criticism has been transformed. . . . Many [critics] now regard social activism as the major purpose of literary criticism, and social activism of a very specific kind: the primary issue in all literary texts is the question of oppression by virtue of race, gender, and class."

He goes on to say that the venerable Fredric Jameson's dictum "everything is 'in the last analysis' political" has become a bedrock assumption, and suggests that although "those in the grip [of race-gender-class criticism] are critical of the Western tradition and define themselves by their opposition to it

. . . the impulse itself is *so much a part* of the Western tradition that the attitudes it generates can be said to be quintessentially Western." Ellis goes on to invoke Tacitus, who in the first century AD measured the decadence of his native Romans against the supposedly democratic and virtuous Germanic barbarians; Rousseau who compared his eighteenth-century decadent Frenchmen to imagined, presocial noble savages; and Margaret Mead, whose "sentimentalized Samoans" were meant to provide an ideological counterpoint to repressive and repressed Americans. Ellis notes that the crimes of which the West stands justifiably accused—racism, sexism, colonialism—are essentially transgressions against the universal rights that were first proclaimed by the Enlightenment, which did indeed take place within the sphere of Western culture, and which led to many things we still all claim to believe in. He writes, "To put the matter simply, when you reduce literature to a single issue, your reasons for doing so must have nothing to do with literature, and consequently neither will your results." The ultimately more damaging effect of race-gender-class criticism is that it reduces the "great range of opinion on social and political questions, as well as on any other kind of question" embodied in literature to a single dimension, a sort of up-or-down vote on the moral value of the author, the work under inspection, or the society that "produced" both. Such attitudes are a return to [as Ellis writes] "an older moralizing tradition . . . that was always mocked as the work of dull, pious middle-class folk who had no ear for what transcended their narrow understanding of the Bible." Such moralizing misrepresents the "canon" as a fixed set of texts that pompously transmits univocal "wisdom." In fact, Ellis notes, "few have ever thought the canon immutable."

John Ashbery, in his introduction to *Other Traditions,* the texts of his Charles Eliot Norton lectures at Harvard delivered a decade ago but only recently published in book form, has this to say about the "canon":

> Most poets, I suspect, have their own ideas of what the canon ought to be, and it bears little resemblance to the average anthologist's. That is why I at first decided to call this series "The Other Tradition," which I later regretted having done, deciding that it was more accurate to call it "Other Traditions." (Though since every poet has other traditions, perhaps it would be correct after all to refer to these collectively as "The Other Tradition.") . . . As I look back on the writers I have learned from, it seems that the majority, for reasons I am not quite sure of, are what the world calls minor ones. Is it inherent sympathy for the underdog, which one so often feels oneself to be when one embarks on the risky business of writ-

ing? Or is there something inherently stimulating in the poetry called "minor," something it can do for us when major poetry can merely wring its hands?

So, while we will never have the perfect and complete anthology of the twentieth century's poetry—not even of that written in U.S. American English—we are free to compose our own.

And as a kind of a model of how it may be we do this, I would like to end this talk, which was supposed to be about "the field" and has turned out to be, at least in part, about how downright impossible it is to delineate that field, the field of U.S. American poetry in the twentieth century— I would like to conclude, as they say, with a couple of quotes from an interview with Alice Notley by Ed Foster published last year in a collection of interviews titled *Poetry and Poetics in a New Millennium:*

The biggest driving force across my life has been the desire to know things directly for myself, without interference of opinion of others. . . . I've been led astray from time to time, into accepting someone else's ideas, but in general I have to find out for myself. I've increasingly come to distrust almost all of society's formulations of the truth, almost all of the language of "the historical context," and pretty much all the language of current philosophies and poetics. I want to stand face to face with whatever reality is and I feel that all the friendly theoreticians in my neighborhood are keeping me from doing this by proclaiming that there is no such reality as is made evident in the works of so-and-so philosopher or poet. . . . A poem is written, and best read, in a different kind of time from historical time, even if it sounds like its time and even if a good part of what the reader gets from it is bound up with what's going on in time. . . . Writing poems gets done in a strangely isolated nontemporal space as all poets know, but I'm not really trying to claim anything "special" for the poet. I think anything we do could be like this, but poetry is especially meditative. The historian could not discuss this terribly well. . . . The historian can't deal with what it feels like to write or read a poem, and that's what poetry is all about.

—Spring 2001

PO/ETHICS

Anne Waldman, Daisy Zamora, Jack Collom, Harryette Mullen, David Henderson

ANNE WALDMAN: Po/ethics refers to a poetics and an ethic of accountability, of owning the word, of standing by the word; a sense of how one might live as a writer, the role one might play as a citizen of a literary, as well as a social, community. These are intense times, as we all recognize, and we all have differing emotional, intellectual, experiential responses to the ongoing occupation of Iraq, to the wasting of the environment, the revelations and the ongoing karma of the 9/11 attack, to the oil crisis, to the situation in Haiti and the Congo, Israel and Palestine, to the PATRIOT Act's offense on civil liberties, to the assault on medical marijuana, to gay and lesbian and cross-gender marriages, to abortion rights, to the treatment of prisoners in our own USA prisons, not to mention Abu Ghraib and others. All these issues, which are really realities, invite us to stay attentive as they increasingly threaten, condition, cause unmitigated suffering the world over. The hegemony of the particular United States of America is quite scary, daunting, dangerous. The people in charge are, I would say, pathological. The mainstream media is, for the most part, shackled; yet the information is out there. It is a far-reaching, complex web of interconnectedness, and no one is immune to these doings. There are incredible webs of deceit and, very offensive to us as writers, the euphemism, the lying, the way the language is used and abused; basically we are talking about foxes in the henhouse and the undoing and unraveling of sanity.

So these rogues in charge can say one thing, put whatever spin on it, act normal, seemingly get away with it under the guise of patriotism or the war on terror. We see the fabric unraveling one day and knit back the next. You get sort of hopeful, and then suddenly Ronald Reagan dies and it's D-Day, and there are opportunities to once again beat the war drum, compare the struggle to the beaches of Normandy, and forget how many innocent Iraqis are being slaughtered daily, how many soldiers are dying. I think they assume our attention span is a matter of seconds, and you can just flip the channel, change the tune, someone can push a computer button somewhere that downs a swatch of rainforest or pollute a stream or ignore global warming, refusing to join the Tokyo accords and [using] terms euphemistically like "Clear Skies Initiative."

When Buddhism speaks of emptiness it means empty of the ego, of manipulation, of solid existence, empty of that individual identity. The view is that everything is co-arising, interconnected; one cannot be insular, cannot operate unilaterally. I noticed in the Sunday *New York Times* magazine the theme this week was "doing well, doing good, doing time." There were articles such as "When a Rich Man Goes to Jail," "The Immortality of Investors," "Do White-Collar Convictions Make Us Happy?" "Who Cheats and Why," and articles on the "ethics of shopping," the "ethics of high-end dining," the "ethics of going bankrupt," etcetera.

So, why a po/ethics? The problem in this country is that it is such a business operation. You travel to other cultures, other places—I remember being in Nicaragua, and there is some value to being a worker of words [there], to being a dreamer and an imaginative person, although that country has fallen on incredibly hard times because of the u.s. engagement there. So, how to speak of this? How does art respond to the hegemony of empire building, to popular culture, to media? How is our art to be in the world? To make it, do we need to hide, do we have to go underground, lay low, keep a low profile, go back into a safe cocoon, get depressed, get high, unplug constantly, write raging texts? It's hard to deal daily with the kind of rage and outrage. But many of the people here, including all this community, many of the students here are teachers, cultural activists, archivists, scholars, doctors, and are putting energy into supporting one another, supporting alternative communities, alternative imaginative projects, and in this ethics of taking back the language, in being able to invent and reinvent and translate, play with it all. We form our own collectives. There is a loyalty, a vow to imagination in language.

Avant-gardism has questioned the very role of art in a bourgeois society. Art has been produced by isolated communities, by isolated individuals, associated with elitism. How do we reconfigure this, how do we think about this? I'll leave you with a quote from the literary critic Fredric Jameson, from about a decade ago:

> The only authentic cultural production today has seemed to be that which can draw on the collective experience of marginal pockets of the social life of the world system, black literature and blues, British working-class rock, women's literature, gay literature, the roman Québécois, the literature of the third world. This production is possible only to the degree to which these forms of collective life or collective solidarity have not yet been fully penetrated by the market and the commodity system.

JACK COLLOM: *Ethics:* Sanskrit roots *sva da*—self, to place. How do you place yourself? Also, self-will and strength have a lot to do with our understanding of the word. In a sense, ethics means exerting oneself contrary to nature: fighting off temptation, jumping up out of sleep and sloth, restraining oneself. There is a sense in which nature is all crammed in the instant, and to think of time, of good, to be ethical, is possibly hubristic, is to go against impulse, against gravity, against nature. But then, it is natural to counter nature.

Interesting subspecies of the ethics question: Poets tend to go for the gesture and to ally themselves with Feeling. Could this tendency put them at odds with the bloodless-seeming Plans of ethics, for selfish reasons? Because you look good being gestural. Because you look good being all warm and poetical.

If you work at your art intensely and honestly, what could be more ethical than that? What could ever do more good than the continuation of bringing what Gary Snyder calls the richly interconnected, interdependent, and incredibly complex character of wild ecosystems into the culture? Good poetry, regardless of content, is intrinsically nutrition for language and mind, thus nutrition for life. What could be more moral than frequent surprise?

Perhaps ethics means you place yourself, but then everything moves on you. The moral duty of an artist is to make and perhaps disseminate images and moves that advance thought. So what about the ethics of propaganda? Of expressivity itself? Is it proper to color language? Can there be falsification for the sake of truth? I say yes, if we take truth to exist but to always be in partial embryo or disintegration states, like the word *nature* is. In other words, *sorta*. In other words, talk as well as you can, but if you then find yourself leading the country, pause and take stock, ethically. In other words, when the scientists try for objectivity, that's o.k., but they shouldn't ever think they made it, or could. In other words, ethics is to keep on dividing the remaining distance into halves, unless you are a Zeno-phobic. Ethics is the particulars of the general theory of good, or even spelling of "good." Ethics could be quitting smoking because you respect yourself biologically enough to do what is possible to continue your work. Or, it could be keeping on smoking because you feel of value in going contrary to sheer quantity. So, ethics is like poetry itself; it certainly depends on uncertainty, it is composed of contradiction, but if you take that as a key you have lost it.

Hauling back from these edges of edges, I would say it is good to partly put one's work in the service of so-called good. But about thirty seconds after you swell up with pride about it, you are hyperventilating, lying on the side of the road—or you should be. Who knows what is good? We feel clear, we in this room and other rooms these days, that we know what is bad, and that's o.k., it's a start. But what is good bounces different ways down the hall of mirrors that represents short times, medium-rare, long, etcetera—immeasurable times. There could even be an ethic that strives for whatever will eliminate humanity the quickest, as being good for life on Earth. I mean, we are too smart for Earth and too dumb for heaven. But furthering that ethic would be too much fun, it couldn't be truly moral. So, ultimately, compromise—which does not mean do nothing. Take a chance.

HARRYETTE MULLEN: I like the distinction between ethics and morality, and I would add law. These are three different things, but they all guide what we are trying to do in our time on Earth, in our struggle to be good and to avoid evil. The problem is that we are not always sure what is really good and what is really evil, and sometimes we do evil with good intentions. The struggle to be good, as a writer, as an artist, is a different thing from the struggle to be good as a human being. Sometimes they do overlap, but one can be an excellent artist and a miserable human being. We've probably all seen examples of that.

I am the first to admit that I often fall short of my own ideal of ethical behavior. I like what John Cage said when he defined his "minimum ethic: do what you said you'd do." That is my constant struggle, and I often fall short due to a lack of attention. It's important to pay attention to what you say and the person you are speaking to when making promises. We can be more ethical and more effective when we promise to do what we actually want to do or are willing to do; when we focus on things that need to be done, and things that we actually have time, energy, and interest to do. Along with attention, it's important to have compassion and commitment. It seems to me these are the keys to the kind of ethics that I would aspire to in my own behavior, in my own dealings with other human beings. Echoing what Jack said about ethics, the basic root of it has to do with your relationship to others and your relationship to your work as well. Does your action make the world somewhat better, even if it is only a tiny increment, or do you make it worse? That is what it all boils down to. Are you enhancing our humanity, your own and the humanity of others, or are you in some way diminishing your humanity and the humanity of others? Every ethical system probably boils down to that.

Acting ethically means paying attention. It means being compassionate toward yourself and others. It also means commitment and persistence, because I fail every day and I have to start over the next day, and try again to be better.

I think there is a critical aspect to being ethical. It requires a certain kind of intelligence, and that is not intelligence in the sense of measuring IQ on a standard exam. I think we all have this basic ethical intelligence, so that we know when we are hurting someone, if we pay attention to what we are doing and the effects of our actions. There is a critical aspect to paying attention and being aware that we are constantly making mistakes. We are constantly falling short of our goals, and we are constantly in need of improvement. There is also a critical aspect to the work that we do as writers. Sometimes writers are disliked because we are characteristically critical. We want ourselves and others to be better. We talk about it. We write about it. We say what we think when things are not right. That takes some kind of courage, but I think it is important.

DAISY ZAMORA: I will start by saying that I believe poetry is the highest art, because poets work with words, and a word is the most elusive tool of all, because it can mean many things and say many things. The wonder of it and the craft of the poet is to say the most with every word in a poem. Humans are chaotic beings, but we search for an articulate world, yet the world is also a set of blind forces. Nevertheless, we like to believe that we are in control of our lives. But if you think about it, the soul of poetry is the same as nature, the same as life. To believe that you can control poetry for your own mundane purposes goes against the soul of poetry. To be a poet is to have a fresh eye for the world, for life, for people. Everything you see on any day—it might be a face in the bus, a set of wrinkles in a face, the sky, trees you're walking by, people or vendors in the street—has to be seen always as if for the first time. Poets should be like walking radars with sensitivity always afloat, ready to capture life. A poet has to be a poet twenty-four hours a day, seven days a week, every day of his or her life. That means you become a dangerous person, not only because you are being vulnerable to the world, but also because you have to say the truth. And if you say the truth, you start a personal revolution with your poetry. You never have to be afraid of saying what you see, and what you need to say. You have to write as much as you can stand, to be honest with what you write, and then leave it there. Afterward, you have to contemplate the words on the page, contemplate your poem as an object, and try again to say what you want to say the best you can. If you don't find a way, keep trying, because when something is haunting you and you don't know what it is, it's because poetry is sending you her messages. It comes to you in waves, like the sea. You're trying to capture the soul of poetry, and you know that you are going somewhere, but need a compass. Humbleness is the compass.

Because poetry is pitiless. She makes the part of you that was not honest come through the lines of the poem. Poetry is about truth, and telling the truth is the only danger of poetry. The poet walks with stilettos in her or his eyes, which go through the surface and into the entrails of things. That's what makes poetry dangerous: poetry is essentially revolutionary because it penetrates to the essence of what is happening, and reveals the truth hidden beneath the surface. But strangely enough, poetry is also a lie, because it is through a lie that you tell the truth.

The Nicaraguan poet Carlos Martínez Rivas said about another poet, Joaquín Pasos, that to write a poem is to plan the perfect crime, because it is to tell the truth through a lie, but a lie that becomes true because of its utmost purity. This purity is the core of poetry; it is what gives poetry its spiritual force in this world. Of course, poetry can be made into a commodity like anything else. But poetry, true poetry, resists any sort of easy packaging, because it bears an obliged relationship to events. For example, Homer portrayed a war in *The Iliad*, but also drew an insightful map of the human soul, because poetry, like the world, is also about the private life, the hidden motive, the contained feeling. Poetry, like the world, is also a matter of details that capture emotions and feelings.

Poems come from the experience of individuals, but this experience, which is so private, transcends the personal, because a poet not only tells what happens on a crowded street or in the solitude of a room, but, also, and simultaneously, explores the most profound layers of the human condition. A poet is also a reporter of the fears, the anguish, and the anxious shifting of consciousness when it dives deep within itself.

When we read such poetry, we cannot not feel as if a lightning bolt has hit our minds and our hearts at the same time. We cannot not feel that familiar sensation of strangeness that reminds us over and over again of the solitude of each individual, the aloneness of a life in this world, and how in that solitude, a world is also drawn and re-created. All the upheavals of history, such as wars, political struggles, or social uprisings against tyrannical regimes, can also be felt and read as metaphors of our inner life. They correspond to, and can also stand for, the individual anxiety of mortality, failure, despair, or betrayal, the whole tangle of thwarted desires, failed expectations, and misplaced hopes that hound all of us. The personal and the political, what is private and what is public, is constantly feeding one another because we are individuals, but we live in families, in communities, and all share the fate of a given place where we were born, its culture and its history.

I said at the beginning that I believe poetry is the highest art because I was born in a country where poetry is the one art that sustains everything and speaks for everything. Poetry is our only possible Utopia, because for us, poetry means Nicaragua. Poetry means our homeland, the place we belong to. My country is known as a "republic of poets," because poetry plays extraliterary roles in the society. Poetry is our ethics, our philosophy, our history, our sacred book. Our poets are our heroes. They integrate in their work our culture and our history, our sufferings, our hopes, and our dreams. Our poets are prophets and natural leaders for our people. Throughout our history we have had poets who killed tyrants and poets who have died fighting for the freedom of our country. That's why our poets are like our patron saints. Our very identity as Nicaraguans comes through our poetry, because we believe that poetry is the guardian of memory. Countries that have no memory stumble through history.

During the Nicaraguan revolution, Ernesto Cardenal, then minister of culture, said that we had to socialize the means of poetic production because poetry should be appropriated by all Nicaraguans. The reason it should be appropriated by all of us is because poetry makes us more human. Nicaraguan people are extensively educated in poetry.

Our poetry vibrates with ancient Greek voices, shines with the splendor of Latin, sings with the cadence of Spanish, weeps with our indigenous languages, and dances with African and Caribbean rhythms. Poetry is our best achievement and our legacy to the world. We are a small country, rich in poetry and natural resources, but made poor first by the long colonial period during which we lived under the Spanish Empire, but mainly by the relentless greed and harassment the u.s. has unleashed on us since the middle of the nineteenth century, beginning shortly after we gained independence from Spain. That's why our poetry has historically been charged with what is understood as [the] "political." Our poetry has been the resource that we, the people, have always used to speak out about our longing for freedom.

To finish, I'm going to read a note that the Spanish poet Miguel Hernández wrote to Vicente Aleixandre. Hernández died in jail during the Spanish Civil War. I think that this note from him synthesizes how we see poetry in Nicaragua. This is a loose translation, directly from the Spanish. He says:

We, who have been born poets among all men, life has made us poets next to all men. We have been springing from the stream of guitars taken in by the people, and every poet that dies leaves a legacy in the hands of another one, an instrument that comes rolling from the eternity of nothingness to our scattered heart. Before the shadow of two poets, two more of us rise, and before ours, two more will rise tomorrow. Our foundation will always be the same, the earth. Our fate is to end in the hands of the people. Only those honest hands can contain what the honest blood of the poet pours vibrantly. [. . .]

We, poets, are the wind of the people: we are born to pass blowing through their pores and to guide their eyes and their feelings to the highest beauty. Today, this today of passion, of life, of death, pushes us in an imposing way, you, me, others, toward the people. The people are waiting for the poets with their ear and their soul lying at the foot of every century.

I wanted to share with you our understanding of poetry, of po/ethics in my country, because it has to do with the idea of doing what you say you will do, so what you do is sustained by your words. This is the way we live our lives as poets in Nicaragua.

DAVID HENDERSON: Ethics. I was panicked about ethics. I was running around asking everybody, "What's ethics?" A lot of people didn't have any answers, either.

I was in San Francisco when Roberto Vargas and Alejandro Murguía, some Latino poets, some Filipino poets, put Augusto César Sandino [Nicaraguan revolutionary, assassinated in 1934, after whom the Sandinista movement was later named] on the cover of a literary magazine. Of course, I didn't know who Sandino was, and they told me. I remember later Roberto Vargas telling me how they had assembled on a hill in Nicaragua, there were maybe one or two hundred people who were committed to taking back the government of Nicaragua. And what a great story that is. The involvement of poets is essential to that struggle. I think in terms of ethics it is a beautiful example. I visited Roberto in Washington after they had succeeded, and went to the Nicaraguan embassy, where the Somoza's art collection was still up, but they had taken it over, there were all these young people, and I had not even known at that time, until I went to the embassy, that Nicaragua had black people. The coast had a connection with the Caribbean Islands. It was remarkable; it opens the world up. Trying to learn about the country of a dictator, from a dictator—obviously I didn't learn very much. But with the Nicaraguan revolution, I learned a great deal about Latin America, about South America, and about the interrelatedness of the people of color there.

The ethics of poets has always been part of my life because I came downtown from the Bronx . . . I was born in Harlem, went uptown to the

Bronx, was living in the South Bronx, and came downtown because there wasn't really anywhere else to go; I was kind of looking for a poet named Ted Joans. He was a Beat poet, but Ted was more into the surreal, dada-istic aspects of the Beat generation. He had something called "Rent a Beatnik," where people from the suburbs could rent a beatnik for a week-end, and people actually got work out of this, it was quite fun. I joined a group of writers called the Umbra poets, having blundered down to the New School to take a class in writing. Ishmael Reed was part of that group, Calvin Hernton, Tom Dent from New Orleans—it was a great mixture of middle-class, working-class, and underclass African Americans and some whites. We were on the Lower East Side, on Second Street and Avenue C, which even today is remarkable because the East Village ends there and you have these huge housing projects, the Hamilton Fish Library, these wide boulevards, but Avenue D, Avenue C and Second Street, looks more like the Bronx than Manhattan. And that's where Umbra hung out. That's where today *Tribes* magazine and Steve Cannon, the Gathering of the Tribes is; that's where the Nuyorican Poets Café is—it's a special area for me. Umbra was a group where we had workshops and read poetry to each other, but we were also existing in this multiculture, this Bohemia; we all knew Ed Sanders and the peace poets; I'd met some poets who had marched from San Francisco to Moscow. It was a beautiful time. We were black national-ists, we were very problack, but we also had white friends and had a very interesting argument with some other black nationalists, who thought that we should not be friends with white people and should go live in Harlem, where I was born. But I said, I'm not going back to live in Harlem, I'm going to stay here, I have friends, I'm happy here, and none of my friends have any problem with my being a black nationalist, if they read about it they would understand. In the early and mid-1960s, that's the time when a lot of the countries of Africa were finally relinquished by the colonialists, to some extent. I learned about Patrice Lumumba then. I was just talking with someone about Richard Wright, and how he had invented a term, as a writer, as a poet, he invented something he called the third world. It had nothing to do with economics, it had more to do with consciousness. We saw before our eyes how the *New York Times* and other entitites usurped this term and made it apply to the economic levels of countries; the meaning Richard Wright had in mind was much too revolutionary for it to be allowed to continue as a concept. What Wright had in mind was that someone who is born somewhere like Asia, Africa, Latin America, or South America, but that lives in the West, doesn't become a dual person, but becomes a third person, something that is a combination and elevation of both of those worlds. That's what he meant by third world. We see it all the time now and it's amazing to me how it has got into the language that way, but not that there wasn't a fight over letting that happen. I remember people were arguing over that term, but there was not a lot of power involved.

At the time that Umbra was evolving on the Lower East Side and in the East Village, Amiri Baraka, who was then LeRoi Jones, whom we were in awe of, was a brilliant Beatnik. Allen Ginsberg and Gregory Corso, Frank O'Hara, they loved Amiri because he was a bright and shining star. He published a magazine called *Yugen* with Diane di Prima; he lived in Cooper Square, right near Cooper Union . . . and all of a sudden one day Amiri changed. The change that was brought about for Amiri as well as others was the fascination of Malcolm X. That happened right after the assassination of John F. Kennedy. I don't know exactly what Amiri thought, though I do in some respects, because he wrote about it in his autobiography, which is a beautiful book. There's a new edition out with a long introduction that had been taken out of the first edition, and he talks about what was in his head. Umbra supported Amiri when he decided to become a black nationalist, changed his name, and was going to move uptown and become part of the black revolution—which he didn't. But Umbra supported him. I think Sun Ra was living down in the East Village; we would all go uptown and do readings, whatever we could do to help Amiri with his Black Arts repertory, and then we would go back downtown. People would say, don't go back downtown, stay here, and we'd say, no, we're happy living in Bohemia. There was always that tension for many years, between the blacks living in Bohemia and the blacks living in the black community. We always felt steadfastly that we would stay where we were.

Amiri comes to mind to me, in terms of ethics, very recently. He wrote a poem called "Somebody Blew Up America," about the 9/11 stuff right after it happened, read the poem for months and nobody said anything until something coalesced with him being named the poet laureate of New Jersey. People asked why he was the poet laureate of New Jersey: it's because he was the best poet in New Jersey, at least [laughter]. They really came down on Amiri—basically New Jersey is withholding the money that came with that award. Now here we are poets on the Lower East Side, after 9/11, noting, noticing clearly that we were really let down by our government, by all the people who were supposed to be in charge of it: the military, the City of New York, even the police and the fire department let themselves down by losing so many because of, to some extent, inadequate planning. There are so many ways we were exploited by that whole situation. To me, Amiri, with that poem—which I think is one of his best poems—was talking about why this happened, who was behind it, and he suffered accordingly. All the media in New York and the national media came out against this poem, and actually started instructing us in how to read poetry. Which I thought was remarkable; I couldn't believe it. Poets are ignored by these people most of the time. And Amiri was pretty much by himself, taking that on. A lot of poets signed the petition [for him], a lot of poets didn't sign it. I found myself in a situation where I was having arguments with poets about poetry. Some of the poets were saying, I didn't really read that poem, but he said this thing about this, and so . . . and I said, look, why don't you read the damn poem? But Amiri single-handedly kept open the whole thing about the 9/11 Commission; the whole idea that there should be questioning and accountability for what happened was born by Amiri, by himself, until the 9/11 Commission got together. Bob Holman did provide a space; Amiri gave a press conference and was able to talk back to the press, and actually everybody came. It was a remarkable situation where finally he was able to confront his accusers and tell them where he was coming from. In Newark, a multicultural bunch of people appointed him the poet laureate of the school system of Newark, and that was a beautiful thing. In terms of that type of ethic, I look to Amiri as being someone of deep ethics who always follows his ideal and who has a lot of courage as well.

So for me, in terms of poets, the 9/11 poets, or we can talk about the downtown poets, all the poets downtown gave one reading and then disappeared, and we're still trying to talk about what we can do or what we should do. One thing I think that all the poets downtown, in the explosion of poetry that happened recently, where we have spoken word poetry, performance poetry, we have a lot of poets, and that's a good thing. I don't think people really need to particularly achieve any level of poetic-ness to be poets; I think it's more by declaration. Those who stand for that, who sign on to that ethic, need to be committed to talking to people, to standing up for what they write, and to help people understand the level of language that is being put upon us. They are putting the public in a position where we accept contradictory terms, we accept lies, and it is affecting our future. To this point in time, where we are right now, I don't think we really have any other choice than to act in such a way, to talk to people, to put ourselves forward, to act individually to deal with this situation. Our backs are against the wall. It's not only about this war, it's symbolic of the problem with oil, and humanity; we're kind of facing things that the public doesn't understand, like these damn tornadoes, funny weather that's coming around from global warming. I think we are in a terrible crisis, and the poets, as representatives of all of the artists, who are perhaps the most comprehensive, who are most interdisciplinary, the poets really have an obligation to be even more ethical, in the sense that we have to stand up for the word, defend the word before our citizens, and help them understand what's happening.

—June 7, 2004

BIOGRAPHIES

SHERWIN BITSUI is originally from White Cone, Arizona, on the Navajo Reservation. He is Diné of the Todich'ii'nii (Bitter Water Clan), born for the Tl'izilani (Many Goats Clan). His poems have been anthologized in *Between Water and Song, Legitimate Dangers: American Poets of the New Century.* He is the author of *Shapeshift* and *Flood Song.*

ANA BOŽIČEVIĆ was born in Croatia and emigrated to New York when she was nineteen. She is the author of *Stars of the Night Commute,* and coeditor, with Željko Mitić, of *The Day Lady Gaga Died: An Anthology of Newer New York Poets.*

NICOLE BROSSARD, poet, novelist, and essayist, was born in Montréal (Quebec). In 1965 she cofounded the influential literary magazine *La barre du jour,* and in 1976 she codirected the film *Some American Feminists.* She has published eight novels including *Picture Theory, Mauve Desert, Baroque at Dawn;* an essay, "The Aerial Letter"; and many books of poetry, including *Daydream Mechanics, Lovhers, Typhon dru, Installations,* and *Musee de l'os et de l'eau.*

RHONDA DAHL BUCHANAN is a professor of Spanish at the University of Louisville in Kentucky, and has been the director of the Latin American and Latino Studies program since 2002. She is the author of numerous articles on contemporary Latin American writers from Argentina, Colombia, and Mexico, and a translator of literary fiction, including the work of Alberto Rúy-Sanchez.

ANDREI CODRESCU was born in Sibiu, Romania; he emigrated to the United States in 1966 and became a u.s. citizen in 1981. He is a poet, novelist, essayist, screenwriter, columnist on National Public Radio, editor of *Exquisite Corpse,* and MacCurdy Distinguished Professor of English at

Louisiana State University in Baton Rouge. He is the author of numerous books, including *Whatever Gets You through the Night: A Story of Sheherezade and the Arabian Entertainments, The Poetry Lesson, The Posthuman Dada Guide: Tzara and Lenin Play Chess, Jealous Witness,* and *New Orleans, Mon Amour.*

JACK COLLOM grew up with a strong interest in nature, walking in the Salt Creek Woods, birding from age eleven. He joined the U.S. Air Force during the Korean War and wrote his first poems while stationed in Tripoli, Libya; spent time in Munich, Germany, then, stateside, worked in factories for twenty years. He has taught creative writing freelance for nearly forty years; most of his pupils are children of all ages, teachers, and college students. He is the author of twenty-five books and chapbooks of poetry and three CDs; his *Second Nature* received the Colorado Book Award in Poetry in 2013.

CID CORMAN (1924–2004) was born in Boston and lived for many years in Kyoto, Japan, where he and his wife ran Cid Corman's Dessert Shop. As the editor of *Origin,* he published some of the major works of the Black Mountain poets, as well as other important work, choosing mostly poems not yet readily available elsewhere: the early poetry of Charles Olson, Robert Creeley, and Denise Levertov with the late works of Wallace Stevens and William Carlos Williams. Corman also published more than seventy volumes of poetry, translated several French and Japanese poets, and published four volumes of essays.

ELSA CROSS was born in Mexico City and teaches philosophy of religion and comparative mythology at National Autonomous University of Mexico. Her poems have been translated into twelve languages and published in magazines and more than sixty anthologies in different countries. Her numerous books of poetry include *El diván de Antar, Moira, Los sueños— Elegías, Ultramar—Odas, El vino de las cosas—Ditirambos, Cuaderno de Amorgos, Jaguar, Bomarzo, Los suenos en la voz de la autora, Nadir, Escalas,* and *Canto malabar y otros poemas.*

VICTOR HERNÁNDEZ CRUZ is a member of the Nuyorican movement of writers. He was born in Aguas Buenas, Puerto Rico, and moved to New York City with his family when he was five years old. He started writing poetry early and at seventeen self-published his first book, *Papo*

Got His Gun! And Other Poems, on a mimeograph machine. Since then, more than a dozen collections of his poems—among them *Snaps; By Lingual Wholes; Red Beans; Rhythm, Content and Flavor: New and Selected Poems,* and *The Mountain in the Sea*—have been published by traditional publishing houses.

BEI DAO is the nom de plume of Zhao Zhenkai. His poems have been translated into more than thirty languages. In English he is represented by numerous collections of poetry, fiction, and essays, including *The August Sleepwalker, Old Snow, Unlock, Landscape over Zero, Midnight's Gate,* and *Waves.* In China in the 1970s and 1980s, he was a leading member of the loosely associated avant-garde movement Ménglóng Shi Rén, or Misty Poets. Much of his early work, as well as that of other Misty poets, appeared in the influential underground journal that he cofounded in 1978, *Jintian (Today).* The journal was banned after two years of publication, and in 1989 Bei Dao was exiled from China for his perceived influence on the protests that led up to the Tiananmen Square massacre.

SAMUEL R. DELANY was born and raised in New York City and began writing in the early 1960s. His 1966 novel *Babel-17* established his reputation as a science fiction writer, and over the next decade he became famous for his provocative futuristic explorations of race and sexual identity in the novels *Nova, Dhalgren,* and *Triton.* His other works include the *Nevèrÿon* series of novels and the novel *Stars in My Pocket Like Grains of Sand.* He has also written frankly about his life as an African American homosexual, and his nonfiction books include *The Motion of Light in Water: Sex and Science Fiction Writing in the East Village, 1957–65* and *Times Square Red, Times Square Blue,* a book about sexual culture.

MÓNICA DE LA TORRE, poet, translator, and scholar, was born and raised in Mexico City. Her poetry collections include *Public Domain, Talk Shows,* and *Acúfenos.* With artist Terence Gower, she coauthored the art book *Appendices, Illustrations and Notes.* With Michael Wiegers, she coedited the bilingual anthology *Reversible Monuments: Contemporary Mexican Poetry.*

LINH DINH was born in Saigon, Vietnam, and moved to the U.S. twelve years later; he has also lived in Italy and England. He is the author of two collections of stories, *Fake House* and *Blood and Soap;* four books of poems, *All Around What Empties Out, American Tatts, Borderless Bodies,* and *Jam Alerts;*

and a novel, *Love Like Hate*. Linh Dinh is also the editor of the anthologies *Night, Again: Contemporary Fiction from Vietnam* and *Three Vietnamese Poets*; translator of *Night, Fish, and Charlie Parker*, the poetry of Phan Nhien Hao; and has published widely in Vietnamese.

DOLORES DORANTES's books include *Querida fábrica* (Práctica Mortal, CONACULTA, 2012) and Estilo (Mano Santa Editores, 2011). Her op-ed pieces, criticism and investigative texts have been published in numerous Mexican newspapers. A bilingual edition of books two and three of *Dolores Dorantes* was copublished in early 2008 by Counterpath Press and Kenning Editions; a new edition with books one through four from the series is forthcoming from Kenning Editions (both books translated by Jen Hofer). *Intervenir*, written collaboratively with Rodrigo Flores Sánchez, is forthcoming as *Intervene* from Ugly Duckling Presse (translated by Jen Hofer). Dorantes lived in Ciudad Juárez for twenty-five years, and currently lives in Los Angeles.

ALLEN GINSBERG (1926–1997)'s first book of poems, *Howl*, published by City Lights, overcame censorship trials to become one of the most widely read poems of the twentieth century. In 1974 Ginsberg cofounded the Jack Kerouac School of Disembodied Poetics at Naropa University with Anne Waldman. Some of his later books include *White Shroud: Poems, 1980–1985, Cosmopolitan Greetings: Poems, 1986–1992; Journals Mid-Fifties 1954–1958; Selected Poems, 1947–1995;* and *Death and Fame: Last Poems, 1993–1997*. His *Collected Poems, 1947–1997* was published in 2007 by HarperCollins.

C. S. GISCOMBE was born in Dayton, Ohio, and currently teaches at UC–Berkeley. His poetry books are *Prairie Style, Two Sections from Practical Geography, Giscome Road, Here, At Large,* and *Postcards*; his prose book—about Canada—is *Into and Out of Dislocation*. A book of essays titled *Back Burner*, on poetry and other cultural topics, was published in 2013.

LYN HEJINIAN, poet, essayist, and translator, was born in the San Francisco Bay Area and lives in Berkeley. Published collections of her writing include *Writing Is an Aid to Memory, My Life, Oxota: A Short Russian Novel, Leningrad* (written in collaboration with Michael Davidson, Ron Silliman, and Barrett Watten), *The Cell, The Cold of Poetry,* and *A Border Comedy*. Translations of her work have been published in France, Spain, Japan,

Italy, Russia, Sweden, and Finland. From 1976–1984, Hejinian was the editor of Tuumba Press, and from 1981 to 1999, she was the coeditor (with Barrett Watten) of *Poetics Journal*. She is also the codirector (with Travis Ortiz) of Atelos, a literary project commissioning and publishing cross-genre work by poets.

DAVID HENDERSON was a founder of the Black Arts Movement in the 1960s and has been an active member of New York's Lower East Side art community for more than four decades. He has published four volumes of poetry, and his work has appeared in numerous literary publications and anthologies. A revised and expanded edition of *'Scuse Me While I Kiss the Sky*, his highly acclaimed biography of rock guitarist Jimi Hendrix, was published in 2008.

CHRISTIAN IDE HINTZE (1953–2012) was born in Vienna, Austria. He was the author of performances, tapes, books, installations, drawings, exercises, Super 8 films, leaflets, posters, CDs, DVDs, and internet sites, as well as an inventor of instruments and the creator of a 7fold poetics. Hintze propagated lowercase writing, organized cross-culture events, and served as the director of the Vienna Poetry School.

JEN HOFER is a Los Angeles–based poet, translator, social justice interpreter, teacher, knitter, bookmaker, public letter–writer, urban cyclist, and cofounder (with John Pluecker) of the language justice and language experimentation collaborative Antena. Her books are available from numerous small presses, including Action Books, Atelos, Counterpath Press, Dusie Books, Kenning Editions, Insert Press, Les Figues Press, Litmus Press, LRL Textile Editions, Palm Press, Subpress, Ugly Duckling Presse, and in various DIY/DIT incarnations. She teaches poetics, translation, and bookmaking at CalArts and Otis College.

ANSELM HOLLO (1934–2013), poet and translator, was born in Helsinki, Finland, and lived in England for many years, working for the BBC European Services. In 1967, he moved to the United States and taught at various institutions, including SUNY Buffalo and the Naropa Institute in Boulder, Colorado. Hollo was the author of more than forty books of poetry, including *Notes on the Possibilities and Attractions of Existence: Selected Poems 1965–2000, AHOE, Corvus, Finite Continued,* and *Sojourner Microcosms: New* and *Selected Poems 1959–1977*. His many translations include works by Paavo Haavikko, *Selected Poems 1949–1988,* and Pentti Saarikoski, for whose *Trilogy* (2003) Hollo received the Harold Morton Landon Translation Award from the Academy of American Poets.

PIERRE JORIS, poet, translator, essayist, and nomad, left Luxembourg at age nineteen and has since lived in the U.S., Great Britain, North Africa, and France. He has published more than forty books and has taught poetry and poetics at the University of Albany since 1992. His translations include *Paul Celan: Selections, Lightduress by Paul Celan,* and *Exile Is My Trade: A Habib Tengour Reader.* With Jerome Rothenberg, he edited the award-winning anthologies *Poems for the Millennium* and *Pablo Picasso, The Burial of the Count of Orgaz and Other Poems.*

BHANU KAPIL, born in England to Indian parents, teaches through memory, the monster, and experimental prose at the Jack Kerouac School of Disembodied Poetics. She loves teaching and is constantly amazed by her students—learning from and with them in a classroom that is half laboratory and two-fifths incubator. She is the author of *The Vertical Interrogation of Strangers, Humanimal, Incubation: a Space for Monsters, Schizophrene,* and, most recently, *BAN: a novel of the race riot—as yet unwritten.*

MYUNG MI KIM was born in Seoul, Korea, immigrated with her family to the United States at the age of nine, and was raised in the Midwest. She earned a BA from Oberlin College, an MA from Johns Hopkins University, and an MFA from the University of Iowa. Her collection of poems *Under Flag* won the Multicultural Publishers Exchange Award of Merit; subsequent collections include *The Bounty, DURA, Commons, River Antes,* and *Penury.*

ILYA KUTIK was a member of the Metarealists in the 1980s in Moscow, where he published a translation into Russian of Alexander Pope's "Essay on Man." He is the author of *Pentathlon of Emotions, Odysseus' Bow,* and *Ode on Visiting the Belosaraisk Spit on the Sea of Azov.*

JOANNE KYGER lives on the coast north of San Francisco, writing poetry, editing the local newspaper, traveling to Mexico, and teaching frequently at the Jack Kerouac School of Disembodied Poetics in Boulder and the New

College of San Francisco. She is the author of more than twenty books of poetry and prose, including *Strange Big Moon: Japan and India Journals, 1960–1964, God Never Dies, The Distressed Look, Again: Poems 1989–2000, As Ever: Selected Poems,* and *About Now: Collected Poems.*

JUDITH MALINA is an actress, writer, director, and cofounder of The Living Theatre. Founded in 1947 as an imaginative alternative to the commercial theater. The Living Theatre has staged nearly a hundred productions performed in eight languages in twenty-eight countries on five continents—a unique body of work that has influenced theater the world over. A lifelong pacifist, anti–death penalty activist, and self-described leader of "the beautiful nonviolent anarchist revolution," Judith Malina's work has continually challenged the forms, content, and style of the theater and its relationship to and with the audience.

HARRYETTE MULLEN was born in Florence, Alabama, and raised in Fort Worth, Texas. Early in her career as a poet, she worked in the Artists in Schools program sponsored by the Texas Commission on the Arts, and for six years she taught African American and other U.S. ethnic literatures at Cornell University in Ithaca, New York. Her books include *Tree Tall Woman, Trimmings, S*PeRM**K*T, Muse and Drudge, Recyclopedia, Blues Baby: Early Poems,* and *Sleeping with the Dictionary.*

EILEEN MYLES was born in Boston and moved to New York in 1974 to be a poet. *Snowflake/different streets* (poems, 2012) is the latest of her eighteen books. *Inferno (a poet's novel)* came out in 2010. For *The Importance of Being Iceland: Travel Essays in Art,* she received a Warhol/Creative Capital grant. She is professor emerita of writing at UC–San Diego, a 2012 Guggenheim fellow, and a resident of New York.

SAWAKO NAKAYASU was born in Japan, moved to the U.S. at age six, and currently lives in Japan. Her most recent books are *Texture Notes, Hurry Home Honey,* and a translation of Kawata Ayane's poetry, *Time of Sky//Castles in the Air.* Her translation of Takashi Hiraide's *For the Fighting Spirit of the Walnut* received the 2009 Best Translated Book Award from Three Percent.

HOA NGUYEN was born in the Mekong Delta and raised in the Washington, DC area. With the poet Dale Smith, Nguyen founded Skanky

Possum, a poetry journal and book imprint in Austin, Texas, where they lived for fourteen years. The author of eight books and chapbooks, she currently lives in Toronto. Wave Books published her third full-length collection of poems, *As Long As Trees Last*, in September 2012.

AKILAH OLIVER (1961–2011) was born and raised in Los Angeles, and was the artist in residence at Beyond Baroque Literary Arts Center in Los Angeles and the curator of the Poetry Project's Monday Night Reading Series. Oliver taught on the faculty of the University of Colorado–Boulder; the Department of Writing and Poetics at Naropa University; Long Island University (as the Visiting Distinguished Author, MFA Creative Writing program); and LaGuardia Community College. At the time of her death in 2011, she was a professor at Pratt Institute in Brooklyn, New York, in the humanities and media studies department, and a PhD candidate at the European Graduate School in Saas-Fee, Switzerland. Her books include *the she said dialogues: flesh memory* and *A Toast in the House of Friends.*

ALEXS D. PATE is the author of five novels, including the *New York Times* best seller *Amistad*, commissioned by Steven Spielberg's DreamWorks/SKG and based on the screenplay by David Franzoni. Other novels include *Losing Absalom, Finding Makeba, The Multicultiboho Sideshow,* and *West of Rehoboth.* He is an assistant professor in African American and African Studies at the University of Minnesota, where he teaches courses in writing and black literature, including a course titled the Poetry of Rap.

TOM PICKARD was directly instrumental in ending the obscurity that surrounded Basil Bunting. He cofounded and for several years managed Morden Tower, a poetry center situated on a medieval city wall in the industrial sector of Newcastle upon Tyne. He also edited the arts magazine *King Ida's Watch Chain* with Richard Hamilton, and cofounded the magazine *Eruption* and the bookstore Ultima Thule. His publications include *Hero Dust, Tiepin Eros, fuckwind, Hole in the Walls, The Dark Months of May,* and *Ballad of Jamie Allan.*

MICHELLE NAKA PIERCE, born in Japan, is the author of seven titles, including *She, A Blueprint* with art by Sue Hammond West and *Symptom of Color.* Awarded the Poets Out Loud Editor's Prize, her *Continuous Frieze Bordering Red* documents the migratory patterns of the hybrid as she travels the floating borders in Rothko's Seagram murals. Pierce is associate professor and director of the Jack Kerouac School of Disembodied Poetics at Naropa University.

WANG PING was born in Shanghai, P. R. China, and received a BA in English and American literature from Beijing University. She received her MA in English literature from Long Island University and a PhD in comparative literature at New York University. She joined the English department at Macalester College in Minnesota as an assistant professor in 1999. Her publications include *American Visa* (short stories), *Foreign Devil* (a novel), *Of Flesh and Spirit,* and *The Magic Whip* (both poetry). She is also the founder of Kinship of Rivers, an interdisciplinary project to build kinship among communities along the Mississippi and Yangtze.

MEREDITH QUARTERMAIN is a poet and novelist living in Vancouver, British Columbia. Her books of poetry include *Vancouver Walking, Recipes from the Red Planet,* and *Nightmarker. Rupert's Land,* a novel, was published in 2013. She is also cofounder of Nomados Literary Publishers, who have brought out more than forty chapbooks of innovative Canadian and U.S. writing since 2002.

MARGARET RANDALL is a poet and essayist who loves teaching at the Jack Kerouac School of Disembodied Poetics, Naropa University Summer Writing Program. She has lived in New York, Seville, Mexico City, Havana, and Managua, and now lives and works in Albuquerque, New Mexico. Among her most recent titles are *My Town, As If the Empty Chair/Como si la silla vacia, The Rhizome as a Field of Broken Bones, More Than Things,* and *Che on My Mind.*

HANON REZNIKOV (1950–2008) was an American theater and film actor, writer, and codirector of The Living Theatre in New York City following Julian Beck's death in 1985. His first contact with The Living Theatre was in 1968, when, as a biophysics student at Yale University, he attended a performance in New York's Lower East Side.

JEROME ROTHENBERG is the author of more than seventy books of poetry, including *Poland/1931, That Dada Strain, New Selected Poems 1970 -1985, Khurbn and Other Poems, The Case for Memory,* and *A Book of Witness.* He has also edited seven major assemblages of traditional and contemporary poetry, including *Technicians of the Sacred,* comprised of tribal and oral poetry from Africa, America, Asia, Europe, and Oceania; *Revolution of the World,* a collection of American experimental poetry between the two world wars; and two volumes of *Poems for the Millennium.* Rothenberg was elected to the World Academy of Poetry (UNESCO) in 2001.

ALBERTO RUY-SÁNCHEZ is a fiction and nonfiction writer, poet, and essayist from Mexico City. His novels include: *Los nombres del aire, Los demonios de la lengua, En los labios del agua, Los jardines secretos de Mogador: Voces de tierra,* and *La mano del fuego.* Other recent publications include: *Limulus. Visiones del fósil viviente/Visions of the Living Fossil* (an album coauthored with the artist Brian Nissen and translated by Rhonda Dahl Buchanan) and *Nueve veces el asombro.* He is also the author of several books of literary criticism, including *Una introducción a Octavio Paz.* Since 1988, he has served as the editor-in-chief of *Artes de México.*

ELENI SIKELIANOS spent nearly two years traveling (often by thumb) through Europe and Africa (from London to Ankara, and from Haifa to Dar es Salaam). She has lived in Paris, San Francisco, New York, Athens, and now, Boulder. Her books include a long poem in and around the history and sites of her home state, *The California Poem;* a hybridized memoir about her father, heroin, and homelessness, *The Book of Jon;* and *The Monster Lives of Boys and Girls, Earliest Worlds, The Book of Tendons,* and *To Speak While Dreaming.*

DANIEL STANIFORTH, originally from England, is a writer, musician, and teacher now residing in Colorado. He is the author of *Weaver in the Sluices* (poetry), *Diddle* (short stories), and *Groundlings of Divine Will* (hybrid), and has edited poetry collections by Will Alexander and Basil King. His various music recordings include a setting of Margaret Randall's poems, incidental theatre music for the Cheltenham Playhouse, independent film soundtracks, and assorted rock/folk/classical CDs. He teaches at the Metropolitan State College of Denver.

JAMES THOMAS STEVENS, a member of the Akwesasne Mohawk Tribe, was born in Niagara Falls, New York. His Mohawk name, under which he sometimes publishes, is Aronhiótas. Stevens's poetry collections include *A Bridge Dead in the Water, Combing the Snakes from His Hair,* and

Tokinish. He coauthored *Mohawk/Samoa: Transmigrations,* a collaborative poetry and translation project, with Caroline Sinavaiana.

BARBARA TEDLOCK is an initiated shaman practicing within the ancient Mayan subtle-energy system. She is also a professor of anthropology at SUNY Buffalo, the granddaughter of an Ojibwe woman shaman, the author of *The Woman in the Shaman's Body: Reclaiming the Feminine in Religion and Medicine,* and editor of the *Journal of Shamanic Practice.*

DENNIS TEDLOCK is an initiated daykeeper practicing within the Mayan system of divination, dream interpretation, and subtle energy. He is a distinguished professor of English and research professor of anthropology and has done field research among the Zuni of New Mexico, the Maya of Guatemala and Belize, the Karajá of Brazil, and the Mongols of Mongolia. His books include *Finding the Center: The Art of the Zuni Storyteller, Breath on the Mirror: Mythic Voices and Visions of the Living Maya, Days from a Dream Almanac, Rabinal Achi: A Mayan Drama of War and Sacrifice,* and *2,000 Years of Mayan Literature.*

LORENZO THOMAS (1944–2005) was born in Panama and moved with his family to New York in 1948. The family lived in the Bronx and Queens, where Thomas, a native Spanish speaker, soon became fluent in English. He is the author of five poetry collections: *A Visible Island, Dracula, Chances Are Few, The Bathers,* and *Dancing on Main Street.* Thomas was part of the Black Arts Movement in New York City and a member of the Umbra workshop. A critic as well as a poet, Thomas also published *Extraordinary Measures: Afrocentric Modernism and 20th-Century American Poetry.*

CECILIA VICUÑA was born in Santiago de Chile and currently splits her time between her homes in New York and Chile. She is a poet, artist, and political activist. She was in exile from Chile beginning in the early 1970s because of her support of the elected president, Salvador Allende, who was murdered by General Pinochet. She peforms and exhibits her work throughout Europe, Latin America, and the United States. Vicuña has authored and published sixteen books, most of which have been translated into several languages. Recent publications include *Saborami, beforehand,* and *Spit Temple.*

ANNE WALDMAN, poet, professor, performer, editor, and cultural activist, grew up in Greenwich Village and founded the Jack Kerouac School at Naropa University with Allen Ginsberg and Diane di Prima in 1974. She is a student of Tibetan Buddhism, has traveled frequently to India, and helped direct Naropa's study abroad program in Indonesia. She has presented her work at conferences and festivals around the world, lecturing at Muslim colleges in Kerala, and worked on educational projects for the Tamaas Foundation in Morocco. Her recent books include *Manatee/Humanity; The Iovis Trilogy: Colors in the Mechanism of Concealment,* which won the PEN American Center's Award for Poetry in 2012; and *Gossamurmur.* She is the editor of *Nice to See You, Out of This World, The Beat Book,* and coeditor of *The Angel Hair Anthology, Civil Disobediences,* and *Beats at Naropa.* She is a Guggenheim fellow for 2013–2014.

PETER LAMBORN WILSON (also known as Hakim Bey) is a political writer, essayist, and poet. He is responsible for proposing the concept of the temporary autonomous zone (TAZ). Recent books include: *Gothick Institutions* (2005); *Orgies of the Hemp Eaters* (2004), coedited as Hakim Bey with Abel Zug; and *Sacred Drifts: Essays on the Margins of Islam* (1993).

LAURA E. WRIGHT has been a poet, librarian, volunteer firefighter, musician, and occasional adjunct faculty member at Naropa University. For a number of years she curated the Left Hand Reading Series in Boulder. She is the author of various chapbooks, *Part of the Design* (poems), and the coeditor, with Anne Waldman, of *Beats at Naropa.*

KAREN TEI YAMASHITA is the author of *Through the Arc of the Rain Forest, Brazil-Maru, Tropic of Orange, Circle K Cycles,* and *I Hotel. I Hotel* was selected as a finalist for the National Book Award and awarded the California Book Award, the American Book Award, the Asian/Pacific American Librarians Association Award, and the Association for Asian American Studies Book Award. She is currently a Ford Foundation fellow and professor of literature and creative writing at the University of California–Santa Cruz.

HERIBERTO YÉPEZ is a Mexican writer, journalist, and psychotherapist, and a full-time professor at the Art School at the Autonomous University of Baja California, in Tijuana. He's the author of more than a dozen books of poetry, experimental fiction, novels, theory, and literary criticism in Spanish, including *Tijuanologías, A.B.U.R.T.O, El órgano de la risa, El Imperio de la Neomemoria, Contra la Tele-Visión,* and *Al otro lado.* His work in translation includes a selection of William Blake's fragments/aphorisms, José Vasconcelos's work in English, a poetry anthology, and a forthcoming lengthy prose and poetics anthology of Jerome Rothenberg.

DAISY ZAMORA lives in Managua and San Francisco and is the author of five books of poetry in Spanish, most recently *Tierra de Nadie, Tierra de Todos (No-Man's Land, Everybody's Land).* She edited the first anthology of Nicaraguan women poets, a book about concepts of cultural politics during the Sandinista Revolution. She has also translated into Spanish a collection of George Evans's poems, *Espejo de la Tierra.* A combatant in the National Sandinista Liberation Front, she was the program director and voice of the clandestine Radio Sandino. She became vice-minister of culture after the triumph of the revolution, and throughout her life has been a well-known political activist and advocate for women's rights.

NINA ZIVANČEVIĆ is a Serbian-born poet, essayist, fiction writer, playwright, art critic, translator, and contributing editor to *NY ARTS* magazine from Paris. She has also edited and participated in numerous anthologies of contemporary world poetry. In New York she worked with The Living Theatre and the members of the Wooster Group. She currently lives and teaches History of the American avant-garde at Université Paris 8.

FUNDER ACKNOWLEDGMENTS

COFFEE HOUSE PRESS is an independent, nonprofit literary publisher. Our books are made possible through the generous support of grants and gifts from many foundations, corporate giving programs, state and federal support, and through donations from individuals who believe in the transformational power of literature. Coffee House Press receives major operating support from Amazon, the Bush Foundation, the Jerome Foundation, the McKnight Foundation, the National Endowment for the Arts—a federal agency, and from Target. This activity made possible by the voters of Minnesota through a Minnesota State Arts Board Operating Support grant, thanks to a legislative appropriation from the arts and cultural heritage fund, and a grant from the Wells Fargo Foundation Minnesota.

Coffee House also receives support from: several anonymous donors; Suzanne Allen; Elmer L. and Eleanor J. Andersen Foundation; Mary & David Anderson Family Foundation; Around Town Agency; Patricia Beithon; Bill Berkson; the E. Thomas Binger and Rebecca Rand Fund of the Minneapolis Foundation; the Patrick and Aimee Butler Family Foundation; the Buuck Family Foundation; Claire Casey; Jane Dalrymple-Hollo; Ruth Dayton; Dorsey & Whitney, LLP; Mary Ebert and Paul Stembler; Chris Fischbach and Katie Dublinski; Fredrikson & Byron, P.A.; Katharine Freeman; Sally French; Jeffrey Hom; Carl and Heidi Horsch; Kenneth Kahn; Alex and Ada Katz; Stephen and Isabel Keating; the Kenneth Koch Literary Estate; Kathryn and Dean Koutsky; the Lenfestey Family Foundation; Carol and Aaron Mack; George Mack; Mary McDermid; Sjur Midness and Briar Andresen; the Nash Foundation; Peter and Jennifer Nelson; the Rehael Fund of the Minneapolis Foundation; Schwegman, Lundberg & Woessner, P.A.; Kiki Smith; Jeffrey Sugerman and Sarah Schultz; Nan Swid; Patricia Tilton; the Archie D. & Bertha H. Walker Foundation; Stu Wilson and Mel Barker; the Woessner Freeman Family Foundation; Margaret and Angus Wurtele; and many other generous individual donors.

ART WORKS.
arts.gov

MINNESOTA
STATE ARTS BOARD

CLEAN
WATER
LAND &
LEGACY
AMENDMENT

WELLS
FARGO

TARGET.

amazon.com